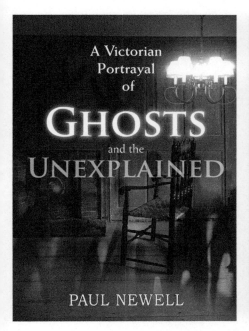

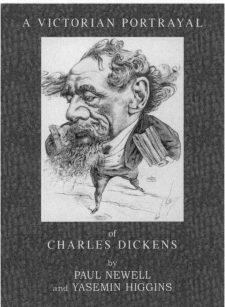

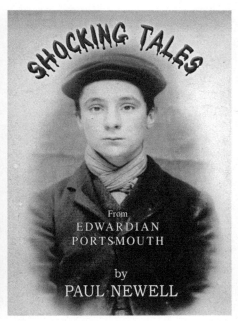

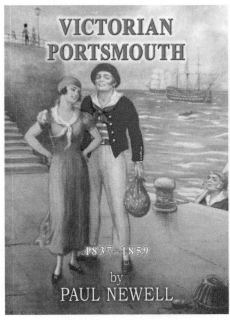

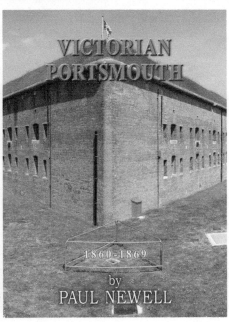

Shocking Tales from Victorian Whitechapel

Shocking Tales from Victorian Whitechapel

by
Paul Newell

Moyhill Publishing

© Copyright 2021 Paul Newell.

First Published in 2021 by Moyhill Publishing.
ISBN 978-1-913529-84-0

A CIP catalogue record for this book is availablefrom the British Library.

Transcripts and Images have been created by myself with thanks to
The British Newspaper archive (www.britishnewspaperarchive.co.uk),
or from my own private collection.

Book Design by *Moyhill* Publishing.

Cover image by publicdomainpictures from Pixabay.com

The papers used in this book were produced in an
environmentally friendly way from sustainable forests.

Moyhill Publishing,
1965 Davenport House, 261 Bolton Rd, Bury, Gtr. Manchester BL8 2NZ. UK

Contents

Contents

Contents

Contents

INTRODUCTION

Whitechapel – the area of the East End of London which gained notoriety the world over during the "*Autumn of Terror*" in 1888 when the infamous "Jack the Ripper" stalked the streets, plying his gruesome trade. But what of Whitechapel during the rest of the Victorian era. The place was already synonymous with crime, destitution, and as a collective for the poor, Jewish and Irish immigrants and the desperate – the perfect representation of the social deprivations as described by Charles Dickens in his novels.

Rapid industrialisation meant that migration from the countryside to the capitol intensified during Victorian times and the Whitechapel slum was a popular destination due to its cheap living quarters. By the 1890's, 250,000 were living in Whitechapel, crammed mainly into single-roomed accommodation, which inevitably led to overcrowding. This, coupled with poor ventilation and sanitary conditions meant disease was rife and crime was common. Poor lighting by single gas lamps led to dark corners, courts and alleys aiding the thief or murderer to disappear into the night. There were also over 200 common lodging houses which provided shelter for some 8,000 homeless and destitute people per night. Many of those seeking refuge were the "unfortunate" class who worked the streets at great risk to earn the fourpence to pay for a bed for a night. There was estimated to be 62 brothels in 1888, with 1,200 prostitutes competing for custom. The poorest areas were considered to be Flower Street, Dean Street, Dorset Street and Thrawl Street, with Dorset Street being considered the worst of them all.

William Booth began his missionary work in Whitechapel in 1865 forming the Christian Revival Society, later to become the Salvation Army in 1878, to try and alleviate some of the suffering.

At the same time, newspapers and penny papers (Dreadfuls) become more readily accessible to the masses and the sensationalism created by publications such as the *Illustrated Police News* fuelled the hype and hysteria, especially during the "*Autumn of Terror*." Each publication had to compete for sales so the headlines became more and more graphic to appease the salacious appetite for gruesome stories and crime. These papers also printed graphic illustrations of murders which gripped its readers and increased demand. There are many examples in this book.

I believe it is true to say that the sensational journalism of the time led to the creation of the image of "*Jack the Ripper*" and indeed, it was the journalists that gave the murderer his moniker, creating an almost supernatural being – a fiend who couldn't be caught. Indeed, it is alleged that in October 1888 a lady called Mary Burridge dropped dead after reading a graphic account of one of Jack's murders.

This book is a compilation of "*Shocking Tales*" selected from Victorian newspapers, reported verbatim to give the reader a flavour of life in those hard times. No book describing Victorian Whitechapel would be complete without a nod to its most famous son, "*Jack the Ripper*" so a separate section has been added entitled "*Autumn of Terror and Beyond*" to showcase the truly sensational nature of the Victorian Press.

Step back in time and wander the dimly lit courts and alleys of Victorian Whitechapel…but keep your wits about you…you never know who may be around the corner.

1838 – WHITECHAPEL FIRE.

At 9 o'clock on Thursday night the inhabitants of Whitechapel were thrown into a state of the greatest excitement by the outbreak of a fire in the extensive sugar baking premises of Messrs. F. Bowman and Son, in Duncan Street, Whitechapel. The fire broke out in what was denominated the casement of the factory, and in a few minutes, owing to the combustibility of the materials therein deposited, had attained alarming ascendancy. The buildings covered nearly two acres of ground, presenting a frontage in Duncan Street of 150 feet, and were raised to the height of five stories.

About half-past 9 o'clock part of the great walls fell in, and their fall forced down a portion of the sugar house of Messrs. Craven and Lucas, which is situated on the opposite side of the street. It is impossible to contemplate the lamentable results which might have ensued had the flames gained possession of these buildings, inasmuch as they are not only more extensive in their range but are somewhat more dangerously situated with regard to the adjacent houses.

The exertions of the firemen, which were unremitting, were about 12 o'clock rewarded by the certainty that they had obtained a mastery over the enemy, which by that hour presented an appearance of total subjection. Various reports are in circulation as to the value of the property destroyed, the most current being that it was much upwards of 100,000l. The backs of the houses in Great Alie Street suffered very considerably. The premises were known as the "Rushhouse," and are said to be insured in several of the offices to a large amount.

Not less than 3,000 persons were assembled, and, amongst others, a young man who slipped, and, falling down, was trampled on by the mob, who were still pushing forward. On being taken up, he was immediately conveyed on the shoulders of four men to the shop of Mr. Cheshire, surgeon, Whitechapel Road, when he was found to be horribly mutilated and quite dead. Deceased appeared to about 28 years of age and was well dressed. Several other accidents occurred.

As soon as the conflagration was somewhat got under, and no further danger expected, several firemen were, by the direction of Mr. Braidwood, employed to obtain for the various insurance companies particulars of the extent of the damage. On Friday morning Mr. Braidwood made the following report:-

At a quarter to nine o'clock a fire broke out on an extensive range of buildings situated on the south side of Duncan Street, Red Lion Street, Whitechapel, known as the Russian Sugar House, the property of Messrs. Frederick Boman and Son, sugar refiners, which destroyed the whole of the same; stock and buildings insured as follows:—Phoenix Fire office, £10,000; Imperial Fire office, £7,000; Scottish Fire office, £5,000; Sun Fire office, £3,000; West of England Fire office, £2,800.—Total, £27,800.

A large sugar house, the property of the same firm, situated in Half Moon Alley, Great Alie Street, much damage to the front of the building, and window casement burned out, stock and contents much damaged by water; insured in the Sun, Phoenix, Imperial, and Scottish Union offices. The premises of Messrs. Craven and Lucas sugar boilers and refiners, opposite those of Messrs. Boman and Son (burned down), considerably damaged in front of the building; fully insured in the Sun and other offices. The premises adjoining, used as workmen's houses, belonging to the sugar factory of Messrs. Craven and Lucas, considerably damaged; insured. The whole frontage of this building was driven in by the front wall of Messrs. Boman's premises falling into the street.

Bell's New Weekly Messenger – 23rd December 1838.

1839 – EXPLOSION IN WHITECHAPEL.

On Monday night a Jury was sworn by Mr. Baker, the Coroner, to inquire into the circumstances attendant on the deaths of Samuel Marshall, aged 15 years, and Richard Sterne, aged 32.

The Coroner and Jury, in the first instance, proceeded to the London Hospital to view the body of Sterne, which was sadly mutilated. They then took a careful view of the premises of Mr. Marshall, where the unfortunate occurrence took place, and expressed much surprise at the scene of devastation which presented itself; and ultimately returned to the Half Moon and Punch Bowl public house, in Buckle Street, to view the body of Marshall, which was placed on a table in an upstairs room, and presented a most frightful spectacle, being most dreadfully mangled. The right arm, which was blown completely off a little above the elbow, was placed on the same table, behind the head.

On the Coroner and Jury reaching the inquest room, the following evidence was given:-

Mr. Joseph Lane, of No. 4, Berner Street, Commercial Road East, deposed that he was clerk and foreman to Mr. John Marshall, steam engine boiler manufacturer in Colchester Street, in that neighbourhood, and whose son, Samuel Marshall, was one of the deceased. On Saturday evening

Master Marshall was employed with Richard Sterne, a workman, in proving a boiler on the premises – a process which all boilers were put through previous to their being sent out. The process consists in putting water into the boiler, and getting the steam up to a certain degree, to test its strength and stability. The intended working of the boiler then under proof was about 40lbs. to the square inch, so that a proof of its capability to 50lbs or 60lbs. was all that was intended to be proved, though, in his opinion it was capable of bearing 120lbs. to the square inch. Some hundreds of boilers had been tested on the same premises in precisely the same manner, by Mr. Marshall, without the slightest accident happening. The boiler in question was 26 feet long, and six in diameter, with a tube of three feet in diameter. Mr. Marshall, Sen., had been present during the greater part of the process of proving, and witness heard him tell the deceased, when the steam had got up to 60, to ease the weight on the safety valve, to let the steam blow off, and slack the fire.

Coroner: Do you know, of your own knowledge, what the power of steam was at the time you heard Mr. Marshall say this?

Witness: I cannot say exactly, but I should suppose from 50 to 60. Mr. Marshall, after giving these directions, walked from the spot; he had been standing close to the boiler, and entered the counting house, where he (witness) was at the time engaged, and had not been there more than from 10 to 12 minutes when a dreadful explosion took place. Master Marshall and Richard Sterne had, a moment before, been close to the boiler, and both were used to, and conversant with such work, as well as the danger attendant upon it in case of negligence. The outward tube was driven eastward, towards Church Lane, about 15 yards, carrying everything in its way along with it, and was ultimately stopped by coming against the end of a wall. The inner tube was forced in an opposite direction, about the same distance, and it also tore to pieces everything opposed to it in its progress. One of the legs of a triangle, a beam of timber 70 feet long, and weighing, at least, eight cwt., was driven 50 feet from its original position, and, in its fall, had stuck a considerable distance in the ground.

A juror here remarked that it must have been forced into the air a great distance, else it could not in its fall have buried its end such a distance in the earth.

The witness further stated that a half-hundred metal weight, and a bar of iron weighing nearly 60lbs., had been blown into the air, and, having passed over the houses, fell upwards of 70 yards from the premises. The body of Samuel was found on a dung heap, at a distance of upwards of 60 feet from where he must have been standing at the time the explosion took place, with a part of the internal tube upon it. It was dreadfully mutilated, with the right arm, which was found about forty feet from the spot, blown off. The body of Sterne was found in the same direction, but about 30 feet farther eastward in Buckle Street. It was some distance beyond the large gates leading to the premises from Buckle Street, and which were blown down by the explosion. He (Sterne), though seriously injured, and perfectly insensible, was not quite dead; but he expired a short time after being brought to the London Hospital. The usual course of proving steam boilers is by hydraulic pressure first, and by steam afterwards; and both tests were tried in this instance. The inner tube became collapsed, but he had no doubt this was the result of accident.

Mr. John Marshall, the father of the deceased Samuel Marshall, who seemed overwhelmed with grief, was the next witness examined. He attributed the accident to Sterne's neglecting to comply with the orders of letting off the steam. He (Mr. Marshall) always proved the boilers at night when the workmen were away, so that it might be done with more regularity, and that the person attending on him might hear his directions.

Coroner: Then is it your opinion that the explosion was perfectly accidental, and from the safety valve sticking?

Mr. Marshall: It is.

Coroner: I believe that, independent of the loss of your son, you are also a serious loser by the destruction of your property? – I am.

The Jury expressed themselves perfectly satisfied, and unanimously returned a verdict of "Accidental Death" in both cases.

The Era – 10th March 1839.

1839 – A NOTORIOUS THIEF.

Yesterday John Brown, a notorious thief and returned transport, was charged before Mr. Hardwick with the following impudent and daring highway robbery.

George William Founds, a sergeant of the City police, No. 322, and who is a tall and powerful young man, stated that having leave of absence from duty on the preceding day, he had been to see some friends in Essex, and on his return about half-past eleven at night, and while passing the end of Essex Street, Whitechapel, a man rushed between him and a friend who was with him, and gave him a violent blow on the left eye. On recovering from the effects of the blow, he instantly put his hand into his fob pocket, and discovered that his watch and appendages were gone, upon which he charged a young man, who stood close to him, with taking it, and the accused person instantly struck him a blow to the back of the neck with his fist, but was secured and taken to the station house.

Mr. James Bishop, a respectable tradesman in the City, deposed that he was walking along Whitechapel on the preceding night, in company with the last witness, when a man passed between them, and struck Founds, and on hearing the latter exclaim that he had lost his watch, he followed and seized the man who struck his friend. A violent struggle took place between them, during which he succeeded in getting his opponent down, and while on the ground struck him several blows on the face, which must have caused him to bleed profusely, as his hand was afterwards covered with blood. The man, however, kicked him so violently on the shins, that he was compelled to relinquish his hold of him, so that he got away.

James Sullen, a cellarman at the Whittington and Cat public house, High Street Whitechapel, said that, on observing the disturbance on the other side of the street on the night before, he crossed over to see what was the matter, and just as he reached the crowd, the prosecutor accused him of stealing his watch, upon which he, on the impulse of the moment, struck him. He was then taken into custody, and conveyed to the station house, when, on the declaration of his master that he had not been out of the house at the time the robbery took place, he was discharged. On his (witness) first going up to the crowd, he saw two men struggling on the ground, and one of those he was certain was the prisoner, who at that time had his coat on.

A witness, named Pritchard, also said he saw two persons struggling on the ground, and on approaching them his foot struck against something, which on picking up he found to be a silver watch and appendages, and which were afterwards identified by the prosecutor as his.

Police Sergeant Carr, H 109, deposed that a short time after the robbery he observed the prisoner without his coat, and knowing his character he took him into custody on suspicion of being concerned in the robbery but he denied all knowledge of it. On reaching the station house he observed that the prisoner's left temple was cut and bleeding, and that his countenance wore other marks of punishment; and on asking him what had caused it his reply was that it had been done by him (Carr) while conveying him to the station house, though he had never as much as laid a finger upon him.

The prisoner denied the charge, and said it was not at all likely that a person of his size would have attempted anything so daring as to rob a man so much more powerful than himself, and that too while accompanied by another, in the public street.

He was fully committed for trial.

Morning Advertiser – 18th September 1839.

1839 – A VIOLENT ASSAULT.

Yesterday, William Sainsby, a dwarfish tailor, was charged with having violently assaulted a respectable looking woman, named Leary, the wife of a porter at the Bank of England.

The complainant stated that at a late hour on the preceding night she was returning home from a party under her husband's protection, when they saw the prisoner at the corner of Goswell Street, in company with two other men. Her husband had occasion to leave her for a moment, which he had no sooner done, than one of the prisoner's friends advanced towards her and began to take the most indecent liberties with her. She called out to her husband, who immediately ran up and expostulated with the fellow, upon which the prisoner struck him a violent blow in the face. On her interposing to protect her husband, she was herself attacked in the most savage manner by the prisoner, who tore her bonnet and cap from her head, and knocked her down twice.

Her husband, in the meantime, was engaged in a struggle with the prisoner's companions, in the course of which he got severely handled. Their cries for assistance at length brought a private watchman to the spot, who secured the prisoner; but his two friends effected their escape. The cap, bonnet, and shawl were completely destroyed, and she lost a new pair of clogs in the confusion.

The complainant exhibited her tattered attire for the Magistrate's inspection, and pointed out some contusions on the neck which she sustained from the prisoner's violence.

Her husband confirmed her testimony, and described the prisoner's conduct to have been most outrageous. He was himself very roughly treated, his coat being torn in several places, and his hat lost altogether.

The watchman part corroborated the evidence, and said that the prisoner had evidently been drinking freely.

In answer to the charge, the prisoner said that he was first assailed by two or three women, who plucked the hair from his head and rolled him in the mud. He declared that he had only acted in self-defence.

Mr. Grove said that the prisoner's conduct had been most disgraceful and dastardly, and had fairly earned the character proverbially attributed to his class, of possessing only a tithe of manhood. He was fined 20s for the assault, or to be committed to the House of Correction for one month, he was also ordered to pay 23s. for the damage done, or to be imprisoned for a further term of fourteen days.

The prisoner was locked up in default of payment.

Morning Advertiser – 18th September 1839.

1841 – THE WHITECHAPEL UNION.

Sir,

In a morning paper of this day there is letter, signed "Medicus," attributing the increase of fever in some unions mentioned to the high price of food, and the most striking instance named by the writer is Whitechapel Union, where out of 5,800 paupers 2,400 are said have been attacked by the disease. Now, Sir, the writer of the letter in question, if he had made proper inquiries, would have found that the prevalence of fever in the Whitechapel Union is owing to a very different cause than that assumed for it, viz., – to the want of sewers.

In the Parish of Whitechapel, which contains upwards of 31,000 souls, there was till within a year or two scarcely a single sewer, although many of the inhabitants have been paying a sewer rate for a century; and when the number of confined courts and alleys in the district is considered, the prevalence of fever will no longer be a matter of surprise. Most parts of the district are still most inefficiently drained, and in some streets the number of cesspools has caused the earth to be completely saturated.

I am sir, your obedient servant,
An old inhabitant of the Whitechapel Union.

Evening Mail – 11th October 1841.

1841 – SPREAD OF FEVER.

"In going over the Whitechapel workhouse I was struck with the statement of the fact, that out of 104 girls resident in the workhouse 89 have recently been attacked with fever. On examining the room in which these children sleep my wonder ceased – all these 104 children, together with four women who have the charge of them, sleep in it. The beds are close to each other. In all the beds there are never less than four children – in many five. The ventilation of the room is most imperfect. Under such circumstances the breaking out of fever is inevitable.

"In another establishment (the Jews' Hospital) not far distant from Whitechapel workhouse, for several years in succession it was found impossible to prevent the breaking out of fever among the young people until the dormitories were less crowded and more perfectly ventilated. I was likewise struck with the pale and unhealthy appearance of a number of the children in the Whitechapel workhouse, in a room called the infant nursery. These children appeared to be from two to three years of age. They are 23 in number. They all sleep in one room, and they seldom or never go out of this room either for air or exercise."

Freeman's Journal – 26th November 1841.

1842 – CORN LAW AGITATION.

Last night a numerous meeting of the members of the Whitechapel and Stepney Anti Corn Law Association, was held at the Grave Maurice Tavern, Whitechapel, for the purpose of expressing their opinions on the ministerial measure of the Corn laws; Mr. Moss, churchwarden, in the chair.

Mr. Bishop proposed a resolution, that "It is the opinion of this meeting that the proposition of Sir Robert Peel, for the modification of the Corn laws, is an insult and an injury to the country; that therefore steps should be taken to obtain a total repeal of all taxes that constitute the sustenance of man." The present government having had time granted them, ought to have been prepared with some remedy.

Mr. Little seconded the motion.

Other gentlemen having addressed the chair, the resolution was put and carried unanimously, followed by loud cheers for repeal and three groans for Sir Robert Peel.

Mr. Martin, a delegate from Leicester, next addressed the meeting, stating that the warehouses of the manufacturers were crammed with goods, for which there were no purchasers.

It was announced that the petition to the House of Commons, for the total repeal of the Corn laws, from Whitechapel and Stepney Anti Corn Law

Association, and which will be presented on Monday night, had nearly 30,000 signatures. A memorial to the Queen (which has already been signed by above 70,000 of the inhabitants) requesting that her Majesty will adopt measures to secure to the people of England a total repeal of the Corn laws, is also in course of signature.

Globe – 12th February 1842.

1843 – JUMPING OUT OF THE WINDOW.

Yesterday afternoon an inquest was held before Mr. W Baker, the Coroner for the eastern division of Middlesex, at the London Hospital, Whitechapel Road, to inquire into the circumstances attending the death of Mary Rowe, aged 52, late an inmate of Whitechapel workhouse, who destroyed herself under the following shocking circumstances:-

Norah Delahunt, a nurse in the workhouse, said, that the deceased was taken into the union in January last as a pauper. The husband of deceased was a pensioner at Greenwich Hospital. On Monday morning last, at half-past 6 o'clock, witness was standing in the same ward in which deceased slept, when she heard an alarm raised, and upon looking round saw the feet of deceased in the air, she having precipitated herself out of the window; and before any person could get to her assistance, she had fallen to the ground beneath, a distance of 30 feet. She was picked up, and a surgeon sent for, but life was quite gone.

In answer to the Coroner witness replied that she never saw anything strange in the conduct of the deceased, who was allowed her liberty in the union the same as any other pauper; in fact, she was not under the least personal restraint whilst in the house, more than being obliged to remain at night in what was termed the "sleeping ward." On the day following that on which deceased was admitted into the workhouse she cut her throat, but from the medical treatment she received she entirely recovered from the loss of blood on that occasion.

On Wednesday last she asked, and obtained, permission to go and see her husband at Greenwich; on her return to the union she told witness that she had injured herself by asking for a holiday, as one of the guardians had told her that she was an able-bodied person, and that she must try and work partly for her living, and that he would allow her a loaf of bread and a shilling at certain intervals, which deceased objected to, and said, rather than leave the union she would destroy herself.

Joseph Edmonds, porter in the workhouse, corroborated part of the above evidence, and added, that deceased was a habitual drunkard, and would, before her admission into the union, spend all her money to obtain drink. Since last January, the time when she attempted to destroy herself by cutting her throat, witness had observed nothing in her conduct to lead him to suppose her mind was affected.

Mr. John Miller, assistant-surgeon to the union, said he was called to see deceased on Monday morning last, a few minutes after the occurrence. On his arrival he found her quite dead. She had fallen upon her head and must have died instantaneously. Witness added that she had made no less than four different attempts to destroy herself. A short time back she had two houses left her, which she sold, and then squandered the money away in drink. Witness could not speak positively as to the state of mind deceased was in at the time she committed the act. He had been told that she had orders given to leave the union, and rather than do so she had threatened to destroy herself.

The Coroner said he had often heard of persons threatening to commit suicide through fear of being obliged to go into a workhouse, but he never before heard of anyone attempting to do the like because they were obliged to leave it. He (the Coroner) thought the previous attempt deceased had made upon her life was quite sufficient to satisfy the Jury that her mind had been disordered; and, although nothing particular had been perceived in her conduct during the last few months to cause her to be watched or put under restraint, yet he thought the same disorder might be lurking within and unperceived.

Verdict, "Temporary Insanity."

Evening Mail – 8th September 1843.

1844 – THE PLIGHT OF THE POOR.

Within these last few days, the number of people, more than half naked, who have for some time past been wandering about the streets, a prey to disease and famine, has been visibly increased. Every winter is attended by the same occurrence. The remote cause is the operation of the corn laws, as we have often shown; but the proximate cause is the cessation of employment in the fields and gardens. There they have further prospect of obtaining food or shelter, and they very naturally flock to those places where princes and merchants "most do congregate," in the slender hope that the casual donations of the benevolent may enable them to prolong their miserable existence until the spring, when they again return to their labour.

There are, as everybody knows, charitable associations, which provide a shelter for the night, with a quantity of bread, for these wretched outcasts, but they appear to be bound by some peculiar law in their constitution. They have not yet commenced their humane work, notwithstanding the urgency of the case, of which any street in the metropolis will furnish proofs. Rather earlier than this time last winter, about the latter end of October, we believe, the *Times* called attention to the horrible fact, that human beings were nightly huddled together in the Parks, and almost beneath the windows of the nobility. This announcement was followed by several good effects, of which one was the immediate opening of the nightly asylums, and another was the provision of workhouse asylums, under certain regulations, by a clause in Sir James Graham's amended Poor Law Act.

There was great need of the latter, because by orders of the Commissioners of Woods and Forests, and the Commissioners of Metropolitan Police, care was taken that for the future no houseless wanderer should make comfortless home in a hollow tree, or under an earth bank in the parks. And apparently, at least, on the face of the Act of Parliament, there is not the slightest reason for any one, however destitute he may be, to pass the night without food and the shelter of a roof.

There must, however, be some very great fault in the working of Sir James Graham's humane clause, for many of the wretches, perishing with hunger, and shivering with wet and cold, at any time more pernicious to life than frost, are still creeping through the streets, as if there was no such thing in the world as a workhouse asylum. What is the reason of this? The public have a right to an answer from whomsoever is in possession of the facts. In the meantime, we can but state what appears in occasional paragraphs and police reports. These concur in representing the work required from the poor, who receive a small piece of bread and a pint of thin gruel, with their shelter, as much too long and laborious for the accommodation. In other words, the poor calculate that too great a profit is made by this official charity. For a quantity of bread (said to be ounces) which is worth about one halfpenny, and one pint of water with something floating in it, worth another, they are required to work two hours in the best part of the day. Hence it is that common vagrants take the relief, but obstinately refuse the work, while those who really stand in need of the former, are, from weakness and illness, incapable of

labour without the quantity of food that is necessary to enable them to go through it.

This is not all; there are others of these poor wretches, who, being very evidently fit subjects for the hospital, are not deemed fit to be taken into the workhouse asylum. Yesterday Mr. Cooke, the keeper of Lambeth Street police court, informed the Magistrate that a poor man was on the outside, "frightfully ruptured," and in a state of the most deplorable destitution; and that he had been dragging himself through the streets for three successive nights, in consequence of having been refused admittance into the Whitechapel workhouse asylum; so that he was now unable to stand. Of course, the Magistrate directed care to be taken of him; but that is not the thing; Magistrates are not relieving officers, nor are police cells asylums for the distresses of poverty. We say again that something must be dreadfully wrong in the practical part of the clause, especially enacted for the relief of the houseless poor, and hope that the proper authorities will forthwith take the steps necessary to give it the effect which it was intended to have. The people now without a home, without clothes and without food, are neither sturdy vagrants nor idle beggars, but hardworking people, whose employment, dependent at best upon the fineness of the weather, is entirely suspended with the close of the autumn. The asylums provided for them by Sir James Graham's Act ought to be constantly ready to receive them, and on easy terms as possible. As for those of charitable institutions, we have no right to interfere with their regulations, but should be glad to see them preventing such heartrending cases as that relieved by the police Magistrate.

1845 – HOARDING AND MISERY.

At the Thames Police office, Wednesday, a most extraordinary case was brought before Mr. Broderip, by Mr. David Warlters, boot and shoe maker, Rosemary Lane, Whitechapel.

Mr Warlters stated that adjoining his place of business was a large cow yard, the gates of which opened into Rosemary Lane, a place which is the abode of more filth, misery, and destitution than any other locality in the metropolis. In the cow yard, in which there was considerable property, dairy utensils, and eleven cows, was a small and very miserable dwelling house, the receptacle of dirt and lumber, in which the owner of the dairy, William Chapman, his sister, Elizabeth Chapman, whose name was over the door, and a brother had for some time resided. They were all far advanced in life, and notorious for their penurious habits. The two brothers, though living in the same house, entertained the most deadly animosity towards each other, and, but for the interference of the sister, one would have been sacrificed to the hatred of the other long since.

About one o'clock that morning Mrs. Warlters was informed by a neighbour that the sister, who was called Mrs. Chapman, was dying, and she dressed herself and went into the house in the cow yard, and found the statement too true; and was so alarmed at the aspect of the woman, and the humble appearance of the dwelling, that she left immediately, and requested him to go in. He did so, and, finding the woman in a lifeless state, he sent for a surgeon in Wellclose Square, who came immediately, and pronounced her to be dead. He then sent a messenger for Mrs. Ruffle, a widow, and the niece of the deceased, who kept a baker's shop at No. 121, Rosemary Lane. She came to the house as early as possible, and, though previously acquainted with the miserly habits of her uncles and aunt, was quite unprepared for the dreadful scene of which she was compelled to be an eyewitness.

In a small, dark, and low-roofed apartment, on the first floor, they found the brother of the cow keeper, in a most wretched plight, covered with filth and vermin. The miserable creature had shut himself up in this room for the last two years, and was never out of it except for a few days last summer. The room had never been cleaned out during that time, and the man had never washed himself. They found him sitting on some rubbish which had formed the materials of a bed. There was nothing on his person but an old jacket, and he had suffered his hair, beard, and nails to grow for years, which gave him a hideous appearance. There was not a vestige of furniture in the room, but the entrance was nearly blocked up by rubbish. The stench was quite overpowering, and the wretched man had remained in this horrible place during the whole of the late severe weather without any fire, and was scantily fed by his sister.

Mr. Warlters added that a more appalling sight was impossible to conceive, and that unless the dwelling was cleansed and fumigated, he was afraid some contagious disease would be engendered. He understood the brother of the cow keeper was the owner of estates in Leicestershire, which realised a considerable income, but the man, who had become imbecile, denied himself the common necessaries of life.

The deceased Mrs. Chapman was for some time preceding her death in a similar filthy state, though she was enabled to command luxuries. She never paid any attention to personal cleanliness, and when she died had nothing on her person but an old gown and a bit of flannel, not worth sixpence, which had been her dress for some time! He asked the cow keeper how he came to let his brother and sister remain in such a miserable condition, and he replied in a surly manner that his brother had property of his own, and that he would not have kept him so long but for his sister. He then asked him if he should apply to the parish authorities, and he said his brother must go somewhere, for he would not keep him any longer.

Mr. Warlters added that the cow keeper was ninety years of age, and his brother was between seventy and eighty.

Mr. Broderip directed Macready, No. 93 H, one of the summoning officers of the court, to wait upon the parochial authorities of Whitechapel, and visit the place.

In the afternoon Macready said the description given by Mr. Warlters fell short of the reality. He was quite horror struck at the appearance of the cow keeper's brother, who was in a very emaciated state, with scarcely any semblance of humanity about him. The room had not been cleaned out for six years, and the creature was quite helpless. An attempt had been made to light a fire in the aperture where the stove had once been. This had failed, owing to the wind blowing down the chimney and scattering the fragments about the room, where they had ever since remained. The room in which he found the cow keeper was also in a filthy state, and the man himself had no razor to cross his chin or soap and water to come in contact with his face for several months. The room in which the sister died was closed, and he was of opinion that if the dwelling were not cleansed and limewashed the remaining inmates would not long survive. He had waited upon Mr Hughes, the relieving officer of the Whitechapel union, who had promised to remove the cow keeper's brother to the workhouse, where he would be properly fed and clothed.

Mr. Broderip said he should leave the case in the hands of the parish officers. Mr. Hughes subsequently visited the place, in company with Mr. Warlters and another person, but such was the noxious effluvia that they were glad to make a precipitate retreat. It would be absurd to compare the abode of a savage with the dwelling in Rosemary Lane, for nothing like it was ever seen among the savage tribes.

In addition to eleven cows and a large quantity of dairy utensils, there is some valuable property in the lower part of the house, but so covered with the filth that has been accumulating for years that its real value cannot be ascertained. The cow keeper is reported to be worth 11,000l.; and his sister, who confined herself to the most spare diet, and refused to send for medical assistance when she was taken ill, is said to have died rich. The Chapmans have been familiarly known as the "three misers."

Westmorland Gazette – 8th February 1845.

━━◉━━

1846 – SUDDEN DEATH IN A GIN PALACE.

About four o'clock on the afternoon of Saturday, a respectable old German, named Jacob Baker, who was formerly master of a vessel, but has recently obtained a subsistence by acting as interpreter and translator for his countrymen, with the addition of a small weekly donation from the German Chapel, in Great Alie Street, Whitechapel, went into the Roebuck gin palace. Cannon Street Road, St. George in the East, London, and asked for a pint of beer in his jug and a quartern of gin in a bottle. Having made his order, he retired to a seat in front of the bar, and instantly expired. Dr. Cory, who resides immediately opposite, was in prompt attendance, but the poor fellow was beyond all human assistance.

Nottinghamshire Guardian – 21st August 1846.

━━◉━━

1847 – THE GIN PALACE.

The gin palace is generally at the corner of two interesting streets in a gin drinking neighbourhood; it towers, in all the majesty of stucco pilasters, in genuine cockney splendour, over the dingy mansions that support it, like a rapacious tyrant over his impoverished subjects.

The doors are large, swinging easily upon patent hinges, and ever half-and-half open, half-shut, so that the most undecided touch of the dram drinker admits him. The windows are of plate glass, set in brass sashes, and are filled with flaming announcements in large letters, "The Cheapest House in London," – "Cream of the Valley," – "Creaming Stout," – "Brilliant Ales," – "Old Tom, fourpence a quartern" – "Hodge's Best for mixing," – and a variety of other entertainments for the men and beasts who make the gin palace their home.

At night splendid lights irradiate the surrounding gloom, and an illuminated clock serves to remind the toper of the time he throws away in dethroning his reason.

Within, the splendour is in keeping with the splendour without; counters fitted with zinc, and a long array of brass tap fittings of the finest Spanish mahogany, beautifully polished; bottles, containing cordials, and other drugs, gilded and labelled, as in the apothecary's shops. At one side is the bar parlour, an apartment fitted up with congenial taste, and usually occupied by the family of the publican; in the distance are vistas, and sometimes galleries, formed altogether of huge vats of the various sorts of liquor dispensed in the establishment.

Behind the counter, which is usually raised to a level with the breasts of the topers, stand men in their shirt sleeves, well-dressed females, or both, dispensers of the "short" and "heavy" the undersized tipplers, raising themselves tiptoe, deposit the three-halfpence for the "drop" of gin, or whatever else they require, and receive the quantum of the poison in return; ragged women, with starving children, match and ballad fill up the foreground of the picture.

There are no seats, nor any accommodation for the customers, in the regular gin palace; exertion is used to make the place as uncomfortable to the consumer as possible, that they shall only step in to drink, and pay; step out, and return to drink and pay again. No food of any kind is provided at the gin palace, save a few biscuits, which are exhibited in a wire cage, for protection against the furtive hand; drink, eternal, poisonous drink, is the sole provision of the whited sepulchre.

There is not in all London a more melancholy and spirit-depressing sight than the area of one of the larger gin palaces on a wet night. There the homeless, houseless miserable of both sexes, whether they have money or not, resort in numbers for a temporary shelter; aged women selling ballads and matches, cripples, little beggar boys and girls, slavering idiots, pie men, sandwich men, apple and orange women, shellfish mongers, huddle pell-mell, in draggle-tailed confusion. Never can human nature, one would imagine, take a more abject posture than is exhibited; there is a character, an individuality, a family likeness common to the whole race of sots; the pale, clayey, flaccid, clammy face, pinched in every feature the weeping, ferret-like, lacklustre eye, the unkempt hair, the slattern shawl, the untidy dress, the slip-shod gait, too well betray the confirmed drunkard.

The noise, too, of the assembled topers are hideous; appalling even when heard in an atmosphere of gin. Imprecations, execrations, objurgations, applications, until at length the patience of the publican, and the last copper of his customers, are exhausted, when, rushing from behind his counter, assisted by his shopmen, he expels, *vi et armis*, the dilatory mob, dragging out by the heels or collars the dead drunkards, to nestle, as best they may, outside the unhospitable door.

Here, unobserved, may you contemplate the infinite varieties of men self-metamorphosed into beasts; soaker, tippler, toper, muddler, dram drinker, bear swiller, cordial tipper, sot.

Here you may behold the barefoot child, hungry, naked, clay faced, handing up on tiptoe that infernal bottle, which made it, and keeps it what it is, with which, when filled, it creeps home to its brutal father, or infamous mother, the messenger of its own misery.

Here the steady respectable sot, the good customer, slices in and flings down his throat the frequent dram; then, with an emphatic "hah" of gratification, drops his money, nods to his friend, the landlord, and for a short interval disappears.

Here you may behold with pity and regret, and as much superadded virtuous indignation as the inward contemplation of your own countenance may inspire, the flaunting Cyprian, in over-dressed tawdriness, calling, in shameless voice for a quartern of "pleasant gin", which she liberally shares with two or three gentlemen, who are being educated for the bar of the Central Criminal Court. You may contrast her short-lived hey-day of prosperous sin with that row of miserables seated by the wall, whose charms are fled, and whose voices are husky, while they implore you to treat them with a glass of ale, or supplicate for the coppers they see you receive in change from the barman; and who are only permitted that wretched place of rest that they may beg for the benefit of the publican, and for his profit poison themselves with the alms of others.

John O'Groats Journal – 29th October 1847.

1848 – A MURDERER'S DEN.

About twelve months ago, the parochial surveyors of Whitechapel condemned several houses in Tewkesbury Court, High Street, as being from age and decay dangerous and unfit for habitation. The premises having passed into a speculative builder's hands, their demolition has revealed some most fearful testimony of the spot having at some period been the scene of horrid tragedies.

The locality in question is known to antiquarians as the spot whereon stood Tewksbury church, but of late years has been better known to the police as one of the worst harbours of crime in the metropolis;

indeed, so intricate were the premises and villainous the colonists, that once in its precincts the refugee, be he murderer, burglar, smasher, or thief, could safely baffle the pursuit of the officers of justice.

The recent discoveries at once explain how this has been affected. In pulling down one of the most notorious of the dwellings, the labourers discovered a cellar, in digging up which the skeletons of children and adults were found; in this cellar they at last came to what appeared, at first sight, to be a cesspool, but what is now found to be the entrance of a subterraneous passage, of sufficient diameter for ingress or egress of adults, but where this leads, or rather terminates, is at present undiscovered, as the work of demolition is not sufficiently advanced for the exploration of the mysterious pit; in this horrid place the labourers found the bodies of two fine fellows in a good state of preservation, attired in the garb of sailors, standing upright in the soil, their appearances giving every indication of their having been the victims of a cruel murder.

Sickening as the above details are, we would willingly, if it were only for the credit of human nature, be spared chronicling the sequel, for after the labourers had dug out the bodies, it appears a council of their companions was called, the issue of which was the bodies were stripped, hacked to pieces with spades and picks, and the mangled remains carted to distant receptacles for the deposit of their rubbish. The only excuse, if any excuse can be entertained for so great a violation of decency and frustration of justice, would appear to be that, if the affair got to the knowledge of the Coroner, as witnesses they would lose their time and pay at the inquest.

The general rumour and which if correct may define the right cause of the outrage, is that the fellows disposed of the clothes and watch which was found on the persons of the deceased. The affair has been diligently investigated by Mackintosh, 98 H., an intelligent and shrewd officer, but it may be readily conceived he is engaged in a difficult task, for, even if he but succeeds in gathering the bones of the unfortunate sailors, all evidence of identity is destroyed; it is, however, to be hoped that some of the mechanics engaged at the time upon the works will come forward and assist the constable in the horrible, mysterious, and disgraceful affair, as it is needless to state that he can get no information from the Irish labourers, who have so brutally frustrated the course of justice.

Beside the discovery above mentioned, we have ascertained that numerous secret recesses found in the building brought to light traces of iniquity in the shape of silver spoons and other valuable property; it is to be hoped that the further exploration of the subterraneous den will not be left to the barbarians who have commenced it, but that if the parochial authorities refuse, the police at least will explore into what one would be led to expect as likely to bring to light evidences of a harrowing description.

Fife Herald – 30th March 1848.

1848 – WHITECHAPEL CHARTISTS.

The Chartists of the district east of Whitechapel assembled shortly before 9 o'clock on Stepney Green. At a few minutes past 9 o'clock the procession started at a good round pace. It was headed by a band of music, and from the numbers on the banners appeared to represent seven or eight lodges. Other banners were intermixed, with inscriptions, such as "Frost, Williams, and Jones, the political prisoners;" "If we will, we can be free." Some of the party had crimson, and others green ribands in their button holes. There were from 600 to 700 persons in the procession. Their general appearance was not particularly prepossessing; but though there might be some whose gait was somewhat free and easy when trudging through the mire of Whitechapel, there were others whose appearance was decent, and whose demeanour indicated earnestness of purpose. A crowd of boys accompanied the procession, increasing, of course, in numbers every minute.

Before reaching Aldgate, the procession diverged to the right, and joining a much larger body of Chartists which had assembled in Finsbury Square at 9 o'clock, proceeded down Bishopsgate Street, Gracechurch Street, through King William Street, and across London bridge. As it approached the shops were closed, to be opened again so soon as it had passed. It sometimes happened, as at the point where Bishopsgate Street, Gracechurch Street, Leadenhall Street, and Cornhill meet, that a deadlock would occur, involving omnibus, cab, waggon, and passengers, in most admired disorder; but generally, the procession moved easily along, exciting some interest and some confusion, but not very much of either.

As the procession emerged from King William Street, it had swollen to some 2,500, walking sometimes six and sometimes ten abreast. Five Chartists of the fair sex were of the procession. There were three tricolour flags and the emblems of several trades, but the most conspicuous banner was one of crimson and green, extended between two poles, bearing the inscription—"The voice of the people

the voice of God." This banner unfortunately fell in the mud at King William Street, but its bearers soon rearranged their gear and regained the procession. We observed only one man who had a stick.

About two o'clock bands of stragglers returning from Kennington announced the issue of the meeting, and the pacific counsels which had prevailed. Both ends of London bridge had been lined by special constables, of whom numbers were sworn in while the procession was in progress. The communication, however, across London was at no period interrupted; and the processionists were soon lost in the masses that usually crowd the city thoroughfares.

Weekly Chronicle (London) – 16th April 1848.

1848 – FATAL CONFLAGRATION IN WHITECHAPEL.

On Saturday morning the inhabitants of Whitechapel Road, in the immediate vicinity of the church, were aroused from their slumbers by the springing of rattles. and a general cry of "Fire!"

In the course of a few minutes, it could be distinctly seen that the premises belonging to Mr. Alfred Frederick Watkinson, a staymaker and milliner, No. 45, Whitechapel Road, were on fire. At that time the inmates, consisting of about half a dozen persons, were in their beds asleep. The police who were on duty in the district commenced knocking violently at the street door, and, after considerable trouble, succeeded in awaking Mr. Watkinson, but not until the shop and staircase were completely enveloped in flame, so that all means of descending to the street door were cut off.

The other inmates having been made sensible of the great danger to which they were exposed, attempted, but in vain, to get down the stairs, and the moment they got on the landing they were met by such a dense mass of flame and smoke as nearly suffocated them. Having retraced their steps to the upper rooms, they opened their window and called loudly to the people below to assist them. Unfortunately, the nearest station of the Royal Society for the Protection of Life from Fire was at Aldgate pump, a distance of considerably more than half a mile, consequently some time was lost before the necessary intelligence could be conveyed to the conductor; and when it arrived the fire had made too great a havoc for it to be of any assistance.

Seeing the perilous condition of the inmates, the crowd called to them to jump out of the window, and that they would catch them. A Mr. Pitt at once obeyed the order, and he fortunately received no injury. Mrs. Pitt, with her daughter and son, a little boy, made to the upper part of the house, hoping there to be secure until the fire escape arrived. In that, however, they were doomed to disappointment, and in the course of a few minutes the room was filled with hot smoke, which compelled them to retreat to a lower floor. Upon getting to this part of the building, Mrs. Pitt beheld a most distressing scene. An elder son, a lad about 13 years of age, was running to and fro in the midst of the flame, and unable to reach his mother. In vain he cried out for assistance, for the flames ascended so fiercely that it was impossible for the unfortunate woman or anyone else to get to him. Half paralyzed with grief and fear the poor creature ran to the window with two of her children at her side. She was repeatedly told to get out and walk along the blind box over the shop front, but this she refused, and said, "she would never leave unless she could rescue her boy, who was in the midst of the fire."

There is no doubt that, had it not been for the praiseworthy and intrepid conduct of Mr. Watkinson. both Mrs. Pitt and the two children would have been burnt to death; as it is, it is extremely doubtful whether she and her daughter will survive the injuries they have received.

Owing to the great quantity of timber used in the construction of the building, but few minutes passed away before the house, from the ground floor to the room in which the inmates were, was in one immense sheet of flame, which rushed through the door and window shutters with the greatest impetuosity, and extended completely over the footpath into the middle of the road. Mr. Watkinson, at this juncture, got upon the narrow lead flat, and, although the flames mounted over his head, succeeded in snatching from the flames a child about four years of age, which he handed to a soldier below. The child fortunately received no injury; but a daughter of Mrs. Pitt, a girl about nine years of age, was clinging to the side of her mother, who was leaning over the window and bewailing the loss of another son. Mr. Watkinson laid hold of this child (her wearing apparel being in flames,) and threw her out of the window. She fell on the pavement below, and was immediately taken to the London Hospital, severely, if not fatally, injured.

Notwithstanding that the fire was burning his hands and face, Mr. Watkinson stood to his post, and by great exertions managed to pull Mrs. Pitt out of the room, when she also fell upon the stone flags, and was likewise removed to the hospital.

Notwithstanding that so much mischief had been done, scarcely ten minutes had elapsed from the time the first discovery was made, and neither fire engine nor escape had time to reach the spot. The premises on one side of the blazing property being the extensive oil and colour warehouses belonging to Mr. Cockman, and known to contain articles of the most inflammable, if not explosive character, the greatest fears were entertained lest they should also become ignited; and the crowd were cautioned from venturing too near them, when the parish engine arrived. This was followed shortly afterwards by several brigade engines, and those of the County and West of England Fire offices. The speedy arrival of these machines allayed in some measure the fears of the inhabitants, and, there being an abundant supply of water furnished by the East London main, the engines were set to work under the direction of Mr. Braidwood and the other chief officers.

The first object sought to be accomplished was to cut off the further extension of the flames, for by the time the engines could be called into operation the premises of Mr. Cockman on one side, and of Mr. Hartley, hatter, on the other, were both on fire. By directing the water from the hose of two or three engines upon the latter-named property the further progress of the flames was cut off. Whilst the firemen were busily engaged, the whole of Mr. Watkinson's premises not consumed by fire fell with a tremendous crash, blocking up the foot pavement, and nearly burying several of the firemen.

After two hours' hard working the firemen succeeded in getting the fire entirely extinguished, and, as soon as the ruins were cool enough, they commenced their search for the lad who was known to have perished. After some time, his body was found on the ground floor, standing almost in a perpendicular position on its head, clearly showing that he must have been in one of the upper rooms, and when the flooring gave way had fallen head foremost into the place where he was found. From the fact of a handkerchief being round his neck, and his stockings being on his feet, it is supposed that he stopped after being alarmed to dress himself, instead of making his escape. The body was literally burnt to a cinder, and has been removed to Whitechapel workhouse, where it will remain until the Coroner's inquest.

Respecting the origin of the outbreak nothing that can be depended upon could be learned. Mr. Hedgers the assessor of losses to Messrs. Toplis and Son, surveyors to the principal fire offices, inspected the ruins during the day, with a view of learning how the calamity occurred. From the statement made by Mr. Watkinson it appeared that he closed the shop on Friday night at ten o'clock, and at half-past eleven he turned off the gas, and retired to rest. At that time there was not the least smell of anything burning. He went to bed along with the unfortunate deceased, and was awoke between two and three o'clock in the morning by a strange noise, and the moment he got up he found the room full of smoke. The first thing he did was to arouse the youth, who was sleeping in his bed, whom he told to escape without a minute's loss of time. The next thing he did was to go upstairs and alarm Mr. Pitt and his wife and family. The lad, he considered, had not done what he told him; if he had he might have escaped. He could not form the least idea how the fire originated.

It is but right to say that when the distance of the fire escape station from the scene of conflagration is taken into consideration, the machine arrived as early as possible. Subjoined is the official report of the damage done:-

No. 45, Whitechapel Road. – Mr. A.F. Watkinson, staymaker, &c. – Building burnt down and contents consumed. Insured in the Legal and Commercial Fire office for stock in trade. A lad named S.T. Pitt burnt to death, and Mrs. Pitt, with her daughter, a girl nine years of age, seriously burnt and taken to the hospital.

No. 44, Whitechapel Road. – Mr. R. Cockman, oil and colourman. Building severely damaged by fire and water. Insured in the Sun Fire office.

No. 46, Whitechapel Road. – Mr. Thomas Hartley, cap maker and hatter. Building similarly damaged. Insured in the Phoenix Fire office.

The cause of fire unknown.

The unfortunate child Priscilla Pitt, who, along with her mother, was so severely burnt at the above fire, expired in the London Hospital on Sunday forenoon at eleven o'clock. From the time the child was admitted very little hopes were entertained by the surgeons of that institution that she could recover. Mrs. Pitt, the mother, who is far advanced in pregnancy, is also most fearfully burnt about her legs and thighs, and it is extremely doubtful whether she will survive. Mr. Watkinson, the proprietor of the premises, who was severely burnt in endeavouring to save the lives of Mrs. Pitt's family is considerably better, and nothing fatal need be apprehended in his case.

Hull Packet – 22nd September 1848.

———————

1848 – THE SANITARY CONDITION OF WHITECHAPEL.

Yesterday an inquest was held before Mr. Baker, at the London Hospital, on view of the body of James Barber, aged 13 years, who died from the effects of fever produced by an impure atmosphere in the neighbourhood of Whitechapel.

Mr. James Brown, Inspector of Nuisances to Whitechapel, stated that on the 24th of July last the mother of the deceased called his attention to her back kitchen, No. 17, Princess Street. The room was overflowed with filthy water, and the effluvium was most dreadful. Witness was directed to call the attention of Mr. Liddle, surgeon of the district, by the churchwardens, and, after examining the premises, he certified that the water flowed through the wall of the kitchen from an offensive drain belonging to No. 8, Moss Buildings, contiguous to Princess Street. Several drains in the same street were also in a bad condition, and the air was very impure. There were several persons suffering from fever, and the effluvium was so obnoxious that the inhabitants were scarcely able to live in the tenements. Witness had applied to the landlord of the premises to abate the nuisance, which had not been attended to, and witness had obtained a summons against the landlord to show cause why he does not remedy the evil.

The Jury returned the following:-

"That the deceased died from fever caused by a noxious effluvium from a privy draining into the back part of the house in which he resided, and the Jurors strongly recommend that prompt and speedy measures be adopted by the parochial authorities for the abatement of the nuisance so caused, to prevent further mischief."

The Coroner said he would write to the churchwardens of the parish and acquaint them with the sentiments of the Jury.

Morning Post – 7th September 1848.

———————

1848 – CHOLERA IN WHITECHAPEL.

Sir,

The very prompt admission which you gave to my two communications relative to the sanitary condition of the poor in the Whitechapel Union encourages me to give to the public, through the medium of your journal, the result of my long experience of the administration of medical relief to the poor.

I have been engaged nearly 16 years in attending the necessitous poor of this densely-populated district; and for several years past, I have visited annually upwards of 2,000 patients, and during the last year I prescribed for 3,531 different pauper cases of illness.

The knowledge of the diseases and habits of the poor which such extensive practice has enabled me to acquire convinces me of the necessity of appointing medical men, whose duty it shall be attend to the poor only, and whose time shall not be encroached upon by the calls of private practice.

The medical officer who is appointed to attend the poor should be independent of the board of guardians, provided with drugs at the expense of the union, and responsible only to a superior medical officer under the Board of Health. However careful the guardians may be of the poor rate, and however praiseworthy their sacrifice of time, there are few among them who are fitted to direct or even interfere with the duties of a medical officer.

Under the present arrangement it is almost impossible for a union medical officer, subject as he is to an annual election, faithfully to discharge his duties as an officer of health, in endeavouring to prevent disease, by urging the adoption of sanitary measures, and at the same time maintain his independence. He must either be silent upon the subject of the physical sufferings of the poor, and allow the most disgusting and degrading state of things to continue, without raising his voice to ameliorate them, or he must resign his appointment.

The health of a population depends upon various causes; among others, the occupation, number, and density of the inhabitants, the drainage of the localities, the ventilation of the houses, and the cleanliness of the people; also, upon the kind, quantity, and quality of the food which is consumed by them.

In some parts of this union much fish is consumed, as well as bacon, pickled pork, and vegetables, a great proportion of all of which is in a state injurious to the health of those who eat them. Over the sale of unwholesome food, the guardians have no control; but this, as well as every other matter relating to the health of the people, ought to be placed under the surveillance of a medical officer.

There can be no doubt that the adoption of those measures which will tend to preserve the health of the poor will be the soundest economy; and for many years past my attention has been directed to the consideration of those sanitary measures upon which public health so much depends, especially in poor neighbourhoods; and the statements which I have, from time to time, made, respecting the unhealthy condition of the neighbourhoods of the poor, have created a prejudice in the minds of some of the guardians of our union, and have at length led to my resignation.

The Whitechapel Union has long enjoyed a most unenviable notoriety for unhealthiness. It contains a population of about 72,000; and during the year ending March, 1848, the medical officers attended no less than 4,113 pauper cases of typhus fever, a proportion of more than 1 in 17 of the whole population.

This appalling fact may easily be accounted for when the wretched localities of this union are examined. The habitations of the poor in the vicinity of Rosemary Lane and Petticoat Lane are indescribably filthy, and totally unfit for any species of animals to live in. The unhealthy courts and alleys have recently

Fig. 1.   The Habitations of the Whitechapel Poor

been placed under the special care of the guardians, by order of the Board of Health, and it is to be hoped that the disgusting scenes which were so recently described in your journal will never again be witnessed.

From the assiduous daily washings, by means of fire engine and hose, of these unhealthy localities, the cholera, which had recently been so fatal, has almost disappeared. A few cases have occurred within the last week, but they have not been nearly so severe; for, all who have been attacked with this disease since the work of purification commenced have recovered.

Your obedient servant,
John Liddle.

Evening Mail – 29th December 1848.

───◆───

1849 – MYSTERIOUS DEATH IN WHITECHAPEL WORKHOUSE.

An inquest was held on Friday, before Mr. Baker, at the Grave Maurice public house, High Street, Whitechapel, touching the death of Mr. Johns James Watts, aged sixty-six, one of the parochial surgeons of St. George-in-the-East, who died from the effects of poison, in the Whitechapel workhouse.

Elizabeth Lewis deposed that she managed the Britannia Coffee house, in the Whitechapel Road. On Tuesday night last, the deceased came to the house, accompanied by an elderly female, and engaged a bedroom for the night. They were shown to a room, and the deceased paid witness 2s. for the apartment. They both appeared quite well and sober. They went to bed, and nothing was heard of them during the night. On the following morning, at ten o'clock, witness, finding that they were not up, sent the servant girl to knock at the door. She returned directly afterwards, and said there was something the matter in the room, for the man and woman were moaning very loudly, and appeared as if they were dying. Witness instantly went upstairs, and called out to the deceased, "What is the matter?" The deceased faintly answered, "Open the door and come in." Witness opened the door, and found the deceased and the woman lying in bed, and seemed as if in great pain and very ill.

The room was in great disorder. Witness asked the deceased if she should fetch Mr. Blackman, a

Fig. 2.   Whitechapel Workhouse

surgeon, and he replied, "No, I'll have no other but my partner, Mr. Broadwater, who lives in Cannon Street, St. George's-in-the-East." Witness immediately went to Mr. Broadwater's, but he was from home. Witness then returned home, and found the deceased and the female apparently much worse. They were both vomiting very much, and witness sent again for Mr. Broadwater, who soon afterwards attended, and eventually Dr. Allison, one of the parochial surgeons, arrived, and gave an order for the admission of the deceased and the female into the workhouse, in consequence of the deceased refusing to be conveyed to his home or to a hospital. By the Jury: Witness found two bottles in the room containing a liquid, which she handed over to Mr. Blackman, and also an empty phial.

Mr. W.J. Broadwater, surgeon, said the deceased was late his partner, and had been so for upwards of two years. They jointly occupied a house in Cannon Street Road. The deceased was one of the parochial surgeons of St.-George's-in-the-East, and he had absented himself from his professional duties for the last five weeks, and witness had never heard of him. It had latterly come to his knowledge that the deceased was in the habit of visiting a female named Sarah Craig, a widow. The deceased was a married man, but was separated from his wife sixteen months after marriage. This was about thirty years ago. The poor law guardians had only lately suspended the deceased from his duties, in consequence of his negligence.

Between ten and eleven on Wednesday morning last, witness received a message to attend Mr. Watts, at the Britannia Coffee house. Witness at first felt a delicacy at doing so, and said they had better call a medical man in from the neighbourhood; but shortly afterwards a second messenger came to his house, and he then went to the deceased, whom he found lying in bed with a female, both of whom were in a sinking state. They were both vomiting most violently, and complained of excessive thirst. Witness then sent for some brandy, which he administered to the deceased in cold water. The deceased had scarcely any pulse, and the whole surface of the body was cold, with a slatey appearance of skin, which is usually found in persons who suffer from cholera. The deceased had violent purging and vomiting; and witness at the time considered the deceased and the female suffering from an attack of the Asiatic cholera.

The deceased, after swallowing a portion of the brandy and water, revived a little, and could just articulate that he was dying.

By the Coroner: Arsenic would produce all the appearances under which they were then suffering. Witness on Thursday last interrogated Sarah Craig, who now lies dangerously ill at the workhouse, and she informed him that she had been taken suddenly ill shortly before entering the coffee house, and that she obtained some medicine from a chemist, some of which she had taken. Witness was unable to find out whether the deceased had taken any of it, or anything else. She afterwards informed witness that the deceased obtained some other "stuff" from some other chemist. From her statement it appeared that they had both been suffering from the want of the common necessaries of life, which had produced an attack of diarrhoea. They had no supper on the Tuesday night, and the deceased paid the last money he had for the use of the bedroom at the coffee house.

William Challis, a labourer, said Sarah Craig was his sister, and on hearing of her illness he visited her at the workhouse, on Thursday last. She then told him that the deceased had given her three glasses, containing a liquid, and desired her to drink it. She did so, and directly afterwards she became very ill.

Mr. Joseph Nash, surgeon to Whitechapel workhouse, said the deceased, together with a female, were brought in about five o'clock on Wednesday evening. They were both exceedingly ill, and from their appearances he treated them for Asiatic cholera. The deceased was sinking fast, and died at half-past three o'clock on the following morning. In the course of the same afternoon witness examined the female, and while he was doing so, one of the nurses handed him in a packet of powders, which she had found in the deceased's clothes, and some of which contained corrosive sublimate, an acrid poison, and one was labelled poison. He had since made a post-mortem examination of the body, and he felt no doubt that the deceased had died from the effects of a mineral poison. The contents of the stomach and the intestines had since been analysed by Professor Letheby, lecturer on chemistry at the London Hospital, who detected the presence of oxalic acid, and corrosive sublimate. Witness had also been informed, that on the Tuesday evening the deceased had procured a small quantity of prussic acid at Mr. Blackman's shop.

Mr. Broadwater here mentioned that the deceased was in the habit of taking a few drops of prussic acid occasionally for a disease of the heart under which he laboured. By the Coroner: Witness would not undertake to say what the female was suffering from, but she was in a very dangerous state, and he did not expect her to survive.

The Jury returned the following verdict:- "That the deceased died from the effects of poison, but how or in what manner administered, or whether taken by the deceased, or otherwise, there was not sufficient evidence for the Jury to say."

Lloyd's Weekly Newspaper – 12th August 1849.

1850 – A CHRISTMAS PRESENT.

On Tuesday a man, having the appearance of a carrier, left a hamper, from one end of which a few pheasant feathers were sticking out, at the house of a person in North Street, Whitechapel, for which he received 2s. 3d. carriage. When the parcel was opened it contained nothing but three old bricks and a quantity of straw.

South Eastern Gazette – 1st January 1850.

1850 – WHITECHAPEL JEWS.

Sir,

Your police report of yesterday, under the head of Westminster, contains some remarks offered by Mr. Broderip, the Magistrate, which appear to me so harsh and so uncalled for, that I am induced to ask your indulgence for a few lines in your valuable columns.

Had I not been convinced of the correctness which characterises your reports, I should hardly have credited that, under the circumstances as you state them, a Magistrate could have made such an attack on a body of people, and I would ask him, "Shall one man sin, and wilt thou be wrath with all the congregation?"

From your report it would appear that a butler plundered the mistress of the house of plate to the value of 50l. The thief was captured. He first denied his guilt, and then admitted it; and "that he took the plate and sold it to the Jews at Whitechapel for 10l." Your report further states, "the Inspector accompanied him to that neighbourhood, but prisoner could not find the place where he had disposed of it."

Your report further states Mr. Broderip inquired whether the plate had been discovered. Mr. Cummings replied it had not. He had exercised the utmost diligence, but without effect; indeed, he had every reason to believe the prisoner's statement to be true, and from first considered that there was little chance of rescuing it, as it was no doubt melted.

Why Inspector Cummings should have "every reason to believe the prisoner's statement to be true" after having gone with him to Whitechapel, and not being able to find the place where he had disposed of it, I cannot tell. Inspector Cummings, no doubt, knows the neighbourhood in Whitechapel, where the Jewish dealers reside, and no doubt the Inspector took him to Middlesex Street or Petticoat Lane, as it is called, and

Fig. 3.   Poor Jewish Quarter Kids – Wentworth Street (Harper's Weekly 1873)

though he could not discover the place, the prophetic Inspector gives credence to the statement of a thief, who "had first denied his guilt," and then admitted it, and to get out of the trouble and the shame which the producing of the theft would put him to, says "he had sold it to the Jews in Whitechapel."

The prophecy of the Inspector seemed to have inspired the Learned Magistrate, and his worship, touched by the sacred mantle of that modern Elijah, Mr. Cummings, delivers the following emphatic speech:-

"Mr. Broderip said, "I cannot suffer this case to pass without observing that it is one the opprobria of this metropolis, that these gangs of Jews should be permitted to carry on their nefarious trade in the heart of the city of London. They are the head nurses of crime, ready to take anything, from the precious metals downwards to the garment, from which one of their haunts takes its name, at enormous discount. They lie in wait to rob the robber, and prey upon the public. In this case 10l. are stated to have been paid for plate worth five or six times that amount. Even the nefarious Jonathan Wild let those who were plundered have their property again upon payment of a fee, but when once property gets into the hands of these harpies, the owner can never hope to see it more. If it be an heirloom held in the greatest estimation by the family who have been plundered, the piece of plate is instantly consigned to the melting pot, and converted into "white soup," as these Israelites term it. Their first act is to destroy all identity, and in this way large fortunes are made with impunity."

Now, I appeal to that impartiality and justice which distinguish the columns of the *Morning Advertiser*, whether these severe strictures are not, to say the least of them, premature and uncalled for. Had the stolen property been discovered in the possession of the "Jews in Whitechapel;" had it been found that it was sold at 10l., and that it was melted down, his worship could, perhaps, have justified his wholesale condemnation by drawing inferences from an individual case. But since nothing was found, since the place could not even be discovered where he alleged he had sold them, might we not ask, did he sell it to the Jews in Whitechapel? Might he not have sold it in Barbican—a neighbourhood where we often hear that refiners also keep melting pots, and "no trace can be discovered" after the plate is out of the hands of the seller.

I should be sorry, Sir, to defend, or even palliate in the remotest sense, the conduct of those Jews who do trade in stolen property. Nor am I prepared to deny that there are, alas, such people to be found among the Jewish persuasion, who are shunned in society, and scouted from every decent Jewish house. But I cannot

admit that this buying of stolen property is a Jewish vice. It unfortunately exists among other creeds also; and the butler's tale became more plausible when he said that he sold it to the Jews in the ears of Inspector Cummings and Mr. Broderip; because deep rooted prejudices will have it that none but Jews are buyers of stolen goods. I doubt not, therefore, that you will agree with me, that his worship's severe remark, "That they are the head nurses of crime; they lie in wait to rob the robber, and prey upon the public," is not justified, either by reason or by the circumstances before him.

I am, &c.,

Mr. H. BRESSLAW, Editor of the *Jewish Chronicle*.

Morning Advertiser – 4th January 1850.

1850 – A MUNIFICENT DONATION.

The Queen and the Prince Consort have given a renewed proof of their earnestness in promoting the welfare of the working classes by transmitting to the committee for promoting the establishment of baths and washhouses for the labouring classes a further munificent donation of £100 towards the funds for completing the model establishment in Goulston Square, Whitechapel, and have thus again testified to the validity of the claims which the poverty of that district has on the sympathy and help of the wealthier quarters of the metropolis.

Illustrated London News – 30th March 1850.

1850 – DWELLINGS OF THE WHITECHAPEL POOR.

Last evening the first annual meeting of the Whitechapel association for promoting habits tending to the cleanliness, health, and comfort, of the industrious classes in the parish of St. Mary, Whitechapel, was held in the room of the society, Whitechapel Road, and was attended by a goodly number of the working classes and others.

The Rev. W.W. Champneys, the Rector of Whitechapel, occupied the chair, and in commencing the proceedings said when the cholera ceased its ravages this association was formed, and its object was by persuasion and kindly argument to induce the working classes to remove such of the causes of disease as they had the power to remove.

During the past year the association had been actively at work. It would be seen by the report that many of the dwellings of the poor had been visited, not once only, but several times. Some of the causes of disease the occupants had been induced to remove, but there were others which they could not remove; and other powers were wanting to place the parish in a proper sanitary condition.

Mr. John Liddell read the report of the committee, which stated that they had appointed a paid agent, by whom every street, lane, and court, every house and room inhabited by the classes whose improvement was aimed at, had been visited. In almost every instance the agent had been received with civility and kindness. Small tracts, expressing in a few words the leading causes of disease, had been largely circulated, and hung up in the rooms visited, and in the public baths.

The principal causes of disease which had been found to exist were insufficient supply of water; the existence of nuisances in and around the dwellings of the poor caused by the want of drainage; the defective state of the pavements, and the neglect of the scavengers and dustmen; the overcrowded state of the tenements, more especially the low lodging houses; the dilapidated conditions of the dwellings of the poor; the want of light and ventilation; and the filthy habits of the people. By persuasion, many persons had been induced to clean their windows, to whitewash their rooms, to frequent the public baths and to improve their dwellings; and it was gratifying to observe, that owing to the spread of information on sanitary subjects, many of the working classes were now aware of the deficiencies in their dwellings, and said they were quite willing to keep their dwellings clean, but that their efforts would be of no use while the roofs, ceilings and drainage were in their present condition.

But there were many of the causes of disease over which the occupants of the houses had no control. One of these was the insufficient supply of water. In many courts the water flowed only an hour at a time, and for only six days in a week. On Sundays the poor people must go without water or make use of that which had been saved from their previous day's supply, and which, from being kept in crowded rooms, was rendered impure. The inhabitants of the courts frequently quarrelled and sometimes fought for their turn to catch water; and on rainy days it often happened that they got drenched before they got the water they were waiting for.

Another matter over which the inhabitants had no control was the want of drainage. In many cases there were filthy privies common to a whole court. In several cases the privies were situate in the basement of the houses, from which the foul miasma arose, infecting the air of every room, even to the top of the house.

There were 91 courts, containing a population of 7,500, which were badly paved, where stagnant water was frequently observed in front of the houses. The majority of these places were private property and were not included in any commission, and there was no law requiring the owners of private property to pave and drain.

Another matter over which the occupants had no control was the dilapidated state of the buildings. A great number of the houses visited by the agent were unfit to live in. In most cases, where the tenants complained they were told by the landlords that if they did not like the house or room, they might leave it; but several landlords had kindly cooperated with the committee in improving the state of the dwellings.

Among other evils was the crowded state of many of the houses. The state of the low lodging houses entirely baffled description. At one of them, 5, Holloway Court, Blue Anchor Road, in a small room on the second floor, 10½ ft. by 13ft., with a sloping roof from 5 to 7½ ft. high, and having only one window, were crowded together 57 human beings, men, women, and children, the majority of whom were nearly naked and very filthy. The smell was intolerable. On the stairs was a tub full of all manner of abominations, the smell of which, on passing by, was suffocating. In this room there were only 20 cubic feet of air for each person, the quantity of air recommended by the Inspector of Prisons being 1,000 feet, as being the least that should be allotted to each person to preserve health.

At another lodging house in Mill Yard, Cable Street, where persons were lodged for 2d. a night each, nine men were found in a room on the first floor, and in another room on the second floor also nine, but from the arrangement of the beds it was evident that the rooms were only partially occupied. The committee attributed a great deal of this crowding to the immigration of Irish.

The total number of visits to families was 7,600; the number of persons induced to keep their rooms clean, 460; number who had been induced to clean their windows, 591; and to visit the public baths, 461. There had been 26 nuisances removed, 7 privies emptied, and 14 rooms whitewashed by tenants. The trustees of the parish had been active in endeavouring to repress nuisances. Within little more than 12 months, 384 persons had been proceeded against for nuisances of various kinds.

Mr. W. Straw moved the adoption of the report, in doing which he dilated on the great need there was of a better supply of water being afforded to the district and stated that when the authorities had applied to the New River Company to turn the water on for public purposes, they had never permitted them to have it except at night. He thought that was not as it ought to be. The East London Company had let them have water in the daytime.

Mr. J.M. Rippingham seconded the motion, which passed unanimously.

Mr. W.H. Black moved a resolution to the effect that, while the working classes were willing to adopt what remedies they could to improve the condition of their dwellings, no voluntary efforts were sufficient to meet the worst and most pressing of the evils. He stated that he was himself the owner of some houses, which in their present state were unfit for human beings to dwell in. But landlords were not so much to blame in these matters as some people may think. In numerous instances he had had rooms forcibly opened by athletic Irishmen, who had appropriated them without his leave for the dwellings of themselves and families. He had had his life threatened by these people. He had been for six months together prevented from getting possession of a room in which no human being ought to have lived, because the parties living in it would neither be clean nor do anything to permit peace and quietude.

In two instances the visitors of this society found two of his rooms occupied by forty persons. He could not get them out or get any rent for six months; but the man who was tenant of them was now dead. Mr. Black then complained of the state of the paving and said there were nine or ten paving jurisdictions in the parish, and there was a doubt as to which district some parts were in, the consequence of which was that those parts were not paved at all.

The meeting was also addressed by Mr. G. Simmons, and a petition to the House of Commons, praying for the passing of a bill constituting parochial paving and sanitary boards and with power to appoint paid agents to visit low lodging houses, and make regulations respecting them, was universally agreed to.

London Daily News – 17ᵗʰ October 1850.

1851 – FALL OF A HOUSE IN WHITECHAPEL.

On Saturday afternoon an old building in Whitechapel fell to the ground. The house in question, with several others, had been condemned by the district surveyor, and accordingly means were resorted to take it down with the two houses adjoining. The contractor for pulling the houses down had sold a large quantity of old timber to the poor persons in the neighbourhood, and while the men were proceeding with the work of demolition, several boys were on the ground floor picking up small pieces of wood, when a loud crashing noise was heard, and the next moment the whole building fell to the ground, carrying with it the several floors. Some police having been procured from the nearest station, as well as other assistance, the bodies of two boys, named Edward Eyers, aged eleven, and John Murphy, aged nine years, and also a labourer named Sullivan, were taken out. The two boys were found to be dead. The man Sullivan, who was much injured, was conveyed to the London Hospital.

Leeds Times – 21ˢᵗ June 1851.

1852 – CRIME IN LOW LODGING HOUSES.

The *Morning Post* of Sept. 8th, in a leading article, observed with much satisfaction the efforts which the police are making to enforce the provisions of that very important law, the Lodging Houses Act.

Our paper a few days ago contained a report of the case of a large number of the depraved and dangerous people who keep these dens of filth and vice, who had been brought up before Mr. Ingham for infringement of the law. We trust the Magistracy will show no quarter to these characters. On no ground have they the least claim to leniency in the administration of the law; on every ground they deserve punishment, and their offence calls for strong and unceasing repression.

It is not necessary to repeat the details of the case to which we refer. It is enough to say that it revealed the most shocking and disgusting instances of misery, dirt, disease, and disregard of common decency. And then, after stating at some length that no sources are so fruitful of crime as the low lodging houses of the metropolis, quotes as an instance of the assertion, the following report of Capt. Williams, the Inspector of Prisons for the Home District:-

"Thomas Dean, fourteen; once apprehended on suspicion, but discharged. Now convicted of picking pockets, and sentenced to 12 months' imprisonment, which expired 9th April, 1852. Father and mother alive; keep a chandler's shop, Arthur Street, Goswell Road; I have been at school, it was the National school; I used not to go there when sent, and used to spend the money given to me to pay for my schooling; I used to go into the fields with bad company; a lot of boys came and took me from home; I went with them to a lodging house in Cates Street, Whitechapel, where the little boys are; I paid 3d. a night; my father found me out, and came after me; the woman's name who keeps it I do not recollect, but I shall in a minute; she keeps a beer shop, and there is a skittle ground; she minds the boys, money and all; I once gave her 8s. to take care of for me; she used to buy the things for the boys; she keeps a chandler's shop also; Sundays they hold a judge and jury in the upper room, and plenty of boys and girls are there; I now recollect the woman's name, it is Mrs. Hurley; father brought a policeman there with him, and said he would pull her house down; I have been very often drunk there; she keeps spirits which she is not allowed to do; there is a fiddle there every night except Sunday; at the judge and jury they try the boys, and you pay a penny for counsellor to speak for you, and another penny if you are found guilty. There are grown-up men there, who take the boys out a thieving. The most I ever got was £5 a purse from a rich woman; I know she was a rich woman, for she had a bonnet with a veil hanging from it; it was a purse, £3 in gold, and £2 in silver; I gave £3 to Mrs. Hurley to take care of, and she wronged me out of £1, saying I had only given £2; I spent the whole in her house; I have been all night tossing for money on the beds; I know Mrs. Sims, she lives in Whitechapel; the boy Wells was at Mrs. Hurley's; her daughter Moggy, keeps a chandler's shop, and when a boy has had a lucky chance, she asks them to buy her a ring or shawl.

The boys used to come to my father's house, and shout out, "Tommy Dean, come away," and the policemen used to bang them about, which I did not like to see, and I went with them. When a boy has a thing which is worth a good deal of money, Mrs. Hurley will always buy it off him, but she won't have anything which is not good. The boys offer her the things; Mrs. Hurley encourages the boys and girls there, which brought me away from home; I should not like to go into the streets again; I never picked pockets of such things as handkerchiefs, nothing but ladies' pockets of their purses. Mrs. Hurley's daughter's name is Margaret; we call her Moggy; I once gave her a brass purse when I had been lucky, and got £2 10s. at one time; I was never sober a night at Mrs. Hurley's. There is drinking, dancing, singing, smoking, and gambling always going on. The girls used to come and kiss me and nurse me when I was drunk and had money; they used to put me to bed and steal my money; I have spent as much as half-a-sovereign there on a night, in beer, ale, shrub, and cigars.

When we went in the morning, Mrs. Hurley used always to say, "I wish you good luck, boy, today." Henry Rogers, who was transported last sessions, and his brother Johnny, live there and are great favourites. Johnny Rogers hires carts, and takes the boys to races. There are four streets there, leading from Whitechapel, where all are thieves, and not an honest woman among them. There were about 50 boys at Mrs. Hurley's. If I was ever to go out from prison, I should be obliged to go a thieving again, for the boys would come and meet me going out, and I should be transported.

I used to be told what a lucky fellow I was, to be thieving so long and not to be taken up. I would willingly go to the Philanthropic and should like to go abroad. I will engage to obey the rules of the Philanthropic, if sent there.

This boy's career has been a most vicious one, but, like others of his class, he is the slave of circumstances, and has no appearance of being naturally vicious. His behaviour in prison has been good. The chaplain and schoolmaster, and other officers of the prison, speak well of him."

Western Courier, West of England Conservative, Plymouth and Devon Advertiser – 22nd September 1852.

1853 – THE MURDER OF MRS. MOBBS

At the Central Criminal Court, on Thursday, Nathaniel Mobbs was arraigned for the murder of his wife. The evidence against him was very complete. Mobbs lived in Enoch Court, Whitechapel; and the dwellers in the court narrated the whole transaction.

On the 23rd August, Mobbs came home tipsy, and his wife took refuge from him in the room of Frances Lancaster. The same night, she again sought shelter; and sat up all the night with Julia Angling, a poor sack maker, and did not go away until her husband fetched her on the fatal morning. Mrs. Mobbs had no sooner reached her room, than screams were heard; she then appeared at the window, and asked Julia Angling to satisfy her husband that she had not been out all night with a policeman. The next scene was the actual deed. All these witnesses heard screams of "Murder!" They ran to the door; they could not open it; a child was heard to cry, "Oh mother, mother!" then a heavy weight was moved from the door on the inside; and Mrs. Mobbs, with hair hanging down, and a bleeding throat, ran out into the court.

She was taken to the hospital, and died. John Featherstone, a policeman, went into the room, and found Mobbs lying on the floor with his throat cut, but still living. The policeman found a whetstone recently used, and Mobbs subsequently confessed that he had whetted the knife before he cut his wife's throat.

The Jury unhesitatingly found the prisoner "guilty;" and Mr. Justice Cresswell, with due solemnity, passed sentence of death.

Bradford Observer – 3rd November 1853.

1856 – A NIGHTLY SCENE IN LONDON.

Under this heading Mr. Dickens describes, in *Household Words* of this week, what he witnessed one night outside the Whitechapel workhouse:-

"On the 5th of last November, I, the conductor of this journal accompanied by a friend well known to the public, accidentally strayed into Whitechapel. It was a miserable evening; very dark, very muddy, and raining hard. There are many woeful sights in that part of London, and it has been well known to me in most of its aspects for many years. We had forgotten the mud and rain in slowly walking along and looking about us, when we found ourselves at eight o'clock, before the workhouse. Crouched against the wall of the workhouse, in the dark street, on the muddy pavement stones, with the rain raining upon them were five bundles of rags. They were motionless, and had no resemblance to the human form. Five great beehives covered with rags; five dead bodies taken out of graves, tied neck and heels, and covered with rags, would have looked like those five bundles upon which the rain rained down in the public streets.

"What is this?" said my companion. "What is this!" "Some miserable people shut out of the Casual Ward, I think," said I. (Mr. Dickens then described his inquiries in the workhouse; he found that the women were shut out simply because the house was full.) "We went to the ragged bundle nearest to the workhouse door, and I touched it. No movement replying, I gently shook it. The rags begun to be slowly stirred within, and by little and little a case was unshrouded. The head of a young woman of three or four and twenty, as I should judge; gaunt from want, and foul with dirt;

but not naturally ugly. "Tell us," said I, stooping down, "Why are you lying here?" "Because I can't get into the workhouse."

She spoke in a faint, dull way, and had no curiosity left. She looked dreamily at the black sky and the falling rain, but never looked at me or my companion.

"Were you here last night?" "Yes. All last night, and the night afore too." "Do you know any of these others?" "I know her next but one. She was here last night, and she told me she came out of Essex. I don't know no more of her." "You were here all last night, but you have not been here all day?" "No, not all day." "Where have you been all day?" "About the streets." "What have you had to eat?" "Nothing." "Come," said I, "think a little. You are tired and have been asleep, and don't quite consider what you are saying to us. You have had something to eat today. Come think of it?" "No, I haven't. Nothing but such bits as I could pick up about the market. Why, look at me!" She bared her neck and I covered it up again. "If you had a shilling to get some supper and a lodging, should you know where to get it?" "Yes, I could do that." "For God's sake get it then."

I put the money into her hand, and she feebly rose and went away. She never thanked me, never looked at me, melted away into the miserable night in the strangest manner I ever saw. I have seen many strange things, but not one that has left a deeper impression than the dull impassive way in which the worn-out heap of misery took that piece of money and was lost.

One by one I spoke to all the five. In every one interest and curiosity were as extinct as in the first. They were all dull and languid. No one made any sort of profession or complaint; no one cared to look at me; no one thanked me. When I came to the third, I suppose she saw that my companion and I glanced, with a new horror upon us, at the two last, who had dropped against each other in their sleep, and were lying like broken images. She said she believed they were young sisters. These were the only words that were originated among the five."

Londonderry Standard – 7th February 1856.

1857 – DEATH FROM DESTITUTION.

A Whitechapel prostitute has been found dead in an open arch of the Blackwall railway, near Wellelose Square, which, despite the frightful weather, was a "nightly receptacle for prostitutes, and other persons who may be destitute of homes!" According to the policeman, the deceased went by the name of "Coarse Mary." The deceased was dressed in a black stuff gown, old brown petticoat, cotton chemise, and black cloth lace-up boots. She had no shawl or bonnet and was evidently in a destitute condition. Two other young prostitutes had passed the night there.

Dr. Payne, of the Whitechapel Road, said that the deceased most probably died from destitution and exposure to the weather. At the inquest last Monday, Mr. Baker, the Coroner, directed the attention of the police authorities to the archway in question, to prevent the recurrence of a similar death, and with a view of keeping destitute persons from inhabiting the wretched place.

The Jury returned a verdict of "Death from destitution and exposure to the weather."

Sussex Agricultural Express – 10th January 1857.

1857 – TURNING THE TABLES.

The attention of the sitting Magistrates at Worship Street Police Court, on Tuesday, was occupied for a considerable time in the investigation of a charge, which excited an unusual degree of interest, against Joseph Phillips, general dealer, in Duke Street, Spitalfields, and a man named John Samuels, who were alleged to have unlawfully purchased a Crimean medal and some military clothing, the property of her Majesty.

In the early part of last week, Reuben Collins, a private in the Royal Artillery, was charged before Mr. D'Eyncourt, on suspicion of having deserted from his regiment. The accusation mainly resting upon the evidence of one Elias Benjamin, a general dealer, in Houndsditch, who deposed that on the afternoon of the previous day he saw the soldier in Whitechapel accompanied by a prostitute, who managed to wheedle him into low beer shop, and suspecting something wrong witness followed them into the house, where he found the Artilleryman engaged in bartering with two Jews for the sale of his medal and uniform. The negotiation apparently terminated in a satisfactory arrangement, as they all left the beer shop together and repaired to a private house next door, from which the soldier emerged soon after in a shabby suit of plain clothes, and was speedily followed by the Jews, each of whom was in possession of a portion of his uniform and accoutrements. Witness immediately stopped the soldier and charged him with being a deserter,

which he strongly denied at first, but afterwards acknowledged in the presence of a policeman, to whom he was handed over, that he had absconded from the Woolwich garrison on the same morning as his company was under orders for India, and he had a wife here whom he liked better than the service.

It having been admitted in court by the soldier that he had left his regiment under the circumstances described, the Magistrate sent him in the usual form to the House of Detention, for the purpose of being delivered over to the army authorities, and directed the police to use their best efforts for the apprehension of the men who had facilitated his desertion by changing his dress.

The defendant Phillips was subsequently charged with being one of the parties implicated in the offence; and although he strenuously disclaimed all knowledge of the transaction, the witness Benjamin, who had given him into custody, swore so positively to his identity that he was ordered to pay the maximum penalty of 5l., under the act 18 Vic., cap. 11, and was sentenced in default to a month's imprisonment.

Shortly after the committal of Phillips, who was unable to raise the money, the other defendant, Samuels, was brought up in custody, at the instance of Benjamin, who charged him as an accessory in the unlawful purchase, and having again deposed to the above particulars in the same clear and connected manner as had characterised his former testimony, the witness was about to leave the box when Mr. Green, a licensed victualler in the neighbourhood of Whitechapel, stepped forward, and expressed a wish to disclose certain facts which would furnish a strong presumption that the witness Benjamin was either equally guilty with the accused parties, or had given false evidence against them.

The Magistrate at once ordered him to be sworn, and he then stated that on the afternoon of Monday se'nnight an Artilleryman was brought to his house by Benjamin, who quietly asked him if they could be accommodated with a private room to enable his military friend to exchange his uniform, for a suit of plain clothing. Feeling satisfied that they were actuated by some improper motive, he refused to comply with the request and turned them both into the street. He thought no more of the affair, until the preceding evening, when he was informed that Mr. Phillips had been committed to prison upon the evidence of Benjamin, for having purchased military clothing on the same day the latter had visited his house, and on coming to this court to ascertain the truth of the report, he was surprised to find another man under examination on the same charge, and conceived it to be his duty to communicate all he knew with regard to the occurrence.

Mr. D'Eyncourt said that after the evidence of the witness Green, the case had assumed such a different aspect that the whole matter must be thoroughly sifted, and in the meantime, he had no hesitation in ordering the detention of the witness Benjamin, which might ultimately result in his committal for perjury. The man Benjamin was manifestly astounded at the untoward turn which the proceedings had taken, and after a solemn asseveration that he was a witness of truth he was removed by the gaoler.

Berkshire Chronicle – 12th September 1857.

1858 – GEORGE YARD RAGGED SCHOOL.

An interesting festival was celebrated yesterday in connection with this school, when upwards of 300 of the children educated in this useful establishment sat down to a sumptuous dinner of roast beef, plum pudding, &c., the generous provision of the Lord Mayor and several noblemen and other wealthy supporters of the institution.

The excellent meat was carved and served chiefly by his lordship and the Rev. Hugh Allen (of St. Jude's, Whitechapel), and we need hardly add that the banquet (for banquet it assuredly was) was vastly enjoyed by the glad children who partook of it.

In the evening a public meeting was held in the schoolroom, at which the Lord Mayor presided. On the platform we recognised many of the ardent supporters of the ragged school system; and the room was filled by a crowded assembly. The business of the meeting having been opened by prayer by the Rev. Hugh Allen, the Lord Mayor briefly addressed the meeting, descanting on the benefits derivable from institutions of this character. He had attended the dinner in the morning with very great pleasure, and the evening's meeting with not less satisfaction; and he had exceeding gratification in lending his aid in the furtherance of this and similar institutions, which had for their object the elevation of the poor lower classes by education on religious bases, without which education was worth nothing.

The secretary, Mr. F.P. Crossley, then read a very interesting account of the origin and progress of the institution, from which it appeared that it had its commencement in 1854, through the instrumentality and exertions of the Rev. Hugh Allen, and that it had progressed gradually and satisfactorily until now. The daily schools were now attended by about

Fig. 4. George Yard Ragged School (Illustrated London News)

250 children. A ragged school on Sundays, too, was very well attended, and a temperance society, that had effected a world of good in its way, met every Monday evening. There was also a ladies' association for caring for the poor women of the locality, which had produced excellent effects.

The financial statement stood thus:- In, January, 1857, they began with a debt to the treasurer of £25 14s. 6d., with rent and taxes owing; they had expended £129 0s. 2d., and they had received £126 6s. 3d., so that they now owed the treasurer £28 8s. 2d. They had, however, some receipts to be paid into his hands, which would make the accounts nearly balance to the end of the last year.

The report, in conclusion, still seriously called for continued support in the future. The expenditure required was not much – some £130 a year—a sum which he trusted would be gladly raised for the prosecution of so excellent a work.

A series of resolutions followed in furtherance of the ragged school system, some of which contained indisputable proofs of the growth and value of these schools. One matter is especially deserving of notice— that every year some 2,000 children are placed out by this system in London alone in situations wherein they are enabled to earn their own livings. It is needless to say that the whole of the resolutions were unanimously passed amidst great approbation, and the meeting did not separate until a late hour.

Morning Post – 15th January 1858.

1858 – BOHEMIANS OF THE EAST END.

Our Continental neighbours denominate that a large portion of the population gaining their livelihood in the public streets—the itinerant vendors of goods—performers, vagrants—Bohemians. It is a title bestowed totally irrespective of its territorial signification. The Bohemians of Paris have little in common with Bohemia as Charles Kean has demonstrated Polixenes to have had, though Shakespeare has thought proper to make that gentleman monarch of the country.

East London has its Bohemians—a people who gain their bread in the open air, an irregular army, who boldly take a position and fight the battle of trade with the regular troops, the ratepaying, taxpaying shopkeepers, who have to contend against this guerrilla warfare, hampered with the heavy baggage of an army in the shape of high rents, heavy rates, gas bills, and inconvenient trade taxes.

Within a threepenny ride of the Bank, the City tradesman may, if he be inclined, find that peculiar gratification which some minds derive in viewing these misfortunes of their brothers, from which themselves are free. Let the City man cause the conductor to set him down about the eighth of a mile eastward from Whitechapel Church, about 200 yards west of the London Hospital, and on the right-hand side of the way, he will find, as he elbows his way through the dense crowd on the footpath, abundant reason to congratulate himself on the immunity from itinerant competition the payment of rates and taxes occurs to himself, but fails to obtain for his East End brother.

For this is the Arab encampment so ably alluded to by our talented correspondent, "Amicus," in our impression of the 26th December. This is the desultory, irregular army of Bohemians that has bivouacked in the open space by the side of the road, and has shown disposition to contest every penny of trade with the established and legitimate dealer on the other side of the footway.

Let us attempt a glance at the scene. It is ten. p.m., Saturday. Take our arm dealer from the City. Happy man! your shop has been closed an hour, but your "down East" fellow must have two hours more labour and bad atmosphere ere his aching head can press his pillow. So, now the distance we have to traverse is not more than a quarter of a mile, yet so thick is the crowd, that it will take us half an hour to accomplish it. Never mind, your good lady will not be particularly alarmed, and the last "bus" for Camberwell starts at half-past eleven; you will catch it easily. So, button your coat, look after your pockets, and come along.

What a din! You are in a perfect fair, a footpath that forms a street, with stalls on the one side, flaring with filthy tallow and oil lamps, many improvised from earthenware pipkins, and on the other blazing gas-lit emporiums, shops, gin palaces, the butcher's, with meat ruddy lean and white fat delicately alternating, from his first-floor window to the pavement; the cheesemonger's presenting as huge a show, but yellow with rich butter and ponderous cheese; the grocer's, with those smart young men behind the counter, revolving under a perfect forest of blazing gas burners; the steaming eating house with its looped and windowed raggedness flattening its nose against the opaque windowpanes; the penny pie shop, with its smart grisettes behind the counter, and hungry customers before it; but it is not with these recognised and legitimate establishments we have to do. It is the itinerants we wish to observe, the skirmishers who are rapidly appropriating the advantages of a regular organisation, while avoiding the harassing inconveniences householding entails.

Itinerancy, most worthy Cit, you are apt to associate with misery, with squalor, with the hard effort to glean a crust in the field where the tradesman is reaping a fortune. Look here, and be undeceived. Is yon fancy repository, gay with toys that would grace the Lowther Arcade, the stock of a peripatetic dealer? See, it occupies about three yards of the pavement, extending backwards another couple of yards, with perfect counter and till, and canvass-covered recess behind the display of goods, in fact, a regular shop; its stock consists of valuable articles; its proprietors seem smart women, or respectable looking men.

Further on, the street jeweller is metamorphosed from Israelitish pedlar we are apt to connect with an itinerant trinket merchant, to the smart, dapper tradesman with a very valuable stock, in a very carefully built canvass place of business, his oil lamps arranged to throw the light to the best advantage on his wares. No department of trade is safe from the incursions of these Bohemians. Body and mind are alike catered for. From the cradle to the grave everything that is required for man's use can be supplied here. Yon hall of baby linen, fitted up with all the elegance of a City shop, symbolises the Alpha of human life. The travelling doctor, with his horrible-looking anatomical preparations is its nearest approach to the Omega. Now a board over an elaborately fitted stall, a board in the most approved sign-painting art, announces the fishmonger's street shop. Then another announcement over a brush and broom stall invites us to buy our brushes of the maker. There the Cheap Jack, with his Brummagen van, and his flaring filthy tallow lights, forcing his cast-iron cutlery down the throats of his gaping audience. There the crockery dealer with a stock equal to the china shopkeeper, before whose door he has perched himself, is emulating Brummagen Jack in noise, and making night hideous with his dreadful din, as he thumps his delf wares hard on the floor of his platform, to demonstrate their freedom from fracture. The street tailor will supply you with clothes of the true Monmouth Street cut. Crispin displays his shining brogues in attractive rows, for the benefit of the barefooted. Bibliopoles may delight themselves with heaps upon heaps of well-thumbed tomes in well-filled street booksellers' shops, whilst those who prefer viva voce recommendations to their studies, may listen to the harangues of the book auctioneer, who emulates Spurgeon himself in strength of lungs and beauty of diction.

And for whom is this market held? Who benefits by it? Not the poor man, for the wares supplied are neither better nor cheaper than they can be obtained at the shops. Not the shopkeeper, for these Bohemians seriously injure his business. Not the poor itinerant, the needy pedlar, the poor creatures who endeavour to gain an honest living by the sale of the scanty stock they carry about with them. No! these poor souls make a thoroughfare—these minor merchants supply many a want it scarce pays the regular shopkeeper to provide for. These poor people secure business to a neighbourhood by their presence; but the Bohemians of Mile End are not the representatives of this class. The street trade of this neighbourhood has by degrees drifted into the hands of men of business and possessing capital, men well able to contend with the shopkeeper on his own ground, so far as regards trade habits, stock, and capital, and possessing this incalculable advantage over him, that the burdens he toils under, they are free from.

We are near the "Gate" now and will take the return "bus" to the City. Yet, first, let us take a glance at the mob. Of what is it composed? The taverns are beginning to belch forth drunken furies, who will brawl about the neighbourhood until long after midnight. Yonder a weeping mother, with two or three little ones tugging at her apron, is endeavouring to induce her reeling lord to return to their miserable home before the last shilling of his hard week's earnings shall have passed over the pewter-covered counter into the taper fingers of the ringleted houri behind it. Matronly women are harrying about with bulky baskets, brobdignag cabbages, and ponderous door keys. Here and there a young couple in the first perplexities connubially are being pushed about by the crowd as they vacantly turn over in their minds the subject of tomorrow's dinner, until at length a sturdy butcher seizes them and forces a huge leg of mutton into their very diminutive basket.

With a stick, tap tapping before him, the blind mendicant feels his way through the mob. With restless, ferret-like eyes, well-greased curls, and slouched caps, active, little, young East End gaimins run like rats in and out amongst the people. How many poor matrons, pockets emptied of the results of their husband's brow-sweat during the past week, will tell when they return home, of the success of this branch of industry? And above all, that hurrying, swearing, buying, selling, pushing, restless mob, ascends the shrill "buy, buy, buy," of the butcher, the bawling, anatomical speech of the street doctor, the vulgar joke of the cheap Jack, the crockery dealer, or the book auctioneer, the crash of the brass band, blaring from the well-lighted first-floor window of a newly-opened baker's shop, where a glass of gin is announced to be given away to every purchaser of a four-pound loaf.

A mile or two away in the marshes of Poplar or Plaistow, or down by the muddy currents of the Lea, purling through Hackney fields, people look with surprise and see the dark sky crimsoned with a bright beam light that looks like the reflection of a distant mighty fire, but they contemplate with indifference, for they know it is only the reflection of the lights from the Saturday night fair at Mile End.

Jump up on your "bus", worthy Cit, and as you roll along towards Camberwell, just revolve in your mind "What if your brethren of Mile End were to lay claim to the camping ground of these Bohemians, and each one, some fine Saturday afternoon, anticipate his weekly vis-à-vis by building up and stocking a booth opposite his own door, with the goods of his own trade?" It would be a novel competition, would it not? We should like to see the capitalist Bohemian's countenance when he brought up his truck full of traps for erection in the evening, and found his stall forestalled, as another source of speculation, as the bus stops at the well-whitened steps of Lupina Villa. Suppose the Bohemians were to take fancy to enter into competition with your brothers of Piccadilly, Knightsbridge, Bayswater, or any other large West End thoroughfare, would Sir Richard Mayne smile blandly, ink his pen, and receive a deputation with "Ah! well. I'm very sorry, but these people must live you know, &c., &c." We wonder!

East London Observer – 23rd January 1858.

1858 – OUR THOROUGHFARES.

Once in a generation there is a great moral awakening. How moral we are all at once. Social evils, great and small, form just now prominent topics of public discussion. The evils of tipcat street cries—organ-grinding—costermonger's stalls—Sunday trading—and the social evil, par excellence—have been well paraded of late.

Paterfamilias in the East rush into print, and tell the burden of their woes; how the peace and quiet of their homes are invaded during the day by the vocal and instrumental music of travelling trades and professions, and at night by tavern broils, and the noisy uproar of the free-and-easy boon companions that meet at the Red Lion opposite. How the windows of his domicile and his eyes are endangered by juvenile sports—how that when he ventures out that offensive corner situation (doing a good business) disgraces the respectability of his street—how he is jostled by the rabble if he seeks the north side of the Whitechapel Road for a promenade—how his virtuous ear is assailed by a perfect babel of profane tongues in our

streets and highways—and, above all, when he retires to his devotions at a quiet Arbour square church, the puny voice of the preacher is drowned by the stentorian lungs of the vendors of stale fish and hot cross buns in the vicinity.

We must stop here, although we have not half recorded the catalogue of annoyances. A fellow-feeling makes one wondrous kind, and paterfamilias and those who think with him arrange a petition, the result of which is, that Justice Dogberry issues orders to his subordinates "how not to do it," in this case, very sensible advice, as the subject is far easier in theory than practice.

Pleasant waking dreams, to imagine the day when boys will not be boys, and the songless street vendors, the street with silent tread, when convivial meetings at the Red Lion, shall have given place to temperance songs around the pump, and chilling draughts from the cup that cheers but not inebriates; and when trades and tongues shall be subject to the baton of a highly virtuous, pure, and moral police. No fear, however, of that at present. Ratcliff Highway, and similar localities; places, where immorality is unbounded, and vice paraded in its most repulsive forms, may still run riot. There are more important things to attend to than the lives and property of ratepayers. If you want 500 Z, he is on political service, though he does not like the term, acts the "spy."

An instance of this ignorant neglect occurred last week during the hearing of a case before the Lord Mayor, when his lordship's attention was directed to the frightful state of Petticoat Lane on Sunday mornings. It was stated that about six or seven thousand persons, two thousand of whom were notorious thieves, congregated in that place and its vicinity to the great terror of the respectable part of the locality. The few police who were there were comparatively useless, as the thieves worked in gangs, and robberies were committed with impunity in broad daylight. The Chief Magistrate of the metropolis professed to be in ignorance upon the subject, and announced his intention of visiting the place. Only think! a live Lord Mayor in in Noah's Ark. Dives of the Mansion House going to visit Lazarus in his rags. There's a good Samaritan going down to Jericho to heal the wounds of the man who fell among thieves. We think it quite likely the complimentary visit will be returned by Moses and Aaron appearing in the Mansion House Dock.

But seriously, we believe, much good will result from the adoption of this inspecting process by our Magistrates. Let them pay a visit, incognito, to the scenes of those disturbances that are brought under their judicial and notice, and there is little doubt both they and society will be immeasurably benefited by the results. The protection of person and property is the undoubted province of the police—now they are comparatively powerless—and often on that account subjected to insult, and placed in danger. We trust that a stronger and well organised force will be stationed in these localities, so that rows in Bluegate Fields, and mobbing in Petticoat Lane may be numbered among the things that were.

Leaving this phase of our thoroughfares, which the authorities are perfectly competent to deal with, we turn to another that requires far more delicate consideration. Down the highways—along the main streets—at the time when "The moon pulls off the veil of light that hides her face by day from sight," the painted butterflies come out to ply their trade of sin. Creatures lost to all sense of shame parade obscenity and profaneness—vices the most hideous—with unblushing effrontery. Coffee houses are open far into the morn. The little hells that are situated in the slums of the vast metropolis, are loose with riot and dissipation.

On the day of rest these scenes are ten times worse. Is it to be wondered at that public attention should be drawn to the Great Social Evil? Is it to be wondered at that some over virtuous minds should have their moral sensibilities so shocked as to run into extremes the most rash and panacea's the most dangerous handing over the victims of our social system to police persecution and the prison scourge in order to stay this growing disgrace?

Such a mode of proceeding might lop off a few straggling branches but would leave the root of the evil untouched. There is little virtue in legislation on these matters. The old adage stands good, "Prevention is better than cure." You may rake up obsolete laws and punish for profaneness—for not attending the parish church, &c. &c., but you will never better the world by so doing. It is all very well to paint a Utopia where such things shall not be, but to be attained, far different means must be used. Fancy a state of society squared and polished by parliamentary regulation. All shops closed and all in with the curfew. Seven days imprisonment for transgressing Lindlay Murray or showing a preference for Billingsgate. No Sunday trading and the whole community neatly dressed, marching under police inspection to a parliamentary place of worship.

All this is very fine to talk about, but is it practicable? Yet such a state of things would be the inevitable result of calling in the aid of legislation to suppress the Great Social Evil. Such would be the full adoption of the principle. We turn with a feeling of pride to a comparison of the state of public morals in Paris, Vienna, Rome, and Naples with our own huge metropolis, although there, restrictions the most severe are laid upon the class alluded to. This fact is enough to prove the inadequacy of legislation to deal effectively with the subject.

Let those who advocate moral police visit homes and haunts of our shirt-working population. In the midst of squalor and wretchedness you may see women with pallid faces toiling from morning to eve at the needle to earn a miserable pittance. As many shillings as they earn farthings would not do much more than keep starvation from the door. Still, this is one phase of life. Here is the cause of the Great Social Evil. Here is the true field where philanthropy may labour for our moral purification. Can we expect virtue to thrive in the midst of poverty? Can we expect purity when virtue is synonymous with starvation and weary toil, and sin is garnished by temptations of ease and luxury? Oh! men with sisters and wives—you who feel strongly upon the subject, try your utmost to raise the price of female labour, to extend the sphere of female employments. Displace the linen lads and counter jumpers, and other equally unnecessary employments for men, and you will do more to cure the evils of society by prevention than all the enactments of legislation have or can do in the matter.

This may do for the future, but how to stay the present evil? Must that be treated harshly? Are those degraded creatures who flaunt their meretricious adornments along our thoroughfares eternally lost? Are they to be reformed by the prison, or are they in the right who think with Thomas Hood that, "Still, for all slips of hers One of Eve's family," is to be dealt with by humane and Christian means?

All honour to those noble-minded men who have sought to deal with the evil in a thoroughly practical manner. Go on with your truly Christian work—extend your missions—increase your refuges and public liberality will not be backward in assisting you. Let these legitimate and charitable exertions be made by the philanthropists of the east, and we shall then have more hope of seeing our thoroughfares decent and respectable, and our population improving in morality, than we shall by the stern exercise of police supervision, which at best can only produce an artificial result.

East London Observer – 8th May 1858.

1858 – A MOORISH GENTLEMAN AND AN IRISH SAVAGE.

At the Worship Street Police Office, Dennis Sullivan, an athletic Irish labourer, of truculent aspect, was brought up in custody of Gee, the warrant officer, charged, under peculiar circumstances with having assaulted and threatened the life of Mr. D.T. Benhouliel, an Algerine gentleman, residing at Priory House, Wandsworth. The imposing appearance of the prosecutor, a majestic-looking man, attired in a richly embroidered military tunic, with Zouave trousers, and Turkish fez of bright scarlet, attracted marked attention.

On being placed in the witness box, the complainant entered into a rather diffuse, but highly interesting account of his early antecedents, from which it appeared that he was a native of Algeria, and being an accomplished linguist, he became attached as interpreter to the staff of General Pelissier during the first campaign of that gallant chief against the Arabs of the desert. He had since followed the fortunes of that illustrious patron whom he accompanied to the Crimea, and attended him through the whole of his memorable engagements until he achieved his final triumph at the Malakhoff from which he derived his present title. His position was of such a character that he was enabled to amass a large amount of money, with which he came over to England at the close of the Russian war, in order to study the language and habits of a country which he had long admired as the cherished home of freedom.

Having determined upon establishing himself there, after a short residence, he employed an agent to invest his funds in household property, and several detached estates, amounting altogether to nearly 200 buildings, were accordingly purchased for him, amongst which was a lot situated in a place known as Mulberry Court, Whitechapel. He was soon afterwards informed by his agent that the last-named property was utterly uninhabitable from dirt and dilapidation, and he gave the necessary directions for a thorough cleansing and reparation of the premises, but all his sanitary efforts were obstinately resisted by the savage occupants, who paid no rent whatever, and insisted upon their right to live at free quarters in their normal state of filth and squalor.

On learning the condition of affairs, he accompanied his agent to the locality in order to remonstrate with the refractory people, but, although he was a great traveller, he never met with such a reception in any part of the world. He was instantly surrounded by a horde of ragged and raging barbarians, led by the defendant, who defied his authority, and subjected him to gross outrage and personal violence before he escaped from their hands.

He had been engaged from early youth in broil and battle among the roving tribes of his own land, the ferocious Calmucks, and the dogged serfs of the Ukraine, but such a desperate tribe as his present tenantry he never before encountered. He was a man of hot blood and ready action, and fearing that some serious mischief must ensue unless he resorted to the protection of the law, he determined to adopt the present proceedings.

In answer to the usual interrogatory as to whether he went in bodily fear from the violence of the defendant, the complainant indignantly replied, "Fear him—Bismillah! no; but I fear my own passion, if he puts upon me the same indignity again, and I don't wish to slay him."

The defendant appeared suddenly to collapse on hearing the magniloquent statement of his aggrieved landlord, and, with the sneaking servility common to Irish braggarts, assured the Magistrate that he meant no harm to "the jontleman forrener," and if he were only let off this time he would "leave the place entirely."

Mr. Hammill said that the prisoner had manifestly conducted himself with the most unjustifiable violence, and he must pay a fine of 10s, and enter into recognisances for his good behaviour for three months.

On learning the decision, the stately stranger expressed his obligation to the Magistrate with oriental ceremony, and after a graceful salaam, stalked out of court.

Westmorland Gazette – 22nd May 1858.

1859 – EAST LONDON ANTIQUITIES.

Whitechapel Road and what is now called the High Street, notwithstanding that the roadway at the city end was as uninviting as we have described it, and far worse in other parts, bearing less resemblance to a modern road than to a mud ditch, spotted with indentations from horses' hoofs and furrowed with ruts from the wheels of vehicles, was from a very early period the scene of considerable traffic, as one of the chief approaches to London.

Strype describes it as "a spacious fair street, and somewhat long, and well resorted unto, which occasions it to be the better inhabited, and accommodated with good inns for the reception of travellers, and for horses, coaches, carts, and waggons." The "Three Nuns," the "Blue Boar," and the "Black Bull," on the north side, are evidently inns of considerable antiquity, though deprived by the introduction of steam propulsion of most of their former glory.

Most of our readers know the old house nearly opposite the church of St. Botolph, Aldgate, with the elaborate carved work on the front, now in the occupation of a wholesale butcher. The carvings consist of the Prince of Wales' feathers, the Fleur de Lys, a thistle, and portcullis. In another place there is a shield of arms almost obliterated, the crest being a dove volent. The initials J.S. are also discoverable. We have not met with any conjecture as to who formerly inhabited this house.

The maps of London, in the latter part of Elizabeth's reign, show continued rows of houses on each side of the road, from Aldgate some distance beyond Whitechapel church; and behind them on both sides fields sparsely dotted with rural cottages. On the north side, Petticoat Lane—of which more hereafter—had houses on each side, along nearly its entire extent; and Wentworth Street, Spitalfields, might be said to exist as a continuation of Artillery Lane from Bishopsgate.

All the other places, now so thickly peopled, and the abiding places of disease and squalor, were green fields, where walked grave citizens to breathe the country air, where turbulent London apprentices cracked each other's crowns at quarter staff, or trained themselves to warmly receive the hated Spaniard, and where courtly gallants, in ruffs and baggy breeches, escorted simple town maidens, "Stealing their hearts with many vows of faith, And ne'er a true one."

On the south, Goodman's Fields shows several houses in contiguity to each other; and Rosemary Lane was built on, on the side nearest Whitechapel. This state of affairs did not, however, continue long; for we find Stow complaining loudly that "both the sides of the street be pestered with cottages and alleys even up to Whitechapel church, and almost half a mile beyond it into the common field, all which ought to lie open and free for all men. But this common field (I say) being sometime the beauty of this Citie on that part, is so encroached upon by building of filthie cottages and with other Pupresters, Inclosures, and Laystalls, that (notwithstanding all proclamations and acts of Parliament made to the contrarie) in some places it scarce remaineth a sufficient highway for the meeting of carriages and droves of cattell, much less is there any fare, pleasant, or wholesome way for people to walke on foot; which is no small blemish to so famous a Citie, to have so unsavorie and unseemly an entire passage thereunto."

Stow's invective is certainly well deserved by some of the narrow alters which abound in Whitechapel, for the contracted size of which, those who erected them could not plead in extenuation, as they might at the present day, the enormous price of land.

We have said that Petticoat Lane had houses on each side in Queen Elizabeth's day, and there appears to have been several scattered houses on the west side at a much earlier period. It had not then received its present—or rather its late—well-known name; but was called Hog Lane—Strype says, "perhaps from the hogs that ran in the fields there"—a supposition that cannot at all events, be called far-fetched. He adds, to explain his supposition, "that the bakers of London enjoyed the privilege of keeping hogs, and 'nourishing' them within their own houses or elsewhere, but not within the city."

However true this guess may be, it must have been a very distant period, that hogs claimed as their own, the lane where now swarm the people who refuse to eat them; for in 1550, it had "on both sides fair hedge rows of Elm trees, with bridges and easy stiles to pass over into the pleasant field, very commodious for citizens therein to walk, shoot, and otherwise to recreate and refresh their dulled spirits in the sweet and wholesome air." "To what base uses may we come!' Arcadia transformed into Rag-fair."

The beauty and healthiness of the spot induced many rich persons to fix their residences in "the lane." Strype mentions a house on the west side, in existence when he was a boy, which was commonly called "the Spanish Ambassador's house," and which he believed was the residence of the famous Count Gondomar, ambassador from Spain to the court of James I. This was the ambassador who procured the legal murder of Sir Walter Raleigh, as an atonement for the insult offered to the Spanish crown. He knew so well how to insinuate himself into the good graces of James, that he rather occupied the position of royal favourite than of the delegate of a foreign power; and he boasted in one of his letters that he had lulled King James asleep, that he hoped neither the cries of his daughter (the ill-fated Queen of Bohemia) nor of her children, nor the repeated solicitations of his Parliament and subjects on their behalf, should be able to awaken him,"—a boast which proved too true.

Strype himself was born in Petticoat Lane, down a paved alley on the east side, (now called Strype's Court) in a "fair large house with good garden before it," which was built and inhabited by Hans Jacobson, a Dutchman, and King James's jeweller. Many of the French protestants who fled from their country on the cruel and impolitic revocation of the edict of Nantes, established themselves in the Spitalfields end of the lane, and carried on their trade of broad silk weaving.

"The lane" can further boast of having once been visited in state by a queen. On the 10th of July 1564, Elizabeth came by water to the Tower to visit the mint, where she coined several pieces of gold with her own hand, and gave them to those about her. Leaving by the iron gate, she proceeded over Tower Hill on horseback, with her trumpeters, heralds, gentlemen pensioners, sergeants-at-arms, gentlemen, and nobles proceeding her—Lord Hunsdon carrying the sword of state—and attended by the jewelled and ruffed ladies of her court. In this order she proceeded, amid the cheers of the delighted populace, by Aldgate, through Houndsditch, and along Hog Lane, and so across the fields to the Charter house, where she reposed till the 14th, and then started her summer progress into Essex and Suffolk. How strangely this incident reads when contrasted with the present everyday life of the same place!

"The lane" was, soon after Strype's time, taken possession of by the second-hand clothes dealers, or brokers, as they were originally called. They first established themselves on the east side of Houndsditch, as we stated in our notice of that place, and gradually extending their quarters, left traces of rural beauties in Petticoat Lane.

Goodmans Fields will claim notice in our next number.

East London Observer – 29th January 1859.

———◦◉◦———

1859 – ROBBING A CUSTOMS HOUSE OFFICER.

Dennis Cocklin, James Hurley, and John Bary, three well-known thieves, were brought before Mr. Yardley, the first named charged with stealing a black canvas bag containing a uniform coat, three shirts, looking glass, brushes, and other articles, the property of a custom house officer named Frederick Townsend.

It appeared from the evidence that on Sunday, the 6th inst., a young man, named Callaghan, was employed by the officer Townsend to carry his bag, containing the articles above mentioned, from a public house opposite the London Hospital, in the Whitechapel Road, to the Fenchurch Street railway station. On the way they were joined by the prisoner Cocklin, a thief named Carty, and others, and they adjourned to a public house in Whitechapel, where nine or ten pots of beer were drunk at the expense of the prosecutor, who soon lost all recollection of himself, and was taken away by two of the party,

leaving Callaghan with the other thieves. Carty demanded the bag of Callaghan, and on his refusing to deliver it to him a violent assault was made upon him by Cocklin and another. They beat him in a savage manner, and Carty took the bag and its contents from him and ran away with it, leaving Callaghan bleeding upon the ground.

On Saturday night, two police constables, named Clements, 210, and Donovan, 212 H, took Cocklin into custody at a beer shop in Waterloo Town, Bethnal Green, and they were bringing him away when the prisoners Hurley and Barry attempted to rescue him, and Hurley was exceedingly violent. Hurley made a rush at the constables and separated their prisoner Cocklin from them, exclaiming, "Now you are clear, run away." He made his escape, but was retaken, and Hurley continued his violence and struck the constables. All the prisoners were ultimately secured. The prisoner Cocklin made a determined resistance, and a great number of Bethnal Green ruffians and Whitechapel thieves attempted to drag him from the officers. Barry, it appears, was not aware that Cocklin was in custody when he interfered. Hurley had been a thief and burglar for years, and was connected with a desperate gang.

Mr. Yardley remanded Cocklin on the charge of robbery until Thursday, committed Hurley to prison for one month for the attempted rescue, and discharged Barry.

Sun (London) – 14th February 1859.

———◦◉◦———

1859 – MISERY AND FILTH OF LODGING HOUSES.

In the year 1851 the Common Lodging houses act was passed, and two years later it was rendered more effective by several important amendments. The condition of the poorer class of lodging houses in the metropolis rendered this interference on the part of the legislature absolutely necessary.

It is a curious fact that the classes of society most liable to be imposed upon are the highest and the lowest. But there is this important difference between them, that the former has it in their power in a great degree to protect themselves, while the latter are, from their extreme poverty and dependence, placed absolutely at the mercy of those who choose to take advantage of their necessities.

The condition of the common lodging houses in the metropolis previous to the passing of the acts in question afforded a striking proof of this painful truth. In these filthy and overcrowded dwelling places of the poor the only object of the landlord was to extract as much from his miserable tenants as they could possibly pay. There were honourable exceptions, of course, but this was the general characteristic of the class in question, and it was this which obliged parliament to set political economy aside, and to interfere on behalf of those who were powerless to protect themselves.

But this was not the only motive for our interference. It was essential to the progress of sanitary improvements that means should be taken to correct the abuses in question. It was impossible to leave the poorer class of lodging houses in the condition in which they were a few years ago without positive danger to the public health. It was in these localities that typhus and cholera were sure to find their readiest victims, and from thence the seeds of pestilence were scattered to other quarters.

We need not be surprised therefore that the measure adopted for the better ventilation and drainage of these dwellings of the poor, and for the prevention of overcrowding within confined limits, have been attended with the best results. To these, and to other sanitary improvements in the metropolis, we believe we may fairly attribute the absence of malignant epidemics for some years past.

But it appears that there are still grievous abuses in connection with the homes of the poor which the Lodging houses acts cannot reach. These, as their title implies, are only applicable to one kind of dwelling. They do not apply to a class of dwellings which are probably the most wretched, as well in a physical as a moral sense, of any in this metropolis. They do not apply to single rooms occupied, or alleged to be occupied, by families; and a return just published discloses a state of things with reference to the occupants of such premises in different parts of London which must shock every friend of humanity, indeed, were the report not issued by official authority, we could not give credit to many of the details, which it contains.

It seems hardly possible to believe that there should be so much misery and filth, and, we must add, revolting indecency, in the greatest and healthiest and wealthiest city in the world. But, in spite of all that philanthropy has done, and is doing, to improve and elevate the humbler classes, there are still numbers of our fellow-creatures living in different parts of the metropolis in a condition which it makes us shudder to contemplate. We have only to quote at random from the report before us in order to convince our readers of this melancholy fact.

The following are a few, and only a few, of the details with which it furnishes us:-

"In a room, No. 4, John Street, Bethnal Green, having space for three persons, were found a man and his wife, one boy, and three girls above the age of fourteen. In a room, No. 5, in the same street, of similar dimensions, were found a man and his wife, three boys and two girls above the age of fourteen. In another room in the same house, having space for only three persons, were found a man and his wife, two boys and two girls above the age of fourteen. In a room, No. 7, in the same street, a man and his wife, three boys and two girls, above the age of fourteen. The houses visited were dirty and unwholesome; the floors, stairs, bedsteads, and bedding filthy, and swarming with vermin. The yards are small and mostly unpaved. There is a closet to each house, but they are so dirty as to be almost unfit for use. Each house has a separate supply of water, but no cistern to contain it. There is a small kitchen to each house, but this is generally found to be without fireplace or copper, and is so full of filth as to be of no service whatever."

"In a room, No. 5, Compasses Court, Whitechapel, having space for three persons, were found one adult male, three adult females, and two girls above the age of fourteen. In another room in the same house, of similar dimensions, were found one adult male, one boy and four girls above the age of fourteen."

Such is a sample of the melancholy report before us. We may add that it contains details of a still more revolting character; but we have quoted enough to show the nature of the evil, which the Lodging houses acts do not touch, but for which it is surely time that some remedy should be found. What are we to expect of a youthful population bred up amid such scenes as those we have just described? Must not an atmosphere so filthy destroy by slow but sure degrees whatever good nature may have implanted even in such children of misfortune? The question is how to apply a remedy to this painful state of things; and we have no hesitation in saying that the legislature alone cannot do it. It has already done much in regulating common lodging houses; but the report before us clearly shows that further interference is necessary for the preservation alike of the public morals and the public health.

Lloyd's Weekly Newspaper – 24th April 1859.

1859 – AN EXCITING SCENE.

On Tuesday morning, between the hours of 1 and 2 o'clock, a fire of a rapidly destructive character, attended with a serious loss of property, took place on the extensive premises of Mr. Lewis Jacobs, wholesale boot and shoe maker, No. 124, High Street, Whitechapel. Samuel Wood, the conductor of the Royal Fire Escape at Whitechapel church, arrived just in time.

Ten persons presented themselves at the second-floor window, and the most piteous cries for help were heard. Wood told them to remain a few minutes, and he would rescue them. He then placed his machine against the burning building, and first brought down six children. He again ascended, and placed Mrs. Jane Henry, aged seventy years, Mrs. Susan Jacobs, Mr. Lewis Jacobs, and the servant, in the machine. The poor conductor now sank under his great exertions, and if it had not been for the timely arrival of Edward Cooke, the conductor of the royal fire escape from Aldgate, he must have fallen victim to his courage.

When Cooke brought his brother conductor down the ladder, Wood was in a state of insensibility, and it was upwards of half an hour before he returned to his senses. Had it not been for the perseverance of the fire escape conductor, the whole ten persons must have been suffocated or burnt to death, as there was no means of escape from the roof and outlet or back yard to retreat to.

The premises were entirely destroyed, and the adjoining houses considerably damaged. The loss will fall on the Sun, County, and other fire offices.

Frome Times – 14th December 1859.

1860 – WHITECHAPEL PAST, PRESENT, AND FUTURE.

On the 13th instant, the Rev. Samuel Thornton, M.A., incumbent of St. Jude's, Whitechapel, delivered a lecture on the above subject, as one of the annual courses in connection with the Young Men's Mutual Improvement Society belonging to his church.

The rev. lecturer after a few introductory remarks referred briefly to the occupation of London by the Romans, which was described by Tacitus as occurring about fifty years after the coming of Jesus Christ, later than the occupation of other parts of Britain. He glanced also at the theories which derived the name of the city from Llyndun or "the Hill Fortress on the Lake," because the river not being embanked formed a lake, flowing over the present Southwark; or from "Long-dinas," "the City of Ships," whence came Londinium, the Roman name. He believed the name had nothing to do with the Temple of Diana, as some thought, and that Sir Christopher Wren had conclusively disposed of that theory.

When the Romans came, they found a narrow slip of ground between the lake or river, and the great moors and fens from which come the names of Moorfields and Finsbury or Fensbury. Eastward were fields or alluvial wastes, and beyond these the mighty forest which stretched out northward and easterly, the haunt of the wild cat, the wolf, and boar, but now has become the scene of many picnics and of the annual Cockney hunt. The eastern part of the narrow slip of ground mentioned was traversed by a fair meandering stream—afterwards called the Wall-Brook—now a stream of carts, cabs, and omnibuses, being the street running from the Mansion House to the river; and this communicated with another—the Langstream or Lang-bourn —which gives its name to Langbourne ward, at Bridge Row, now Budge Row. The principal street ran from the western side of the City along the line of Watling Street, branched off at the London stone—probably a Roman standard from which the milestones were reckoned—to Aldgate, and then straight off through Whitechapel to the forest beyond. Another street ran from Dowgate to the northern boundary of the City at Cripplegate. An interesting proof of these facts was to be met with in "Archer's Vestiges of old London," but time would not permit him to enlarge upon the details.

He passed on to A.D. 306, when London was walled in by the Romans for protection from attacks made on it by the unsubdued islanders outside. Beginning at the Tower, which they were aware was a Roman fortress, the wall ran along the west side of the Minories to Aldgate, then took a bend and ran by the west side of Houndsditch to Bishopsgate, passed then to Moorgate, and ran along the street called Barbican, from a remarkable rampart or bastion there on the wall; then making a bend on to Cripplegate; and on till it reached the Fleet river, running where Farringdon Street stands; and down by the site of the present large warehouses in Blackfriars; being connected again with the Tower by a wall running along the side of the river. The remains of this wall were distinguishable at no distant date from the present day. Not long since when digging in the Minories, a portion was discovered; and relics had been found in Cripplegate and elsewhere. It was composed of alternate layers of brick and ragstone, being no less than nine feet broad at the foundation, and diminishing to two feet at the top. Temple Bar, and Whitechapel Bars, and Holborn Bars were not stations on the wall, but were marks which enclosed the Liberties of London, and were once, no doubt, really bars, or posts with chains attached to them.

The teeming regions in which they now were, if then inhabited at all were tenanted by the dead. The Romans brought their dead outside the walls, and did not wait till the year 1850 to pass an extramural act; moreover they robbed the dead of any miasmatical or pestilential influence by burning them, so to enclose their ashes in a small funereal urn—a custom which may seem to us at first sight heartless but for sanitary objects he could not help wishing they could see their way to some such method of disposing of the dead as this.

Eastward, immediately under the City wall lay Spitalfields where had been found considerable relics of Roman sepulchre, and in Goodman's Fields many of these records of the mortality of a day gone by were also dug up.

He mentioned three of the most remarkable relics of Roman antiquity found in Whitechapel, remarking that wherever that great people went they left relics of their industry and skill. He was not quite certain where the street called Whitechapel Lane ran, but conjectured it was from Mile End gate to near the bottom of Great Prescott Street; and near this last-mentioned place was found a monumental tomb dedicated to the memory of a soldier of the Legion. The second relic was dug up in Petticoat Lane about 17 feet below the surface. It was a beautiful torso or the trunk of a Roman slinger executed in white Parian marble, sunk down below the sewers and only by accident brought to the light of day. The third relic was found at the bottom of Commercial Street, about 20 years ago when the street was being excavated for the purpose of sewerage, nearly opposite the pump which stands in front of one of the beer shops which infested this district, and between it and the elegant obelisk with lamps which adds so much to the beauty and effect of the street. It was a Roman urn or amphora, eleven inches broad, and was found to contain inside four vases of a very elegant shape, one radiated like the Etruscan vases and bearing the figure of a dog roughly executed in the middle, and partly filled with charred bones. Many antiquaries were called down to explain its story, but it was exceedingly simple. It was the Roman custom not only to burn the body of their deceased, but take out the vital parts and insert them separately in smaller vessels; and as pastes of various degrees of redness were found in these inner vases, no doubt they contained the heart, liver, lungs, and other interior parts of a human form—some family enclosing therefore in this little urn the vital parts of one who was dear to them.

It was impossible to trace the changes in Whitechapel century by century. He therefore took a leap over many ages to the reign of Richard II., the imbecile and unfortunate victim of Bolingbroke, afterwards Henry IV. They must then conceive Whitechapel as presenting the features of a sequestered country hamlet, traversed by the broad road to Essex, with occasional Inns where travellers could stop for refreshment, and here and there a family mansion of a superior order to the general houses, and a few dwellings gathered together into a kind of street as they approached Aldgate, but this only on the South side of the road cultivated fields being to the left and right—namely the Hospital fields or Spital fields on one side and Goodman's fields on the other, with blossoming hedge rows and clusters of beech and hawthorne; and to the right hand of the high road, as one left the city, peering up among the trees a small spire white as snow, marking the little church of that little village. So small was it that though it bore the name of the church of St. Mary Matfellon it was wont to be commonly described by the less imposing name of the Whitechapel. It was erected in 1329, in the reign of Edward II., and dedicated to St. Mary.

The appended name of Matfellon has received various explanations. One is that a certain Frenchman barbarously murdered a lady of fortune and piety living in this neighbourhood, to whom he was indebted for his education and support in childhood, and that being pursued he succeeded in crossing the river, but had to reach St. George's before he could make sanctuary—that he was arrested and brought back, and that the women of Whitechapel pounced upon him and, an old writer says, "having flung on him, much dirte and filth of the street, did prick him to death with their bodkins." How, even if this story were true, the name of Matfellon arose from it—whether it meant that the Whitechapel ladies were a match for the felon—he did not know. The story is proved to have had nothing to do with the name. One hundred years before the date assigned for the event—namely in 1336, the murder being stated to have been committed in 1428—the London register speaks of the church by the name of St. Mary Matfellon. This difficulty seems insuperable for the believers in the story; and the way being thus cleared for another explanation the name is conjectured to be a corruption of the church Maria Matris Filii, of Mary the Mother of the Son; but the commonly received explanation derives it from the Hebrew word, Matfel, signifying one lately become a mother, so that it would be dedicated to "Mary recently the mother," as distinguished from the other Mary and the Magdalene.

Two hundred years ago, the original Whitechapel was pulled down in consequence of a fire destroying a portion of it; and the present unsightly structure was erected in its stead. In 1711, the living was bought by Brasenose College and has since passed into the hands of the Bishops of London. He need not enter into the comparatively recent dispute about tithes, the result of which as they all knew was the obtaining of a rule of Court which declared that the rector was not entitled to tithes, further than to say that the character of the late excellent rector, and the esteem and regard in which he was held, did not suffer at all from proceedings which might have been conducted with much animosity and bitterness.

It was difficult to imagine the pent-up abodes of a crowded population were once green fields where the lark carolled, but had the audience ever thought of the derivation of the name Plough Court, Greenfield Street, Fieldgate Street, Great Garden Street—where once no doubt there was an extensive cultivated garden separated from the adjacent meadows—or Barley Mow Court? It was its sweet odours that gave a name to Rosemary Lane—part of which by the bye was called Hog Lane, which added rather to his argument—in Bull Stake Court, bulls were once tethered—sheep lowed in Green Street, and grazed at pleasure over Goodman's fields—leaning upon Goodman's Style the shepherd told his tale of love to the rosy milk maid; and afterwards wandered to hear the notes of the sweet songbird in Nightingale Lane! What's in a name? people sometimes ask. The whole history of a neighbourhood is in the names of its streets; and though names change and their meaning cannot always be traced, they do not bear their names without a reason. In Wood Street, there were once trees, Mulberry Court mulberries grew.

Sometimes the name is derived from the shape and appearance of the place, and thus they had in Whitechapel, Short Street, Horse-shoe Alley, and Sugar Loaf Court. Many retain recollections of the old signs of very prominent houses, for every shop had a sign, stretching often half across the road, till in 1768, by order of the King they were obliged to be removed as dangerous to passengers and impediments to the circulation of fresh air. Thus, we have Five Ink Horn Court (abbreviated to Acorn Court) Half Moon Alley, Green Dragon Yard, Boar's Head Court, and others take their name from the business carried on there, such as Tripe Yard, Bakers' Row, and Butcher Row. His recourses failed to discover the origin of Greggs Alley—probably Mr. Gregg was the original owner; Heneage Street was so-called from a celebrated minister of the time of Charles II., and Wentworth Street, as they would see, from the family of the unhappy Earl of Strafford.

Whitechapel changed but little in the years between the date last mentioned, and the period of the plague and fire of London, 1665-6. They would remember the couplet with which Defoe concluded his narrative of events of the plague year, which, if it did not possess great poetic beauty, was written in a spirit of pious thankfulness to Almighty God for his mercy:-

A dreadful plague in London was, in the year '65,
Which swept a hundred thousand
souls away; yet I'm alive.

Defoe resided this year in Whitechapel, and gives one fearfully vivid picture of the panic which had seized everybody, to read his description of the crowds of fugitives which by the house where he had determined to continue his residence, seeking to escape from the horrors of the apparently doomed city. Carriages, carts, wagons, vehicles of all kinds filled the broad highway of Whitechapel from morning to night, fleeing in the terror and disorder of a French army pursued by a Wellington: and truly it was a terrible enemy they sought to escape from. Entire neighbourhoods in plague stricken London were stripped of their population; grass grew in once crowded thoroughfares; fearful silence reigned in the highways, the city palaces become a city of death; and the silence was only broken by the cry of neglected animals which ran about in large numbers, the screams of persons in the houses where the red cross on the door and the watchman before it, marked that the plague had seized upon its victims, or the rumbling of the death cart as it moved slowly on, and the fearful cry of the attendants of "Bring out your dead."

Amidst the mortality from this scourge, which reached the appalling number of 100,000 deaths, Whitechapel was comparatively lightly afflicted. The weekly returns of deaths never exceeded 300, even at the end of the plague, when the eastern part of London suffered most, for the plague moved from west to east. Probably this small mortality as compared with other parishes was due chiefly to the thinnest of the population in Whitechapel. London outside the walls would naturally, at that period, be thinly peopled compared to the city within; and, indeed, through a well-meant, but mistaken policy, the construction of houses outside the walls was discouraged by the several successive governments.

In 1580, for instance, Elizabeth prohibited by royal proclamation the construction of houses within three miles of any of the city gates. Of course, the edict was not obeyed, such edicts never are, though when the Lord Mayor came to take the oath of allegiance, he had to make a solemn oath to strictly carry them out, and demolish all prohibited structures. Stowe recorded that in his time they had marred the open fields which were the beauty of the city on the east, and there were no longer the pleasant and wholesome walks he remembered in his youth. There were also strong complaints of the badness of the roads, and by the reign of James II., factories began to be complained of, which emitted "foul and filthy smoke and stench," as they do still—the parish, more shame for those who caused it to be so, being omitted from the operation of the general Metropolitan Smoke Act.

The fire of London, it was well known, began at Pudding Lane and ended at Pie Corner. Consequently, it did not reach Whitechapel; in fact, the fire was the making of Whitechapel. Houses began to be built right and left of the highway along its whole extent, to accommodate those who were left houseless by the fire, and who could not recommence building within the city till a general plan was approved of by the authorities. On the return of the inhabitants their recollections of the plague and fire made them afraid to go again into the denser parts of the city, and business obliged them to live as near as possible outside the walls: while the rebuilding of the city brought many people to the metropolis who took up their residence outside. Whitechapel rapidly ceased therefore to present the appearance of a country village—trees were cut down and converted into butchers' blocks, and the pruning hook was turned into a pole axe.

Having briefly traced the general progress of Whitechapel from British morass to a Roman burial ground—then to a sequestered hamlet—and finally to a teeming limb of the modern Babel—it was necessary to examine it in more detail. He began at Petticoat Lane, the Jew's quarter, which might be said to extend on the east to Commercial Street, on the west to Houndsditch, on the north to Artillery Street, and the south to the Tenter ground of St. Mark's; he promised that he would not in this part of his subject attempt to keep any defined separation of Whitechapel past and present. He said this was emphatically the Jew's quarter of London; and within the area defined, the stranger might fancy himself transported to Frankfort or Warsaw or the Jewish quarter of any other continental city where that peculiar people abound.

Why the Jews settled in Petticoat Lane was not clear to demonstration, but it seemed probable in the case of London, as of other cities, a particular quarter was allotted them outside the city walls; or being excluded from the city, and finding an indisposition on the part of the inhabitants to mix with them, they might have selected the vicinity of Aldgate for its proximity to the haunts of business, for as surely as a vulture to the carcass, so surely does the Jew fly to the scene of commercial activity.

There are 18,000 Jews in London, and they must once have been more numerous, for in 1287, under the reign of Edward I., by an arbitrary edict, 15,600 were banished in one day from London. Petticoat Lane must have looked deserted and dreary indeed. It by no means had always the same mean appearance as at the present day. Traces have been discovered there of buildings of considerable size and pretensions to elegance. A few doors from where a flaming gin shop now stands—the rent from which, by the bye, goes to pay the lecturer of St. Olave's, Jewry—singular source for the stipend of a minister of the gospel, and curious it would be to inquire whether he saves most souls or the gin shop sends most to destruction—traces of such a building were found on digging for the foundation of the present house. That Petticoat Lane has seen better days is known to very many persons. A friend of his (the lecturer's) was passing along some years ago, when in digging below the surface portions of a large building had been discovered, and he stopped to comment on it to the navvy. "Oh, sure," was the reply he received to his remark, "don't your honour know that this was the west end of the town at one time."

Leaving "the Lane," and passing down Whitechapel Road, they would find on the left-hand a series of streets and alleys, the names of which recalled the occupation of the site where they at present stand by a residence of the luckless Earl of Essex, the favourite of Elizabeth, and who was afterwards beheaded by her warrant. Near the site of his stately mansion are now Castle Street, Castle Court, Kent and Essex Yard, and New Castle Street. There was an Essex Street, Essex Court, and Essex Alley, before the formation of Commercial Street, when many narrow places gave way to that broad thoroughfare. In Castle Street were started the model baths and washhouses, the first of the kind opened in London. They originated in the meeting together of some benevolent people, and their belief that the poor might be advantageously initiated into the mysteries of soap and water more than they were. In 1844 they succeeded in getting the matter taken up by parliament, and an act was passed encouraging the erection of baths and washhouses. Another building was then bought and the model establishment in Goulston Street was erected, He regretted to say it was at present not a very profitable speculation, though it deserved cordial support and sympathy.

Going eastward from this place they came upon a population which was well described in a celebrated speech by the late Bishop of London, Dr. Bloomfield, when advocating the building of new churches in Bethnal Green, as "one of the poorest and most neglected and miserable in all London, inhabited by the lower kind of artisans, thieves, and costermongers." He (Mr. Thornton) must protest against the connection of the honest costermongers with thieves; but there was no doubt of the truth of the Bishop's description of the locality.

Passing through Commercial Street, and going down Whitechapel Road, they would observe, he hoped with sorrow, that there was a public house at every few doors. He had looked in Whitechapel High Street, in vain, for a single honest downright bookseller's shop, but every three or four doors there were these flaming gin palaces; and he asked himself what reason there could be for this abundance, while for a bookseller's an inhabitant had to go down to Mr. Gladding's or to Paternoster Row. Alluding to the sign of one of those houses in the High Street, the "Angel," he could only hope for the sake of his temporal and eternal welfare, the working man's Angel visits might be few and far between.

A large proportion of the people living in the courts and alleys between those houses subsist by begging, and (it was a sad thing to say, but he felt it was true) the crowding of the place and overstocking of the labour market made it difficult to suggest to many of them any other mode of living. He had heard an estimate which fixed the beggars of London at about 15,000, two thirds of them being Irish, and he believed that nearly a third more must come from his own district.

He had remarked that Wentworth Street revived in its name memories of the unfortunate Earl of Strafford, who was the chief of an unpopular administration under Charles I., and being impeached for high treason basely betrayed by the King into the hands of his enemies, and executed in 1641. What the Irishman said in reference to Petticoat Lane was in a sense true, for the Earls of Strafford had a mansion where there is now the squalor and misery of Wentworth Street. There is a curious proof of this in the old singularly-written leases by which some of the houses there are held, which are all for 500 years, the object being to prevent the Earl's property from getting into the hands of his enemies by confiscation. The leases have now from 200 to 300 years to run.

Passing to the Eastern extremity of his district they came to Osborn Street and there was a curious fact connected with this. Brick Lane was formerly connected with Whitechapel by two narrow thoroughfares forming a fork, and meeting at Wentworth Street. One of these was called Brick Lane like the lower portion; the other rejoiced in the euphonious and suggestive name of Dirty Lane. A Magistrate named Osborn was the means of building over Dirty Lane, and made the entrance to Brick Lane wider. There was a proof of this in the absence of a No. 73, Whitechapel Road, which was pulled down to make the extension and Whitechapel certainly owed something to the memory of Sir William Osborn (he believed that was the name) for his improvement.

They came now to the old workhouse site, where bones were lately discovered, and people imagined they were the bones of poor people starved by the Guardians. No doubt they were the remains of the days of pestilence, when people were buried in many unusual places and in great numbers. He would not say much of the workhouse system. He would only draw attention to the singular fact that benevolent people found it absolutely necessary to band together to form a voluntary association for the relief of destitution in the metropolis. If the Poor law did the work it was designed for, what need could there be for societies like this, which he hoped the public would take up more generally, giving their money to be dispensed by benevolent kind hearted people instead of by the master of a workhouse. He made these remarks in no antagonism with the Board of Guardians, many members of which he deeply respected and esteemed, and who he was sure would not permit of rules and systems essentially oppressive of the poor; it was in the carrying out of these, by inferior officials, that cruelty was not seldom exhibited.

Leaving the workhouse, or rather its site, for the building was no longer there, he passed on to Court Street, opposite Meggs Alms houses, where there used to be a prison for debt similar to the Marshalsea in Southwark. Connected with this was the memory of a benevolent individual of the name of Coulston, who died in 1721, and whose custom was to release annually on a certain day all persons imprisoned there, by payment of their debts. The benevolence was commemorated, in the following lines:—

He feeds yon alms house, neat, tho' void of state,
　Where age and want sit smiling at the gate;
Him 'prenticed lads and friendless orphans bless
　The young ones labour, and the old ones rest.

Coulston distributed £17,695 in the course of his life in charity. His setting at liberty the debtors in the prisons, perhaps, had this one bad effect, that people were a trifle more careless about keeping out of debt. One time the Churchwarden of Whitechapel received £1,000 as a gift from an unknown donor towards the relief of destitution which afterwards proved to be from Coulston. He sent £20,000 to some benevolent scheme without any signature whatever. Coulston was a single man, and when asked why he did not marry he said "he considered every widow his wife, every orphan boy his son, and every miserable friendless girl his daughter." He died leaving £100,000 to his relatives—a beautiful illustration of the truth of the Scripture passage:-

"There is that gathereth and yet increaseth,
　And there that withholdeth more than is
　　meet, and it tendeth to poverty."

A little way down the road from the place last mentioned, and at the bottom of Paradise Row is the house where Guido Fawkes was said to have been born. Further on they came to Whitechapel Gate which stood to date within twenty years ago and still further on in the middle of Whitechapel Road, Wat Tyler in the reign of Richard II., at the head of the rebels against the obnoxious poll tax, met the King and made their demands which he promised to satisfy. Close by Mile End Gate formerly used to stand the old Whitechapel pound. The London Hospital, which they came to before reaching this, dated from 1740, being originally established in Great Prescott Street, and called the London Infirmary. The house which it left was occupied by the first institution for the reclamation of young women—the first Magdalen—established in the metropolis. It took in 100 girls, and of these one-seventh were under 15; and the institution grew so rapidly that it was transferred to larger premises at Great Surrey Street, Blackfriars Road. It is curious to read that at the time of its institution the girls wore, as a suitable uniform, the high mop caps and large black chip hats and long black mittens.

Adjoining the London Hospital, where now stands Mount Terrace, there used formerly to be the Mount Terrace. Various delusions prevail in reference to this. There is an idea abroad that its increase of height above the surrounding district was caused by the burial there of persons who died of the plague. Another that it was raised in connection with some scheme of fortification of the City; another that it was formed from the debris of the fire of London. None of these suppositions was true. Some time ago the mound was removed and levelled, and there were found no bones or other relics of mortality, and nothing but a few fragments of pottery. The rest of the mount was dirt. It had been, in fact, a common lay stall or receptacle for the filth of the City, of which there were several others on its outskirts. In 1703, we find it designated in not very complimentary terms, "The Dunghill."

Returning to the Church, they found some curious entries in the parochial books, relating to the time of the Protectorate, when everything was brought down to the level of commercial flatness. They read that the "banns of marriage of Julius Wood and Jane Smith were published in the market place at Leadenhall, three several market days, 16ᵗʰ, 18ᵗʰ, and 26ᵗʰ of October; so that the entire business was got over in about a week." Another entry was this, "Richard Allison of this parish was published three several times in the public meeting place, commonly called Mary Whitechapel in the county of Middlesex."

In Whitechapel Church there used to be a very curious painting as an altar piece, painted by Fells. It represented the Last Summer, and Judas was drawn sitting in an armchair with a cap, and gown, and brands, and having a striking likeness to Dean Kennett. Dr. Weldon was then rector, and it is said he wanted to paint the portrait of the Bishop of London as Judas, but the painter refused, and he had to be content with Dean Kennett. The painting is now in the possession of the Antiquarian Society. In reference to it, the following lines were written, he knew not by whom:-

> "To say this picture does to you belong—
> Kennett—does Judas and the painter wrong;
> False the image, the resemblance faint—
> Judas, compared to Kennett, was a saint!"

Rosemary Lane, a rather notorious place at the present day, has a close connection with the execution of Charles I. Richard Brandon, "a rag man of Rosemary Lane" was the one who cut off the head of that ill-fated monarch. On receiving payment of his wretched office, he went back to Rosemary Lane to enjoy it, and it was said that while relating the circumstances to his wife he suddenly lost his speech, and died in three days after, regarding it a visitation of the Lord. The people pelted the coffin along Rosemary Lane, and through Leman Street into Whitechapel—the body having been buried in Whitechapel churchyard—with rotten eggs, mud, and dirt, crying out, "Hang him, dog, away with him;" and they were with great difficulty restrained by the sheriff from further violence.

In Bull Stake Court, of bull-baiting memory there was at one time a meeting house of Seventh Day Baptists. In the reign of James II., one John James preached there, and was heard to say that Jesus Christ was the King of Great Britain, France, and Ireland. He was torn from the pulpit by an officer sent to watch the proceedings, hanged, drawn, and quartered at Tyburn, and his head stuck on a high pole in the middle of Whitechapel, High Street, nearly opposite Mr. Francis's house of business.

He must not omit to notice, as a leading feature in Whitechapel present, the bell foundry of the Messrs. Mears. He understood that no less than 188,000 bells had been cast there. Big Ben of Westminster, Big Ben of Montreal, Big Tom of Lincoln, the big bell of Leicester, were among the number. He was informed that there had been 80 tons weight of molten metal in the place at one time.

No. 76, Whitechapel Road – a house now removed was pointed out as a place of royal residence. Outside was the Prince of Wales's feathers, the fleur de lys of France, and the initials H.R.

Goodman's Fields formed originally part of the manor of the Nonnee Minores or minon nuns of St. Clare, whence we get the Minories. It got into the hands of a man named Barnes and let to a farmer named Trollope and then to one Goodman. In 1692,

Sir William Leman whose wife's name was Maunsell left to his grandchild his interest in this place, and the names of this family are perpetuated in Leman Street, Maunsell Street, Ayliffe Street, and Buckley's Mews.

In 1850 a man assuming the name of Sir John Leman made a claim to this property, installed himself in one of the houses, and got up a company to recover it. But one fine morning the office clerk suddenly disappeared with the bag, and there was an end of Sir John Leman, unless it was true what he had been told, that he was to be found clearing bricks in Whitechapel.

In 1720, Goodman's Fields theatre was built, and in 1741, Garrick made there his first appearance on any stage as Richard III. This theatre, now rebuilt in Leman Street had been opened innumerable times, but it was a remarkable fact that it never filled except when it was opened for public preaching of the word of God. Part of Goodman's Fields was called the Tenter Ground. In 1572, Benedict Spinola, a charitable Spaniard, came from his country with the object of benefitting the condition of poor people here, teaching them the art of preparing cloth by stretching it on tenter hooks.

Prescott Street, they would read in many books, was derived from Peas-cod Street, because peas cods grew there, but rather it was originally so called, as he found the name of Prescott among the numerous connections of the Leman family. Before speaking of Butcher Row, it might be interesting to note the prices of some articles of consumption five centuries and a half ago, namely in 1317. The prices were famine prices, but nevertheless they would not alarm the most frugal housewife of the present day: best goose 3d., best capon 2½d., best hen 1½d., best chicken two for 1½d., eggs 20 for one penny!

In the midst of the butcher's market was a very respectable wine merchant's, kept by a person of the name of Newton. Through this house ran the division line between the parishes of Aldgate and Whitechapel. A man died in the house who was liable to burial in the parish, but unhappily the boundary line of the parishes ran directly through the bed where he died. Part of him therefore died in Whitechapel and part in Aldgate. Each parish refused to undertake the burial; the Overseers came down and there was a regular fight over it; the result being that the corpse remained unburied and decomposed while a decision of a Court of Law was taken upon the question; the decision being that the parish in which the vital parts of the man are found must take the responsibility of the burial. It was found that Aldgate had the lungs and heart, and Aldgate had to carry the body away and bury it. The dispute was repeated elsewhere in the case of a man who fell dead in a fit in the street across the boundary line; and the same rule was applied.

The lecturer caused great amusement reading a humorous description of the Butcher's market, and of another peculiarity of the road—the shop which periodically makes "alarming sacrifice" being found shut up for three or four days previously, as if retired within itself to contemplate the projected act of self-devotion.

Leaving Whitechapel future, of which he had much to say, to another occasion, the rev. gentleman concluded his able lecture by describing one of the most interesting features of Whitechapel present – the sugar refiners' premises. He had heard many reasons why this manufacture was almost exclusively in the hands of Germans, but in reality, it had nothing to do with the willingness to work for lower wages, nor entirely to greater ability on the part of Germans to stand the heat, to which he had heard it ascribed. It was in fact a monopoly, handed down from father to son, and the employment of strangers was regarded with great jealousy. The various processes of the rough unrefined sugar to the sugar loaves of the grocer's windows were successively pointed out, and illustrated by specimens and drawings.

East London Observer – 24th November to 15th December 1860.

1861 – A HUNGRY MOB.

The distress in Whitechapel and St. George's-in-the-East is assuming a tenuous character, numerous baker's shops have been visited by hungry mobs demanding bread; and in some cases, breaking and carrying off all the loaves on the premises.

John Bull – 19th January 1861.

1861 – OGRES OF THE WORKHOUSE.

On Tuesday, at Worship Street Police Court, Henry Warner and Mary Warner, man and wife, were charged before Mr. Knox, with being found at night in the open air, destitute, and without any visible place of abode.

The subject matter of the above charge is this:- About a fortnight since the woman Warner preferred a charge of assault against a gate porter, named

Coxall, at the Whitechapel workhouse, for violently assaulting her. Mr. Knox, after an attentive hearing and corroborative evidence on a remand, ordered that Coxall should enter into recognisances to appear and answer the charge at the Middlesex Sessions, at the same time desiring it should be signified to the authorities of the workhouse that it would be advisable for them to protect the mother and child until the result of the proceedings against their servant should be known.

That this humane suggestion was not acted upon appeared from the testimony of Police Constable Gerrety, 159 H, who had the conducting of the present case. He deposed, "Last night, about ten o'clock, I saw this man and woman, the latter having a child in her arms, sitting on the steps of Whitechapel workhouse. In answer to my inquiries, they said that they had been denied entrance. Coxall, the porter, came up at the moment, and I referred them to him. He said, "You will not be admitted here. Go to the, casual ward." The woman then observed, "You know, Mr. Coxall, that Mr. Knox, the Magistrate, told you he should wish us to be admitted every night while the charge against you was pending." To which Coxall replied, "Who is Mr. Knox? I would care about as much for him as I would for you." He then went in and shut the door, but opened it almost immediately, and said, "Constable, the master wishes to speak to you." I then went into the workhouse, where I saw the master, who asked, "What do you want here?" I replied, "The porter invited me in." He continued, "I am master in this house, and you have no business here without my permission." To this I answered, "Well, sir, I shall go out if you please," and I put my hand on the door to do so, but he called out, "Let that door be." He then got between me and the door, and again asked, while he held it fast, "What business have you here?" I told him as before, and then I left. I took the man, woman, and child to the station; it was raining at the time.

I was there directed to take them to the casual ward, and saw a man named Lambert, whom I told that admission was required for the three. He said, "We are full of men, and I can't take the man in at all, but as the child is ill, they say, why you shall have an order for the doctor." He then gave an order to Dr. Richardson, the house doctor, and I took the poor things there. The doctor examined the child, and gave an order for admission to the house. I then took them back and gave Coxall the order. He kept us waiting about ten minutes, then returned, and said he would not admit them. It was one o'clock. I again saw them to the station, and learning that they had not eaten anything all day I supplied them with tea and bread and butter, and they remained there until I brought them to this court."

Mr. Knox directed Mr. Wood, one of the officers of the court, to see that the husband, wife, and child were provided for under this emergency until the issue of the charge against Coxall was known. Such conduct on the part of the parish authorities he said was disgraceful in the extreme, and the more so on account of the vindictive feelings displayed. One step he (Mr. Knox) should most certainly make, and that was to communicate immediately with this president of the Poor Law Board.

Reynolds's Newspaper – 9th June 1861.

1861 – THE WHITECHAPEL WORKHOUSE AUTHORITIES.

In the House Commons on Monday evening, Lord Robert Cecil asked the President of the Poor Board whether his attention had been called to the case of two poor women, brought to the Worship Street Police Court on Friday last, who had been found in a state of great destitution on the pavement in front of the Whitechapel Workhouse, having been refused admission by the master, and to the remarks of Mr. Knox, the Police Magistrate, who was reported to have said that such cases were of constant occurrence, and whether he had caused any inquiry to be made?

Mr. Villiers said that the Magistrate in question had been communicated with, and that he stated he was incorrectly reported in the report referred to. He did not cast any reflection at all on Workhouse authorities in general, but simply referred to a particular workhouse, which was the Whitechapel Workhouse, and in regard to which he said that he had reason to complain on two or three occasions recently of its authorities. The superintendent of the casual ward was examined, and he admitted that the two women were brought to the ward on the evening in question, but that there was no room, and he was unable to take them in.

With respect to what was stated in the report that the policeman then took them to the Workhouse, and that they were refused, the person in authority denied that they were brought there at all, and asserted that when the police brought such cases, he invariably admitted them; in proof of which he referred to a book which showed that within the last six weeks he admitted no less than 18 cases of the kind brought by the police.

East London Observer – 22nd June 1861.

1862 – SHOCKING DEATH FROM DESTITUTION AT WHITECHAPEL.

Yesterday Mr. H. Raffles Walthew, the deputy Coroner for East Middlesex, opened an inquiry at the Sir George Osborn's Head public house, Princes Street, Whitechapel, on view of the body of Elizabeth Carey, aged 54 years, who died under very distressing circumstances at a wretched place situated at No. 10, Eagle Place, at the back of the Pavilion Theatre, Whitechapel Road.

Jane Harris, a lodger in the house, deposed that the deceased was a widow, and had obtained a scanty living by making slop shirts. She rented a small room and paid 1s. 6d. per week. The place was void of furniture, and the deceased had nothing to lie upon. She would not apply to the parish for relief, but had been visited by the parochial surgeon for illness. On Saturday last, witness went into deceased's room and found her in a very weak and dying state, lying upon a heap of dirty rags in the corner, on the floor. The place was in a wretched and filthy condition, without food or firing. Witness questioned the deceased, but she could scarcely articulate. She told witness that she had not had any food for nine days, and was starving. A neighbour was called in who gave her a little weak brandy and water, while a messenger ran for Mr. Champneys, the medical officer, who attended, but the deceased had expired before his arrival.

Mr. Alexander Champneys, the parochial surgeon to the Whitechapel Union, stated that he was called to the deceased on Saturday last, and found her in a shocking condition and lifeless upon a heap of filthy rags. The body was much emaciated, and thinly clad. He had made a post mortem examination of the body, and had found the stomach perfectly empty. On opening the head, he found an effusion of serum in the ventricles of the brain. Death had, no doubt, been accelerated by want of the common necessaries of life, and long exposure to the inclemency of the weather. He had attended the deceased some months back when she was lying ill with fever, from which she recovered. He then tried to persuade her to go into the workhouse, but she declined, although living in such a wretched condition.

Other witnesses were examined, and the Jury, after a brief discussion, returned a verdict, "That the deceased died from effusion of the brain, accelerated by want and exposure to the weather."

Reynolds's Newspaper – 13th April 1862.

1861 – THE BLIND BEGGAR'S HOUSE.

About the year 1578, John Kirby, a rich citizen, built a house on the green, which was frequently called Kirby Castle, and for which the proprietor was much ridiculed by the wits of the day. Years afterwards popular tradition pointed to it as the residence of the renowned Blind Beggar of Bethnal Green, and affirmed that in one of the towers he deposited his store of gold, accumulated by his mendicancy. But Old Stowe shrewdly remarks, "Kirbies house, I make no doubt, is that now called 'The Blind Beggar's House;' perhaps Kirby beggared himself it." The old house was in more modern times a lunatic asylum.

The legend of the Blind Beggar (whose memory is yet preserved in a public house sign, and, if we mistake not, on beadle's staves in the parish) forms the subject of a fine old ballad; and Sheridan Knowles founded on it, in our own times, a capital play.

The story went that Henry de Montfort, son of the great Simon de Montfort, Earl of Leicester, who was defeated at the battle of Evesham, in August, 1265, by the King's forces under Prince Edward, afterwards Edward the First, was, with his father, left for dead on the battlefield. A noble maiden, compassionately visiting the wounded, discovered signs of life in the young Henry, and bore him from the field. The usual result of plighted love followed; but as the bridegroom would infallibly have lost his head if he had been known to be alive, and she had no property whatever, his inheritance having been forfeited by his treason to the Crown, the young couple were rather embarrassed as to their means of future support. A bright idea occurred. Henry adopted the disguise of a blind beggar, and choosing the hamlet of Bethnal Green, as an obscure dwelling place, sat for many a long year by the roadside, and by such means accumulated enormous wealth; of which, however, his daughter, "the pretty Bessie," was so ignorant that she set forth to seek her fortune. Of course, her rare beauty soon gained her many suitors. According to the ballad:-

It was a blind beggar, had long lost his sight,
He had a faire daughter of bewty most bright,
   And many a gallant brave suiter had shee,
   For none was soe comelye as pretty Bessee.

But the suitors, all save one, fell away when she told her history. It was the old story over again. A young Knight alone loved the beggar maid for herself; the others were mercenary wooers, and no more was heard of them after Bessee had sung:-

My father, shee said, is soon to be seene.

The seely [silly] blind beggar of Bednall Greene,
That daily sits begging for charitie –
He is the good father of pretty Bessee.
His markes and his tokens are known very well,
He always is led with a dogg and a bell;
A seely old man God knoweth is hee,
Yet hee is the father of pretty Bessee.

Of course, the generous lover was rewarded the hand of Bessee, and away rode with her to Bednall Green. But his relations, who could not reconcile themselves the misalliance, waylaid the happy pair, and endeavoured to separate them by force of arms. The gallant Knight did his duty bravely, and at an opportune moment the old Beggar made his appearance and offered to prove the equality of the match by covering every gold crown which the objecting parties would lay down. They accepted the proposal, and produced their purses. For every crown they produced the Beggar put down three, and when their store was exhausted capped the affair by a handsome present to the young couple. At the banquet which followed, he told his story, and satisfied everybody that the pretty Bessee was descended of noble blood of the old line of De Montfort.

Shoreditch Observer – 14th September 1861.

1862 – TWO FATAL ACCIDENTS.

On Monday a fatal accident happened in High Street, Shadwell, to a man named John Harwood, aged fifty-five, a chimney sweep, residing at North Street, Whitechapel. While crossing the carriageway he was knocked down by a cart, and one of the wheels passed over his body. He was raised up and taken to the London Hospital, where he was found to be dead.

Another fatal accident occurred to a female named Ann Denny, aged sixty-six, who lately resided at No. 2, John Street, Whitechapel. She was crossing the roadway in the Whitechapel Road when she was knocked down a horse ridden by a man who was passing at a rapid rate. The animal trod upon her body, and when raised up she was found to be insensible. The man on horseback succeeded in getting clear off. The poor woman was carried to the hospital, where she expired shortly after her admission.

Penny Illustrated Paper – 26th July 1862.

Fig. 5.   Kirby Castle – The Blind Beggar's House (Old and New London, 1876)

1864 – DEATH IN THE STREET.

Mr. Walthew held an inquest last night at the London Hospital on the body of Mary Barrett, a poor old woman of 74, who died on Thursday night last, upon a doorstep, on her way to the Whitechapel Workhouse. She had during the last three months been living in a cheap lodging house, at which she paid threepence a night for her bed—the money she got begging in the neighbourhood of Whitechapel. Disease of the heart was the cause of her death, which had been hastened by exposure and destitution.

Globe – 19th January 1864.

1864 – WHITECHAPEL RAGGED SCHOOL VISIT TO HAMPSTEAD.

In a narrow Whitechapel court, at noon yesterday week, we witnessed one of the pleasantest sights to be seen by a Londoner on a beautiful summer's day. Under the direction of an active young man—Taylor by name—troops of little children were streaming from the George Yard Ragged Schools into the vans which were to take them for a pleasure trip to Hampstead.

Accompanying Mr. Holland, the able superintendent, into the spacious room wherein the most useful knowledge is daily imparted to these poor children, we learnt that it is by voluntary contributions he and a few assistant teachers are enabled to carry on their good work, in what used to be one of the worst neighbourhoods of the metropolis, but which is now scarcely to be recognised. What were once

Fig. 6.   Visit to Hampstead (Penny Illustrated Paper)

the infamous haunts of thieves and vagabonds have become happy homes.

Undoubtedly, the cause of this great change for the better is mainly owing to the superintendent's course of action, which is first to win the hearts of the children, and thereby reach the hearts of their parents. As a means of effecting this object, nothing can be better than giving the little ones a holiday in the country. This was clearly proved by the glad faces of the children, their sparkling eyes and voluble tongues; while the neat manner in which they—ordinarily in rags—were clad, together with the gratified look of the mothers who had come to see them off, proved how highly the pleasure in store for their darlings was appreciated in another quarter.

There being a delay in the arrival of all the vans, and as we felt rather "peckish," we took the opportunity of visiting another Whitechapel institution, no less useful in its way, no less worthy of imitation, than the George Yard Ragged Schools. The institution in question was the No. 1 branch of the London Restaurant Company, situated in Commercial Street. First paying his or her money to a comely young lady at the door, anyone can have a dinner of broth and bread for 1½d., in a large, airy room of the restaurant; or dinner of beef, potatoes, bread, and a slice of wholesome plum pudding, with a glass of fresh spring water for 4½d.; or, if he or she be an epicure, a richer dinner still may be had for 6d.; or for 1s., which will pay for very little at an ordinary dining room, a dinner fit for an Alderman may be had. Indeed, should a City dignitary, coming to this establishment, be compelled to eat and drink all that would be put before him for half the sum he is supposed to expend daily for his dinner, the consequences could not fail to be appalling. Without following the painful train of thought further, let us leave the "London Restaurant Company, Branch No. 1," with the remarks that breakfasts, teas, and suppers may be obtained proportionately cheap there, and that, notwithstanding the extortionate waiters' tax is not levied, the attendants – clean and active youths – are more attentive than those who are in the habit of pocketing fees.

Returning to George Yard we found the vans filled by their living freight, many of whom were being supplied by loving affectionate brothers and sisters with apples and pears, homemade cakes, and other toothsome delicacies. The elder children with their parents—1400 in all—made holiday, it should be mentioned, early in the month, when they were treated by train to Epping Forest. So, on this occasion only the infants—those just beginning the A.B.C. – were taken.

Directly the vans started, "The men of merry, merry England" was struck up by our cornet, there was a farewell waving of arms from the mothers and a burst of cheering from the little ragged children left behind, while the young excursionists sung one of the songs they had learnt at school so vigorously and joyously that anyone not knowing that they lived amidst misery and want would have put them down as the merriest children of "Merry merry England." Eight or nine shoeless lads started at the same time, and as street after street, road after road, was passed they still ran a neck-and-neck race with the vans. Thus, they trotted on all the way to the Vale of Health, Hampstead, arriving there simultaneously with the conveyances.

Playing on the heath for an hour under the guidance of the fatherly Mr. Holland, the two hundred little ones took in enough of the country air to well sharpen their appetites for the bountiful tea provided. It is as they appeared while enjoying this meal and with their attentive superintendent in their midst, that our Artist represents them on the preceding page. The round and a half of thick bread and butter given to each, with a cup of tea made their little eyes glisten again; but the glances which they now and then gave in the direction of "M. A. Varnell's Vale of Health Tea Rooms" seemed to imply a knowledge of something good yet to come. A chorus of "Ohs!" which involuntarily came from the youngsters at the sight of Mr. Taylor bringing forth a plate full of thick slices of plum cake at once solved the mystery. Plateful after plateful was handed round until each infant was supplied with a quarter-of-a-pound junk of good cake. The bread and butter having disappeared, most of them fell to eating the more delicious compound; but one plump faced little fellow put his junk inside his coat, saying, "I'll save mine for my brother." Like other good intentions, however, this one was not carried out, for, seeing the zest with which his companions were munching away, he, by-and-by followed their example.

Tea over, they once more rambled about the heath, enjoying themselves to their heart's content, until it was time to return home. Then they were safely packed inside the vans, while room was found outside for the poor little fellows who had trudged all the way to Hampstead on foot, and to whom, of course, a good tea had been given. An hour or two later Whitechapel was reached, and many a blessing was, no doubt, bestowed that night by grateful parents on those who had kindly subscribed the funds necessary for the trip, as well as upon those who had so successfully conducted it.

Should the Engraving we give of the above excursion enlist the practical sympathy of our charitable readers for those Ragged Schools yet to be treated, we shall feel that the Illustration has done some good. Not far from our office are the Clare Market Day, Night, and Sunday Ragged Schools, the hon. Secretary of which writes on behalf of the poor children attending them:-

"We wish to take them for a day away from the smoke, dirt, and misery which they are, alas! too familiar with, and to drop them for a few hours in some pleasant country spot, where their little lungs may be filled with pure air, and their blanched cheeks coloured with the health-giving rays of the glorious sun. Will not fathers and mothers help these children to have a day's pleasure? I believe they will, if only as a thank-offering for the strong limbs, the plump, rosy cheeks, the clear eyes, the ringing laugh, and healthy playfulness of their own dear little ones. It is the painful experience of many friends belonging to ragged schools to witness delicate human flowers droop and die because they are unable to command the means for strengthening the stems upon which they bloom. This is as sad as it is unnatural; and I appeal to the kindly sympathy of your numerous readers to assist in casting a ray of sunshine—if only for a day—over the gloomy existence of 200 of the poor destitute children of this overcrowded metropolis.

I am, Sir, your obedient servant,

JNO. Palmer, Hon. Secret Clare Market Ragged Schools.—Colonnade, Clare Market."

Penny Illustrated Paper – 3rd September 1864.

1865 – SAD DEATH OF
A SACK STITCHER.

On Saturday an inquest was held in Leman Street, Whitechapel, on the body of Mary Calahan, aged fifteen years, who died at a wretched place, situated at No. 1, Christopher Court, Royal Mint Street. The deceased obtained a scanty livelihood by stitching large sacks for a City warehouse, at 2d. each. On St. Valentine's Day she was unable to continue her work. On the following day she expired suddenly. The surgeon who had made the post mortem examination said that death resulted from disease of the lungs and congestion of the brain, accelerated by want of proper nourishment. The Jury returned a verdict of "Natural death, accelerated by the want of proper food."

Penny Illustrated Paper – 25th February 1865.

1865 – THE GREAT
BURGLARIES IN THE CITY.

Ten of the eleven prisoners charged with the great City burglaries are represented on the preceding page as they appeared on the 14th inst., before the Lord Mayor, at the justice room of the Mansion House. Their names are David Roberts, William Henry Jeffrey, Martha Jeffrey, Thomas Casely, Ann Casely, Thomas Brewerton, Louisa Brewerton, James Hurley, William Brown, otherwise Millar but better known by the sobriquet of "Scotty," and Frederick William Wilkinson.

One only of the eleven prisoners was absent – namely the wife of Hurley, and a letter was received by the Governor of Newgate, stating that she had given birth to a child there on the previous Saturday, and was in the infirmary of the prison.

As on the previous occasions the court was crowded during the examination. Besides the Lord Mayor, there were present on the Bench Alderman Sir Robert Carden and Alderman Lusk, Colonel Fraser, the Commissioner of City police, and Mr. Nelson, the City solicitor. Mr. Lewis jun., solicitor, again conducted the prosecution; Mr. Beard defended the women; the rest of the prisoners defended themselves. Mr. Davis, from the office of Mr. Howell, was present watching the examination on behalf of Messrs. Bennock, warehousemen, of Wood Street, Cheapside, who, in November last were robbed of 11,000 yards of silk and Mr. Webb, of Euston Road, solicitor, whose iron safe, containing money, plate, and securities for money and property, was bodily carried off from his offices there on the night of Christmas Day, attended to watch the case on his own behalf.

Some of the prisoners are charged with being concerned in Mr. Johnson's robbery, some in that of Mr. Walker, and some in both.

From the first, during the examinations, the conduct of the prisoner Casely has been marked by a reckless effrontery. He is a good-looking young man of about twenty-four, wearing a light overcoat, and in other respects fashionably dressed. At a judge-and-jury club, which he frequented he was known by the sobriquet of "Counsellor Kelly," and when before the Lord Mayor he cross-examines the witnesses for the prosecution in a very amusing manner, but seldom with discretion.

Some of the police, especially Inspector Potter and Constable Ranger, appear particularly obnoxious to him, and he never loses an opportunity of exercising his wit and sarcasm at their expense. On the last occasion, when Ranger was making his way to the book to be sworn, he said, "Here he comes, crawling like a dog." He strongly objected to Potter being in court until he was called as a witness, and the Inspector was requested to withdraw. At one part of the exanimation, when he fancied the evidence of Inspector Brennan was tending to implicate him in Mr. Johnson's robbery, he amused the whole audience by saying, "I have alibis in my pocket, my Lord Mayor, showing that I could not have been concerned in Johnson's affair. One of the alibis is a certificate from the chaplain of the new prison at Birmingham stating that he had a conversation with me on the day Johnson's robbery was committed. What the other alibi is I am not obliged to state now, as the police might try to upset it." This sally occasioned some laughter. Again, he chuckled greatly when a locksmith, who had been called to identify another of the prisoners as having spoken to him when he was engaged putting a lock on a door at Mr. Johnson's shortly before the robbery, pointed to him (Casely) as being the man. It was known to the police, as had been incidentally

stated in evidence, that he was at that time in prison for another offence, and therefore could not have been the man. Addressing the puzzled witness, he said, with a look of scorn, "You can go down; you have for once made a grand mistake, and you'll have no share of the £1,500 reward, I can tell you." When he speaks of his wife, who stands near him at the bar, he always calls her his "old woman."

The prisoner Hurley is a man of immense physique. From the first, all the rest have stood aloof from him in the dock, as if they suspected that he, if any, would be the man who would turn against them; and it will be seen by the evidence of Superintendent Durkin that they were not deceived. Brown, or Millar, otherwise "Scotty" is about thirty-five years of age, and is said to be the captain of the gang. He contrived to evade the police for some time after he was suspected of being concerned in the jewel robbery in the Strand. Two of them at last tracked him to a house in Hackney and surprised him in bed, upon which he sprang out

Fig. 7.   The Prisoners at the Mansion House

and waged a desperate struggle with the officers, one of whom, Inspector Brennan, a powerful young man, he tried to strangle. The rest of the male prisoners are slightly-made young men, presenting nothing remarkable in their appearance. The prisoner Roberts, who is a poor, cowed-looking creature, is said to have no actual hand in either of the robberies; but he was found trying to dispose of two of the stolen watches shortly after that of Mr. Walker.

On Tuesday they were again brought up at the Mansion House and were again remanded, the Lord Mayor fixing Friday for the next examination. Casely and Jeffreys as they were leaving the dock kissed their wives, and told them to "cheer up," as they were "all right."

There must be great sorrow in Rascaldom over this wholesale raid. There must be wailing in Whitechapel for the far-famed "Velvet Lad;" and the braw Land o Cakes, or at least the felonious portion thereof, must be sore distraught at the tribulation which has overtaken the adventurous "Scotty." With the different degrees of turpitude of these rogues it is not just now our purpose to deal. Let their crimes be brought home to them, and it will then be time to sing their elegy. That they are all arrant thieves, however, seems clear. The merciful theory of the English law assumes a man to be innocent until he is proved guilty; but, in the case of a gang of desperadoes who are found crammed to the gullet with gold watches and chains, all stolen, it would be stretching politeness a little too far to treat them merely as persons arraigned on suspicion. It is clear that the metropolitan police have pounced upon and broken up as hardened and atrocious a horde of bandits as ever merited the application of Jedburgh justice or Halifax law.

Leaving aside for the moment the great question of the burglaries, and the manner in which each particular crime can be fixed on each particular prisoner, the reader will find much to instruct him in studying the features and manners of the miscreants unearthed in the pie shop in Whitechapel.

It may be interesting to the honest part of the community to know what an out-and-out thief is like, where he lives, how he passes his time, what are his habits and amusements. There could certainly be no better corrective to a most false and mischievous notion, inculcated about a century since certain writers of fiction, than the revelations made by the police as to the way in which they captured this knot of ruffians. We find no Jack Sheppard in a laced coat, cocked hat, and velvet mask, carousing over egg-flip with Poll Maggot and Edgeworth Bess in plumed hats and embroidered riding habits, the while Blueskin, pipe in hand, chants "Jolly Nose." We find no Captain Macheath, leaving the Rose or the Mitre to mount his

bit of blood for a gallop to Finchley or Hounslow; no Claude Duval the "gentleman highwayman," as he has been wickedly and mendaciously described, to the ruin of innumerable apprentices and shop boys. Or, rather, we find the real Sheppard and his real paramours, the actual Blueskin, the genuine Macheath, the substantial Duval, as they are figured forth in the grimly prosaic pages of the Old Bailey Sessions papers.

It may not be generally known that the "gentleman highwayman" of whom so much stuff has been written, was a gentleman's footman, stripped of his livery for infamous conduct; and that Mr. John Sheppard, so far from having been arrested at the funeral of his mother, as related in Mr. Ainsworth's romance was taken in a filthy kitchen near Fetter Lane, waiting for half a pint of gin for which he had sent his mamma in question.

Or, if we must go to fiction to help out the illustration of fact, we find in this Whitechapel pie shop Bill Sykes and Nancy. There is Bill, crowbar, jemmy, velveteen jacket, false hair, and all. There is Nancy, staunch to the last, grappling with the Inspector, tugging him by the whiskers, trying to secrete the stolen property and in all doing her best to secure the escape of her beloved "bloke." Then the Inspector himself figures in a curiously characteristic manner. Collaring a couple of vagabonds, he does not thunder out in stem accents, "Jeffrey and Parker, in the Queen's name and the law, I arrest ye both." There is nothing of the exempt or the alguacil about Inspector Potter; he mildly remarks, "Ned and Billy, you must consider yourselves in custody," and collars them accordingly.

The captives—after a little preliminary kicking, biting, and tugging at the whiskers of their captors—seem to be on the best of terms with them. As Mr. Casely was being removed, securely handcuffed, to the station house, he asked the Inspector quite in a friendly way, how many robberies he was going to "buff" to him. On reference to the copious "Slang Dictionary" of Mr. Hotten, we find that to "buff" means to accuse, and the phrase is as old, in its cogenerate sense of boasting, as the reign of Queen Elizabeth. It is refreshing to find that the Lingua Balatronica shows no signs of dying out in the East End. Mr. Casely's subsequent remark that he was "doing time"—that is, suffering a term of imprisonment at Liverpool when one of the robberies was committed—we do not, however, find in the volume to which we have alluded; but no doubt thieves' lingo, like the dialect of commerce and the language of nations, grows with the progress of events and the development of ideas.

It will be observed that we have frequently referred to the district, Whitechapel, and the house, a pie shop, where the most notable of these thieves were taken. It is not astounding that these wretched criminals seem tied, as though by fascination, to the very neighbourhood where they know the agents of justice will come to look for them, and to the very haunts they might be expected to inhabit. This ostrich-like cramming of their heads into the sand, and exposing their great hulking bodies to the full glare of the policeman's bull's-eye, would really seem to bear out Mr. Carlyle's theory, that the root of all crime is stupidity.

In a city of three million inhabitants, with hundreds of trains leaving London at all hours of the day and night, these people seem not to have the sense to disperse, to go away, to put the breadth of the Channel between themselves and their pursuers. The police know them to be Whitechapel, or Westminster, or Drury Lane birds, as the case may be; and to Whitechapel, to Westminster, or to Drury Lane they go to find them. "Scotty" is just canny or just patriotic enough to deposit a portion of his plunder in the Royal Bank of Scotland; but others of the gang thrust large sums into the Whitechapel branch of a London joint stock bank. They have not even the sense to go to a West End branch. They seem to invite discovery and court capture.

Rendering every credit to the astuteness and energy displayed by the police in this affair, it is not difficult to guess at the modus operandi they have pursued in hunting down prey. A policeman generally begins his evidence with "From information I received;" which means that when a great robbery is committed, he makes the rounds of all the haunts of all the thieves of his acquaintance, and very soon discovers how many Neds or Billies are missing from their accustomed taverns, concert halls, bagatelle rooms, coffee shops, or skittle grounds; for, be sure, the thief can no more dispense with his amusements than the half-pay officer with his club. But there are other ladies and gentlemen frequenting these places, not yet in trouble or "wanted," with whom Ned or Billy may wish to communicate. These people are discreetly followed. Moreover, Ned's wife or Billy's mistress must go out to do the marketing, or to dispose of a little stuff; and, hovering about the familiar haunts, she is "spotted and followed," the inevitable catastrophe speedily supervening.

The sole reason why Agar and Jem the Penman enjoyed for so many years complete immunity was that they were men moving in a somewhat superior grade of life, and at least did not, as in this Whitechapel case, migrate from an oyster stall in the New Cut to a pie shop in Whitechapel. They kept themselves to themselves, and were mistaken for a long time for respectable folk; and from this fact arises, perhaps, the most curious consideration of all to which we have endeavoured to draw attention. It is perfectly patent to the police that there in the low districts of London a swarm of public houses, coffee shops, and saloons which are as notoriously the habitual resort of thieves as the Guards' Club is the resort of Guardsmen, and Brookes's of ancient Whigs. All these places are licensed, and the Magistrates could sweep them away with little difficulty. The police maintain that to tolerate them is useful and even necessary, because, so long as these places exist, they know where to find the thieves when they want them, or at least to gain information respecting them.

But from this view suggests another grand question—whether, if the haunts of vice were demolished, the vicious beings who haunt them might not be demolished likewise. Do away with the slums of Whitechapel, and we might do away with the thieves. When we wish to get rid of wasps, we destroy not only the wasps, but likewise the nest.

Penny Illustrated Paper – 25th March 1865.

1866 – A DEN OF INIQUITY.

The *Morning Post* says that not many nights ago several Inspectors of police, accompanied by a squad of Sergeants, escorted a party of gentlemen of the highest and social position into the Whitechapel district. Deep into the purlieus of vice this party penetrated, and their interesting inspection did not end until the "wee small hours of the morn."

In this portion of London there is, as it were, a distinct nationality in existence. The kingdom of thieves is there firmly established, and the argot of the cracksman and his associates, male and female replaces the sonorous accents of our mother tongue. In that dank and fetid atmosphere, in hovels and dens bordering upon our dirty Thames, the contrast was vivid between the visitors, accustomed to all the refinements of life in its moral and social views, and the inmates, who regard no laws nor morals excepting those laid down in the thief's code. Thousands of thieves, some with their wives and families—others with their mistresses and the attendant train of low characters, who, though not actual criminals, consort with these prostitutes—nightly congregate in the various dance houses, drinking shops and other dens with which that district abounds. Those who have practised their profession during daylight meet to divide the spoils, or to spend it in debauchery. The midnight prowlers come early to their rendezvous to concert their plans of action; but all, united in a common bond, prepare to wage war against that society which declares them outcasts for their crimes.

The life of a woman, after reaching the Whitechapel district, was computed by the Inspector to average about eight years. And with all efforts she could scarcely earn, in the highest prosperity of her horrid life, more than 3s. per day. Imagine the minimum when the wretched creatures are near the close of their miserable career. The liquor in this district is almost poisonous. Stomachs which endure it must really be coated with some rough substance to resist the action of the acids which undoubtedly exist in all these liquids. The beer even was impregnated with a substance similar to cayenne, which burnt the throat of the unaccustomed drinker. It seemed to have been thus adulterated for the purpose of exciting thirst.

We spend millions in philanthropic efforts to convert the heathen, who lives in contented ignorance thousands of miles from our shores. And yet here we have, under our very eyes, a heathen far more pitiable and far more deserving of our attention. Think of the hundreds of little children, who should be innocent by nature, and whom education might fit for worthy members of society, actually being reared by their parents or protectors with the single design of preying upon their fellow men, and boys to become ruffians in time, and grace the prison or the gallows, and the girls to be thieves or prostitutes early in life, and to descend into premature graves. Here is a field for labour pointed out, and inestimable returns may reward the efforts of kind hearts whose attention might be turned thereto.

Clerkenwell News – 4th January 1866.

1866 – A VISIT TO WHITECHAPEL CASUAL WARD.

Whitechapel is in strong contrast to St. George's East in its treatment of the casual poor. The "wards"—as we suppose we must call them by way of courtesy—are situated on a piece of ground that stretches behind the site of the old workhouse in Whitechapel Road, and that has been for many years used as a stone yard by the guardians. The entrance is from Pavilion Yard, through a gateway, and the opposite end of the yard abuts upon a flagged court or cul-de-sac leading from Old Montague Street, the last house in which has been taken by the guardians for the residence of the ward superintendent and his wife.

Immediately within the gateway there stands a small wooden box, where the casual who has been allowed inside presents himself for the particulars of age, ordinary occupation, last night's lodging and next day's destination to be duly entered in the prescribed register—two old paupers appearing to superintend this portion of the business of admission. He then crosses the open yard towards some sheds of the very roughest description. What was the original purpose of these erections we are not in a position to say. They were built "before the time" of the Master of the Workhouse or the superintendent of the wards, so they can give no information concerning them. They could not be intended for stables, for they are too cold and comfortless, and they are scarcely sufficiently watertight for haylofts. These are the "casual wards."

On the threshold of one of these, covered overhead, but otherwise unprotected from the weather, and standing on the bare unfloored ground (save when, as we are told, in very bad weather some straw is spread for him to walk on), the casual strips, and consigns his clothes to the care of an attendant, who rolls them in a bundle and places them away in a cupboard. A padlocked door being then unfastened, he enters his "ward," gets to bed, and the key is turned upon him. If we were at all disposed to conjure up sentimental grievances, we should certainly make a point of this locking up.

The Whitechapel casuals from the moment they consign themselves to the "wards" are close prisoners. We are not quite sure that Mr. Gladding, although he has a hand in the doing of it, would regard this as altogether constitutional. Regarded, however, as a practical measure, it is doubtless necessary, and though a sensation might easily be made out of it, we wish everything in Pavilion Yard were equally unobjectionable on the score of comfort. The offices of the superintendents—male and female—are near, so that a knocking would soon attract notice in case of necessity.

The "ward" in which the casual finds himself padlocked is a rude, primitive erection of wood and brick, with an open tiled roof, dingy and black. The snows of January have found out the defects in this roof notably in the female ward—and poured down the end walls, which look and feel still saturated, though the leakage has long been stopped. Here, in barrack bedsteads—the best idea of which will be conveyed by comparing them to broad egg boxes—the casuals lie side by side, their bunkers close together, but with a sufficient separation to keep them apart unless they desire not to be so. There are twenty-five of these sleeping places in the men's shed, and twenty-one in the women's. Ten of the former are occupied at the time of our visit, which is about nine o'clock at night, and eight of the latter.

Only twice since the passing of the Houseless Poor Act, we understand, have the wards been full. The beds immediately adjoining the wet wall are out of use, and we are told are kept so since the rain came in. The sleepers are closely enveloped in a rug or railway wrapper of more than usual warmth and thickness, and each has a stout nightgown in addition. The beds are the usual straw bags. Once stretched upon them, and swathed in their wrappers, the casuals are doubtless perfectly safe from the winter's inclemency, even under such wretched circumstances as those the Whitechapel Guardians have placed them in. When not asleep, they are able to lie and gaze upon the blackened grimy rafters overhead, or at the grotesque figures the rain has formed upon the whitewash; and may indulge in curious reflections upon the various modes in which metropolitan guardians interpret the obligations the law has imposed upon them. Those of them who have been in gaol may also cogitate on the superior treatment of English criminals as compared with that of such of the honest poor as may sink to a Whitechapel casual ward.

The description we have given applies equally to the male and the female wards. They are some short distance away from each other, but except that the shed for females is the smallest, and has suffered worst from the weather, they are "much of a muchness."

Most of the inmates were far away in the land of dreams when we entered. It would be a tempting theme for an imaginative writer to inquire what scenes and circumstances in a chequered life, commencing, perhaps, in many cases with a happy childhood, the drowsy god had summoned to the pillows of these wretched outcasts. But we have forsworn imagination in these articles! One man has been awakened and recalled to the hard realities of life by the turning of the key in the padlock, and the grating of the gate upon its rusty hinges.

The Master of the Workhouse asks him if he is warm?

"Oh, yes, Sir, quite warm," he replies, without uncovering his face, which is almost wholly nestled in his rug.

"And do you want anything?"

"I should like a basin of skilley."

This brings us to the question of the fare of the vagrants, and we learn, greatly to our astonishment, that five ounces of bread and water for supper and the same for breakfast is all that is allowed—six ounces of bread and a pint of "skilley" being the allowance at each meal in St. George's, Mile End, Bethnal Green, and, indeed, not at most metropolitan parishes! In the women's shed the same questions were put by the Master to some of the waking occupants.

"Are you warm?"

"Yes, Sir."

"And quite comfortable."

"We'd be more comfortable if we had some skilley," said the spokeswoman of the party; "we do have it at some places now."

Not, however, in Whitechapel! There the rule applied to casuals appears to be in all respects consistently hard and harsh. The task of work exacted is, however, proportionately less—like the food—than in other places, three-quarters of a pound of oakum for men, and half a pound for women—only about half the task exacted elsewhere.

And about the bath? is probably a question that has risen in the reader's mind. There is here another deviation from the uniform treatment. Casuals in Whitechapel are not bathed. The sheds in Pavilion Yard are a little paradise for the great unwashed. They lie down exactly as they are, and unless some special providence governs the distribution of nightgowns, the poor respectable clean tramp or wanderer of tomorrow has the reversion of the covering of the frowsy, filthy vagabond of tonight! We started a difficulty on this score, which led to an explanation of the course adopted. Each week as many clean nightshirts are served out to the superintendent as there are beds in the "wards;" and as the beds are very rarely more than half full, this would allow a change of shirt say twice a week. But sometimes you get a very dirty person? Yes, in that case the shirt can be washed at any time. How far this fact, however, affords a security against what we have indicated, the reader will judge.

Such are the Whitechapel casual wards, and such the treatment of vagrants by the Whitechapel guardians. We believe that no fault lay in carrying out the regulations. The Master of the Workhouse is a man calculated to inspire confidence in his humanity, as well as in his powers of management and sense of responsibility. He appears to feel the inadequacy of these miserable sheds for lodging human beings, however degraded. We have his assurance, too, that the guardians feel it; and without doubt in their individual capacity, they are men all of whom would revolt at subjecting fellow creatures to the harshest possible construction of a law designed to be a humane one. But how happens it – and here comes the question that so often arises in dealing with the acts of public bodies – how happens it that the individual responsibility is so completely merged in the general responsibility as to allow of these gentlemen, when they meet as a board, permitting such things within their jurisdiction? Admitting, for the sake of putting the question more cogently, all they urge of their difficulties in providing new and better wards—we ask how comes it that such easily preventable pieces of harsh management as this condemning of the poor to bread and water should continue many weeks after the recent exposures first directed public attention to casual treatment, and a month after they were in receipt of the circular of the Poor Law Board, based on the resolutions of the conference of guardians, at which the chairman of their Board was present, recommending the adoption of a uniform diet of gruel and bread throughout the metropolis.

What is the answer of the guardians? Do the simply plead as their excuse a *laissez faire* policy or have they some theory for the repression of vagrancy by cold and semi-starvation? It would be curious to hear the explanation which gentlemen so estimable, and, we say in all sincerity, so full of kindly sympathy for their fellows as Mr. Powell, or Mr. Gladding, or Mr. Craven, or Mr. Brushfield—we might run through the whole Board of Guardians, indeed—would give of their active or passive participation in the upholding of a regime for which they alone, as guardians of the poor, are responsible.

A fortnight ago we announced that we had been informed the certificate of the Poor Law Board had been withdrawn from these wards. Having visited them at the time we made the announcement, we saw no difficulty in believing the statement nor in admitting the justice of the withdrawal. It would appear, however, from the letter of one of the guardians which we inserted last week, that the statement was not strictly true. The certificate was not withdrawn, though Mr. Farnall entered in the visiting book an intimation that it was his duty to request the Poor Law Board to withdraw it, adding, "I have waited for several months to see the guardians' new wards for the houseless poor, but as nothing is really done, and the present wards are insufficient, I must take the course adverted to."

The explanation of our correspondent apprises us therefore in advance of what is the guardians' answer to many of the facts we have stated. They blame the Poor Law Board for the delay that has taken place in the provision of proper wards, for the erection of which they have purchased a site in Thomas Street, adjoining the workhouse, alleging that the plans were sent up twelve months ago for the necessary approval, and have only just been returned sanctioned. This is to some extent an exoneration of the union authorities, but not wholly.

Much might certainly have been done to lessen the rigour of the temporary treatment of the casuals, and for neglecting this the guardians have, so far as we know, no excuse. They have not loyally applied themselves to do their best; and unless a great improvement is at once made, we trust the Poor Law Board, notwithstanding their own fault in the matter, will have the courage to adopt Mr. Farnall's advice and withdraw the certificate. It is little short of an imposition upon parishes which

properly carry out the act, as well as a cruelty to the casuals themselves, to ask them to maintain places such as these at Whitechapel.

Before leaving Pavilion Yard we encountered some "specimen casuals" of a kind different from those we met at St. George's. Three young men, all under thirty, applied at the gate and were admitted. They were decently dressed like mechanics, and, whatever else they may be, looking far too clean to take their chance in the sheds we had just inspected.

They described themselves as "tramps"— boilermakers by trade, coming from Oldham, and had slept last night at St. Albans. They had been out of work for five weeks. When in work each admitted his weekly earnings to be thirty shillings. They only had threepence between them, and therefore could not get a lodging.

"Well, you can come in, but you'll have to do a task of work after breakfast," said the superintendent. The announcement evidently staggered them. There was a moment's pause.

"Didn't you know that?"

"No, we never slept in any of these places before." Then there was a consultation aside, ending with a surly, "Well, we'll come in." And they sauntered to the little office to be entered in the books, hands deep in trousers' pockets—lazy, hulking, mean-spirited, despicable characters—lacking the spirit to be honest, independent workmen; and, to all appearance, lacking even the energy and boldness to be thieves. Here, at least, we said, are three fellows that even the Whitechapel casual wards are too good for.

East London Observer – 3rd March 1866.

━━━◦●◦━━━

1866 – THE SICK WARDS IN THE WHITECHAPEL WORKHOUSE.

Mr. Ernest Hart writes to the *Times* a statement of the result of an examination of two of the sick wards of the Whitechapel Workhouse, which he made on Friday evening last in the presence and with the sanction of Mr. Farnell. The inquiry was made in consequence of a communication received by Mr. Hart from a person of superior education, who had lately been an inmate of the sick wards, and who had made horrifying statements respecting them.

Mr. Hart was surprised to find the dreadful statements confirmed in every respect. The first ward he entered was one containing ten beds, in two ranges, with one range of windows high in the wall. In the left-hand corner, he found a bed-ridden patient of middle age lying on a very wet, hard straw mattress. On lifting him up they found extensive bed sores; they were only covered with a bit of wet rag. The details are too disgusting to be entered into, but the suffering to which the patient is exposed by night and day, by sheer neglect, is hardly to be expressed in words. He eheis never cleaned or changed at night.

Two beds beyond him lay a poor fellow with a sinus on the thigh, and inflamed glands of the throat. He believed the doctor had ordered him something the day before, but he had on the thigh at the time they saw him nothing but a piece of rag, and no application or medicine whatever had yet been given to him.

Passing on to Ward 5, a miserable little passage room, quite unfit for the occupation of any sick person, they found three persons, one a raving lunatic, of filthy habits. He had been in the habit of disturbing the other wards by night, and like the man first mentioned, was never cleaned or changed. He was lying in a state of neglect and dirt, raving incoherently, and with a form set against his bed to prevent him from falling out. Next to him was another poor fellow, half paralysed, inarticulate, and half imbecile, of dirty habits, who was sitting on the edge of his bed, and had a coloured handkerchief tied over a sore place on his foot. The third inmate was a decent old man, possessed of all his senses. He had a somewhat extensive ulcer of the leg; it was dressed with a dry rag (which had been wet), which adhered firmly to it, and was tied on with a piece of string. This was called a water dressing. There was no oil silk or waterproof tissue to keep the rags moist.

Mr. Hart says it is needless to go on multiplying instances, but most of the patients stated that they were hungry, one or two that they were half starved. If patients got money from their friends, the nurses expected to share it. Many were on a diet which allows meat for dinner only three times a week, soup three times, and bread and cheese on one day. The patients also craved for stimulants, but none were allowed save two or three ounces of gin for a dropsical patient. The medicines were irregularly administered, and frequently not given at all.

Mr. Hart saw enough to convince him that it was a mockery to call this "place of torture" a sick ward, and the method of procedure the "nursing of the sick," and hopes, in conclusion, that the present Parliamentary session may not pass away without some measure being made law to secure the sick poor from continuance of such needless and irrational cruelty and neglect.

Carlisle Journal – 26th June 1866.

1866 – REFUTATION FROM THE WHITECHAPEL WORKHOUSE.

A short time ago we gave in our columns the particulars of a visit paid by Mr. Ernest Hart to the above workhouse, in which some startling instances of alleged neglect and cruelty appeared with respect to the patients in some of the wards.

Since that time Mr. G. Adams Farr, the clerk to the Whitechapel Guardians, has addressed a letter to the Poor Law Board, in intended refutation of Mr. Hart's statements, and this letter has been published in the *Times*.

The case of Joseph Hill, referred to by Mr. Hart, is reported to be not so bad after all. True, this man was bedridden, suffering from bed sores, and lying on a straw bed; but the clerk of the guardians assures us by way of amelioration that, "this man is paralysed, but his sores were only superficial and were healthy." It is also asserted that he had been changed and cleansed three times on the day of the visit, and that he was in the possession of many advantages, the wet rags even having been applied by the direction of the medical officer as a means of cure.

The alleged woes of Samuel Partridge, who was found suffering from sinus, are met by the assertion, which may or may not be a complete answer to the case, that he has been a frequent inmate of the workhouse from that affection, from which he has been suffering for eleven years, and, the medical officer states, requires nothing but rest!"

"As to the raving lunatic, Matthew Morris, referred to in Ward No. 6," the clerk denies that he was filthy, or that the ward was unfit for the occupation of any sick person. The clerk is bound to admit that the imbecile, John Sayers, was unfortunately in the state represented as to paralysis, but nothing is said of the manner in which he was found, and the public is consoled with the assurance that Sayers has only "a small sore about the size of a sixpence, covered by a dry scab, on one of his toes, and to prevent his picking this off a handkerchief was tied over his foot."

Jeremiah Crawley, it may be some satisfaction to learn, who was found afflicted with a bad ulcer, has been accustomed to and is quite capable of wetting the rag, and applying the lotion supplied to him himself. The clerk further states that "the poor fellow referred to as sitting up on the bench in Ward No. 6, suffering from dropsy (Matthew Gallavan) prefers sitting as he was found"—this, of course, irrespective of the question whether it may be good for Matthew Gallavan—"and gets excited and irritable if endeavoured to be kept in bed."

It appears that oiled silk or other waterproof is not used in the workhouse, as the medical officer considered that the heat and prevention of evaporation caused by its use are not beneficial. The charges that some of the patients were hungry, and one or two half-starved, are met, the latter by passing over its "absurdity," and the former by the statement of the medical officer that he doeth what he liketh with meats and drinks, to which he adds, "I order extras and stimulants according to the condition and disease of the patients, and as I, as a medical man, think they require it—not according to their cravings!"

The clerk asserts that the medicines are properly dealt out. He also calls the attention of the Poor Law Board to the fact that Dr. Smith had a very short time previous gone over these wards with Mr. Farnall, pulling down the bedclothes and examining the patients for himself; and that all that Mr. Barham and the master (whose services were declined on the occasion) heard were Mr. Hart's assertions, and neither of them were asked for or permitted to give any explanation, or make any statement, which the master could readily have afforded and made, and shown the injustice and impropriety of Mr. Hart's remarks, and perhaps removed the impressions he entertained.

Mr. Farr concludes his letter by stating that the guardians are of opinion that Mr. Hart ought not to have been introduced into the workhouse by Mr. Farnall, as he was on the occasion referred to, and that his statements, had opportunity offered, could have been readily shown to be untrue.

This morning, a lengthy letter from Mr. Hart appears in the *Times*, reviewing the communication of Mr. Parr, and alleging that most of the painful cases cited are admitted to be true, the guardians "justifying them on various pretexts" (as we have shown and summarised above) "and calmly describing arrangements revolting to humanity, in language which seems to indicate that the guardians are prepared to continue them." We shall not again enter into these cases, as we have done so somewhat fully in the preceding paragraph.

Mr. Hart, however, says that he reaffirms every particular of his former statement, which was carefully restrained and not exhaustive. In reply to the charge of prejudice, Mr. Hart says, that he has prejudices against practices such as those which are avowed to exist at the workhouse, against the cruelties to which they give rise, and the shocking neglect of the sick. He deliberately proposes to retain those prejudices, and seeing that they are pretty universally shared, he has no small hope that they will triumph over what he must now call the prepossessions of the guardians.

In conclusion, Mr. Hart says, that the clerk is seriously in error in alleging that no explanation was invited from the officials, for Mr. Farnall did so invite explanation, in his presence, from the master, the matron, the one paid nurse, and the guardian present. He also thinks that the clerk's letter itself will prepare for the death warrant "of a system which is founded on principles obsolete and so barbarous, which admits of an accumulation of atrocities, and is supported by a defence which is itself a most damaging exposure."

Globe – 12th July 1866.

1867 – DISTURBANCE AT WHITECHAPEL WORKHOUSE.

At Worship Street, James Parsons, a carman, was charged with disorderly conduct, causing a mob to assemble outside the Whitechapel Workhouse, and inciting them to violence.

On Friday evening, a loud knocking was heard at the gate, followed by a smashing of glass, afterwards ascertained to be broken windows. A mob had assembled, and Parsons was urging them to do as he was doing. When called upon to leave, he refused, and tried to persuade the mob to steal from a baker's shop.

Benjamin Skeet, in charge of the union gate, said that at the time in question some persons were applying for a lodging. He desired them to apply at the police station. This, possibly on account of refusing instant admission, occasioned a little excitement among those who did not hear what was requisite to be done first.

Harmer, 101 K, swore that he heard defendant call out, "Let them in," and to the mob, "Don't go away, don't go away," as also, "Smash in, smash in."

Defendant, through Mr. Abbot, his solicitor, wished it to be understood that he had not purposed either offence or disturbance; most certainly he interfered for the admission of two apparently destitute persons, who appeared unable to get admission, and did not conceive he was doing wrong. Mr. Newton, with most suitable caution, inflicted a fine of 40s., which was immediately paid.

Herts Guardian, Agricultural Journal, and General Advertiser – 23rd February 1867.

1867 – ATTEMPTED WIFE MURDER IN WHITECHAPEL.

On Saturday, at Worship Street Police office, John Bishop, about thirty years of age, a vendor of dogs' meat, at 2, North Street, Whitechapel, was brought before Mr. Newton by Inspector Honey, K Division of police, on a charge of feloniously and wilfully cutting the throat of Ann Bishop, his wife, with intent to cause death thereby.

The first witness called was Eliza Bishop, a young woman and sister of the prisoner, who deposed:-

"He (prisoner) came to my sister's house in Summerfield Street, which is not far from North Street. It was ten minutes to three o'clock this morning. He went direct upstairs and sat on the side of the bedstead. His wife was walking up and down by his side with the baby in her arms. I could see into the room from the top of the stairs. I did not see him do anything. He said to me, "You go home and shut the street door directly; I will follow you." I did not go directly, but told her to put the baby on the bed, then take off Jack's boots, and come down to the door to me. She said, "No, I will let him come to the door." I then threw the key of the front sitting room door on the bed, said, "good night," and left the house, closing the street door behind me. As I reached the corner of the street, I heard a cry of murder in my sister's voice. My mother was with me, and also heard it. I ran back with her and met the prisoner, who was coming out of the house. He said, "Mother, mother, I have done it." He then ran away in the direction of the station house. I had not seen him and his wife quarrel."

Sergeant Freeland, 21 K said, "At ten minutes to three o'clock this morning, I heard cries of murder in the direction mentioned and hastening there saw the prisoner's mother. I asked her who was calling "Murder." She replied, "Oh, it's my son and his wife

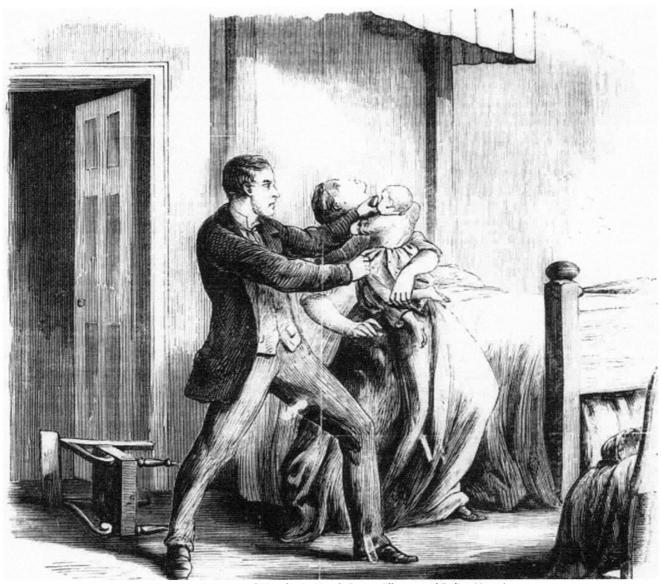

Fig. 8.   Attempted Murder in North Street (Illustrated Police News)

quarrelling." Subsequently, I found a woman lying on a bed in a back upper room. She held an infant in her arms; only a few spots of blood were on the floor and bed clothing, but a real quantity about the child's face and neck. The woman had evidently pressed it close to her while the wound was inflicted – it is not injured. After conveying the woman to the hospital, I sought for the prisoner and caught him locking the door of his own house in North Street. I took him into custody, and told him it was for cutting the throat of his wife. He observed, "If you had found your wife with another man you would do the same." He said, "Mind, I am giving myself up, don't knock me about. I will give you the knife I did it with." He then took from his breeches' pocket a clasp knife, close and clean, which he handed to Constable Vincent, 318 K. There was not any blood on the prisoner's hands. I took him to the station house. He said nothing more."

The evidence of the second constable was similar, and, in reply to Mr. Newton, it appeared that the wound was completely round the throat, or, as described, from one boundary to the other, and doubtless must have been fatal, but for the interposition of the infant's body and clothes, which the latter were completely saturated.

Prisoner, who declined to say anything, was remanded. For if possible, the attendance of his wife.

At the Central Criminal Court on Wednesday, John Bishop, 30, brush maker, was charged with feloniously wounding his wife, Anne Bishop, with intent to murder her. When the prisoner was called upon to plead to the charge, he replied that he knew nothing about it, and the Learned Judge directed that a plea of not guilty should be entered. The prisoner and the prosecutor lived at No. 2, North Street, Bethnal Green, and on the morning of the 13th of September they were in the bedroom together, the sister of the prisoner being also present. The prisoner told the latter to go home, and immediately after she left, and while the prosecutrix was in the act of undressing herself to go to bed, the prisoner went up to her and inflicted a wound upon her throat.

The prisoner appeared to have gone out into the street after committing the act, and he exclaimed, "Mother, mother, I have done it." and upon his being taken into custody he told the policeman that he would give him the knife he had done it with, and he pulled a knife out of his pocket and gave it to him. The knife with which the wound was inflicted was one which was used by the prisoner in his business as a dealer in dog's meat, to cut the skewers with.

Anne Bishop, the wife of the prisoner, who was very much affected while giving her evidence, and who repeatedly entreated for mercy for her husband,

deposed to the circumstances under which the act was committed, and said that she had not had any quarrel with the prisoner that night, and he was generally kind to her, except when he had been drinking. They had been out together in the evening before, and the prisoner had drunk a good deal of gin and beer. It appeared that the wound was now nearly healed, and that no serious consequences whatever were likely to result from it. The prisoner when called upon for his defence, said he had no recollection having wounded his wife. They had been out drinking, and were both the worse for liquor, and he did not remember anything that happened after they left the public house. He said he was very sorry for what had occurred, and he would not get drunk again.

The Jury found the prisoner guilty of unlawfully wounding. The Learned Judge told the prisoner that the Jury had taken a very merciful view of the case. He had committed a very serious offence, and the least sentence he could inflict upon him was eighteen months' imprisonment with hard labour.

Illustrated Police News – 21st September 1867.

1867 – SHOEBLACK BOYS.

Patrick M'Quin, a boy who has been for some time a shoeblack with a box and brushes in Leman Street, Whitechapel, was brought before Mr. Paget charged with violently assaulting Mr. Abraham Woolf, a gentleman of the Jewish persuasion.

The prosecutor is a traveller and jewel manufacturer, of 13 Everard Place, Back Church Lane, Whitechapel. For some time past, on leaving home in the morning he has been pestered by the prisoner and other boys with boxes, brushes, and blacking to clean his boots. He had told them repeatedly that he did not want his boots cleaned, as they had been done at home. He was generally received with derision and laughter, his foreign dialect was mimicked, and the boys at last resorted to threats and abuse.

On Tuesday morning the prosecutor was assailed by the prisoner with the usual old cry of "Clean your boots, sir, clean your boots, only a penny." Mr. Woolf told him he did not want his boots cleaned, on which the prisoner struck him down. Mr. Woolf was immediately surrounded by other shoeblack boys to the number of six or seven. They hustled him, and the prisoner kicked him on the mouth and cut it. The complainant immediately seized the prisoner and took him to the station house.

Mr. Woolf's mouth was cut, and blood was issuing from it while giving his evidence.

Mr. Paget: When did this take place?

The prosecutor: At ten o'clock this morning – only an hour and a half ago.

The prisoner, whose face was scratched and bruised said that Mr. Woolf beat him, and clawed his neck and face.

Police Sergeant Fry, 653, A, said that the scratches were old ones and were quite dry. They had been made some time ago.

Mr. Paget looked at the prisoner's face and neck and said Fry was quite correct. He commented on the conduct of the prisoner, and said he had no right to annoy or molest people who would not have their boots cleaned, but he would allow him and other boys to civilly accost people who wanted their boots

cleaned. A flagrant and cowardly assault had been committed, and he sentenced the prisoner to one month's imprisonment and hard labour.

Illustrated Police News – 2nd March 1867.

1868 – OPIUM DEN IN WHITECHAPEL.

We find the following in M. Albert Wolff's experiences of a night in London, which are just now appearing day by day in the *Figaro*. The locality, it should be remarked, is Whitechapel:-

"We stopped before one of these hovels; the police officer pushed open the door, which was ajar.

Fig. 9.   Assault by Shoeblack Boys (Illustrated Police News)

"Who's there?" demanded someone inside. "Don't be frightened, Jack; it's only me!" replied our Hercules. Whereupon we enter a small room; a strange nauseous odour pervades the apartment, and we quickly beat a retreat. "Wait awhile," says the policeman. "It's only opium."

By the flickering light of the fire burning in the grate I perceive the individual addressed as Jack. It is a Chinese who keeps this wretched hole where one can get intoxicated for a few coppers. The room we enter is so low that we are unable to stand upright. Lying pell-mell on a mattress placed on the ground are Chinamen, Lascars, and a few English blackguards who have imbibed a taste for opium. Some stretched at full length to abandon themselves to the fumes of intoxication in its different stages, while others are only just commencing to light their pipes at a kind of night lamp which is placed on the side of each smoker.

Jack, the master of the house, jabbers a little English. He inquires of us if we wish to smoke, and points to some pipes, which have been already in a thousand courteous mouths, and which he will be happy to offer us, lying on a table between a pile of potatoes and a few bits of charcoal. The police officer explains to this devil's tapster that we have come simply to look on. "Is there no one upstairs?" inquires he. "Yes, there is one woman." "Whereabouts is upstairs?" ask I, looking around. "Why, there is no staircase." Jack fetches a little ladder from the yard, and places it against the wall, where some cats' and rats' skins are hanging; he mounts a few steps, and, pointing to a hole in the ceiling says, "Here." "There is not room for all of us there," remarks the police officer. "You follow the Chinaman, and I'll wait for you below."

One by one we climb the ladder and mount through the opening. Seated on a mattress, in a room lighted by a dim lamp, is an old woman with dishevelled white hair, thin face, and dull looking eyes, blowing a cloud of smoke and coughing every now and then like a person in the last stage of consumption. She casts a stupefied gaze upon us, then throws herself back and continues to puff away at her pipe of opium. The room where she is is a small loft, encumbered with a multitude of objects, belonging to the excellent Jack, but, beyond the mattress on which the old sorceress is reclining, there is not a single piece of furniture.

The atmosphere is so tainted with opium that, being on the point of suffocation, I break the only windowpane, through which, by the way, a kitten would find some difficulty in passing. The fresh air inundates the room, rousing up the sorceress, who gives vent to a volley of complaints in unintelligible jargon A shilling flung on the unclean couch mollifies the old woman, who opens her eyes to their full extent by superhuman effort. She seizes the coin with her long bony fingers and contemplates it with delight. A new attack of coughing, more formidable than the former, seems to tear her lungs as we retreat through the little hole and down the ladder steps."

Tower Hamlets Independent and East End Local Advertiser – 23rd May 1868.

1868 – THE POOR LAW BOARD AND THE WHITECHAPEL UNION.

An agitation emanating from the Poor Law Board has been carried on recently with the view of creating a District Asylum Board, and the erection of an asylum for the sick and infirm poor belonging to the Whitechapel Union. It is also rumoured that the Whitechapel Union is to be united with some other parish or union in the new project. To this proposal the Guardians of the Whitechapel Union have strenuously objected, and the reasons for their objection are stated at length in a memorial addressed by them to the Poor Law Board. We have been favoured with a copy of this memorial and willingly lay the same before our readers

To the Honourable Poor Law Board. The humble Petition of the Guardians of the Poor of the Whitechapel Union, in the county of Middlesex, the esteemed minister of the place. Sheweth:- That your petitioners having been informed by Mr. Corbett, Poor Law Inspector, that your honourable Board is desirous of uniting this Union with some other parish or union for the purpose of raising and establishing an asylum for a portion of the in-door poor, in consequence of the overcrowded state of the Union Workhouse, your petitioners cannot but feel surprised at such an intimation and respectfully submit to the Poor Law Board some particulars on the subject.

Within the last fifteen years your petitioners erected a workhouse for the Union capable of holding 900 inmates, at a cost of nearly 50,000l. The plans and all particulars connected therewith had your sanction and entire approval. The work was carried out to completion with your concurrence, and the payers of rates in the Union were satisfied to bear the large demand upon them, deeming it to be a complete and perfect establishment, capable of meeting all the requirements of the Union. But if Mr. Corbett is right in his statement this large outlay has been made almost in vain, and an additional burthen must be laid upon the already heavily-taxed ratepayers of this Union, for the purpose of doing that which your petitioners consider to be perfectly unnecessary.

To examine the facts of the case, the Workhouse at present contains 814. Of this number 101 are imbeciles, 51 children, and 61 able-bodied. Your petitioners (with regard to the imbeciles) have reason to believe that the District Asylum Board is now about to erect establishments for this class, and for the fever and smallpox cases—at an outlay of nearly one million sterling—and with regard to the children, additional accommodation is now being made at our school establishment in Forest Lane, to which the children in the Workhouse may be sent. And as to the able-bodied, your petitioners trust and hope that the suggestions made by them on many former occasions may be carried out, and institutions formed where this class may be provided for, and subjected to a system of management and discipline, which cannot be obtained in a house containing so many infirm and aged persons as the Whitechapel Workhouse does.

These points and ends accomplished, your petitioners respectfully submit, will entirely supersede the necessity of an additional tax upon this Union, to meet even the altered scale of requirements of space, &c., and do most respectfully but most earnestly request you honourable Board will take these points into serious consideration, and find reasons to spare this heavily-taxed district from any new exactions. Your petitioners have always willingly adopted any rules, orders, or suggestions made by your honourable Board, and are ever willing to do all that can be done for the comfort and wellbeing of the poor under their care, and believe that the Whitechapel Workhouse will bear favourable comparison in that respect with any similar establishment in London or elsewhere, no persons having visited the Workhouse at any time without leaving expressions of approbation and often of admiration at the arrangements and provisions made for the inmates; and if with such arrangements and such attention to all their real wants be added the present sanitary state of those inmates, your petitioners cannot see on what reasonable grounds it can be urged that any change is needed.

For many years your petitioners have paid every attention to the discharge of its important duties, and has endeavoured, to the best of its ability, to carry out the Poor Laws in perfect integrity, and your petitioners believe have accomplished all the requirements for which it was constituted. Not one single complaint of neglect of duty has ever been established against your petitioners, and they cannot but feel these threatened alterations in the mode of dealing with the poor as a reflection on them amounting almost to a charge of neglect or indifference to the wants and comforts of the poor.

Thus, the intimation of the Inspector comes upon them with surprise as well as regret, as they are decidedly of opinion that these continued changes, in the views of officials, as to the management of the poor must, if carried out, be productive of very serious evils. To carry out these notions and suggestions, provisions would be made for the inmates of workhouses which would secure to them comforts and indulgencies that even many of the payers of poor rates, much less the independent labourer, cannot in many cases obtain. So partial a system must have a direct tendency to encourage pauperism, and engender in the minds of the industrious poor feelings of indifference to the retention of their independence.

As Guardians, your petitioners are most anxious to secure the comfort and happiness of the poor under their care, but as reasonable men and members of society, the Guardians cannot forget the great trust placed in their hands, and cannot forget those who contribute the funds, and who confide in them for their wise and proper dispensation.

Your petitioners hope these statements will receive due consideration from your honourable Board, and justify you in not pressing the adoption of any such changes as those in contemplation, the carrying out of which will produce much dissatisfaction, and, your petitioners believe, without any beneficial result.

Tower Hamlets Independent and East End Local Advertiser – 12th September 1868.

1868 – A CLEVER CREATURE.

Elizabeth Welsford, with twenty aliases, a respectably-dressed woman, about forty years of age, was charged on remand with having defrauded several persons, and obtained money by false pretences.

Mr. Wontner, jun., appeared to prosecute the prisoner on behalf of several persons, who were present to prefer charges against her, Mr. B.J. Abbott, solicitor, again appeared for the defence.

Mr. Wonter proposed to go into three more cases against the prisoner, and after shortly detailing the facts of those cases, called the necessary evidence, which showed that, in addition to the fraud she perpetrated on Mr. Hampton, which was proved last week, the prisoner had, in June last, called upon Mrs. Ann Bristowe, of 1, John's Cottages, Charles Street, Hackney Road, and representing herself as the widow of Lieut. Colonel Luxmore, took apartments there saying that she had only just arrived from Cambridge, where she had been staying with a Jewish lady, who had recently died and left her all her plate and property. She had come to town for the purpose of drawing her pension, as an officer's widow, from the Horse guards, and also to see Miss Burdett Coutts, who was the executrix under her father's will of her property to the extent of 30,000l. She also represented that all her luggage was at the railway station, and requested Mrs. Bristowe to lend her some articles of wearing apparel, which she did, and prisoner remained in her house till the 3rd of July, when she left, saying that she was going to draw 180l, from Miss Coutts.

At the time of leaving, she had on a dress and jacket belonging to Mrs. Bristowe, and which she was now wearing, a similar piece of which the witness produced. Prisoner, of course, never came back. During her stay with Mrs. Bristowe, that lady had introduced her to a Mrs. Gallon, a corset maker, and from that person the prisoner afterwards obtained several articles of underclothing and goods on credit to the value of 24s. and several sums of money, all of which Mrs. Galton let her have on the faith of various false representations.

On one occasion she had obtained 1l. from Miss Galton to pay for her cab hire home, as she said she had her pocket picked as she came up Shoreditch, at the same time saying that next Tuesday she was to draw 130l. from Gurney's bank. On another occasion she obtained a second advance of 1l., by false representation.

Her adventures were continued by defrauding and robbing Mrs. Cecilia Crichton, of 37, East India Road, where about the 5th of July the prisoner went to see some apartments, representing that she was the widow of Lieutenant-Colonel Sir Henry Stevens, and making other false statements. When asked for references she produced a number of letters purporting to come from her Majesty the Queen, having the black private seal attached, and others from the Prince of Wales, Duchess of Sutherland, Baron Rothschild, and numerous other ladies of title. She was allowed to occupy the apartments, repeatedly mentioning that she had 4,000l., in Rothschild's Bank and 4,900l., in Coutts's bank. She borrowed several sums of money, amounting to a total of 9l., from Mrs. Crichton, on various pretences, and on the 27th of July she left, and never returned.

After she left it was discovered by Mrs. Crichton that half a dozen silver spoons had left also; and two days after she received a letter, which came from the prisoner, who addressed her as "Dear Cecilia," and stated that she had taken the spoons out with her and raised 1l. 2s. 6d. on them till she came back, but she

returned her the ticket, and said she could get them out herself.

The spoons were produced by an assistant to Messrs. Dicket and Scarlett, who said they were pawned in the name of Mary Crichton.

Mrs. Crichton identified the spoons as her property

The prisoner was then farther remanded, six or seven other cases being ready to be charged against her.

Tower Hamlets Independent and East End Local Advertiser – 12th September 1868.

1868 – THE WISE WOMAN OF WHITECHAPEL.

Louise Kingherst, alias Rebecca Spiller, 26, living at 7, Old Cable Street, Whitechapel, where she had been gaining a living as a fortune teller, has been charged before Mr. Newton with having obtained several sums of money and goods with intent to defraud.

Two cases having already been proved against the prisoner, one other case was now gone into, wherein she obtained money and articles of wearing apparel from Alexander Schwartz, a, tailor, of Plasten Street, Mile End New Town, who deposed that about the commencement of the present year he was passing the prisoner's house, when she called him in, and asked him to have his fortune told. He consenting she shuffled a pack of cards, counting and muttering, and then said that she had read great things for him, and that a power was placed in her by which she could make him very rich, and make all the girls love him. He paid her 6d. for telling his fortune and said that he should like to be rich and loved by the girls. She then said that if he would give her something to charm with, she would do it for him, and he believed it, and gave her a woollen shirt, value 10s., which she said she would return next day.

When he went the next day, she said it would not do, that she must have a linen shirt, which he gave her, although she did not return the woollen one. That shirt, which was worth 5s. 6d., she promised she would return in two days, but when he went again, she said she could not charm unless she had some money, and at her request he gave her 30s., which she was to refund in two days after she had worked the charm. He went to her house in two days but although he heard her speaking, he was told she was not at home. In the consciousness that he had been "done" he repeatedly called at her house, but she was never at home, nor did he see her till that day, having ceased to call for about three months past.

In answer to the Magistrate, witness said, amidst much laughter, that he believed the prisoner when she said she could make him rich and make all the girls love him.

In cross examination by the prisoner, the witness declared that he had never sent a young girl to her with money to get her to charm the heart of a girl named Dingwell, and that he never got either of his shirts, nor his 30s., back again.

William Ives, a pawnbroker, of Leman Street, Whitechapel, produced a signet ring, which was identified by the prosecutor, from whom she had obtained it for the avowed purpose of charming, and then pledged it for 26s. in the name of Ann Spiller.

Sergeant Kenwood, of the H Division, proved that in July 1860, the prisoner was charged before Mr. Mansfield, at this court for stealing a pair of boots off a drunken man's feet while he was lying in the street. She was then sent for fourteen days' imprisonment.

The prisoner said that was all a lie, and the depositions being completed she was sent for trial on three charges.

Illustrated Police News – 17th October 1868.

1869 – BREAKFAST IN WHITECHAPEL.

On Sunday morning we had the opportunity of attending a breakfast, to which 800 and 900 of her Majesty's subjects sat down.

The company was select, none but those occupying a certain station in society, and only a small portion of them having been selected.

Although this was a grand and important occasion to those chiefly concerned, and although so large a company was expected yet neither were any carriage regulations issued by the authorities, nor was any order given as to the garb in which the invited were to come. No confusion was anticipated, and no confusion ensued on this account. The fact was, that few of that multitude would have been able to read such regulations, and if they had been sufficiently advanced in letters to do so, they could only have looked upon them as a bitter sarcasm.

Instead of possessing a brougham, probably not one could boast at having a hand barrow that was his own; and as we approached the crowd assembled round the doors of the East End theatre, we found

that a black coat and the orthodox tubular procured as much respect as the Court dress at a Lord Mayor's banquet. We had only to essay to pass through, and half-a-dozen voices exclaimed, "Make way," not "for my Lord So-and-So," but "for the gentlemen – make way for the gentlemen!"

We were scarcely aware of the nature of the entertainment until we reached the theatre, when we were besieged with applications for tickets for the breakfast. Passing along with the others, we observed that as they entered the inner door each received large and thick slices of buttered plum cake. It was then within a few minutes of 10 o'clock, and the pit was almost filled with adults. Three or four seats next to the stage were occupied by women, and the others were almost entirely in the possession of men. All were furnished with cake, and most of them had brought tin cans, or mugs, or jugs, or cups, and one or two were fortunate to be able to bring both a cup and a saucer. The gallery was filled with a similar assembly.

In the dress circle and on the stage were a few visitors and benevolent ladies and gentlemen who had been instrumental in providing the breakfast. Shortly after 10 o'clock grace was said, tea and coffee were quickly served out, and the hungry multitude devoted themselves to the despatch of the food before them.

The scene presented to the visitor was impressive. The congregation before him consisted of the "residuum" of the population. They had come from the back slums – from fetid courts and alleys, from the casual wards, from the registered lodging houses, from sleep on doorsteps and in railway arches, from highways and byways. They were a mixed multitude: the negro, the mulatto, and other denizens of distant countries were there. Every variety of features could be pointed out, from the noble and intelligent countenance down to the most repulsive and debased.

The agreement, however, as may be imagined, was pretty general in the matter of dress. All were thinly clad, the bulk in rags and tatters. Here and there were to be seen babies at the breast. Good order was preserved throughout and everybody seemed grateful for what he was receiving. One poor fellow was heard to exclaim, "God Almighty knows when I had such a breakfast," and when he was told that he should thank God for it he said, "I do sir, with all my heart."

Another man, between 30 and 40 years of age, said he had come from Canada West to take possession of some property, which, he said, belonged to him. He had worked his way hither a few weeks ago, but on reaching Doctor's commons as he had not 2s. 6d. in his possession he was not permitted to see a copy of his grandfather's will. He was, he said, the eldest grandson, and he did not believe he had been disinherited. In his remarks about the property, he employed the common

Latin phrase *non est inventus*, which he was careful to translate for our benefit, and observed that he was master of four languages, but about this, subsequent questions led us to entertain grave doubts.

The tickets for the breakfast had been left with the people wherever they were found, whether at their lodgings or when attending the district meetings. One man, however, informed us that he had purchased his at the lodging house for a penny; and we may consider that he made a capital bargain, for the tea and the cake so liberally supplied were far superior to that procured at what are called "shilling teas" at a very popular if not the most popular place of resort of Londoners.

An hour and a half having been occupied in this kind of refreshment; proceedings of a different character commenced.

The entertainment we have attempted to describe was given by a few friends connected with the East London Christian Mission, the headquarters of which are at Whitechapel. The society has fourteen mission stations for the purpose of carrying the Gospel to the poor; and out of doors and indoors 170 services are held weekly. There are fifteen paid labourers, and, of course, a great deal of voluntary help. On Sunday four theatres or music halls are engaged, and what was formerly a "penny gaff" at Limehouse has recently been purchased for the mission. Every species of agency for reaching the poor that can be put into operation is employed; and the whole is carried on at an expenditure of some £60 a week.

Addresses were delivered by Mr. Smithers, who officiated as Chairman; Mr. Hamilton, Mr. Blest, Mr. Morgan, Mr. Lean, and Mr. Bastin, who were heard with much attention; but when Mrs. Ashworth, a member of the Society of Friends, rose to speak, she was listened to still more intently. The object of the lady was chiefly to address the female portion of the congregation; and her simple, natural, persuasive utterance, beautiful in the choice of words and its sentences, created a profound impression.

The proceedings did not terminate before half-past one; and, although they had occupied the long period of three hours and a half, all but a very small proportion remained to the end. No disturbance whatever occurred; indeed, it would scarcely seem credible to any but eyewitnesses that such a tatterdemalion, poverty stricken, vicious looking crowd could be marshalled in such order and sit with such quiet as did the meeting at the East End theatre.

We should say that these services are of an entirely unsectarian character, and that on the stage mingled members of all denominations.

Mr. Booth, who is the life and soul of the Mission, was announced to preach later in the day, and the company then separated.

The theatre was gratuitously placed at the disposal of the Mission for the day by Mr. Abrahams, the proprietor.

Illustrated Police News – 10th April 1869.

1869 – DOWN WHITECHAPEL WAY.

In the strange region generally spoken of as "Down Whitechapel Way," there is so much to attract the student of human nature that it would be difficult to do more than indicate the peculiarities of the inhabitants in the short space our disposal.

Taking the line of the main road from Aldgate to Mile End, the stream of life runs fast and carries on its surface so much flotsam and jetsam, so many waifs and strays of our poor humanity, such multiform objects for suggestion and reflection, that we are bewildered at the very outset of our journey, and require a strong head to keep us on our course without turning aside into all sorts of by-ways, and losing our reckoning among unknown bays and quicksands.

Furniture dealers, brokers, bookstalls, herbalists, itinerant preachers, temperance lecturers, dealers in old clothes, old hats, old boots, old cutlery, old ironmongery, old keys, crockery, ginger beer, fried fish, pickled whelks, hardbake, pills, and haberdashery line the pavement; Jew and Gentile hustle each other as they pass in knots from place to place; the gin shop doors are perpetually on the swing; the temples devoted to drinks which are announced to be "all iced" attract thirsty wayfarers from the blaze of the April sun, which thus early seems to bake the very pavement.

There are all sorts of reminiscences, too, down Whitechapel way; old stories of the Three Nuns, the Black Bull, and other remnants of the old coaching times. The Blue Boar, where Mr. Weller, senior, put up, with its sign like "cerulean elephant," is an extinct animal; but the ancient Bull survives, good old quiet shadowy place, suggestive still of the ancient glories of the road when "commercial gents" drove their own traps, and the four-in-hand went "spanking" down long country roads (like the Brighton coach of the present day) with the guard blowing his head off at an attempt to perform "Rule Britannia" on his post horn.

The Three Nuns, with its queer picture for a sign, has gone to decay, its once cosy parlour being turned into a concert room, where everything looks as though the place had been furnished out of a "clearance lot" when the old inn was sold up. "Gentlemen and lady amateurs" are requested to attend and contribute to the harmony in this hall of sweet sounds, which, being an apartment of limited dimensions, having once been no more than the snug parlour already referred to, must be rather trying to a singer with a "powerful organ," and slightly redolent of tobacco smoke when the "select company" are in full force—say, on a benefit night.

Much might be said of the queer outlying streets of this region—not Tiger Bay, not Fashion Street, and Flower and Dean Street and The Kate—the worst of London and thieves' quarters, all of them most graphically portrayed in Mr. Thomas Archer's "Pauper, Thief, and Convict"—but of "the marts" and the busy hives of men; old clothes men, and marts for renovating and retailing those cast-off garments which are collected daily by the peripatetic Israelite.

Much, too, might be recalled of the days when a fair was held at Bow, and the irrepressible Irish population fell upon the show people and the gipsy encampments; and the fun of the fair ended in broken heads and the glory of the shillelagh, until, the news reaching the Whitechapel butchers and the slaughter house men of Aldgate, they determined on deadly reprisals. A butcher boy, mounted on a swift pony, acted as aide-de-camp to the expectant force; and, when the Irish came out again to renew their attack, swift as the wind rode the eager youth—his horse all foam, his face red as the beef he carried—to bring the Whitechapellers to the rescue, armed with ox-goads and those "supplejacks" which were then the pride of the drover who knew his trade. Then every son of Erin who had grown "blue mouldy for want of batin'" had his fustian jacket dusted to a tune that made him doubt the quality of his own ribs.

Those times have passed away, let us hope, never to return. Fairs have been abolished; and, had some more rational amusement been substituted for them, or had they been regulated instead of being abolished, we might have rejoiced. As it is, however, nothing is more hopeless, dreary, and painfully suggestive than a holiday where people have no holiday influence and no holiday occasion to keep them from the fusty tavern and the bar where they set themselves on fire with poisoned gin.

It is true that down Whitechapel way the Hebrew element makes the street gaudy with gay dresses and cheap ornaments when "the people" make holiday; but the Gentile's notion of festivity seldom takes the

Fig. 10.   Down Whitechapel Way (Penny Illustrated Paper)

form of external decoration; a flower chewed in the mouth, or a clean shave and an extra polish to his boots, is the extent of his recognition of the Graces. We are speaking now of the festivity which keeps him to the streets; for his ordinary notion of a holiday is to be "on the fly," which is the Oriental phrase used down Whitechapel way to signify the absolute freedom of a gala season and its appropriate fluttering from bar to tap room. They are very dingy moths; but then there are so many candles, and they are so often singed.

Penny Illustrated Paper – 1st May 1869.

1869 – THE MORAL CONDITION OF WHITECHAPEL.

On the 9th inst. Mr. Mitchell, the Vestry Clerk of Whitechapel, with a numerous deputation of the trustees and other ratepayers, who nearly filled Thames Police Court, waited on Mr. Paget to represent to him the annoyance caused by the assemblage of disorderly prostitutes, reputed thieves, crimps, and unlicensed shoe blacks.

Three Irish prostitutes named Mary Sullivan, Mary Johnstone, and Bridget Bryant, having been placed in the dock and charged with disorderly conduct on the previous Saturday night, Mr. Mitchell addressed the Magistrate at considerable length. He only asked the Magistrate to put the law in force and suppress the nuisance. A similar representation had been made to a Magistrate at the Worship Street Police Court relating to another part of the parish, and the evil had been abated. Two police constables of the H division proved that the prisoners were notorious prostitutes, who had frequented the streets for a great length of time; and that on Sunday night, the 8th inst., when the congregations of the parish church, the German Chapel, and the Zion Chapel, were leaving those places of worship, the prisoners spoke to men, and were leading them off to houses of bad repute, when they were taken into custody. A gentleman said he could not send his daughters out without their ears being assailed with the vilest of language.

Mr. Paget said the design of the respectable deputation now present was a very laudable one. No one could doubt the existence of a very great evil, and that the prisoners were common prostitutes. He could not, however, punish the prisoners for what others had done. He must confine himself specially to the evidence of the police constables, which proved that there was no particular aggravation in the conduct of any of the females. That being so, the case failed, and they must be discharged.

Mr. Paget then addressed the prisoners at considerable length and said if ever they conducted themselves in a disorderly manner, or in any way contrary to law, or to the annoyance of the public, he would punish them with great severity. In conclusion he could not help saying, that the horrible dens in Whitechapel and other parishes in his district where these wretched creatures were encouraged to assemble should be abolished. The keepers ought to be prosecuted with more rigour and more frequency than had been.

Mr. Mitchell was not unmindful of the importance of prosecuting the owners and keepers of the place in question. He had been recently successful in one case committed from that court, and two persons were convicted and sentenced to imprisonment and hard labour.

Newcastle Guardian & Tyne Mercury – 14th August 1869.

1869 – WHITECHAPEL FAMINE.

The appearance of that grim minister of death, the "famine fever," amongst the impoverished thousands of the East End gives dreadful note of the horrors to be endured by the unemployed of the metropolis during the winter now close at hand. Already *the star*ving multitude has been ravaged by the pitiless destroyer, and unless measures are promptly taken of a character commensurate with the dire emergency the devastation of the hungry masses must inevitably attain to a gigantic proportion.

It appears by communication from the medical department of the Privy Council, received during the sitting of the Whitechapel Board of Works on Monday evening, that from July, 1868, scattered cases, principally of Polish Jews and poor Irish from courts in Whitechapel, had been admitted to the London Fever Hospital, until in May of the present year there was evidence of the disease having become epidemic, and since then it had increased both as regarded its amount and the area of its distribution, 140 cases having been treated at the Fever Hospital from the 1st of January to the 15th of October in this year.

This is certainly a gloomy picture which affects us with a gloomier foreboding for the future, and the clouded aspect is intensified by the exceeding difficulty which lies between us and the discovery and application of a timely antidote; for whilst we all see clearly that the fatal malady is a terribly palpable fact, opinions differ widely as are the poles asunder as to cause and effect, disease and remedy. Whilst some allege that want of food and other privations are the precursors of the disease, and that, the residents in the district being unable to bear the pressure of increased local taxation, an equalization of the rates is the only remedy, others maintain that the fever is the result of the immorality, degradation, and vice in which too many of the sufferers have passed their lives, that no individual, though rich as Croesus, could alleviate the scourge by the ordinary means of charity, and that those necessarily progressive reforms in the habits and lives of the people alone furnish the true panacea.

It is but too painfully true that little can be expected in the way of additional monetary aid from ratepayers who are themselves suffering most severely from the protracted paralysis of trade in the eastern, and indeed in all the districts of a metropolis which has long been deprived of Queen and court, and these incentives to manufacturing operations which in by-gone years made the position of London artisans synonymous with the idea of industrial prosperity. But in the persistent absence of these blessings, it remains only for the Whitechapel and kindred boards to do their duty manfully by rigidly enforcing the various sanitary acts, promptly insisting upon the cleansing, ventilation, and disinfection of the dwellings of the poor, and the strict prevention of overcrowding and judiciously distributing amongst the afflicted and distressed such a liberal modicum of food and medicine as the parochial treasury can possibly afford.

The need of a mortuary building can be nowhere in the metropolis so strikingly apparent at the present time as in the poor and plague-smitten district of Whitechapel. As a means of obstructing the spread of infectious maladies the public mortuary is important to an extent which can scarcely be exaggerated, and yet in Whitechapel, with poverty and contagion rampantly flourishing in the polluted air of the crowded courts and alleys, the living and the dead must sojourn together until the parochial hearse bears off its ghastly load.

One of those revolting illustrations of life amongst the lowly, which are good only to the extent of leading the public mind to a perception of the necessity for reform, has just come to light. The Inspector of Nuisance in Whitechapel reported to the District Board on Monday evening that he had visited a certain house in Tenter Street South, where on the 16th inst. lay a child dead from scarlet fever. This corpse, he was informed, would of necessity be kept until the 22nd, or nearly seven days, in an underground room in which father, mother, and three children lived and slept, several other families also living in the house! With such an example

before us of 19th century civilisation in the British capital, is it to surprise us that indigence is so largely supplemented by malaria of the most virulent character in Whitechapel and its crowded surroundings? It is rather a matter for much genuine astonishment that with such unpardonable omissions the extent of epidemic visitations there is not more serious than it is.

The Rev. Brook Lambert has given notice of his intention to point out at the next meeting of the Board the necessity for a public mortuary, and if the reverend gentleman's colleagues should permit a spirit of short sighted economy to override so obviously rational a proposal, they will be no longer entitled to lay claim to an honest solicitude for the bodily welfare of the poor creatures who at the present time stand so sorely in need of the counsel and assistance of a judicious local administration.

Clerkenwell News – 27th October 1869.

1869 – INAPPROPRIATE REMOVAL.

The Whitechapel Board of Works appears to have discovered in a recent act of the Coroner for the eastern district a degree of indifference to the sanitary exigencies of a poor and densely populated locality, which, assuming the published statement to be authentic, is as reprehensible as it is in direct opposition to that fastidiousness in the interests of the public health which Coroners generally profess.

At the meeting of the Board on Monday evening last a member adverted to a report of certain proceedings at the meeting of a neighbouring Vestry from which it appeared that the dead body of a man taken out of the water at Shadwell basin, after having lain three or four days in the dead house of the parish, was removed under an order of the Coroner, to a house in one of the close and crowded courts in Royal Mint Street.

There seems to be no doubt that the corpse, in an advanced state of decomposition, was so removed, and that an inquest was subsequently held relative to the man's death. The medical officer of the Whitechapel district, Dr. Liddle, confirms the statement, and expresses an opinion, obvious to the understanding of even the dullest unofficial mind, that "there could be no doubt whatever of the great impropriety of a decomposed body being kept in a house, such as that of Christopher Court, a very narrow place, and densely crowded with inhabitants."

It may be supposed that the Coroner merely gave up the body to the relatives for the purpose of burial, but if that were so, why was not the inquest held first, and whilst the unfortunate deceased lay in a building constructed expressly with the view of saving the healthy from infection against their will? Apart, however, from the sanitary aspect of the case—and that is as decidedly unpleasant as it can well be—it would be interesting to know from whence a Coroner derives his power to remove a corpse which comes within his official cognizance from one place to another.

That, we believe, is a business which rests solely with the parochial authorities; and though, as a whole, those powers are by no means unexceptionably wise in dealing with such matters as pertain to the security of the public health, their control of sanitary affairs is admirable solicitude, compared with the thoughtlessness of a Coroner – a medical man, too, we believe – who could arrogate the right to house a putrid body amidst a mass of living beings in a narrow and ill-ventilated court in the vicinity of the Mint.

Clerkenwell News – 27th October 1869.

1870 – BRUTALITY BY THIEVES

An illustration of sharp and brutal practice on the part of some Whitechapel thieves was given on Wednesday at an inquest on the body of a poor man, who on Boxing Day fell upon the slippery pavement and fractured his skull. Although he was apparently dying at the time, several ruffians pounced upon him, tore open his pockets, and robbed him of every penny. The victim of this outrage survived his injuries ten days, and at the inquiry yesterday a verdict of "Accidental death" was returned.

Berkshire Chronicle – 15th January 1870.

1871 – ASSAULT ON THE POLICE.

Mathew Bryan, a labourer, was charged with assaulting Frederick Moorhouse, 10 H, in St. Peter's Court, Whitechapel, on Christmas night. The police constable went to quell a serious riot, of which the prisoner was the ringleader, and most dangerous, and threatened to rip all the constables up. The prisoner had a knife in his hand, or what the police said looked like one, but fortunately things did not come to extremes with that weapon.

On the way to the station house all the low characters of Whitechapel turned out and threw all kinds of missiles at the police, and the officer in this case had his helmet completely smashed in, and his head miraculously escaped being smashed in too. The prisoner threw the same constable twice heavily to the ground, and he seemed in great suffering.

Mr. Lushington sentenced the prisoner to four months' imprisonment and hard labour.

Clerkenwell News – 28th December 1871.

1872 – WHITECHAPEL GUARDIANS AND ORPHAN CHILDREN.

The question in this case – whether Jane Barrett, a child whose parents, now dead, were Roman Catholics, and who is now a pauper inmate of the Roman Catholic Orphanage of St. Mary's Asylum at North Hythe in the county of Middlesex, should be withdrawn from that asylum by the Poor Law Guardians of the Whitechapel Union, and transferred to the Metropolitan Police Orphanage—is one of considerable public interest.

Mr. Denman, Q.C., moved for and obtained a rule nisi on the 25th of this month calling upon the master and matron of St. Mary's Roman Catholic Orphanage to show cause why a writ of habeas corpus should not issue to them to bring up the body of the child, Jane Barrett, now under their care in that orphanage, that she might be delivered to the Guardians of the Whitechapel Union Workhouse, who moved upon a legal right under the statute, with a view to their handing her over to a newly instituted asylum, the Police Orphanage at Twickenham.

Mr. Day, now opposing the rule, entered into a detailed narrative of the circumstances under which the child had become a pauper orphan in the Whitechapel Union Workhouse, and was transferred thence by the Guardians to St. Mary's Catholic Orphanage for care, maintenance, education, and religious training in the doctrines and faith of the Roman Catholic Church, of which her father and mother were members. The father was a policeman in the metropolitan force, and had nine children, all of whom he and his wife had had baptised in the Roman

Catholic Church. He unfortunately for his children, fell sick, and died, and up to the time of his death none of them had been in receipt of pauper relief. His wife did not long survive him, and the younger children, bereft of their natural parental support, had no security for maintenance and shelter but the workhouse.

Those parties who knew the father and mother, and some of whom stood in the selection of godfathers and godmothers to the children, and were desirous to have them brought up in the Catholic faith, applied to the Poor Law Board to transfer them from the Union workhouse to St. Mary's Catholic Orphanage, in which they would be brought up in the faith of their parents. The Poor Law Board, under the provisions of an Act of Parliament (25th of Victoria) constituting them in *loco parentis*, having power to make an order to transfer orphan children, no matter of what denomination, to an orphanage in which they might be trained in the religious belief of their parents — such as their parents would wish them to be trained up in — made an order directing the Guardians to send two or three of the children to St. Mary's Orphanage, and the Guardians, in compliance with the order, placed them in the orphanage.

The father of the children had shortly before his death — perhaps not more than a couple of months before — become a member of an institution founded as an orphanage, and designated "The Police Orphanage," for the education and maintenance of their young children in the event of their (the fathers') deaths. The school of the orphanage was, however, not a certificated school, and the commissioners or inspectors were not entitled and had no power by law to visit the school, and there was no security that the orphan children of Catholic parents would be trained up there in the religious principles of the Catholic Church — those of their parents, and in which their parents desired them to be brought up.

The Police Orphanage had been only in existence a few years, and the father of the children had been only a few months a member of it at the time of his death, and had not paid more than three or four shillings to its fund. The Guardians of the Whitechapel Union were bound, when the order was made by the Poor Law Board for the removal of children to any orphanage — no matter of what denomination — to pay a sum per week out of the rates for their maintenance to the institution, to which the Poor Law Board, in conformity with representations made to them of the religious belief of the parents, ordered them to be transferred, and that requirement had been complied with by the Guardians up to the last few days, when the writ of habeas corpus was moved for.

There were two children of the deceased in St. Mary's Catholic Orphanage, namely Jane and John, and it was proposed by the Guardians to remove Jane only, and thus separate her from her brother and those children of kindred ties of religion with whom she was associated. When the writ of habeas corpus was served upon the authorities at St. Mary's Orphanage to bring the child up to this court that she might be delivered to the Guardians, the parties in whose care she was said they would relieve the union parish of Whitechapel from all further expense for her maintenance, and maintain, clothe, and educate her themselves.

The Lord Chief Justice thought there was a cruelty in the effort being made to separate the children, and was apprehensive that there was religious feeling at the bottom of it.

Mr. Day said the father of the children, according to his information, had only paid three or four shillings to the Police Fund, the smallness of which could scarcely give him a claim, and yet it was now sought by the Guardians, or whoever put them in motion, to take this child from an orphanage she was associated with her brother, where there was a guarantee that she would be brought up in the religious faith of her parents, and in which an offer had been made to bring her up at the expense of private charity, and altogether relieve the poor rates from the cost of keeping her.

There were several hundred Catholic orphans in the orphanage, about 300 of which were paid for out of the rates, and 120 of whom were maintained at the expense of private charity. It was said by his learned friend who moved for the writ that the Guardians had a legal right to demand and get the custody of the child; but they could not retain the child in their custody. He submitted, looking at all the circumstances, seeing that the Police Orphanage was an institution originated only within the last few years, and that its school was not a certificated school, and that there was not therefore any power in the School Board to visit it, that the rule obtained by his learned friend ought to be discharged.

Mr. Denman, in support of the rule, submitted that the Guardians had a power under the statute to demand the custody of the child.

The Lord Chief Justice: But why wish to separate the children? Why do the Guardians only wish to take one of them from the orphanage in which they are now?

Mr. Denman: the child in question has been elected by the directors of the Police Orphanage to be received on the foundation; and if not now received she will in a few days have passed the age, nine years, at which children can be eligible to be admitted to the benefits of the institution. It is true it has not been founded many years, but it is becoming a most valuable asylum, and being under the auspices of the Commissioners of Police there is no danger that wrong will be done in the religious teaching of the orphans. The subscriptions of membership are only a penny per week, and although the father of this child had only paid three or four shillings to the fund, his child was eligible to be elected to the advantages of its foundation.

The Lord Chief Justice: But when St. Mary's Catholic Orphanage proposes to relieve the poor rates from the cost of her maintenance, and to bear it themselves, why do the Guardians come to this court to get custody of her.

Mr. Denman: They have the power under the Act to demand and obtain custody of her.

Mr. Day: But they have no power to detain her in custody. This application is for other objects.

Mr. Denman: The object of the Guardians is for the benefit of the child. She has been elected to the Police Orphanage, and if not presented in the next three days' she cannot be admitted. The institution is one in which orphans – the children of policemen who have subscribed to the fund – are brought up in the religion of their fathers.

The Lord Chief Justice: But why separate the brother and sister – why not ask for both?

Mr. Denman: It is intended, my lord, to try and get the brother, and, indeed, to get three of the children into the Police Orphanage. He had an affidavit of one of the friends of the father, declaring that the father had, on his death bed, expressed a hope that his children would be received into the Police Orphanage; and the Poor Law Guardians, having power under the Act to which he had referred, to demand and get custody of the child in question, he (Mr. Denman) submitted that the girl was now a pauper; that the offer of the orphanage to relieve the parish rates from the cost of keeping her was eleemosynary and, as to its permanency, uncertain; while, on the other hand, on the foundation of the Police Orphanage, she would not be brought up either as a "pauper" or a "recipient" of eleemosynary aid, and would have a right, without any danger of perversion of the religious belief in which her parents wished to bring her up. He submitted, therefore, that the rule should be made absolute.

Their lordships having conferred together for a considerable time, the Lord Chief Justice said at first, he thought that the object of the party who moved for the writ was for a purpose of proselytism, and to any object of that kind this Court could not lend itself. The Court was not constituted for any such object. In the course of the arguments, however, the Court discovered that the father – whose children were not paupers during his lifetime, those children

whom he and their mother desired to bring up in the faith of the Catholic Church, of which they were themselves members – had expressed a desire on his death bed that his children might be adopted and brought up by the Police Orphanage, to which the fact of his having been a subscriber gave them a claim; consequently the Court was of opinion that the rule ought to be absolute.

The other Learned Judges concurred—the child to be brought up tomorrow.

Rule absolute accordingly.

East London Observer – 3rd February 1872.

1872 – EAST LONDON HOSPITAL FOR CHILDREN.

We heartily recommend to public charity the support of this Institution, the "East London Hospital for Children and Dispensary for Women," which is situated at Ratcliff Cross, near Stepney railway station, and close to the Thames, with its crowd of commercial shipping. It was started, about four years ago, by the enterprising benevolence of a newly-married pair, the late Mr. Nathaniel Heckford, sometime house surgeon of the London Hospital, and his wife, a lady who had been a volunteer nurse in an East End Cholera Hospital.

With the aid of the Rev. S. Burnaby, Rector of Wapping, and a few other friends, they found means to purchase an old house, which they fitted up with ten beds for infant patients. They made their own abode in a single room on the premises; while Mr. Heckford took upon himself, unpaid, the duty of house surgeon, and Mrs. Heckford that of matron. The Institution grew, for its service was much wanted in that poor neighbourhood. An adjacent sail loft, a building of three stories, was annexed to the house; and forty beds were provided, which were soon filled, as they have since continued to be, while many cases have been rejected for want of room. A dispenser and several nurses have been engaged.

In July, 1870, Mr. Heckford, whose health had been completely broken down by his devoted labours, conveyed the property of the hospital to a committee of trustees. He and his wife then removed from the premises; and he died shortly before last Christmas—surely not having lived in vain, if his example be remembered, and if the good work he commenced obtain its due measure of substantial aid.

The total number of patients treated since the opening of the hospital in January, 1868, is about 20,000, of whom 1,460 were in-patients, the remainder out-patients. The number of in-patients received in the last twelvemonth (incomplete) since April 30, 1871, is 324, and the out-patients 5,517. Not more than thirty-four beds can at present be made up, while the applications to be admitted increase daily. The out-patient department, however, is a great boon to the neighbourhood; the number of new out-patients averages 500 a month. No charge whatever is made; the medicines and advice are supplied cost free. Convalescent children are sent to different convalescent homes, Tunbridge Wells, Brighton, Guildford, and St. Leonards.

During the past year fifty-six children have been sent to these places, as against nineteen in the year before. A gentleman who wishes his name to be kept secret has lately offered to establish, near London, a convalescent home where he will always keep ten patients of the East London Children's Hospital free of charge. The Institution, of which Lord Enfield, M.P., is President, and Mr. F. Peek and Mr. W.R. Winch are Vice-Presidents, is directed by a general with a committee of management that meets weekly, including some of the ship owners and other men of business in the district, the clergy, and medical men.

The ordinary annual expenditure is about £2,800. Mr. E.S. Norris, of Shadwell, is treasurer; the Rev.

Sherrard Burnaby is honorary secretary; and Mr. Ashton Warner, at the hospital, is acting secretary. The house surgeon is Mr. J. Lawrence Bullock; Dr. R. Barnes, Dr. Andrew Clark, Mr. Shillitoe, Mr. Caesar, Baron von Seydewitz, and others are of the medical staff.

The annual meeting of the supporters of this Institution will take place at the London Tavern next Tuesday afternoon, at three o'clock. It is proposed to appeal to public liberality for a fund to build a new hospital, at a cost of £10,000, upon a site in Broad Street, Shadwell, to be purchased for £1,900 from the Peabody trustees. This will give accommodation for one hundred inpatients; and every visitor to the present hospital must be convinced that, notwithstanding the skill and care of its internal arrangements, the rickety old buildings at Ratcliff Cross are not suitable. Our Artist, in the drawing we have engraved for this Number, gives a view of the scene in one of the wards, and the little patients, some in their beds, others on the floor, with their simple playthings for it is a great point to amuse them.

Illustrated London News – 27th April 1872.

Fig. 11.   East London Hospital for Children (Illustrated London News)

1872 – MODEL BABY FARM IN WHITECHAPEL.

On Thursday afternoon Mr. Richards held an inquest at the Sugar Loaf Tavern, Mile End, Newtown, London, touching the death of Sarah Chiddick, aged one month, the illegitimate child of a matchbox maker.

The evidence showed that when the deceased was fourteen days old it was placed with a Mrs. Fooke, of Edward Street, Whitechapel. This person was a widow who lived with her six children in one room on the second floor. The eldest "child" was a woman of 20, next to whom was a young man of 18, then a youth of 16, the remainder of the family being boys and girls from seven years upwards. The house was in a most deplorable state, the room containing nothing but two beds, one chair, one table, and a heap of miscellaneous filthy rags, which covered the wretched inhabitants at night. Into this place the little deceased was taken, "because Mrs. Fooke was known to be very careful in bringing up her children," but it gradually pined and died for want of breast milk.

Mrs. Fooke told the Coroner that she did her best with the deceased, receiving 4s a week from the mother for her care and attendance, and that the kind treatment the child had received, and the wholesome, clean place where it lived ought to have kept it alive.

The Coroner, in summing up the case, said that he had never seen a place where soap and water had been more needed than the filthy room in King Edward St., and the fact that young women and men were herded together like pigs in a stye was, in his opinion, a great evil, and that something should be done to put a stop to such a disgraceful system.

With regard to the deceased, he thought Mrs. Fooke was greatly to blame for having taken charge of the deceased, and it was for the Jury to say whether she was answerable for its death. The Jury ultimately recorded a verdict of "Death from want of proper food and nourishment."

Belfast Telegraph – 27th May 1872.

1872 – WHITECHAPEL ROAD ON A SATURDAY NIGHT.

But few of the well-to-do who live in London know how the poorest section of the poorer classes travel through life – that enormous number of unskilled labourers who were left out of Mr. Scott Russell's scheme for the social redemption of the working classes. This multitude of individuals, whose whole lives are struggles against extreme poverty, is considered unworthy of the attention of our social reformers. And yet the condition of these unskilled labourers – which is hardly better than that of the recipients of parish bread – requires immediate attention. Unfortunately for them, they cannot afford to devote sixpence each week out of their scanty earnings towards the support of an organisation to protect their interests. The great struggle is to make one Saturday's pay carry them to the next without getting into debt and but few succeed in the feat.

The Saturday night, although the pay night, brings with it greater hardship and pain than any in the week. Then the accounts with the baker and the grocer have to be squared, and meat bought for the family for Sunday's dinner – the only meat day in the week. When this is done, so little remains in the purse that it is doubtful whether the other items of family use can be provided for the beginning of the week, certainly not for the end. Before the week is out the old system of credit must be recurred to. But fortunately, there are markets in different parts of the metropolis where this class of poor can obtain their goods on Saturday night a shade cheaper than they can at the shop.

In Whitechapel Road, between the church and Mile End Gate, on this night everything is to be bought from the stalls which line the roadway, especially on the left-hand side going towards the Gate from the City. Amidst the flaming naphtha lights can be discerned toys, hatchets, crockery, carpets, oil cloth, meat, fish, greens, second-hand boots, furniture, artificial flowers, &c. Round every stall are eager women, bartering with the salesmen. It is evident that the poor mother must husband her farthings. The meat must be bought, and so must those boots for her young son; his old ones are so worn that they cannot keep out the wet any longer. Here are women chaffering in good-humoured content because their husbands have been able to give them a shilling or two extra this week; others with difficulty restraining the tears which are welling to their eyes because the price of meat at the stalls is so high that the dear little ones at home will not be able to taste any again this week. But farther on is one worse off than even these. Groping in the slushy mud, surrounded by a crowd, is a neat little woman with unmistakeable tears running down her cheeks. She has lost half a sovereign all her husband has earned this week and she has bought nothing for tomorrow's dinner. But there are sympathising hearts close by. A gentleman stoops down, as if he, too, were looking in the mud, and slips something into her hand – an example that is instantly followed by two decently-dressed working men. There is no doubt of her gratitude, although protestations of it are absent.

Whitechapel Road is well furnished with a variety of entertainments, of a cheap description, and not of a refined class. "The Pavilion" theatre is the most pretentious in its bill of fare. It is the home of the melodrama, where any number of mortal combats take place in one night. Music halls are plentiful, and almost all the public houses have harmonic meetings on Wednesdays and Saturdays. But why is the man in that doorway jumping up and down, backwards and forwards, shifting on to one leg and then on to the other, bawling himself hoarse, while another man a few yards behind him in the passage is turning a tune out of a barrel organ. The man who is skipping about as if he were on hot bricks is dressed like a coachman, but the breast of his coat is faced with crimson satin, trimmed with silver lace. His friend at the organ is a greater man – perhaps Lord Chesterfield himself resuscitated although one can scarcely imagine that nobleman playing "Hop light, Loo," on such an instrument, in powdered wig, with his rapier at his side. "Hi, hi! only one penny! The Gallery of Varieties! Walk in! Walk in! Now exhibiting! Only one penny! The best waxworks in London!" bawls the lively man in the doorway.

Inside, ranged round the three sides of an oblong room, are a number of figures, which the showman assures his audience are all wax, and not, as stated, made of wood. "This finger is broken off to prove it. And you will observe, on removing General Garibaldi's cap, that he is bald, on purpose to show that there is no deception here it is, all wax," feeling his head.

Notwithstanding the opinion of the Press (to which there was no name attached) ostentatiously displayed outside, we could not recognise the likeness of some of the figures. Indeed, we had reason to believe by a second visit that some of them did duty for different notorious personages, according to the exigencies of the hour. The lady who fell down dead in Whitechapel Road, from the effects of tight lacing, on the first occasion, afterwards went through the same performance at the Prince of Wales's hall. "This is Benjamin West's celebrated picture of 'Christ healing the Sick in the Temple.' Originally cost 3,000/." There must be a mistake somewhere. "This is a portrait of Benjamin Lincoln, the President of the United States, painted by Benjamin West, a celebrated American artist. This is another painting by the same man. It was sold for 10,000 guineas, and exhibited in America at half-a-crown a head. It is very valuable, although it is so old that it looks like a piece of rotten canvas varnished."

After having Jane Shore, Lady Jane Grey, Count Cavour, and Old Daddy, of the Lambeth Casual Ward, and many others pointed out to us, we were invited to step upstairs to the Chamber of Horrors, where, for one penny, we should see "all the celebrated murderers of many bygone years, including that beautiful piece of machinery of a man in the agonies of death." This was rather too bad besides, as the invitation to go upstairs was given, the organ encouraged us with "Down among the dead men."

The farther the hours got into the night the busier the stalls and shops became. The Cheap Jacks and quack doctors put forth all their powers of cajolery. Certain cures for every disease flesh is heir to, were to be bought remarkably cheap. The functions of the different parts of the human body were explained minutely with Latin words of "thundering sound." Youngsters were shooting away their halfpence at double-quick time for Barcelona nuts. Men and women are thronging the public houses, talking in loud keys over their beer and gin, as if to drown their boon companions' voices at the same time they down their own sorrows. But these persons that crowd and elbow one another to get to the bar are either of the spendthrift class or those without encumbrances. Some, no doubt, are drinking away the money which would be better spent in providing food and clothing for those at home, or for themselves. The women especially are poorly clad; their quantity and quality of clothing evidently being at the minimum.

"Clear out of the way! Hi, hi!" shouted some voices as we were absorbed in the contemplation of a quack doctor's list of medicaments, and phrenological and physiological diagrams. "Clear out of the way!" Turning round, we discovered a costermonger's barrow issuing from Green Dragon Place, towards which we had previously had our backs. Saturday night is not a favourable one for moving from one habitation to another, especially at half-past ten o'clock at night, if any idea of comfort on Sunday is entertained, but it is certain that this family will not be troubled much in arranging their furniture. Half-an-hour or so will put their things to rights. The barrow drawn by the man contains what chairs and tables there are, while the wife walks at the side with a dilapidated small doubled up mattrass under one arm, swinging a bundle of things, which are wrapped up in a bird's-eye handkerchief, from her hand, and carrying a very small washstand innocent of paint by the other.

Every Saturday night there are many shows. Mysterious creatures exhibiting in enclosed square spaces about six feet each way. Hairy men, hairless dogs, gorillas, Aztecs, and giants. Beyond the Mile End Gate, the young English giant is located. By his own account he is 7 ft. 4 in. high, and has been presented to Queen Victoria and the Royal Family. He also asserts that "the trimming which you here see all round the wainscoting of this room was round the audience chamber of Maximilian of Mexico before he was shot – a fact which will brand the name of Mexican for ever. Wishing you are all satisfied and will recommend me to your friends, I bid you good night." But it was evident all were not satisfied, for one individual had ventured to kick the giant's legs, having doubts of their genuineness. Unfortunately, he touched the wrong part, and brought down an invitation on himself to "feel that there was no deception." This tall individual was certainly very narrow, particularly about the waist, and scarcely knew how to fill his clothes out.

The Graphic – 1ˢᵗ June 1872.

1872 – A NIGHT IN WHITECHAPEL.

Leman Street, Whitechapel, is not an attractive thoroughfare. It is not a place, for instance, in which one would care to spend one's honeymoon, except, perhaps, on the homoeopathic principle of counteracting one sort of dreariness by another. But of all the quarters of the metropolis this is in some respects the most interesting. For squalid misery it is outdone by Bethnal Green, where hundreds of the descendants of the old Flemish weavers live in a condition of abject poverty and are only kept from starvation by their annual gains on the Kentish hop grounds.

It is not a Quartier Breda, like parts of Pimlico. It has not an almost exclusively seafaring or ship-serving population, like Limehouse or Stepney. It is not exactly an Alsatia, for the metropolitan police are paramount even here. But for a combination of queer social elements, of squalid poverty and boisterous amusement, of crime and mutual charity, of vulgar vice and of elevated sentiment, Whitechapel is unequalled. And as one of that half of the world which has to confess its ignorance how the other half lives — and dies — l was not sorry to seize a recent opportunity of passing a night in exploring the district.

When I say that we visited five or six theatres, two or three "penny-gaffs," half a dozen music halls, dancing saloons without number, lodging houses of every sort, more than one thieves' kitchen, opium smoking establishments kept for the benefit of Lascar sailors, and restaurants where stewed eels formed the principal pabulum, that we climbed up to garrets which our guide described as the very worst in London, and assisted at the wake of a sailor killed in a street fight, it will be admitted that we made the most of the occasion. I venture also to think that an account of our experiences may possess some interest for your readers.

At half-past eight in the evening, we left the Leman Street Police station with the Inspector and Sergeant who were to be our guides; and more cheery, pleasant, intelligent companions could not easily be found. They knew every nook and corner of the district, they took us down courts and alleys into which, if any lone stranger should chance to penetrate, he would be not indeed murdered, for nothing would be gained by that, but robbed of whatever he might chance to have about him — possibly not even excepting his clothes. If in his sober senses, indeed, perhaps he might be spared this last indignity, but it is no uncommon thing in a certain neighbourhood for the police to find a sailor wandering about the streets in the early morning in the costume of our first parents, having been stripped of his clothes, he knows not where, by some harpy, he knows not whom. Even the veriest teetotaller would run great risk of being hustled and robbed and would have small chance of recognising his assailants in the crowd of dirty faces.

The police, however, find that the most predatory and most dangerous inhabitants take good care to keep on good terms with them. "I have never been insulted in all the years I have been here," said our Inspector; the Sergeant added, "Why, if I were to say in that thieves' kitchen that I wanted my pocketbook which I had left at home, 20 of these lads would start up and offer to get it. And what is more, any one of them would bring it safely." By the whole population Inspector and Sergeant were received with the greatest cordiality, and we obtained a reflected popularity with everybody, from theatrical managers down to opium smokers.

Our first visit was to the "Garrick" Theatre in Leman Street — as pretty a little house as one would wish to see. For the small sum of one penny, you may here have your marrow chilled and your blood frozen in the gallery, while admittance to the more aristocratic parts of the house may be obtained for a threepenny bit. The piece seemed to be a melodrama; but, though during our short stay there were one or two dagger thrusts and pistol shots, I fancy that Sir Charles Young's "Montcalm " would beat the east end drama in murders and seductions, and not a single character talked about "kisses that kill and beauty that betrays." The high moral sentiments were cheered by the "gods" to the echo, and the occupants of the penny gallery showed the keenest appreciation of the great lesson illustrated by the triumph of Virtue and the repulse of Villainy as effected by means of a horse pistol.

However, the entertainment was really too good to be allowed to detain us long from our explorations;

and we made our way to one of those public houses with music rooms attached which appear to be much in vogue in this part of the town. But the Licensing Act, if it has not made people virtuous, has at least cast a gloom over the purveyors of cakes and ale; and a little dwarf with a large fiddle was almost the only occupant of a room which had been the scene of many a merry meeting in the days before Mr. Bruce held the seals of the Home Department. The dwarf was loud in his complaints. His occupation was gone. His trade was ruined. He should "want a 'lead' himself now, 'stead of helping other people in theirs." What was his occupation, we inquired, and what on earth was a "lead?" "Well, you see, if any of 'em here gets into trouble (this is the euphuism for being brought under the arm of the law) they wants a trifle when they goes in, to keep the family out of the workus', and then perhaps they wants a trifle when they comes out to start fresh with like. So, they sends round a card to their friends and has a meeting at a public; I plays a tune or two, and what with a bit of singing and perhaps a bit of dancing, the friends gets their pecker up and comes down with the dust free enough. I've knowed a man's friends so rally round for his 'lead' as he'd collar three or four 'quid' (sovereigns) from it. But Lor', with your licenses, and your beaks, and your police – no offence, sir – them 'leads' is pretty well knocked on the head. Like a few cards, sir?"

We took some cards, and very queer productions they are, all with a sort of family likeness to each other, and appointing meetings for the benefit of some unfortunate person who has either been sent to prison, or is in hospital, or has a lost wife or child and wants money to bury them. Each card is usually headed with a few lines of doggerel; for instance:—

"Stretch forth your hand as a brother,
Remember that life's but a span,
'Tis our duty to help one another
And do a good turn when we can,"

which appears to be a great favourite. Then follows an announcement that, "A friendly lead will take place on Monday next, at the Spotted Boar, Colchester Street, Whitechapel, for the benefit of Bridgett Shea, who has been laid up with a bad hand, and needs your kind assistance. Chairman, Little Teddy; vice, Ike Oakley; conductor, Young Mad Tom. The smallest donation thankfully received! Sometimes the phrase as to the "bad hand," which may be interpreted as conveying graceful allusion to certain gyves vulgarly known as handcuffs, is more or less varied. "William Cole, better known as Nubley," simply announces himself as "in trouble." "James Green " is "in a difficulty." Somebody else has "had a misfortune."

The precise extent of the misfortune of "Charles Wigg, better known as Bummy," is indicated by a statement that he "has been laid up for six months;" but most of the beneficiaries merely announce that they "need your kind assistance" without entering into details.

Then there are the appeals on behalf of those whose crime is not moral, but, like that of the inhabitants of "Erewhen," actually physical. "John Limber, better known as Jack Knifey," has "suffered from a long illness, and has a bad leg, which prevents him from following his employment." "Knifey" appears, like Messrs. Moses and Son, to keep a private poet, who is just the reverse of the modern poets whose grammar is perfect and their sentiment unintelligible. In this case the grammar is unintelligible and the sentiment obvious:-

"You Muses assist me, and lend me your aid;
Tis for poor Knifey, a good-hearted blade.
He needs your kind assistance, to
his friends now he write,
He hopes you'll gather round him on this
night with a good heart's delight."

One likes to see how the lines grow longer and longer, as if expanding with the poet's sympathies, until at last the slowest Alexandrine would not be long enough to express his feelings.

Then there are lead cards for Andrew Marshall, "who has unfortunately met with an accident while dancing;" for a lady who has a "smashed toe;" for "the aged parents of John Whybra, who was unfortunately drowned;" for the funeral expenses of children, husbands, wives, and so on. We were unable to be present at one of these leads, but from all we could learn about them there seems to be no doubt that they afford opportunities for the display of much of that mutual helpfulness of the poor, which is so general, and that the contributions of the friends in proportion to their means are often enormous. It may seem odd that this generosity should require strains of a fiddle to evoke it; but after all, in another class of life there are such things as fancy fairs, and contributions for the most worthy object are often only forthcoming under the pleasing titillation of a fashionable preacher. However, if our friend the dwarf may be credited, the days of leads are doomed, for under the new act the publicans fear lest the notes of music should imperil their license — a license which does not permit the tripping of "many twinkling feet " on the sanded floor.

It is astonishing how early the streets in the east become quiet. Here, perhaps, there is some altercation, generally ending amicably, between a policeman and a more or less drunken sailor, and there a man is cursing his wife for drinking his earnings and interfering with his work. If the Education Act had been a little longer in existence, he would probably describe her as

"An Evil Genius, all his plans deriding.
Doubling his troubles, and his cash dividing."

As it is, he is obliged to stigmatise her in language which could only be reported by an extensive use of blanks.

Abstaining from taking part in this domestic difference, we pass on to a great lodging house in the neighbourhood of Ratcliff Highway. The ground floor is occupied by 40 or 50 men who are smoking their pipes or cooking their supper. Thursday is, it should be remarked, rather too near the end of the week to admit of the repast being very luxurious. Those men that earn regular wages generally have them paid on Friday or Saturday, and on those days, they will bargain with the butcher for some "stickings," or will even give a shilling for a pound of steak. But this style of living cannot be kept up throughout the week, and we saw little but bread and tea in course of consumption on the occasion of our visit.

All round the room are lockers for clothes and other property. You may hire one of these lockers for 5d. and have 4d. of that sum returned on giving back the key. This seems at first rather an elaborate way of paying a penny; but, of course, it is meant to prevent the loss or the theft of the key. For a bed 3d. has to be paid, and we ascend into a big room for single men, which contains 23 beds. It has been newly whitewashed — every bedroom in a lodging house under inspection is whitewashed in April and October — and appears pretty clean. The Sergeant turns down a counterpane, and, as far as can be seen, no small game is to be found in this covert. The sheets are dingy, as might be expected from the occupations of the people who tenant them and their imperfect appreciation of the virtues of soap and water; and, considering too, that these sheets have always to serve for a fortnight, and, frequently, it was admitted, for a month, there was nothing to shock one; and the ventilation was so good that an old gentleman in spectacles who was reading in bed in the middle of the room complained of the draught, and expressed his decided preference for breathing air warmed in other people's lungs rather than that coming direct from the winds of heaven.

From this we went to the quarters of the married people, each pair of whom were in a sort of box something like the high pews in vogue before the days of ecclesiastical restorations, the sides being carried up to the height of 7ft. or so but admitting a free current of air to pass over them. For each of these boxes a charge of 6d. a night is made, and the use of fire and of hot water ad libitum, in the kitchen below, is thrown into the bargain.

The lodgers in this house are of almost every class. That old man, without shirt or coat, and stretching bare arms through his waistcoat as he deals greasy cards on the table, is a general "cadger," doing a day's work at the docks occasionally, but not very often. He is playing at "twenty-fives," the favourite card game of these people. That stripling with a ferret-like face has been "in trouble" once or twice but earns a pretty regular living now as a "long-shore" man. As for the burly man in the corner who is cracking jokes to an admiring party round him, nobody knows how he keeps himself. He has had plenty of ups and downs, and just now is the time for the downs, but he evidently bears his misfortunes cheerily. Numbers of the company are known to our guides, not, for the most part, as guilty of any grave crime, but possibly as having upon one or two occasions in their lives transgressed the limit which separates the "drunk" from the "drunk and disorderly." But if we are to get on to the gaffs and the opium smoking, we must quit our friends in the kitchen.

It was an abrupt change from the lodging houses of the waifs and strays of society to that most gorgeous place of entertainment, the Cambridge Music Hall, Commercial Street East. We emerged from a nest of dimly lighted courts and wretched alleys to find ourselves in a wide thoroughfare, with large houses, conspicuous among which was this the favourite resort of the more aristocratic of the Eastenders. The interior of the hall is singularly handsome and elaborately decorated, there is a stage of ample proportions, and the entertainment seemed popular enough to ensure a very good "house." A glee was being sung — and very well sung — as we entered and was encored with much applause and jingling of glasses. It was the well-known "Men of Harlech." Then came a lady of exceedingly prepossessing appearance, who figured in the bill as Miss Minnie Howard, and who sang so many songs, appeared in so many different costumes, and danced so many fearful and wonderful breakdowns in such a very short time, that the impression of the performance which is left upon one's memory Is somewhat blurred and confused by the versatility of her talents. Here, as elsewhere, Offenbach's music was predominant, and the Gendarme's song, from "Genevieve de Brabant," found especial favour with the audience.

Quitting these halls of dazzling light, we drove to a public house which is one of the great resorts of the foreign sailors, especially the Germans, whose ships are in the Pool or the Docks. A conspicuous notice, in German, warned us that knives must not be taken into the dancing saloon, but left with the landlady at the bar. "A delicate way of saying that no eating is allowed there?" we inquired. "No, sir, a delicate way of saying that no stabbing is allowed there; for it doesn't take much to make a quarrel, and if you get 20 or 30 foreign sailors in a room, each with a bowie-knife hanging by a lanyard at his side, you may have two or three dead men on the floor before you know where you are. But take their sting away, and they can't do much harm."

The fair partners of Hans and Fritz at this special place had the reputation, we were informed, of being especially fashionable by reason of the lowness of their dresses, and we had been prepared to avert our eyes from a sight like that which, on a memorable occasion, gave rise to Archbishop Whately's joke. "Did your grace ever see anything like that?" was the shocked inquiry. "Never since I was weaned," was the reply, which being archiepiscopal may of course be quoted. But our apprehensions were relieved, for Moll and Sue were not nearly so *decolletees* as scores of the most refined people whom one sees every night in West End ballrooms, and their demeanour was irreproachable.

A dead set is now being made against dancing among the lower classes, and it is quite possible that there may be special evils which are more or less fostered by it. But here at least there seemed to be real enjoyment and hearty fun without any *arriere pensee*; and one cannot help doubting whether anything is gained by stopping the fiddles. Just at present Jack is not educated up to the pitch of spending his time in port in reading *Good Words* and the *Leisure Hour*. It would, of course, be a very good thing if, after passing his day in discharging cargo in foul-smelling docks, he was to occupy his evening in improving his mind in the ii "fok'sle" of his ship by the light of a halfpenny dip. But the fact is, that after his day's work he wants his evening's amusement; and if you shut him out of places where publicity is to a great extent a check on vice, he will betake himself to far worse resorts. I wonder whether the experiment has been ever tried of providing entertainments at a "Sailors' Home" which are within the limits of Jack's capacity. The introduction of dancing would probably be rather too bold a step; for there would be a difficulty as to the character of some of the partners, which could scarcely be surmounted by the issue of vouchers from lady patronesses of Ratcliff Highway.

But when you look at an average Mechanics' Institute or Working Men's Club, very dingily and drearily respectable, and compare it with the brilliantly lighted gin palace, or the saloon where the fiddles are making a merry noise, you cannot wonder that the dullness of the one is less attractive than the cheerfulness of the other. And before we close all places of entertainment that we are pleased to consider unhealthy to morals it would be well to devise some substitute; otherwise, we drive people from dancing, which may possibly lead to vice, to vice itself, and this is scarcely a gain.

When we arrived at Bluegate Fields and saw for ourselves what "home" means there, we could scarcely be astonished that the inhabitants were not very domestic in their habits. Here is a court of which half is, fortunately, sentenced to be pulled down as unfit for habitation, and which is reeking with a smell foul enough to engender any amount of zymotic disease. Its owner has "left his country for his country's good," and during his seven years' absence the trustees have allowed the property to fall into such a state of dilapidation that the parochial authorities have at last stepped in and condemned it. But in part of it, people are living still.

A little farther is another court, in which the houses appear just as bad, if not worse. But this belongs to a leading vestryman. We enter one of the houses and knock at the door of a room. It is opened willingly, for the inmate sees in our coming the chance of getting something towards paying for tomorrow's breakfast. The room is just about six feet square, and one can only just stand upright in it. A young man of 18 is asleep on the floor. It is his mother who has admitted us, an old woman whose features are sadly thin and careworn. The son does a day's work at the docks or along shore — when he can get it — but he has no regular employment. The mother now and then earns a few pence by begging. For this, their sole room, they pay a shilling a week. The rain drives in through the rickety casement, but this, they think, cannot be helped. They are too miserable to express any discontent.

Not so a respectable-looking woman in the next room, with a handsome son of about four years old asleep on the bed. She points to the places in the crazy ceiling where the rain comes through almost everywhere, and heartily wishes that "they" would pull the house down. "And if they did where would she go?" Well, she couldn't say; anyhow she couldn't go to a worse place than that. In this we agreed with her.

Not far off we reached an opium smoking establishment, which is said to be exceedingly popular among the Chinese and Lascar sailors, who are frequently to be found here in parties of 12 or 15, intoxicating themselves with the fumes of that most fascinating of drugs. Unluckily, however, there are scarcely any of these sailors in the port of London at the present time, so that we were unable to be present at one of these symposia. The only occupant of the room was the proprietor, a swarthy Asiatic, who smoked as if years had not palled the sense of ecstatic enjoyment which the habit is said to produce.

A little bit of the opium, which is just like treacle in appearance, is heated at the end of a needle in the flame of a spirit lamp, and is then placed in a huge pipe, specially constructed to keep it alight as long as possible, inasmuch as it only burns with great difficulty, and the pipe must be replenished every three or four minutes. The smoker inhales all the fumes, which seem, however, to ooze gradually out of him and to impregnate the atmosphere of the room so thoroughly that a stay of less than a quarter of an hour is quite enough to give one a queer sensation like that induced by ones first inspiration of chloroform.

From this we went to a rival establishment of which Sally Graham, the old woman described in Dickens's "Edwin Drood," is the proprietress. In this, too, we heard complaints of the badness of trade from the want of ships from China, and Sally and her husband were the only smokers. Sally assured us that though, having been a hard drinker in her youth, she had been able to give up drinking entirely, she found herself utterly unable to give up opium smoking. "Perhaps you've been under the 'lectric machine," she said, "and have felt your nerves a-working. Well, whenever I leaves off the smoking my nerves is all 'on the work' just similar, and so I goes on again. Yes, all on the work and all on the shake, that's how it is. And I've done it 21 year, and it's no good a-trying nothing fresh now."

"Where are the white mice?" inquires the Inspector. "Why you used to have scores of them running about the room and over the bed." "Ah, we're poor now, and them few little darlings up there is all we've got. And this ain't a right pipe, this ain't. This is a pipe as I made out of an ink bottle, and very hard it is to get a hole made in the side of a ha'penny ink bottle without breakin' of it. But there's a man as comes here, a tinker, and he has the tools for borin' 'em, and he'll allus do it for me," and she sucked away at her ink bottle, and ladled the opium out of a little spoon, and gave little jerky laughs of enjoyment which seemed to show that even the strong narcotic could not quite still that nervous "working" of which she had told us. "And his cough is bad, very bad," she said, pointing to her husband, a very handsome half-caste, who lay on the straw paliasse dreamily contemplating us, and who was, we heard, in an advanced stage of consumption.

On a shelf were the white mice, and there was a string down which they ran from it to the floor and over the bed. The only decent piece of furniture in the room was a clock which she pointed out to us with pride as having been preserved when all the rest had gone to the pawnbroker. "It was once meant for him to take to sea, " she said; and even the effects of the opium could not quite conceal the pathos of an utterance which plainly showed how well she knew that the only journey which he could ever take must be to that unknown country from which there is no returning.

Leaving the court of opium smokers, we trudged along wretched alleys, past dilapidated tenements, till we arrived at a little square, where a blaze of light in one house told us that something special was going on. We approached and found ourselves at the door of a small room, richly decorated with prints and paintings and crockery shepherdesses, which covered the walls, and with flowers, which lined the wainscoting.

A girl of singularly prepossessing appearance, and of very modest address, invited us to enter, and when we did so we found that one side of the apartment was occupied by — a coffin. It was a wake. The dead man, a fine young fellow of 25, who had been stabbed in a sailors' quarrel a fortnight before, and had died in hospital, was the girl's lover, and it was she who had rescued the corpse from the indignity of burial by the parish and had assembled her friends to honour the occasion. They had had one of those "leads" of which I spoke yesterday to aid her in defraying the funeral expenses and had thus collected 45s. And this girl, with the corpse of her lover in the room, sat through the livelong night, happy in the thought that she expressed in this tangible way her firm affection for the dead. She and her friends the "wakers" told us the story with much rude pathos, and then we left reverently with rather a choking sensation in our throats.

This is another illustration of how the poor stand by one another, and how much they will sacrifice to keep themselves or their friends from parish aid. If children are left orphans, it is the commonest thing, we were told — especially if their parents were popular in the court in which they lived — that they should be adopted by people almost on the border of pauperism, who take this additional burden on themselves for sheer love of doing a good thing.

I have already said something of the extent to which the thieves at large help those who come under the strong arm of the law; and the fact of a man's being "wanted" is a sure passport to the aid of his friends.

In Ireland, a couple of years ago, a regular business of getting food and lodging for nothing was established by a class of loafers who went round to the small farmers and represented themselves as being hunted down by the police. They were, of course, enthusiastically welcomed, and it was not until they had carried the game rather too far that it was discovered that they had never done anything to bring them within the pale of the law — except, perhaps, having obtained board and lodging under false pretences; and for this, under the circumstances, they could scarcely be prosecuted. It is probable that a pseudo-thief would be entertained in the same way in Whitechapel, though it may be that the people there are connoisseurs in roguery sufficiently acute to distinguish the real from the spurious article.

I should weary some of your readers and disgust others if I were to attempt to describe some of our visits. It would certainly weary them if I were to narrate our experiences behind the scenes of three or four theatres. That region, to which it is always the great desire of your country cousin to penetrate, and which he invests in his imagination with a halo of brilliancy, is really exceedingly uninteresting. Put that country cousin against a newly painted "set," with a fairy of forty asking him to stand a treat, and a swearing sceneshifter thrusting a plank into his stomach, and he will feel, and rightly feel, that his land of enchantment has vanished, and that he is in a place where a serious business is being carried on in a serious way, and where he is an interloper. Here, then our experience was neither novel nor amusing, and an account of a certain round of visits which we paid afterwards would be too revolting for publication. Being bent, not from mere curiosity, on exploring the east, we thought it worthwhile to do so thoroughly, even at the expense of some shock to our senses of delicacy. But as to this part of our peregrination it is best to be silent.

Of course, the thing would not be complete without a supper in the east to finish up with. Need it be said that we went to "Dick's," the celebrity of whose establishment extends from Barking to Custom house Quay, and whose eel soup is unequalled. On this point I agree with Mr. Frank Buckland. It was excellent, with very small taste of fish, but not at all unlike that *"potage a la bonne femme"* which figures on a good many menus. What the price of this soup was l am unable to say. I only know that we had two basins of it, and that the bill for the entire banquet, including five bottles of lemonade, reached the enormous sum of eighteenpence — which was certainly not extravagant. Having indulged in this luxury we reached our place of rest before 4 a.m. and slept the sleep of the blest after our night in Whitechapel.

Morning Post – 7th & 8th October 1872.

1873 – FALL OF A CHURCH DOME.

On Wednesday morning at four o'clock the dome of the church of St. Boniface, Union Street, Whitechapel, fell in with a fearful crash. The neighbourhood around were much alarmed, and were afraid the shock was the result of an earthquake, but happily such was not the case. The building has seen some strange vicissitudes. First a music hall; then a Baptist, or some other sectional, chapel; finally, a Roman Catholic church, and now a heap of ruins. We understand it is intended to raise on the site a building worthy of the denomination to which the original church belonged.

East London Observer – 3rd May 1873.

1873 – GREAT FIRE IN THE WHITECHAPEL ROAD.

A red sky down East, at such a time of night as does not find London asleep, is sure to draw crowds in the direction of the lurid glare; and, following the beacon, throngs of people from all parts of the town converged on Friday night on that put of the Whitechapel Road in which the plain brown brick parish church is situate. The fire that broke out opposite that church, in one of the numerous courts leading off the broad foot pavement on the northern side, proved in a short time terribly destructive.

The place, which is called Size Yard, is, or was, occupied by three large industrial establishments — Mr. Thomas Little's building and timber yard, Mr. George Brown's cabinet manufactory, and Messrs. Davidson and Sons' waste paper warehouse. Whether on these last-named premises, or in the stables at the rear of Mr. Little's yard, the fire broke out could not be ascertained; but there is little doubt that it had been smouldering for some time before its visible outbreak, at a few minutes past ten o'clock; and then the old and disgracefully common complaint of a want of water was heard for at least twenty minutes before so much as a pailful could be obtained.

Meanwhile the flames were getting such a hold on the inflammable materials that it was plain they must burn themselves out, and that the only thing left for the firemen, working gallantly under one of the chief superintendents of the Metropolitan Brigade, Mr. Gatehouse, was to isolate the disaster and save as much of the surrounding property as possible.

Scarcely had all the engines, from the newest and most approved of the steam apparatus to the parochial hand-pumping machines, which are still found serviceable, been got to work, before the roof of Mr. Little's premises fell in; and the sight gained by mounting on the piles of timber, and looking through the openings as the volcano within, was grand beyond description.

By directing copious streams of water on the wooden planking, piled on end in such a manner as to threaten a vast augmentation of the blaze, the firemen succeeded in saving a large amount of valuable property, which, had it caught fire, would have endangered the neighbourhood. Hemmed in by a close network of courts and alleys at the back, Size Yard was the very place to have been amply supplied with water and good watchmanship.

One of the courts or alleys in question was Montague Place, a very poor and teeming spot of ground, despite its rather aristocratic name. Here the sight was pitiable, for the hardworking inhabitants, many of them German sugar bakers, had brought out their household goods, which were being spoiled, or rendered useless for a time, by the water and the falling sparks. A poor woman in a corner house, close against the brick wall on the other side of which the flames were raging, had but just given birth to a child; and she and her infant were removed in haste to a neighbouring place of safety.

The Czarewitch and a distinguished party, who had been to inspect the Sailors' Home, at an early period of the day, were looked for with great eagerness by those bystanders who had got an eligible position near the entrance of Size Yard. If his Imperial Highness came at all, it must have been when the flames had exhausted themselves, and there was very little for him to see except the smouldering ruins.

By midnight the fire had been got well under, and all apprehension of its spreading was at an end. The poor sugar bakers and other inhabitants of Montague Place might have gone to rest without dread of further alarm. They, however, lingered outside their close and oppressive dwellings long after the redness in the sky had cooled down to a dull murky purple tint, and the only spark showers and flame and smoke came from the steam engines. Still, the body of flame left in possession of the building was fierce enough to need subduing, and it was many hours before the fire was extinguished.

Nottinghamshire Guardian – 18th July 1873.

1873 – A ROOFTOP DISCOVERY.

A fresh dose of horror is served up this morning from Whitechapel in the announcement of the finding of a human head on a roof in Whitechapel. The owner of the house, No. 3, Mill Yard, Whitechapel, was examining a leak in the roof when he discovered a basket containing the skull of an adult, with half the scalp attached. He at once placed it in the hands of the police. The finder has occupied the house for several years, and he states that he was last on the roof in 1871.

Globe – 17th September 1873.

1875 – SUICIDE IN WHITECHAPEL WORKHOUSE.

An inquiry took place on Monday, before Mr. Humphreys, Coroner, in the Board Room of the Whitechapel Workhouse, relative to the death of Rebecca Davis, aged 26 years, who committed suicide by cutting her throat on Thursday last.

The circumstances connected with the case were of a painful nature. The deceased, a member of the Hebrew persuasion, resided with her husband, who also belongs to that faith, at 5, Union Court, Spitalfields, and had been confined in Colney Hatch Lunatic Asylum for mania. On the 20th ultimo she attacked her husband by stabbing him, and he was in consequence obliged to be removed to the London Hospital. She was then charged by the police with cutting and wounding him, but on the certificate of the divisional surgeon, Dr. Phillips, she was removed to the lunatic ward of the above union.

Being the time of the Passover, when the removal took place, it was intended merely to detain her in the union until it had passed, and then to send her again to Colney Hatch. Upon her admission to the union, which, on account of her violence, could only be effected by the united efforts of five policemen, she was placed in a ward with seventeen other patients, most of whom, according to the evidence, were aged and imbecile, and it was stated she used to run up and down the apartment, at the same time striking her head against the wails.

About a quarter to eleven o'clock on Thursday morning last she asked to be allowed to clean the taps of a sink where the work of cleaning the knives and other articles was performed, and about three minutes afterwards was observed to be bleeding. The attendant, thinking that the blood proceeded from deceased's nose, procured some water for the purpose of bathing it, and she then discovered it arose from a wound in the throat. Dr. Ilott, the resident medical officer, was immediately summoned, and that gentleman on seeing the deceased pronounced life to be extinct, death being due to haemorrhage consequent on an incised wound in the throat, which had cut through the windpipe and the whole of the arteries on the left side.

Miss Wright, the paid attendant, and the person who had charge of this ward, stated that the knives used by the patients at dinner were placed in a box, which she kept locked in her own room. She was unable to account for the deceased having obtained possession of the knife, which belonged to the house.

Another witness, one of the pauper keepers in the ward mentioned, named Reed, was also unable to state by what means the knife was procured by the deceased; but another keeper, named Smith, stated that the box had been kept in the ward after the knives had been used, and that it was her duty to clean them near the spot al which the knife was found.

The Coroner having commented on the case, the Jury, after a brief consultation, returned a verdict that the deceased committed suicide whilst of unsound mind.

East London Observer – 8th May 1875.

1875 – THE SENTENCING OF HENRY WAINWRIGHT.

On Wednesday the prisoners Henry and Thomas Wainwright were placed in the dock at the Central Criminal Court at ten o'clock, when the Lord Chief Justice commenced the summing up.

The Judge, after remarking on the close and unflagging attention which the Jury had given to the case, said they started with a fact of primary importance— that on the 11th of September the prisoner Henry Wainwright was found in possession of the mangled remains of a body that had been severed by some rough instrument, that those remains had been recently taken from a grave on the prisoner's premises, and that the death of the person whose remains they were had been occasioned by pistol shots.

The Jury would have to inquire whether the life thus taken by foul means was taken by the prisoner. There could be no doubt in this case that the life

Fig. 12. Scenes from the Case (Penny Illustrated Paper)

was taken by violence; the question for the Jury was whether it was the prisoner by whose hands that life was taken. Incidentally, another point was as to the identity of the person murdered; for, although the law held a man responsible for the life of the stranger, yet if the identity was established then the existence of some motive for the crime became essential.

The question therefore of whether the remains, in this case, were those of Harriet Louisa Lane, was of very great importance. The evidence to establish the identity was twofold—partly direct, consisting of marks on the missing woman and portions of her clothing, and partly circumstantial, consisting of the facts and history of the case. Every event in the case was important, and he would now trace the circumstances that had been proved.

Considering, first, the narrative of Harriet Lane's association with Henry Wainwright, her bearing children to him, going by his assumed name, as his wife, and living at lodgings which he took for her, he (the Judge) found that everything appeared to be comfortable between them up to May 20th of this year, when the story entered a new phase. On that date Harriet Lane pawned her wedding ring, and from that time until September she parted with everything she could dispose of. It did not appear that the prisoner had ever an intention of deserting the woman, and they must look for the cause of the change that occurred early this year in the alteration that had taken place in his circumstances.

Up to the end of 1873, Henry Wainwright appeared to have carried on a successful business. Whether from extravagance or from those losses which would occur in trade, he was pressed by his creditors and obliged to have recourse to liquidation. On May 15th a meeting of creditors took place, and it was resolved to accept a composition of 12s in the pound in three instalments, the first of 6s, to be paid within one week. The papers showed that the amount of his debts was £3,250, besides a considerable debt to his brother William. The first dividend was not paid until July, and the prisoner was, therefore, in a state of great pecuniary difficulty. He had to keep up his own establishment in Tredegar Square, where his wife and five children lived, and, moreover, he had to keep the unfortunate Harriet Lane, who, having before been maintained by his liberality, or it might be extravagance, in a condition of comparative comfort, upon an allowance of £5 a week, appeared to have had no disposition to have recourse to her own industry to support herself and her children.

The prisoner, in these difficulties, apparently did not go near Harriet Lane from May to September, although he sent to her; although she knew his place of business, and was there, according to Mrs.

Rogers, more than twenty times. Scenes of anger and recrimination occurred between her and Wainwright. Rogers and his wife spoke to one remarkable time, when an altercation ended in the prisoner writing a letter threatening to commit suicide, and Mrs. King full fainting on the floor. The defence suggested that those witnesses had committed perjury; but he (the Judge) saw nothing to show that the Rogers had committed such an atrocious crime and accepting the story as true it proved the unfortunate position of the two parties.

There could be no doubt that Harriet Lane was a heavy burden to him, and that she was in his estimation a constant source of danger. He had not enough to satisfy her; she was clamorous and apt to be ill-tempered. He was, therefore, living on the edge of a volcano both in respect to his domestic life and his public life. Whether all these circumstances afforded anything like an adequate motive for taking the life of the unfortunate woman was a point upon which the Jury must exercise their judgment. Undoubtedly in August, or early in September, the prisoner desired to get her out of the apartments at Mrs. Foster's and place her somewhere else – to make some arrangements which might pacify if they did not satisfy her.

This, his Lordship remarked, introduced a curious episode, which had been called the Frieake episode. Without throwing any reflection upon Mrs. Foster, she did not appear to be the most intelligent witness they had had. But Humphreys proved that the prisoners were at his house on the 5th of September, when Thomas Wainwright took out two bottles of champagne. This was the same night that Mrs. Foster borrowed champagne glasses because "Mr. Frieake" had called to see Mrs. King (alias Miss Lane). It was also that night in the week (Saturday) when Thomas Wainwright would have least difficulty in getting away from business early. Whoever "Mr. Frieake" was, he had been introduced to Mrs. King by Henry Wainwright and the latter's letter of September 5th said, "E.F. would call upon her that evening." What was the motive of this introduction of Mr. Frieake to Mrs. King? This was one of the most mysterious parts of the case.

The prosecution suggested that having resolved to murder the woman and fearing he would be thought responsible for her disappearance, he had concocted a plan which would lead her friends to suppose she had gone off with another man. Was no other theory admissible? He (the Judge) thought there was. Henry Wainwright might have desired to assist her by some scheme whereby she might obtain her future subsistence, and she might have required some substantial guarantee that she would bs aided—for instance, in a millinery business, until she could carry it on alone.

If Henry proposed his brother as such guarantee, she would have laughed him to scorn; but she would have been satisfied with the name of Mr. Frieake, whom she knew to be a respectable man, and a friend of Henry Wainwright. Another hypothesis was that Henry might have got his brother to assume this name, without any intention of carrying out his promise of help to her, but merely to pacify her for the time. Her letter to Mr. Frieake led him (the Judge) to the conclusion that some scheme had been proposed to her, to which he had not been willing at first to accede, but having well considered it, she wrote that if he and ''Harry'' would come again, "things might be satisfactorily arranged." Was this scheme proposed *bona fide*, or with the intention of deceiving her, but to pacify her for the time? Either theory was consistent with the evidence. Some scheme was surely contemplated, for, if Mrs. King was going into any business she would want to be somewhat free from the children, and on the 3rd of August negotiations were opened with Miss Wilmore by Henry Wainwright to take a house jointly with Mrs. King. Miss Wilmore declined to do that but undertook the charge of the children.

At that time could the Jury suppose a plan had been formed for a murder to be committed, and for Thomas Wainwright afterwards to cover her disappearance in the name of Frieake? If not, then the charge against him of being accessory before the fact failed. The disturbance in the street led to Mrs. King receiving notice to leave her lodgings. She could not go on September 9th, when the notice expired, because she had not paid what she owed; but on the 10th Wainwright had got some money and given it to her, with which she redeemed her things out of pawn, paid her bills, and bought, among other things, some buttons for her dress, of which two remained over, and were put in a stay box. When she left Sidney Square on the 11th with a nightdress only. she undoubtedly thought she had some future, if not a brilliant one, before her. She must have told Miss Wilmore what her prospects were; but unfortunately, our rules of evidence, which sometimes stood sadly in the way of the investigation of truth, prevented it being stated what she had said. They could infer, however, what she did not say. It was clear that she was not going a long distance, and that her stay was not to be protracted; she could not have been going to Brighton, for Miss Wilmore's exclamation on hearing the story was, "Why, she has got no clothes." What became of her?

Undoubtedly a body was buried on Henry Wainwright's premises, which corresponded in many particulars with Harriet Lane, a body which by a singular coincidence the prisoner exhumed and removed on the anniversary of the day that Harriet Lane disappeared. Between those two dates came the inquiries by Miss Wilmore and Mrs. King's friends as to what had become of her. Henry Wainwright first said he had given her money for an outfit and she had gone away, and yet only just before he had found it difficult to provide her with money enough to leave Sidney Square, since she had had to borrow £2 from Miss Wilmore. Subsequently his story was that she had gone away with his friend Edward Frieake. Then followed the letter in that name, which was undoubtedly written by Thomas Wainwright. If the letter was a false one, it was most craftily devised to stop enquiries. On receiving it Miss Wilmore went to Henry Wainwright, who showed her a similar letter. Then followed the telegram saying that Frieake and Harriet Lane had gone to Paris. That also was taken to Henry Wainwright by Miss Willmore, and he produced a similar one. It was not material from whom these telegrams came. The letter undoubtedly came from Thomas Wainwright, but the telegrams might not; but they were part of a plan to lead Mrs. King's relations to believe that she had gone off with Teddy Frieake.

So, matters remained until at the suggestion of Mrs. Taylor the witness Eeles, who is a kind of detective officer, took up the enquiry. On the 16th January, he had an interview with Wainwright, who reiterated the story as to Mrs. King having gone to Paris with Teddy Frieake. Subsequently, Mr. Eeles had an interview with Mr. Freake, the auctioneer, who entirely repudiated all knowledge of Harriet Lane or Mrs. King and accompanied Eeles to Wainwright's place to have the matter explained. An interview took place, and then Wainwright said, "It is not you, it is another Frieake whom I have met in Purcell's and at the Nell Gwynne," and then further described the man as about 24, with no whiskers, but a slight moustache, who had lately come into a fortune. So, the matter ends, but on reaching home Mr. Freiake talks the matter over with his family, and then the letter which he received in the early part of the year, signed "H. King," is thought of and after a search discovered.

Eeles and the father of Harriet Lane wait upon Wainwright once more, and showed him the letter, but he still sticks to his story. It is for you to decide whether his story is true or not. If there be another Frieake it is curious that he does not come forward, for if in almost any part of the *globe* he must know the peril to which Henry Wainwright is now exposed, and from which his simple testimony could deliver him. Besides, if the other Freiake were in the habit of frequenting certain billiard rooms, nothing would be easier than to produce someone who knew him as an habitue. Such evidence has not been produced, and you must draw your own conclusions as to why it has not. It is true, as the learned counsel for the prisoners said, that it is for the prosecution to have negatived the existence of this Frieake, and that until they have negatived his existence you are bound to assume it is a fact. For certain good reasons it is true the prosecution have to prove everything necessary to establish the guilt of the accused; but when they have made out a *prima facie* case, when they have shown that there are grounds to believe that stratagem, deceit and falsehood have been resorted to for the purpose of concealing guilt, and when the whole superstructure which they have built upon that foundation is capable of being shivered to atoms in a moment by the production of some proof which it is in the power of the accused to give, you may reasonably expect that he will meet the case which has been brought against him by the production of that proof, which would immediately clear him of such accusation.

We now come more specifically to the charge of murder against Henry Wainwright. The inquiries after Harriet Lane were discontinued some time in 1875, but all the while they were going on, the body of a woman was lying in a grave in the back premises of 215, Whitechapel Road, silently undergoing a process of decay which would render its identification all but impossible. There it might have remained, but Henry Wainwright's pecuniary embarrassments forced him to mortgage the premises to a client of Mr. Behrens and seeing in July that proceedings in bankruptcy had been instigated against Henry Wainwright, Mr. Behrens took possession of the premises in the name of his client. A man named Francis, and subsequently a Mrs. Izzard were put in possession, and the latter remained until August 22nd. During this time the prisoner could of course do nothing towards removing the remains, though he had a key to the premises.

Now, it so happened that at this time Thomas Wainwright had in his premises in the Borough a cellar opening out of a larger one, the passage from one to the other being by means of a hole knocked in the wall. In the farther and smaller cellar there was a quantity of earth, altogether three cart loads, though how it came there we have no evidence to prove. It became necessary for Henry Wainwright to remove the remains from the Whitechapel Road, and it appears to have struck him that this cellar of his brother's would afford a convenient hiding place for them. Before doing so it was necessary to divide the body into small portions for convenience of carriage. To aid him in this work be bought the axe, also the spade and chopper, and in addition purchased some American cloth wherein to wrap the pieces of the mutilated body.

Then comes the conversation with Stokes as to the selling of the spade and chopper to Mr. Martin,

a circumstance which seems to tell somewhat in favour of the prisoner, as, on the supposition of his guilt he would hardly have been likely to have offered the instruments which he had been using to dismember the body for public sale. The day after this conversation— that is, on Saturday – Wainwright asked Stokes to assist him in carrying two parcels from No. 215 to the Borough. Stakes consented, and the two proceeded to the premises, where Wainwright produced the two parcels from under some straw, where he had, he remarked, placed them a fortnight before — an obvious untruth, as the American cloth in which they were wrapped had only been purchased some 24 hours previously. Then Wainwright directed Stokes' attention to the spade and chopper, and the latter remarked on the offensive nature of the matter adhering to them. Then came the journey to the Borough, the discovery made by Stokes of the contents of the parcels, the meeting with Alice Day, and the arrest of her and of Wainwright by the police, who, on examining the parcels, found the contents to consist of mutilated human remains. The police then, on hearing from Stokes that the parcels had come from 215, Whitechapel Road, proceeded thither, when the discovery of the grave and of the chloride of lime was made.

At this point the court adjourned for luncheon,

Upon re-assembling after luncheon, the Lord Chief Justice briefly referred to the statement made by Henry Wainwright at the police office, explaining how he came into possession of the parcels, and pointed out that that statement was utterly untrue. He then passed on to consider how the person whose remains he had been dealing with had come by her death. Two bullets were found in the brain and one in the hair-pad, and the throat had been cut. It struck him that the probability was that the murderer came up from behind and fired a shot at the back of the head. The hair-pad prevented the entrance of the bullet which, however, stunned her. Then, finding the shot had not taken effect, the murderer fired again behind the ear. The action of the heart had probably stopped before the throat was cut, and therefore there would be little or no flow of blood. Death having been occasioned by the shots or the knife, or by both together, who was the murderer? The body was found in the possession of Henry Wainwright who was in the act of concealing it; must not, in common sense, the presumption be that he who was thus acting was the murderer, unless he could give a reasonable explanation of circumstances so fraught with suspicion? The presumption was reasonable that the man removing the body from one hiding place to another was the one concerned in the original offence. By our law we could not interrogate a man charged with an offence, nor could he offer on oath evidence which might tell in his favour. But he might call witnesses, and give explanations through them; and, after listening to all the learned counsel had urged in the prisoner's behalf, he (the Judge) had heard no explanation offered in this case, except that the woman committed suicide. But it was clear that that was not so; therefore, the only explanation given for the prisoner fell to the ground.

Was, then, the body found in the possession of Henry Wainwright the death of which had been occasioned by a pistol bullet or bullets, the body of

Harriet Lane or not? The remains corresponded with the description of Harriet Lane in these particulars; the age, about twenty-four; the frame slender; the height 1¼ in. less than Lane's, probable height, a difference accounted for by the shrinking of the tissues and by the drying of the inter-vertebral cartilages; the hair of the same colour; the decayed tooth in the upper jaw; the scar below the right knee, which the surgeons only found after Harriet Lane's father had said his daughter had such a scar; and evidences that the deceased had

Fig. 13. Scenes form the Story (Illustrated Police News)

borne children. All these things put together showed that the body closely corresponded with Harriet Lane.

The second class of evidence as to identity related to the dress. The hair-pad found with the remains corresponded in colour with that which Miss Wilmore assisted Harriet Lane to make. The missing woman wore a velvet band; a velvet band was found in the grave. Two jet buttons were taken out of the ash heap within two yards of the grave; two buttons of a perfect similarity were found in the stay box that had belonged to Harriet Lane. A wedding ring and a keeper were found in the grave; the missing woman wore exactly such rings when she left her lodgings on September 11th.

The indirect evidence of identity arose from all the circumstances of the case, the disappearance of a woman attached to her friends and children, who had not been heard of since, and who, if she was living still, must have come forward to rescue the man with whom she had lived on conjugal relations from the peril of his life. If the Jury should find that the body was that of Harriet Lane, what was the fair and legitimate inference from its having been buried on the prisoner's premises? It was impossible to doubt that the body was buried in that secret place by Henry Wainwright.

The body was covered with chloride of lime, which the prisoner purchased on September 10th. The shots which caused death were those of a revolver, and the prisoner possessed a revolver. As the body was buried at No. 215 the death probably took place there; and three shots fired in rapid succession would most likely be heard by any person working near. The two Kays and young Wiseman might have heard the shots and mistaken the work upon which they were engaged at the time. But at any rate, three shots were fired from a revolver, and the body was buried by Wainwright who had a motive for the disappearance of Harriet Lane. And after she was missed, the prisoner was engaged in a systematic course of deception to cover her absence.

The Jury was now to consider whether the body was that of Harriet Lane; if it was, Harriet Lane was killed by the hand of an assassin; and they must say if they had any honest, reasonable doubt that she fell by the hand of Henry Wainwright.

With regard to Thomas Wainwright, he (the Judge) had already made some observations bearing upon the question of his being an accessory before the fact. As to his being an accessory after the fact—still a serious thing for him—it was clear that he lent himself to a scheme for turning aside enquiry. But the argument urged in his favour, that his brother induced him to aid in stopping the enquiries, telling him the woman had gone off somewhere, he did not know where, might be true; the Jury must say if it was consistent with the evidence. Thomas Wainwright had obtained possession of the key to the premises he had left and lent it to his brother; and he bought the spade and axe for Henry. If he knew for what purpose access to the Hen and Chickens and the tools were required, he would be an accessory after the fact. If he did it under the impression that his brother had got into some scrape, but did not know of the murder, then, although guilty of the gravest indiscretion, he was not guilty of the charge. If they thought he knew of the murder, they must find him guilty.

"Gentlemen of the Jury," concluded the Lord Chief Justice, "the case is now in your hands. Of one thing I am quite certain, and that is that you will discharge your duty to the best of your ability and to the satisfaction of your conscience. You will let the world know that never did a Jury fail in giving more devoted and undivided attention to a case than you have done during this protracted trial, with the desire to arrive at a just and righteous conclusion."

The Jury retired to consider their verdict at a quarter to four o'clock.

The Jury returned into court at twenty-two minutes to five o'clock, and having taken their seats, they were called upon by Mr. Avory, the Clerk of Arraigns, to answer to their names.

This ceremony having been completed. Mr. Avory put the question, "Have you agreed upon your verdict?" to which the formal reply was given, "We have."

Mr. Avory: "Do you find the prisoner, Henry Wainwright, guilty, or not guilty, of the indictment which charges him with wilful murder?"

The Foreman: "We do all say he is guilty."

Mr. Avory: "Do you say that Thomas Wainwright is guilty of being an accessory before or after the fact?"

The Foreman: "Not guilty before; but guilty after."

Mr. Avory: "And that you say is the verdict of you all?"

The Foreman: "It is."

The Lord Chief Justice: "Call upon them."

Mr Avory: "Prisoner at the bar. You have been indicted for the crime of wilful murder, and to that indictment you have pleaded "Not Guilty", and have thrown yourself upon your country, that country has proved you guilty. What have you to say why judgment today should not be pronounced against you?"

The convict Henry Wainwright, who spoke with great firmness and admirable elocution, then said, "I should like to make one or two observations, and they shall be very short indeed. I have first to express my deep obligation for the untiring energy and ability of my counsel during this protracted trial. I thank him and all who have assisted him deeply. My thanks are due to the very many friends who have with such promptitude and alacrity come forward to give their valuable and substantial assistance. I have not been able to reply to all the persons…"

The Lord Chief Justice: "I cannot allow you to make a speech. You can only reply to the question whether you have anything to say why sentence should not be passed."

The Prisoner: "Then I will only say, standing as I do now upon the brink of eternity, and in the presence of the God before whom I shall shortly appear, that I swear that I am not the murderer of the remains found in my possession. I swear that I have never in my life fired a pistol. I swear also that I have not buried these remains, and the proof that I have not exhumed those mutilated remains has been proved before you by witnesses. I have been guilty of great immorality. I have been guilty of many indiscretions, but for the crime of which I have been brought in guilty I leave this dock with a calm and quiet conscience. My Lord, I thank you for your kindness in allowing me to say these few words."

The Lord Chief Justice: "Prisoner at the bar, you have been found guilty, in my opinion, upon the clearest and most convincing evidence of the murder of Harriet Louisa Lane, which has been laid to your charge. No one, I think, who has heard this trial can entertain the slightest shadow of a doubt of your guilt, and I can only deplore that, standing as you surely are upon the brink of eternity, you should have called God to witness the rash assertion which has just issued from your lips. There can be no doubt that you took the life of this poor woman, who had been on the closest and most intimate terms of familiarity and affection with you, who had been the mother of your children. You inveigled her into the lone warehouse. The revolver was not there before, but it must have been taken for the purpose, and with that she was slain. The grave was dug then for her remains, which were those you were removing when arrested, and about that no one can entertain the shadow of a doubt. It was a barbarous, cruel, inhuman, and cowardly act. I do not wish to say anything to aggravate the position in which you stand, nor dwell upon the enormity of your guilt, further than by way of rousing you to a sense of the position which you now occupy, in which the hope of earthly mercy is cut off. The only hope and consolation you can have is in the future, where truth cannot be mistaken, where no assertion of yours will stand you in any stead; though where if you seek for mercy, it must be through sincere repentance for the crime which you have undoubtedly committed. I have to warn you

Fig. 14. Passing the Sentence of Death (Penny Illustrated Paper)

against any delusive hope of mercy here as long as the law exists which says that he who takes the life of a fellow creature with malice aforethought shall answer for it with his own. This is a case to which it would be impossible that mercy could be extended; therefore, prepare for the doom which awaits you. I have now only to pass upon you the dread sentence of the law, which is that you be taken from hence to the place whence you came, thence to a legal place of execution to be there hanged by the neck till you shall be dead, and that your body be buried within the precincts of the gaol in which you shall last be confined after your conviction, and may the Lord have mercy upon your soul."

"Thomas George Wainwright, the Jury have, in my opinion, correctly acquitted you of the heavier crime of having entered into the scheme conceived by your brother with the view to the murder of Harriet Lane. Their opinion, and they have pronounced it by their verdict, is that having become aware of the crime committed by your brother, you lent yourself to assist him in its concealment. No fraternal affection, no regard or sympathy which one brother should have for another can excuse you in the eyes of the law by assisting him in his endeavour to escape from the consequences of justice. Your offence, although lighter, and one far short of being an accessory before the act, is one which ought to be punished with proper severity; for by concealment of such crimes, they have sometimes been perpetrated with impunity, and safety and human life is thereby endangered. I am ready to believe that you were actuated under the influence which your brother had over you, without which you might not have done what you did. I have taken that into consideration, as I believe you to have been his dupe and his tool, and he has, in some degree, your crime to answer for practically, as well as his own. You yielded weakly and wrongly to his influence and his greater age, but although that does not in any way mitigate the character of the offence, I think, on the whole, that justice will not be satisfied with a less punishment than l am about to inflict. The sentence of the Court is that you be imprisoned and kept in penal servitude for seven years."

After the prisoners had been removed from the bar, the Lord Chief Justice said, "I think it right to exercise a power which I have vested in me, sitting here upon this trial, by Act of Parliament, to order that a reward be given from the proper fund to the man Stokes. His conduct and his energy on the occasion of these remains being removed from Whitechapel to the Borough, and his perseverance in following up the cab in which those remains were being conveyed, have in reality led to the discovery of this crime, and the conviction of the offender concerned in it. I shall direct, therefore, that he shall receive from the proper fund the sum of £30."

The Lord Chief Justice, in conclusion, paid a high compliment to the sheriffs and under sheriffs for the excellence of their arrangements during the conduct of the trial.

Nottinghamshire Guardian – 3rd December 1875.

1875 – SUNDAY MORNING IN PETTICOAT LANE.

In the core of the City, on a Sunday morning, there are streets as silent as sepulchres. When you disturb their hush with your echoing footfall, you do not see another human being, except, perhaps, some weary watchman or housekeeper looking down with lacklustre eyes on the bare pavement of the deserted close-shuttered thoroughfares, or into a disused churchless churchyard, walled in, like the bottom of a well, with towering warehouses.

It is startling to cross from that drowsy calm into the brawling bustle of the Aldgate and Whitechapel Jews' quarter.

In and about Houndsditch shops are open and watchmakers are at work, heedless of the chaff upon their screwed-up eyes shouted in at them by filthy young roughs hanging before their windows. Every now and then someone passes with a garment or hat in his hand, or a clothes bag on his back. Phil's Buildings and Cutler Street are choked with buyers and sellers of old clothes – male and female, pouring in and out of the old clothes exchanges like very dirty bees at the entrance of very dingy hives. The atmosphere of those densely thronged marts does not remind one of "spicy breezes blowing soft from Ceylon's isle" – it is redolent of oleaginous malodours of a general dusty, musty, fustiness. And yet what energetic bargaining is going on over the old garments! Though some of them look fit for little else than scarecrows, how voices are raised to seabird screeches, what elegancies of very composite English – Cockneyese plus Irish brogue, Jewish enunciation, and a splutter of foreign gutturals – are exchanged, how arms are pump-handled and fists are clenched in the transfer of these fallen leaves of use and fashion. Some of the chafferers look very much as if they were going to fight. Hard by in their Meeting House the Friends are sitting silent as sleek uncooing doves. London is rich in contrasts. By the bye, do Quaker hats, coats, and breeches ever find their way into Rag Fair? And if so, who buys them to wear again?

On the other side of Houndsditch street sellers are coming with their baskets and their barrows from the fruit market in Duke's Place and Mitre Street. The busiest of the marketing is over; in front of one of the unglazed stores stands a chaise with a white pony, which gleams like moonlight, and a scarlet-lined rug which glows like fire from their contrast to the dinginess of the sloppy, rubbish littered square, on which the gloomy, grimy Synagogue frowns down. The chaise is waiting, I suppose, to carry the storekeeper, with his portly gold chained mother in Israel and black-eyed little children of Israel into the country, but most of his fellow tradesmen and their wives linger in somewhat slovenly undress, as if they expected to do a good bit of business yet in their papered pale golden lemons, their brown walnuts and Brazil nuts, their monkey faced, shaggy haired, cocoanuts, and rocky lumps of conglomerated dates. Some flashily dressed young fellows stand talking before the Jew public houses. Their talk is of business – no mere time, and therefore money wasting chaff. Indeed, everybody in this part of the world seems to want to make a deal of some kind. "Vat do you think of it, Mosshy?" shouts a woman to her husband, who is leaning with his back against the wall on the other side of the street. Mrs. Mosshy has been redeeming a spare five minutes in bargaining for something she had not the slightest intention of buying before the would-be vendor chanced to pass her way, and wishes for the marital approval of her proposed investment.

But Petticoat Lane on Sunday morning will give the most vivid idea of the greed of gain, or the hard struggle to make a living, there is in the neighbourhood I am writing about.

Petticoat Lane on Sunday morning is a very striking but by no means a beautiful sight. It is not the place an Englishman proud of his country would take a foreigner to see, unless he were simply proud of his countrymen's business energy. Cramped Middlesex Street is then crammed with, for the most part, a very frowsy throng. When two persons with clean faces and in moderately decent clothes meet there, they give one another an astonished stare. The one or two burly policemen who stand at corners-black breakwaters in the struggling tides that flow from Whitechapel to Bishopsgate Street, and vice versa, look sulky when a "respectably" dressed person passes them.

"What on earth brings you here, to increase our bother?" they seem to say. "Perhaps, you'll get into a scrimmage, and then what can we do for you, or you do for yourself?"

On the whole, however, the Sunday crowds sidle, with their arms down, through the Lane without breach of the peace, and with a general display of rough good nature; though now and then a sturdy, stubbly-chinned denizen of the locality scowls on the "respectable" intruder on it as if he would like to pitch into him for his impertinence. Stunted squalor, however, rather than sturdiness is the general characteristic of those with whom you most literally rub shoulders in Petticoat Lane. Those who object to contact with the Great Unwashed should give it a wide berth; otherwise, they will feel inclined, like Mr. Pendennis in his dandy days, to take a perfumed bath. Little children, however, manage to get through the crowd without being crunched like snails. Of course, horseplay goes on. A favourite joke, when a jam occurs, is to seize one of the street sellers' barrows which still further block the very narrow street, and drive it like a ploughshare with a wild "Hi! Hi! Hi!" through the obstructing crowd. When these crushes take place, the explorer of the Lane must not be astonished if he should be cannoned through the open doorway or window of a shop, or find a sticky seat on a confectionery barrow.

The way in which both street sellers and shopkeepers expose their goods in a place in which, if an organised dash were made at them, it seems as if it would be impossible for the owners to preserve them from plunder or wanton mischief, is one of the curiosities of London life.

The barrows are freighted with the usual eatables and drinkables, flimsy toys and flimsier gimcracks of East End alfresco trade. The specialities of the Oriental-looking open-fronted shops are fried fish, greasy looking tarts and cakes, little tubs of cucumbers pickled in piccalilli mixture, second-hand tools, and all kinds of second-hand integuments for man, woman, and child. There are swaying lianas of hats and caps, ranks of "restored" boots, trayfuls of bright-hued babies' shoes, piles of gaily coloured handkerchiefs – some, perchance, in Pistol's sense, "conveyed" – and groves of dusky garments in which, here and there, a footman's old livery, a stained soldier's coat, or a faded silk or satin gown shines faintly, like a dust-dimmed king parrot, ibis, or macaw.

Salesmen shout at the top of their voices, "Buy, buy, buy;" "What gentleman'll stand treat next?" &c., &c. Those who come to buy, and those who only come to look, keep themselves warm, and "enjoy company," or to wile away the time until the public houses open, are almost all making a noise of some kind or other. And so, in two conflicting turbulent tides, little dreamt of by many a neighbouring church and chapel goer, the motley, tobacco scented crowd forces its way up and down. How sweet the Sabbath thus to spend!

Graphic – 20th December 1875.

1875 – EXECUTION OF HENRY WAINWRIGHT.

On Tuesday morning Henry Wainwright suffered the extreme penalty of the law within the walls of Newgate, at the hands of the common hangman. It is unnecessary to recapitulate the shocking details which successive exhaustive inquiries have revealed respecting the crime for which this man was punished, for they are familiar to all who take the alighted interest in passing events. Let it therefore be sufficient to state that nothing occurred since the death sentence was passed to induce the authorities in the slightest degree to modify their opinion that Henry Wainwright was the murderer of the unhappy woman, Harriet Lane. His protestation of innocence when at the bar of justice was, as might naturally be imagined, unavailing, nor were the subtle concoctions subsequently addressed to the Home Secretary more successful.

Thus, it came to pass that the grey light of this December morning witnessed the painful spectacle of a man, neither influenced by any sentiments of conjugal propriety, nor restrained by any of those considerations which are commonly supposed to operate upon educated minds, undergoing the most humiliating punishment comprehended in our penal code.

Even so early as seven o'clock, while it was yet dark, a crowd of individuals whose dress and demeanour indicated their station in life, had assembled outside the walls of Newgate, and, as the minutes passed, the number swelled until, at eight o'clock, an assemblage of many thousands occupied the space in front of the prison. That portion of the public which had orders for admission was allowed to enter Newgate at half-past seven o'clock, where, passing through the various corridors, they gathered in the execution yard. This space, surrounded by the grim walls of the prison, was divided by a barrier into two parts. In a corner of the inner one was a small penthouse, lit by a couple of lamps, which threw an oily glare on the white beam, from which, on the suspending links, a new rope, about four feet in length, hung trimly, the noose resting on a hook projecting from the apparatus.

The spectators numbering some 50 or 60, huddled against that part of the barrier opposite the scaffold, and here for half an hour they waited, mostly in silence. From above, in intervals of a few seconds, the chapel bell sounded while, in the intermittent moments, the fainter pealing of dis-church bells passed softly overhead. A solitary inspector of police passed up and down within the demarcation line, and a few constables were stationed in a convenient corner. The uprights supporting the crossbeam were visible for a distance of about four feet above the half-doors that concealed the lower interior of the gallows house from the outside gaze, but the portion nearest the main wall was kept open.

At a few minutes before eight, the dismal clang of the prison bell was heard, and then, before the clock struck, it was a repetition of chapel bell, distant church bell, prison bell—deep toned, soft toned, harsh toned. The spectators grew more quiet as the hour of doom drew nearer. The cry came, "All hats off;" and, at the instant, the clock chimed eight o'clock. Every head was uncovered, and every eye strained in the direction of the door from which the prisoner was to proceed. A grey-haired man, in black officiating robe, repeating sentences from Holy Writ, revealed the chaplain. Behind him a figure neatly, but plainly dressed, the hair of whose uncovered head was carefully combed, and whose hands were tightly pinioned behind, needed no one to ask the question, "Who is he?" for all knew that it was Henry Wainwright.

With a countenance as composed as at any time during the several examinations—in fact, less anxious looking than on the last few days of his trial—with slip firmly set, and an unbleached face, the culprit entered the place of his doom, followed by the Governor of Newgate, the Sheriffs, the executioner Marwood, and other officials. The chaplain, leaning against the half-doors before mentioned, read passages suitable for the occasion; Marwood conducted Wainwright to the assigned spot; and the Governor of Newgate placed himself almost in front of the prisoner, while the sheriffs stood a little aloof. Twice Wainwright looked in the direction of the spectators, but the glances were swiftly taken, and the expression had no meaning beyond a seeming desire to fully comprehend the circumstances of his appalling situation. Then Marwood, a thin, spare man, of sharp countenance and determined mouth, raised the white cap and covered with it the head of his victim, who, without the faintest indication of emotion, submitted to the process. Deftly unhooking the noose, the executioner placed it round Wainwright's neck, and, having occasion to slightly raise the white covering, one could see beneath it the still unchanged face of the unhappy man. It seemed that Marwood was needlessly prolix in adjusting the rope, for he turned, and twisted, and smoothed, and folded it several times before its position pleased him.

At length, however, he drew the running knot taut, and thereupon, immediately withdrew from the immovable figure round which for the last minute or so he had been busied. He disappeared, and there was a moment of profound stillness. Then, a crash. Wainwright sank out of sight and the tightly stretched rope told its own tale. A petrified stillness prevailed in the yard at this instant. The officials gazed into the depth concealed from the spectators; the latter regarded only the strained and slightly quivering rope. But dumbness and inanition were soon awakened to speech and action when the waves of cheering from the crowd outside, which had seen the black flag hoisted, billowed into the yard. All within the penthouse was silent as the grave, but from without came the roar of the busy London world quickening into activity with the advancing day and urging the spectators to the immediate dispersal which followed.

After hanging an hour, the body was cut down and duly examined by Mr. Gibson, the prison surgeon. Having pronounced it dead, the representatives of the press were requested to adjourn to what is called the Board room.

About 11 o'clock on Monday night Wainwright placed in the hands of the Governor a statement, an abstract of which is supplied to the press by Mr. Smith. In this document he appeals to the loving kindness of a merciful God that his transgressions may be blotted but for the sake of the Blessed Saviour whom he had so long neglected. He then acknowledges the justice of his punishment, and says he deserves it, though he does not absolutely confess to the murder. He next expresses his sincere thanks to the Governor and to the officials for their attention, and to his loving friends, known and unknown, who have with Christian sympathy, rendered assistance to his family. He hopes and truly believes that their many prayers for his eternal happiness and peace have been answered by a gracious and forgiving God and concludes by commending his family to the hands of the Almighty Father, who is the Protector of the widow and the fatherless.

After about an hour, the body was cut down, and placed in a shell, coloured black. The members of the press, and the other persons present, then defiled past, and viewed the remains. There were no marks about the neck; the features were perfectly placid; and, in the opinion of Marwood, the executioner, death must have been instantaneous.

Poole and Dorset Herald – 23rd December 1875.

1876 – DEATH FROM STARVATION.

The Middlesex Coroner held an inquest on Friday at Whitechapel respecting the death of James M'Cormack, aged 72 years. Elizabeth Spicer deposed that she had known the deceased for many years. He

had been a famous pugilist. On Christmas Day she called at his lodgings, and found him and his wife huddled upon the floor in a mass of rags. There was not a particle of fire in the grate, and nothing but two chairs in the room, except a few rags that they slept on. She at once went home and brought in food from her Christmas table, which they gladly received. She then obtained an order for the removal to the infirmary.

Dr. Staff, resident medical officer of the Whitechapel Infirmary, stated that two persons were admitted in a dying condition. Everything was done that possibly could be, but deceased died on Monday. On making a post mortem examination he found a terrible state of things. The bones were protruding through the skin, and the blood was like water. The cause of death was starvation. The woman was still lying in the Infirmary, suffering from the effects of long privation.

The Coroner remarked that this was the worst case of the kind that had ever come before him. Deceased had died from sheer want, and he left the verdict in the hands of the Jury. The foreman remarked that to see such a terrible case before them was quite distressing. A verdict of "death from starvation" was recorded.

Dundee Courier – 10th January 1876.

1876 – HOME RULE IN WHITECHAPEL.

Home Rule has been tried in Castle Alley, Whitechapel, with the most discouraging results, and Saxon tyrants have been forced to interfere after one of their myrmidons had got a broken head for venturing into a little colony of the Regans, Readys, and Donovans. The inhabitants of the colony are all one family, but the reporter is correct in saying that it is not a happy one. On June 9th three ladies of the Regan family had an argument with one of the Readys, which naturally resulted in wounds. An uncle of the Miss Ready who came to grief, not having the good fortune to meet any of the Regans just as his longing for revenge was most ardent, came across one of the Donovans, a cousin of the ladies who had failed to agree with his niece. The Donovan in question was speedily wrecked, and after easily breaking the head of a constable who had the bad taste to interfere, Ready felt better until the whole party were sentenced to six months imprisonment.

Since then, an armed neutrality has been observed, and hostilities, though often threatened, did not break out until Friday night, when Miss Mary Ready, after applying every epithet but the right one to Margaret Kelly, knocked her down, while Mrs. Ready, Mary's mother, rushed to the assistance of her offspring, and gave effectual aid by biting Margaret Kelly through the right cheek. Mother and daughter have consequently been sent to prison after the cousins, the Regans.

It is somewhat odd that the war chiefly rages amongst the female portion of the colony; but it is clear from this case – one of many similar cases – that when the sons and daughters of Erin dwell together, they do not at all resemble birds in their little nests.

Renfrewshire Independent – 8th July 1876.

1877 – TREATMENT OF THE POOR IN WHITECHAPEL.

In more than one instance we have had occasion to allude to the hard and fast line of policy adopted by the Whitechapel Guardians in dealing with the poor, and on last Monday week a case was brought before Mr. De Rutzen which will serve to illustrate our meaning in the public interest.

Thomas Vallance, a namesake of the Clerk to the Board to which we have referred, was prosecuted for refusing to perform the task of labour given to him. On the case being heard, it was stated that there was some sort of relationship between the defendant and the Clerk to the Guardians, who certainly bears the same name, and that a degree of spite was manifested by the prosecution on this account, as there were many more suitable candidates for the dock at the police court now in the South Grove Workhouse than the one selected.

It furthermore appeared that the accused had occupied a different position in society, having been the proprietor of public houses both in and out of the district, and in that respect a large contributor to the rates. He was by trade a tailor's cutter and had been employed in that capacity at the establishment of Messrs. Gardiner, at the junction of Commercial Road and High Street, Whitechapel.

Since his confinement in the Workhouse, it was deposed that he had performed every task allotted to him, and that on one occasion he had called for the doctor, who found him suffering from a particularly painful disease, necessitating the provision of surgical appliances. The charge was founded on the refusal of employment procured for him by the Rev. S.A. Burnett, the incumbent of St. Jude's, also a member of the Whitechapel Board of Guardians, and distinguished as an advocate of the Charity Organisation Society.

It was proposed that the unfortunate man should take a situation in the shoe black brigade at twelve shillings, possibly, per week we say "possibly," Vallance being fifty-six years of age, and suffering from a complaint which ill-fitted him to kneel on the pavement but added to this was the degradation that he was to be compelled to do this in front of the very shop where he had been employed as a cutter, and in the vicinity of the house where he had formally dwelt as a respectable tradesman.

The case was of such a peculiar nature that the Magistrate twice adjourned it, and ultimately consented to strain the law against the individual only upon pressure from the prosecuting solicitor, prompted by representations from the Local Government Board, of which Messrs. Vallance and Burnett are the representatives. When the case came before the Magistrate this week, this poor victim of ill fortune and surname was sentenced to seven days' imprisonment, without the option of a fine, because he declined to make an exhibition of himself in a neighbourhood where he was well known, and for the satisfaction of the Rev. S. Barnett, of St. Jude's, and Mr. Wm. Vallance, the clerk to the Whitechapel Board of Guardians.

It was said that the defendant had been an inmate of the Whitechapel Workhouse on nine previous occasions; but, instead of this being placed to his detriment, to our thinking it is much to his credit, for it proves that he has struggled to exist outside the walls of the parochial establishment.

The facts as stated by us are a singular comment on the decision of the Whitechapel Board of Guardians to exclude the Press from their meetings, and, if true, indicate a want of feeling for an invalid we should have hesitated to credit them with but for the facts as given. Notwithstanding the beautiful and charitable services of the Church of England, with which Mr. Barnett must be well acquainted, and the humane intentions of the Act "43rd of Elizabeth," which are certainly not unknown to Mr. Vallance, all we can say, with such a case before us, is, "From all such Guardians, good Lord deliver us!"

East London Observer – 28th April 1877.

1878 – SHOCKING CASE OF ATTEMPTED WIFE MURDER.

On Saturday night, about eleven o'clock, a desperate attempt at wife murder was made in Maypole Court, High Street, Whitechapel. Shortly after the time mentioned a police constable named Robert Hill was on duty in the neighbourhood, when a little boy named Daniel Moore came running up to him, and stated that his father had stabbed his mother with a knife. Hill immediately proceeded to No. 2, Mayple Court, where in a room on the first floor he saw a woman named Mary Moore lying on the ground bleeding from a terrible wound in the side. Her husband was standing in the room, and as soon as the constable entered, he said to him, "I want to give myself up for stabbing my wife. I did it, and am very sorry." The constable at once sent for assistance. Moore then said, " You can do what you like with me, officer. I shall not try to get away."

A cab was then procured, and the injured woman, who appeared to be very bad, was taken to the London Hospital attended to by the house surgeon. The man Moore was taken to the Leman Street station, where the little boy, his son, said that his father and mother had been quarrelling all the night. About half-past ten they sent him out for some pickles. They were quarrelling when he went out and quarrelling when he came home again. His mother got up to take some pickles out of the plate, and his father then stuck a knife in her side. Moore was then told that he would be charged with attempting to murder his wife, and was cautioned in the usual way about saying anything. He then made a statement to the following effect:—

"I was at home about eleven o'clock tonight, the 23rd. I had a knife in my hand, and was going to cut some cheese. My wife kept 'jawing' me because I had not been to work all the week. At last, she slapped me in the face twice, and I said, 'Mary, don't hit me, for if you I shall hit you back again.' She then came forward. I met her and plunged the knife in her side. After I had done it, I sent my youngest boy Daniel for a policeman."

The prisoner was then locked up.

East London Observer – 2nd March 1878.

1878 – OVERCROWDING IN WHITECHAPEL.

Mr. John Liddle, in his report for the fourth quarter of 1877, in the Whitechapel district of the metropolis, has some observations on overcrowding which bring out in a remarkable manner the difficulty of sanitary administration in parts of this vast overgrown capital. Out of the 8,313 houses which lie in the district over which Mr. Liddle exercises supervision as medical officer health, not less than 4,500 are let out as tenements—that is, for occupation by two or more families—and many of these, it would appear, are let by the room, each room containing a family.

But the difficulty of dealing with overcrowding, in amount such as is indicated by these figures, is augmented by the kind of occupants. It would appear that there has recently been a large immigration of foreigners, principally from Poland, into East London. These foreigners arrive in a state bordering upon destitution, and are received by their countrymen, who usually possess but little more means, but who give them shelter, even to a portion of their own room it may be, until the newcomers can get work. This gives rise to most unmanageable states of overcrowding and other unhealthy states.

A curious movement of the population has taken place in Whitechapel. The English and Irish, who formerly lived in the district to which the Poles chiefly flocked, have gone elsewhere, and a tendency of different nationalities to isolate themselves in separate quarters has become manifest.

Mr. Liddle sees in this immigration of almost destitute people from the Continent into East London a serious and difficult social problem. It has complicated extremely the sanitary administration of the districts inhabited by the foreigners, and he appeals for help to voluntary organisations, such as were established in 1848, and during the cholera epidemic of 1866. But it must be obvious that the poverty of the immigrants interposes a most formidable obstacle to effective sanitary relief whether public or private.

East London Observer – 27th April 1878.

1878 – MURDER WITH A POKER.

At the Worship Street Police Court, on Monday last, Joseph Cantor, twenty-six, described as a cigar maker, and Charlotte Cantor, forty-six, his mother, both living at 7, Nelson Court, Little North Street, Whitechapel, were charged, before Mr. Joseph with feloniously and of malice aforethought of killing and slaying John Grayburn, by beating in his head with a poker, and both prisoners with attempting to murder Jane Grayburn by beating her about the head with a stick and poker.

Inspector Wildey stated some of the facts in connection with the case. It appeared that at about a quarter to one a.m. on Sunday, the parties, having been drinking till a late hour, met in Nelson Court, the deceased living at No. 4, and the prisoners at No. 5. A quarrel commenced over a girl, a daughter of the Grayburns, who were known only by the name of Crane, and from words the female prisoner and the injured woman got to blows. A stick was brought out of the prisoner's house, and Jane Grayburn was struck on the head once or twice with it before it broke. The men had then joined in the affray, and a poker was used, Joseph Cantor being seen to strike Grayburn, a man of about fifty-three, on the head with it. He must have received two or three blows, and fell insensible, when Cantor ran away. Mrs. Grayburn was also seriously injured, the court presenting "the appearance of a slaughter house" in the morning light. Both the injured persons were removed to the London Hospital. The man died there about twelve hours afterwards. The woman was lying in a dangerous state in the hospital. The female prisoner was charged with assault soon afterwards, but the man had escaped. He remained in hiding until Monday morning, nine o'clock, when he went to the Commercial Street Police Station, and gave himself up to Sergeant Wells, 17 H. He then made a statement, which was taken down in writing as follows:

"About 12.45 on Sunday morning I went to the bottom of the court, and said, "Mrs. Crane, what do you want making a noise round my door?" She said, "What is that to do with you?" I said to her, "It is all to with me." She said, "Who are you, and what are you?" I said, "I am as good as you." She said, "You!" and spat in my face. I said, "Don't spit in my face," and she done it again. Then John Crane said, "You ____ , I've got it in for you and your brother," and he then struck me in the neck. I tried to return the blow, when I received a blow to the head with a poker. I took the poker away, and struck them both back again." (Signed) Joseph Cantor.

Inspector Wildey said that the case was in a very incomplete state, and there were only three witnesses to the occurrence in the court. There was medical evidence as to the nature of the injuries.

Mrs. Emma Chivers, living at 8, Little North Street, was examined. She stated that she saw the man struck across the face with the poker, and he reeled away, being also struck on the head.

Inspector Wildey also deposed to having been officially informed of the death of the man, and a remand was then asked for.

Mr. B.J. Abbott appeared for the prisoners, and said that of course there must be a remand, and this was acceded to.

On Wednesday morning Mr. Humphreys held an inquest at the London Hospital on the body of Joseph Grayburn. Evidence was tendered similar to that given before the Magistrate, and showed that the prisoner had struck deceased over the head with a poker, causing serious injuries. Dr. Fenwick now stated that the weapon had fractured the skull and brought on compression of the brain, which terminated fatally twelve hours after the wound was given.

The Jury at once returned a verdict of manslaughter against Joseph Cantor, and the Coroner issued his warrant for the accused to take his trial on that charge at the next sittings of the Central Criminal Court.

Leighton Buzzard Observer and Linslade Gazette –
16th July 1878.

1878 – RAID ON A GAMBLING HOUSE.

At the Worship Street Police Court on Monday, Girshon Hirschfield, of 4, Boar's Head Yard, Whitechapel, and Mina Hirschfield, his wife, were charged before Mr. Bushby with keeping the house for the purposes of gambling. Sixteen men, named Fisher, Berlinski, Groossman, Jacobs, Alexander, Green, Lilberger, A. Jacobs (son of the other prisoner of that name), J. Cohen, B. Cohen. Poyser, Lubinski, Levi, Richards, Maskovitz, and Goldberg, were also put into the dock charged with being found in the said house for the purpose of gaming.

Superintendent Arnold, H division, stated that, acting under a warrant issued by the Chief Commissioner of Police for the Metropolis, he, at one o'clock on Sunday afternoon, went with Inspectors Abberline and Older, Sergeant Foster, and a number of constables, to Boar's Head Yard, Whitechapel, and surrounded the house. He tried to enter, but the door was fastened. An officer in plain clothes knocked, and after a moment or two the door was opened by the male prisoner Hirschfield. Witness at once went in, and Hirschfield was taken into custody. Witness, with the other officers, went upstairs to a room on the first floor, and forced their way in. He saw 11 men sitting at two tables, on which were piles of money and cards. There was an immediate rush, some making for the door, others for the window, and some scrambling for the money on the tables. When quiet had been somewhat obtained, and the men told they were all in custody, the room was searched. Large quantities of playing cards were found in the table drawers, 125 were also picked up from the floor, and 32 were found in the room below. In all over 18 packs of cards were found. Witness saw John Fisher, Harris Berlinski, Henry Groossman, Henry Jacobs, Samuel Alexander, A. Jacobs, the two Cohens, Alfred Poyser, David Maskovitz, and Goldberg among the prisoners in the room. They were at the tables.

Inspector Abberline gave similar evidence, and said that he took Hirschfield to the station. He had £2 18s upon him, some lottery tickets, and loose playing cards. A disturbance took place at the house some time ago, and witness then cautioned Hirschfield about allowing people to meet in his house, and he, on the way to the station on this occasion, said that if had taken witness's advice this would not have happened.

Inspector Older said that as the street door was opened, he, with other officers, went into a room on the ground floor and found there the prisoners Lewis Levi, Samuel Lutinski, Emanuel Lilberger, Barnard Richards, and Morris Green. Mrs. Hirschfield was in the room, and the men were sitting round a table, and the woman standing looking on. Green, on seeing witness, rushed to the door, but was stopped. Witness stopped the woman, and opened her hand, in which he found 1s. 3d. copper money.

Superintendent Arnold here asked that the prisoner Goldberg might be discharged and made a witness.

After hearing the evidence of Detectives Foster and Newman, Mr. Bushby consented to this course, and Goldberg was put into the witness box. He said that he had been in the habit of going to the house and playing cards, that the house was used as a gambling place, and he (witness) had lost in three weeks there no less than £25. The place was principally used on the Sundays; but witness had been there every day in the week.

After some further evidence, Mr. Bushby fined Hirschfield £50, discharging his wife. The other prisoners were fined £5 each. Some of the fines were paid, but the majority of the prisoners were locked up.

East London Observer – 31ˢᵗ August 1878.

1880 – BURNING OF ST. MARY'S CHURCH, WHITECHAPEL.

The parish church of St. Mary Matfelon, Whitechapel, which was restored, four or five years ago, at a cost of £30,000, chiefly by the munificence of Mr. Octavius Coope, M.P., was unfortunately destroyed by fire on Thursday last week. This disaster is believed to have been occasioned by the carelessness of some persons employed about the organ. They had gone away; and presently, some part of the organ catching fire, the flames were communicated to the woodwork above, and thus gained hold of the roof, which appears to have been composed of beams bare and polished.

The alarm was given at half-past one in the afternoon, when some workmen entered. A few minutes afterwards, one half of the roof burst into flames. Although a principal station of the Metropolitan Fire Brigade is in an adjacent street, and engines were quickly on the spot, little could be done to stay the destruction except with respect to the tower and belfry.

As soon as the engines had arrived and water could be obtained, a hose was taken into the tower and carried by the men to a window in the belfry, from which a stream of water was thrown on the parts of the main building that adjoined the tower. By half-past two, however, the work of destruction was complete. The roof had fallen in all along, the windows were out, and the doors swung wide, while at the gable ends the higher walls threatened to fall at every moment. Fortunately, the firemen had ample space for working, as the open churchyard is at the rear of the building. The police of the H Division stopped all traffic, which here includes the tramways; and the firemen, under Mr. Gatehouse and Mr. Holmes, superintendents, were enabled to do their work.

Our Illustration of the scene during the fire shows the eastern gable of the church, with the tower, and the engines playing on it, while the molten lead was pouring down from the roof. At that time, it was feared that the tower must fall with the rest of the edifice, but it has been saved. Its destruction would have involved the total loss of all the registers of the parish, and of much valuable matter besides.

St. Mary Matfelon has been a parish church for over 200 years. It was originally a chapel of ease to the parish of Stepney, before Whitechapel became a separate parish. The origin and meaning of the name "Matfelon" cannot be certainly known, but it seems to have been used in the twenty-first year of Richard II. Stow mentions the anecdote of a Frenchman or Breton, who had murdered a widow, his benefactress, in this parish, about the year 1428, and who sought refuge of sanctuary in the Church of St. George, in Southwark; but having been overtaken and captured, was brought back to Stepney, and was there killed by the women of the place attacking him with stones and mire in the street. It has been imagined that *matar*, the Spanish word for "killing," or *ammazare*, the Italian, might serve, together with "felon," to explain the name given to the parish church. But this is clearly an erroneous supposition.

Illustrated London News – 4th September 1880.

1880 – HOW WE LIVE AND DIE IN LONDON.

On Monday, Mr. John Humphreys held two inquests at the Weavers' Arms, Baker's Row, Whitechapel, on the bodies of persons who had died from starvation. The first case was that of George Smith, sixty-nine. It appeared that the deceased applied for admission to the Whitechapel Infirmary on the 6th inst., when he stated that he had been staying at a common lodging house in Flower and Dean Street, Spitalfields. He was at once admitted by Dr. Hett, who, from his vast experience in such cases, saw that the man was dying from sheer starvation. Everything was done for the

purpose of saving his life, but without avail, and he died on the 9th. Dr. Hett stated that he had never seen a worse case of destitution and misery. The skin was of all colours, there was a total absence of subcutaneous fat, the blood was like water, and a post-mortem showed incontestably that the unhappy man had been starving for some very considerable time.

The next case was that of William Cootes, aged forty-two years, an agent for a firm in Mark Lane, who had been missing for several days, and who was ultimately found dying in the stable of his employer. He was at once taken to the infirmary, where he died on the following day. In this instance also Dr. Hett was clearly of opinion that death had resulted from cold, exposure, and want of food, a post-mortem giving precisely the same result as in the first inquiry.

A verdict of "Death from starvation" was returned in each case.

But we trust these deplorable occurrences will lead to a thorough overhauling of the system of out-door relief in Whitechapel. Death from starvation in a city abounding with wealth and luxury! It is monstrous that such a public scandal should be tolerated an instant longer!

Penny Illustrated Paper – 16th October 1880.

Fig. 15. The Fire at St. Mary's (Illustrated London News)

Fig. 16. The Church after the Fire

1881 – THE SALVATION ARMY IN WHITECHAPEL.

The reputation of this eccentric religious organisation for good or evil has of late been very widely spread through the medium of reports of their processional demonstrations in the streets and their highly emotional services in the open air or within doors, and also unfortunately by the frequent appearance of its members at the police courts either in the character of complainants or defendants. Whatever may be thought of this peculiar method of evangelisation or of the spiritual value of its results or their permanence, it is undeniable that the statistics of the association are very remarkable.

"General Booth is the commander of a volunteer army numbering 445 "officers" and 12,000 "soldiers," male and female; the number of stations throughout the country is 250, the number of weekly services

4,300, and the number of people preached to weekly in these and in the highways and bye ways is estimated at considerably over 3,000,000. The funds, too, are in a flourishing condition, money being readily subscribed for the general purposes of the work to the amount of nearly 60,000l, a year; whilst towards a special fund of 20,000l. for the erection of a Training College and Congress Hall at Clapton contributions amounting to 9,200l. have already been promised.

Our artist gives the following account of the meeting which forms the subject of his sketch: "The service commenced with hymns and prayers, after which members of the S. A. gave their experiences and accounts of their conversion. After this an appeal was made to sinners to come out of the Burning Pit. At first no one seemed to respond to the call but after a time one stepped forward, then another, until at last they mustered fifteen. Each convert was then attended by captains and captainesses, exhorting and expounding,

Fig. 17. Meeting at the Whitechapel Road Salvation Army Headquarters (The Graphic)

until his or her conversion was acknowledged when the fact was announced to the meeting (see the tall figure in the centre of the sketch), 'Our brother or sister does believe,' followed by a deafening chorus of 'Hallelujah,' 'Praise the Lord,' &c., &c., from the 'soldiers.'

It worked up to such a state of excitement at last, people sobbing, crying, and shouting, that I began to think I should wake up in bed and find it was a nightmare. The men and women captains have brass letters ('S') on their collars, and some of the women have a badge round the arm with Salvation Army on it. They seemed of a respectable class – small shopkeepers, artisans, &c. I did not see any of the Whitechapel roughs there, as I had expected."

The Graphic – 31ˢᵗ December 1881.

1882 – A PITIFUL DEATH.

An inquest was held last Monday by Mr. George Collier, Deputy-Coroner for East Middlesex, at Spitalfields, on the body of a man unknown. A constable stated that about six o'clock on Saturday evening his attention was called to the man, who was lying in the roadway in Underwood Street, in an insensible condition. Witness took him to the Whitechapel Infirmary. The general appearance of the man was very dirty, and he had no shirt on, and only a few rags covered him. He was covered with flour, which appeared to have been thrown over him.

Eliza Ryder, nurse at the Whitechapel Infirmary, stated that the man was under her charge from the time he was admitted, and he remained unconscious till his death. He was in a very dirty condition. In addition to having no shirt on he was without socks, and altogether presented the appearance of a tramp. He had a bruise on the nose, and what things he had on were nothing but rags, and were very wet.

Mr. Case, resident medical officer at the Whitechapel Infirmary, stated that when he saw the man he was in a state of coma, and witness tried to rouse him, but could not. The left eye was black, and there was a bruise and graze on the right elbow. He had made a post-mortem examination and found the stomach and intestines entirely empty. He was about forty-three years of age, and had the appearance of being a Jew. The cause of death was pneumonia, brought about by the want of the common necessaries of life. In fact, he died from starvation.

The Jury returned a verdict in accordance with the medical evidence.

Penny Illustrated Paper – 2ⁿᵈ September 1882.

1884 – TERRIFIC HURRICANE.

At seven o'clock on Saturday evening, the front wall of some premises in Dock Street, Whitechapel, about sixty feet high, fell with a tremendous crash into the street. Some of the debris struck a man named James Donovan on the head, injuring him severely. He was taken to a neighbouring surgery, where his injuries were attended to, and he was then taken home by his friends.

About the same time a wall about twenty feet high, which formed a portion of the brewery of Messrs. Mann and Crossman, was blown down by this wind; the debris falling into Bath Street, Whitechapel, and burying three persons who were passing in the ruins. As soon as possible the sufferers were extricated and conveyed to the London Hospital, where they were attended to by Mr. Alfred Peskett, the house surgeon; one of the three, a man named Richard Fuller, aged thirty-two, of 15, Collingwood Street, Bethnal Green, succumbed to his injuries shortly afterwards, and died in great agony. Of the other two, Jane Saunders, aged twenty-five, of 7, Scott Street, was found to have sustained a fractured thigh and other injuries, whilst Emily Smith, aged twenty-four, of No. 9, Scott Street, Bethnal Green, had one of her ankles fractured and her head severely cut.

About 7.45 on Saturday evening a man, whose name is believed to be Robert Sewell, was crossing High Street, Whitechapel, when a sudden heavy gust of wind took him completely off his feet and threw him under an approaching tramcar, the wheels of which passed over him. He was picked up, and conveyed by the police to the London Hospital, where he was attended to by Mr. Alfred S. Peskett, the house surgeon. Upon examination it was found that the unfortunate man had sustained severe internal injuries and contusions, in addition to compound fractures of the leg.

Penny Illustrated Paper – 2ⁿᵈ February 1884.

1885 – EXECUTION OF THE WHITECHAPEL MURDERER.

At the Central Criminal Court, Henry Alt, 31, baker, was indicted for the wilful murder of Charles Howard; and on a second count he was indicted for wounding Ann Eliza Russell, with intent to murder her, in Rutland Street, Whitechapel Road, on the 18th March last. Mr. Poland briefly opened the case for the prosecution, and then called Mrs. Ann Eliza Russell, who stated that she was a widow, and resided at 25, Rutland Street, Whitechapel. Her husband had been a police constable.

On the night of the 18th March, she went out and met the deceased, Charles Howard. She had known him for a short time. She had previously known the prisoner, who had asked her to marry him, but she had declined to do so. She afterwards promised to marry the deceased man, Charles Howard. As she was going home with Howard, they met the prisoner, and went together into the White Hart public house in Turner Street, a short distance from her lodgings. They only stayed a short time. A friendly conversation took place. They had a little drink, but they were all sober. They left when the house was being shut up. Prisoner was at that time lodging at a public house in Whitechapel Road. They crossed the road together, and, in the hearing of Howard, the prisoner asked her to marry him, to which she replied, "No, sir; as I said before, I am going to marry Howard."

Her landlord and landlady came up, and after some conversation the prisoner stabbed Howard two or three times in the side. Howard had not done anything, and then prisoner got hold of witness and swung her round, after which he stabbed the witness six times in the chest and three times in the back. He said nothing at the time. Howard had gone away to the corner of Rutland Street, after he was stabbed, and she saw him there after she was stabbed. Alt again ran to him and stabbed him again. Her landlady took her into the house, and she was at once taken to the London Hospital, where she remained for nine weeks. While Alt was stabbing her, her landlady went into the house and shut the door. Alt was on friendly terms with her late husband.

In cross-examination by Mr. Besley, witness said she had never told prisoner she would marry him, but she told her landlady that she would marry him at the end of twelve months from her husband's death. She had never taken poison and asked prisoner to give her an emetic, or done anything else to induce prisoner to marry her. The other witnesses, whose evidence was fully reported when the case was on several occasions before the Magistrate, were called.

Mr. Poland afterwards summed up the case on behalf of the Crown, and contended that was either a case of murder or nothing. Mr. Besley next addressed the Jury in defence of the prisoner. He pointed out what he alleged were discrepancies in the evidence. He put it that at the utmost the Jury could only give a verdict of manslaughter. He said that the prisoner had had much provocation. Mrs. Russell had promised to marry him. He had, after that promise had been made, entrusted his bank book to Mrs. Russell, and then she, his affianced wife, took up with another man, and a quarrel ensued about this. By a sudden impulse, after they had all been drinking together, and in the course of an angry dispute, this occurrence took place, which proved that it could only be one of manslaughter.

The Learned Judge then proceeded to sum up. He first explained the law as to what was murder and what was manslaughter. He then analysed the evidence with great care, and left it to the Jury to decide. At ten minutes past three the Jury retired to consider their verdict. In the course of 25 minutes the Jury returned with a verdict of guilty, but with a strong recommendation to mercy on the ground of extreme provocation.

Mr. Justice Stephen then, in the usual form, passed sentence of death, and said the recommendation of the Jury should be conveyed to the proper quarter.

Henry Alt, a German journeyman baker, aged thirty-one, was executed on Monday morning at eight o'clock, at Newgate, for the murder of a man named Charles Howard, by stabbing him with a dagger. The prisoner and the murdered man had been courting a woman named Russell, a policeman's widow, but she had expressed her intention to discard the prisoner and marry the deceased. All the parties were out drinking together on the night of the murder, and the woman Russell positively told the prisoner that she did not desire to have anything further to do with him, and intended to marry Howard.

This appeared to have driven the prisoner almost into a state of frenzy, and he drew a dagger he was in the habit of carrying about with him and inflicted several deadly wounds on the deceased, from which he soon after expired. The prisoner also wounded the woman Russell very severely with the same weapon, and for a considerable time her life was despaired of. She, however, ultimately recovered, and was the principal witness against the prisoner at his trial. The Jury strongly recommended the prisoner to mercy on the ground that he committed the acts of violence while under fearful excitement from jealousy. The prisoner since his conviction appears to have conducted himself exceedingly well, and he seemed to be a remarkably quiet and harmless young fellow. He repeatedly expressed his sorrow for what he had done, and declared that he had no recollection of anything that occurred on the terrible night when the murder was committed.

He seems to have come to England to seek his fortune, and had no relatives in this country. The only persons that have visited him, are a few of his countrymen who are employed in the same business in which he was engaged. He appears to have listened most attentively to the exhortations of Mr. Duffield, the chaplain of the prison, and he has frequently expressed to that gentleman his sorrow for the dreadful deed. The prisoner has also been visited by the Rev. Mr. Welbaum, a German clergyman, to whom he made the same expression of sorrow. It would seem that the German Ambassador has been in communication with the Home Secretary with a view to procure a remission of the capital sentence, but the offence was considered to be of such a character as to preclude the authorities from interfering with the law, and a communication to that effect was made by the Secretary of State on Friday.

The prisoner, who appears to have been prepared from the first for this result, was informed on Saturday that there was no chance of a respite, when he appeared quite resigned, and said that he was prepared. The Rev. Mr. Duffield was with him nearly the whole of Sunday, and the Holy Communion was administered to him. He slept tolerably sound for three or four hours on Sunday night, and at six o'clock on Monday morning he was visited by the Rev. Mr. Duffield, who remained with him to the last moment.

Mr. Sheriff Phillips and Mr. Under-Sheriff Metcalfe came to the prison shortly before eight o'clock, and at once proceeded to the prisoner's cell, where the ceremony of pinioning was performed by Berry, the executioner. The prisoner was asked if he wished to say anything, and he replied, "Nothing." A procession, headed by Captain Kirkpatrick, the Governor of Newgate, and comprising Mr. Sheriff Phillip, the Under-Sheriff, and the warders, was then formed, and the prisoner, who appeared quite calm and composed, walked firmly to the scaffold, the Burial Service being read by Mr. Duffield. When the rope was placed round his neck the prisoner exclaimed, "This is all through that wicked, deceitful woman." The drop fell, and he appeared to die instantaneously. The prisoner, who was only five feet four inches high, had a fall of eight feet six inches, and death took place without the slightest struggle. A gentleman connected with the German Embassy was present at the execution by special request.

Alcester Chronicle – 4th July 1885.

1885 – ROYALTY IN WHITECHAPEL.

The Princess of Wales, who was accompanied by the Prince of Wales and their eldest son and daughter, paid a visit on Saturday afternoon to the east end of London, where the Princess opened the new Working Lads' Institute, which has been erected in the Whitechapel Road, nearly opposite the London Hospital.

The entire length of that road, from the corner of the Commercial Road, was gay with flags and mottoes of welcome, and despite the rain which continued throughout the day, there was immense assemblage of people along the roadway through which the Royal party had to pass.

The Institute, which has a bold front elevation of four floors, is of red brick, with Portland and Ancaster stone dressings, a prominent feature being a three-sided oriel window, with bay windows on either side upon the first floor. The interior arrangements include reading and conference rooms, gymnasium, classrooms, laundry, mechanical workrooms, dormitories, and kitchen. Only twenty-four beds are ready at present, but there is room for sixty when the necessary funds are obtained.

The Royal party arrived at the Institute at four o'clock, and were received by the Lord Mayor and Lady Mayoress, Mr. Alderman and Sheriff Evans, Mr. F.H. Bevan (treasurer), Mr. Hill, Sir James Tyler, Dr. Tyler, and others, with a guard of honour with the band of the Tower Hamlets Rifle Brigade, under Colonel Mapleson. Their Royal Highnesses, who were attended by Lord Colville of Culross, Colonel A. Ellis, and Miss Knollys, were conducted to a prettily decorated canvas pavilion in the rear of the building, which was well filled. A bouquet was presented to the Princess of Wales by Mrs. Hill on behalf of the boys of the Institute, and the proceedings having been opened with prayer, Mr. Hill, the honorary secretary, described the purposes of the Institute, which was the development of a very small beginning nine years ago. The effort then made to attract young working lads from the streets, and the evils of low music halls, theatres, and penny gaffs, had been eminently successful; so much so, that in the period referred to 1,620 lads had taken advantage of the old Institute.

After detailing the difficulty they had experienced in procuring a suitable site when the removal and enlargement became imperative, he said the estimated cost of the whole Institute, which would accommodate over a thousand boys, was £12,000, of which one half was still required. The amount they had received had been expended in erecting the building about to be opened, but to that they intended to add, upon the ground occupied by the pavilion, the second portion, which would include a swimming bath and lecture hall.

The Princess of Wales then, amidst the cheers of the company, declared the new building opened and devoted for ever to the welfare of the working lads of London. The Prince of Wales briefly addressed the meeting, and expressed his interest in the objects of the Institution. Mr. Bevan spoke to return thanks to their Royal Highnesses for this visit, and took the opportunity of announcing subscriptions promised that day to the amount of nearly a thousand pounds, of which £450 had been collected by Mr. Arrowsmith.

A number of ladies and children presented purses, each containing five guineas, to the Princess of Wales, and the Prince of Wales awarded a cup to a lad named Cooper, the champion swimmer of the Institute, after which the National Anthem was sung, and the Royal party retired for an inspection of the building. The Princess graciously acceded to the reading room being known as the "Alexandra Room," and the Prince of Wales promised to place a clock in it. As their Royal Highnesses left the building, they received another great demonstration of goodwill from the crowd.

During the afternoon some of the pupils of the Guildhall School gave a selection of music.

Illustrated London News – 7th November 1885.

1885 – THE HORRORS OF WHITECHAPEL.

To the non-Londoner, how can Whitechapel be described. It is the abode of misery, sin, dirt, squalor, coarseness, and vice. Dante, in the lowest depths of his "Inferno," knows horrors equal to these. And, oh! the pathos of it! The little children, with the old, old faces, their troubles and wants much the greater and more pathetic because that they are children; the boys and girls, with the look that says so plainly, "We have known no youth;" the old men and women, combining in themselves all the suffering and wrong-doing, wrong inflicted, of childhood and youth—the helpless pain, shame, and woe! We must see it all to understand it.

Dundee Evening Telegraph – 29th December 1885.

Fig. 18. Visit to the Working Lads' Institute (Graphic)

1886 – CHRISTMAS AT THE EAST LONDON CHILDREN'S HOSPITAL.

The annual festivities for the enjoyment of the children inmates of the great hospital in Whitechapel Road were given yesterday. The Christmas trees—for there were two—were set up in the Queen Victoria Ward and the Princess Beatrice Ward, that in the first-named being a presentation from Princess Christian, whilst the second was laden with toys sent by Mr. Leopold Rothschild, Mr. Bartley, Mr. Labouchere, and the clerks—male and female—in the Post Office Savings Banks, as well as other sympathisers with the good work here performed.

The walls of the wards in which the chief festivities took place were clothed with evergreens, beaded with berries, wrought into pleasingly suggestive monograms and other designs. Each gift upon the trees was labelled with the name of the child for whom it was intended. The pleasing duty of presenting the gifts devolved upon Mr. F.C. Carr-Gomm, Chairman of the House Committee, who was assisted by Mrs. Carr-Gomm, Princess Ghika

(wife of the Rumanian Minister). Mr. J.H. Buxton (the Treasurer of the Hospital), Sir E.H. Currie and Lady Currie, General Melulion, and Mr. H.E. Beddington. As the little ones were conveyed back to their wards, they were each given a sponge cake and an orange, together with some warm article of clothing.

It should be mentioned that this is the largest children's hospital in London, and yesterday it accommodated 150 sufferers. When the entertainment came to an end the numerous visitors were entertained to tea by the matron, Miss Lucas in the chief room of the New Nursing Home, which has recently been erected, and which is fitted with 102 separate bedrooms for the accommodation of nurses and probationers, who will be instructed in the science of nursing, and so fitted, not only for hospital work, but also to take their places in the homes of private families. Altogether the hospital possesses 800 beds, of which, as a rule, about 650 are occupied.

London Evening Standard – 6th January 1886.

Fig. 19. Decorating the Tree

1886 – A PUBLIC PLEA.

A hideous object under the designation of the "elephant man" is at present an inmate of the London Hospital, and Mr. Carr Gomm, the chairman of the hospital, in a letter which has been authorised to address to the *Times*, makes an appeal for public assistance on behalf of the unfortunate creature.

The human being in question is one Joseph Merrick, who is "so dreadful a sight" that any detailed description of his infirmities cannot be given. His recent career has been that of a monstrosity under the charge of a travelling showmen. In Europe he managed in this way to scrape together fifty pounds; but, like poor Jo, he was compelled continually to move on, and his manager, an Austrian, finally decamped with all his savings.

At last, he found himself in the London Hospital, his existence in the streets being impossible, owing to the curiosity of the mobs. "Terrible though his appearance is—so terrible, indeed, that women and nervous persons fly in terror, from the sight of him, and that he is debarred from seeking to earn his livelihood in any ordinary way—yet he is superior in intelligence, can read and write, is quiet, gentle, not to say even refined in his mind.

He occupies his time in the hospital by making with his one available hand little cardboard models, which he sends to the matron, doctor, and those who have been kind to him.

Through all the miserable vicissitudes of his life he has carried about a painting of his mother, to show that she was a decent and presentable person, and as a memorial of the only one who was kind to him in life until he came under the kind care of the nursing staff of the London Hospital and the surgeon who has befriended him.

At present Merrick occupies a private ward; but it is necessary that his case, which is incurable, must be hidden away elsewhere.

Dublin Evening Telegraph – 17th December 1886.

Fig. 20. The Elephant Man

1887 – MYSTERIOUS POISONING CASE.

At the Central Criminal Court, on Friday, before Mr. Justice Stephen, Israel Lipski, twenty-two, a young Polish Jew, was indicted for the wilful murder of Miriam Angell, a Jewess, on the 28th of June. Mr. Poland and Mr. C. Mathews prosecuted for the Public Prosecutor, and the prisoner was defended by Mr. M'Intyre, Q.C., and Mr. Geoghegan. M. Karamelle acted as interpreter, the prisoner not being acquainted with English to fully understand what took place.

Mr. Poland, in opening the case, said that the circumstances under which the charge was preferred were of a very extraordinary character. The deceased was a Jewess, a married woman, who resided with her husband at 16, Batty Street, Whitechapel, and the prisoner occupied a garret in the same house. The husband of the deceased was in the habit of going out to his work every morning about six o'clock, and the prisoner, no doubt, was aware of this fact.

On the morning of the murder the husband of the deceased went out as usual, leaving his wife in bed and apparently asleep. Nothing more seemed to have occurred until eleven o'clock, when, in consequence of something that took place, some of the other lodgers went to the room occupied by the deceased and found the door locked on the inside. It was forced open, and the deceased was discovered lying on the bed quite dead. A further examination of the room led to the prisoner being discovered under the bed in an unconscious state. The result of a medical examination was that it appeared that the death of the deceased was the result of the administration of nitric acid, and the condition of the prisoner appeared to be ascribed to the same cause. The actual circumstances under which the poison was administered were, of course, enveloped in mystery, but the suggestion on the part of the prosecution was that after the husband had left, the prisoner had entered the bedroom of the deceased with intention to commit a criminal assault upon the woman, and that, failing in this subject, he had forced the poison down the woman's throat, and then attempted to destroy himself by the same means, but did not succeed in consequence of not sufficient poison being left in the bottle. When the prisoner was apprehended, he appears to have made some extraordinary statements with regard to the manner in which he became possessed of the nitric acid, and upon these facts the charge of wilful murder was preferred against the prisoner. It appeared that shortly before the murder the prisoner had purchased one pennyworth of nitric acid, representing that he wanted it for his business as a stick maker, and he was told at the time that the acid was a poison. The learned counsel then gave a narrative of the facts he proposed to put in evidence, and the following witnesses were examined.

A plan of the premises was first put in, and proved to be correct.

Isaac Angell, the husband of the deceased, said he was a boat riveter, and came from Warsaw. He had been ten months in England, and resided with his wife at 16, Batty Street, where they occupied the first-floor front room. It was his custom to leave home to go to his work at a quarter-past six every morning, and he did so on the morning of the 28th of June. Neither himself nor his wife knew the prisoner. When he left the house, his wife was in bed, but he did not think she was asleep, and she appeared to be in good health and spirits. The window blind was partly drawn down and the window was quite closed. At the time he left he had a new coat hanging up in the room, and on the following morning he saw marks on the coat apparently caused by some burning fluid. The witness went on to say that he had never had in his possession a bottle similar to the one that was found in his room. When he left his room on the morning of the 28th of June, he merely shut the door and did not lock it, and the key was inside the room. He came home to dinner about twelve o'clock on this day, and he then found that his wife was dead, but they would not let him go into the room to see her till the following day. At the time of this occurrence his wife was six months gone in the family way.

Mr. Philip Lipski, the landlord of the house, who, though having the same name, was not related to the prisoner, deposed that he was a tailor, and occupied the ground floor of the house 16, Batty Street. The deceased and her husband occupied the first-floor front room, and two women named Rosenberg and Rubenthal occupied the first-floor back room. The prisoner occupied a room at the top of the house,

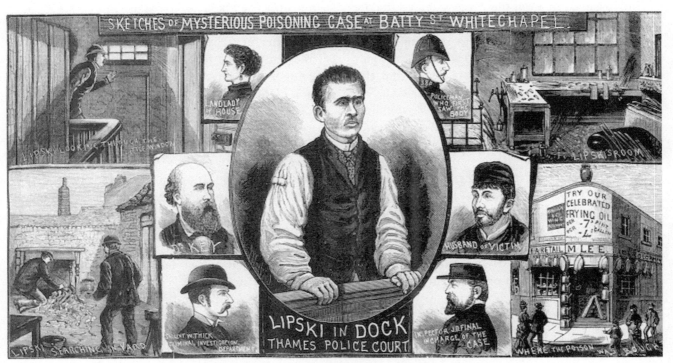

Fig. 21. Scenes from the Case (Illustrated Police News)

which he used as a workshop. On the morning of the 28th June, he saw the prisoner in the back yard, partly dressed and barefooted. After a short time, the prisoner went indoors and proceeded to his room, and witness went out to his work, shutting the street door after him when he left. He did not hear what had occurred until about twelve o'clock on the same day.

Simon Rosenbloom, a native of Poland, said he had been in England about twelve months. He was a stick maker by trade, and he had worked with the prisoner at that occupation. He saw the prisoner on the 25th of June; he told witness that he had got a workshop, and offered to give him employment at regular wages, and it was arranged that he should come to him on the following Tuesday, the 28th of June. Witness got to Batty Street about seven in the morning. The prisoner let him in, took him to his room at the top of the house, and the prisoner went to work for a few minutes, He then went out to buy a vice and some tools that were necessary for the business of stick making. He came back in a few minutes, and said the shops were shut, and he resumed his work. The prisoner went out again about eight o'clock, and while he was away a man named Schultz came into the room, but he left before the prisoner returned, and witness did not see him again until after the discovery had taken place. Witness remained in the prisoner's room until he heard the disturbance downstairs upon the discovery taking place. He heard loud knocking and screaming downstairs, and he went into the bedroom of Mrs. Angell and saw her lying dead on the bed.

In cross-examination the witness denied that he and the other men who had come to see the prisoner on the morning of the murder were standing outside the bedroom door of the deceased when the prisoner returned the first time. He also swore that the bedroom door was not partly open at this time. He said he knew nothing about it because he was not there at the time. He swore positively that he did not go into the bedroom until after an alarm had been given. He also swore that he had not got a small parcel in his hand, and, when the prisoner entered the house, he did not say, "Here he is; come in." He and the other man did not seize the prisoner directly he came in, and they did not try to force something in his mouth. He was not a strong enough man to do such a thing.

Richard Pitman, a lad who had been in the prisoner's service, said that on the night of June 22nd the prisoner told him to come to his workshop in Batty Street, and he did so. He continued to work for him until June 28th, and he corroborated the evidence of the previous witness as to what took place in the workshop on that morning.

Mark Schmidt deposed that he kept a shop in Back Church Lane, which was frequented by foreign Jews. On the morning of June 28th, the prisoner came to his shop and purchased a vice, Witness was acquainted with the stick making business, and he knew that aquafortis was used in preparing the varnish that was put on the sticks.

Isaac Schultz deposed that he was a native of Odessa, and until recently he had been working at Birmingham. He said he was in the shop of the last witness when the prisoner came in and engaged him to work for him at stick making, and the prisoner showed him where he lived in Batty Street. He went to the prisoners on the morning of June 28th, and he described what occurred and what was done by the prisoner on that morning previous to the discovery of the murder.

In reply to questions put in cross-examination, this witness said that he did not go into the bedroom of the deceased woman on the morning of June 28th. He also denied that he and Rosenbloom were at any time in the bedroom of the deceased. Before he went to Birmingham, he heard that the prisoner had been taken into custody upon this charge, and that he had been under examination by a Magistrate. It was after this that he went to Birmingham. The reason he never went back to the prisoner's room was that he did not see any chance of getting work with him.

Madame Lipski, the wife of the landlord of 16 Batty Street, said that to her knowledge the prisoner was not acquainted with the deceased woman. She said she remembered the morning of the 28th of June, and she saw the prisoner in the kitchen on that morning, He asked her to make some coffee for him, and she did so. The prisoner wanted to borrow 5s. off of her, and she told him she had not got it, and told him to get it from the mother of the girl he was going to be married to. Witness went out about half past eight on the morning of the 28th of June, and returned about nine. At this time the prisoner's coffee was on the table, and he had not partaken of it. About eleven o'clock, in consequence of something that she heard, she went to a little window and looked into Mrs. Angell's bedroom, and saw her lying on the bed. The bedroom door was then burst open, and the deceased was discovered to be dead. She was lying on her side, and part of her person was exposed. In cross-examination the witness said that when she went out the house was left in charge of her mother, Mrs. Rubenstein.

Lina Angell, the mother-in-law of the deceased, proved that she was in the habit of coming to her house to breakfast, but she did not do so on the morning of the 28th of June, and witness in consequence went to Batty Street, and tried the door of her daughter's bedroom, but could not open it. They knocked, but could not obtain any answer, and the door was then broken open, and the deceased was found lying in bed, quite dead, and in the position that had been described. The furniture of the room was not at all disarranged.

Some further evidence was then given with regard to the circumstances under which the discovery took place, but no new facts were elicited.

Mrs. Rachel Rubenstein gave some confirmatory evidence as to what occurred in the house on the morning previous to the discovery taking place, and she stated positively that while she was left in charge of the house no stranger came into it.

Lazarus Dywyen deposed that he was passing the house in Batty Street on the morning of the 28th of June, and, hearing a noise, he went in and proceeded to the bedroom of the deceased. He noticed that the bolt of the lock of the door had been shot, and the door could not be shut until the lock had been unlocked. Witness looked about the room and under the bed, and found the prisoner lying on the floor. He had no coat on and his waistcoat was unbuttoned, He was quite unconscious, and was not able to stand when he was discovered. Witness afterwards found a bottle on the bed, and there was no cork in it.

Mr. W. Piper, assistant to Mr. Key, a, surgeon in the Commercial Road, proved that he went to the house about half-past eleven o'clock on the 28th of June and saw the deceased lying on her back in the bed. He described the position of her clothes, and said that her chemise and nightclothes were rolled up above her waist. Several persons were in the room, and he ordered them to leave. A glass was on the table, which appeared to have contained beer or stout. He noticed some yellow marks on the clothing and on the face of the deceased, which appeared to have been caused by burning. He was subsequently shown a bottle containing a small quantity of liquid, which appeared to be aquafortis.

Cross examined: There were several women in the room when he went in, and they were all in a very excited state.

A police constable proved that after the prisoner had been taken from under the bed, he looked at the deceased for an instant and then fell down insensible.

The trial was then adjourned.

On Saturday last the evidence for the prosecution was continued. Inspector Final, H Division, said that on the 28th June the prisoner was brought to the Leman Street Police Station partly insensible. He rallied shortly after the divisional surgeon had attended him. A few things, including a pawnbroker's ticket, were found upon him. Witness afterwards went to the house in Batty Street, which was then in charge of the police.

The lock of the bedroom door of the deceased was in perfect order, but the bolt had been shot, and the door forced open. A bottle with some liquid in it was afterwards shown to him.

On the evening of the same day the witness went to the London Hospital and saw the prisoner, who at this time appeared to be quite sensible. An interpreter was present, but the prisoner made a statement quite voluntarily. On the 2nd July the prisoner was formally charged with the murder at the London Hospital, and he made no reply, but when he came to the police station, he made a reply, which was taken down in writing.

Dr. J.W. Key said he saw the deceased first about twelve o'clock on the day of the murder. She was lying on her back, and a stream of yellowish water was pouring from her mouth. There were several stains on her caused by aquafortis. He noticed that there were splashes of blood on the feather bed, but there were no marks of violence on the body, and in the witness's opinion the deceased had been dead about three hours.

Mr. Calvert, house surgeon at the London Hospital, proved that he examined the prisoner, but did not discover any traces of violence. In reply to a question put by Mr. M'Intyre, Mr. Calvert said that he observed some indications in the appearance of the mouth of the prisoner that some foreign substance had been forced into it.

Charles Moore, manager to an oil and colourman in Back Church Lane, proved that on Monday, the 27th June, a boy named Pitman, whom he knew was in the service of the prisoner, purchased some various articles at his shop – such as were used by stick makers. On the 28th a man whom he believed to be the prisoner came to his shop about nine o'clock in the morning and purchased a pennyworth of aquafortis. He brought a bottle with him, into which the acid was placed, and witness told him that it was poisonous. He asked the prisoner what he wanted the acid for, and he said he wanted it to colour sticks with. Witness heard on the same day what had taken place in Batty Street, and he therefore gave information to the police, and was taken to the London Hospital, where he identified the prisoner as the person who had made the purchase of the aquafortis at his shop. Witness was cross-examined as to the identity of the prisoner, but his evidence that he was the person to whom he sold the acid was not shaken.

A Jewess named Lines deposed that on the day before the alleged murder the prisoner borrowed a sovereign of her. Prisoner was engaged to be married to her daughter, and she said she always considered him to be a respectable, well-conducted young man. This closed the case for the prosecution.

Mr. M'Intyre said he did not intend to call any witnesses for the defence. Mr. Poland accordingly proceeded to sum up the case for the Crown. He said it appeared to him that the facts were clear, and that upon the evidence that had been given the Jury could only come to one conclusion. At the time the deceased lost her life she and the prisoner were the only persons in the room, and on the very day on which the occurrence took place the prisoner had purchased the acid, which was, undoubtedly, the cause of death. He remarked that, as to the question of motive, it was perfectly immaterial, but upon the facts it was reasonable to suppose that the prisoner might have intended to commit an outrage upon this young woman, or to commit a robbery, but the Jury were not called upon to consider the question of motive, and the only point they had to direct their attention to was whether the evidence made out to their satisfaction that the prisoner was guilty of the crime that was laid to his charge.

Mr. M'Intyre then addressed the Jury for the prisoner. He said he should be able to show that the evidence in this case was not of such a conclusive and overwhelming character as to leave no doubt that the prisoner was guilty. It had been proved that the prisoner was a respectable, well-conducted young man, and there did not appear to be the slightest motive for his committing such a horrible crime. A suggestion had been made that the prisoner intended to commit an outrage upon the person of this young woman, but the medical evidence practically negatived this suggestion. He reminded the Jury that in an ordinary case a prisoner was sentenced to imprisonment or penal servitude, if it should afterwards be discovered that there had been a mistake, the prisoner might be set at large and restored to his friends, but in a case of murder a verdict of guilty could only end in the result that the prisoner's life would be forfeited, and the decision of the Jury was irrevocable.

He then referred to the facts, and said that although on the part of the prosecution it was said that the crime must have been committed by the prisoner, he was unable to discover at what period of the morning it was alleged he had gone into the room of the deceased and destroyed her. If any cries had been uttered by the woman they must have been heard, supposing the crime to have been committed by one man, but he said it was a very different thing if the outrage was attempted by two men, one of whom might have struck the deceased while the other held her and prevented her giving an alarm. He concluded by asking the Jury to come to the conclusion that the evidence was not conclusive, and on this ground, he asked for the acquittal of the prisoner.

Mr. Justice Stephen commenced summing up at twenty minutes past two o'clock. He said no difficulty of a legal kind existed in the matter, and the only question for the Jury was whether the evidence established the guilt of the prisoner. The act was clearly wilful murder by whomsoever committed, and the only thing they had to consider was whether the prisoner was the person who had committed that murder. He then observed that they had nothing to do with the motives for committing such a crime. They had only to say whether the accused was proved to have committed it. If the crime had been prompted by lust, and there had been resistance on the part of the woman, a feeling of fury might have ensued, and this might have led to the commission of the crime.

His lordship then carefully directed the attention of the Jury to the evidence. This case was undoubtedly one of the most extraordinary character that he ever remembered to have occurred during his experience.

The Jury retired at a quarter to five o'clock to consider their verdict. They returned in a very few minutes and found the prisoner guilty. When the prisoner was called upon to state whether he had anything to say why judgment should not be passed upon him, he replied, "I am Innocent. I did not do it."

Mr. Justice Stephen having put on the black cap, addressed the prisoner, and said he had been convicted of the crime of wilful murder, and by the law of England the punishment for that crime was death. All that he (the learned judge) had to do was to pass upon him the sentence of the law, and his lordship then delivered the usual formal sentence. The sentence was explained to the prisoner by the interpreter, and he listened with apparent great earnestness. When the interpreter had concluded, the prisoner walked away from the bar without saying a word.

Illustrated Police News – 6th August 1887.

1887 – IMMIGRATION OF FOREIGN PAUPERS.

The Whitechapel Union Board of Guardians having made a protracted and thorough examination with regard to the question of the continued immigration of foreign poor into the metropolis, state that there can be no doubt that the number of foreign residents—chiefly very poor—in the Whitechapel Union and adjacent districts is largely on the increase, and that each year sees some new locality or localities invaded by the foreigner and abandoned by the English poor.

It is not a mere redistribution of poor, and the substitution of one class for another in a certain locality; it is the immigration into the district of a class of foreign poor who seem heretofore to have existed on the mere borderland of civilization, who are content with any shelter, and share that shelter with as many of their class as can be crowded into it.

In considering the question, however, from their standpoint as poor-law administrators, the Whitechapel guardians are confronted by two main difficulties—first, that of showing by statistics the effect of immigration upon local pauperism; and, secondly, that of tabulating facts in regard to the results of immigration. They are, however, led to infer that a considerable number of indigent foreign poor do land in this country, and either become the recipients of legal or private charity or elbow out English workmen and workwomen in certain departments of labour. At the same time, the active nature of the competition of English labour in foreign markets must not be lost sight of, nor the right of asylum which has for centuries been extended by England to the victims of political persecution abroad.

The conclusion to which the Whitechapel guardians have come is, that while nothing should be done to shut out the foreign workmen from the English labour market, something might be done to prevent the landing of foreign paupers—that is to say, such foreign poor as must, by reason of indigence or physical or mental weakness, necessarily, within a short period, become burdens upon the public rates for support.

St. James's Gazette – 9th November 1887.

1888 – MURDER AND SUICIDE.

A terrible murder, followed by the suicide of the murderer, has been committed at 147, back Church Lane, Whitechapel, a poor thoroughfare running out of the Commercial Road, London, and inhabited mostly by a low type of foreigners and small shopkeepers.

The house before mentioned had among its occupants a boot finisher named Louis Cohen and living with him as his wife was a young Russian Jewess, whose name, as far as can be ascertained, was Potstami. It is stated that the female came to England from Russia about five months ago in company with her husband, who, it is alleged, had married her from a house of ill-fame. Two months since she left her husband, and went to live with Cohen, and the husband, though much distressed, kept himself at a distance, not even disclosing his address.

The other morning, however, a man, in calling at Cohen's for 2s. that were owing him, remarked that he had seen the woman's husband in the street. No particular notice was taken of this, and at about one o'clock the woman went out to buy some provisions. Soon afterwards Cohen heard the woman screaming, and, on rushing down the stairs, was just in time to see her lying in the middle of the road with her throat cut from ear to ear. She was just able to point in the direction of Commercial Road, and then became unconscious.

Meanwhile some people saw the husband running away and pursued him; but in passing along Greenfield Street, after crossing Commercial Road, he noticed constable 6 HR coming towards him, and, turning his back upon the policeman, he immediately cut his own throat with a shoemaker's knife. The constable at once procured a cab and took the man to the London Hospital, but he expired on the way. Whilst this was taking place the woman had been removed to the same hospital in a barrow; but she also died before arrival at the hospital gates.

Although no one actually saw the murder committed, it is evident that the man attacked his wife and cut her throat at the foot of the stairs as she re-entered the house, and that she ran out and fell down in the road, as the floor at the foot of the stairs had a quantity of blood upon it, and the provisions which the woman was carrying were strewn in all directions. The murderer was in the same trade as Cohen, and the knife with which he committed the deed is now in the possession of the police. It is an ordinary boot finisher's knife and was secured by the constable at the time the man committed suicide.

The affair has naturally created great excitement in the neighbourhood, and Inspector Thrasher, who has the case in hand, is now collecting evidence and endeavouring to ascertain where the murderer has been living.

Jarrow Express – 3rd February 1888.

1888 – FATE OF A LUNATIC'S CHILD.

On Thursday, in the Queen's Bench Division, before Mr. Baron Huddleston and Mr. Justice Manisty. Mr. A. Glen moved, on behalf of Sir W.H. Wyatt. the chairman of the committee of visitors of the Middlesex County Lunatic Asylum at Colney Hatch, for a rule nisi for a mandamus calling upon the Guardians of the Barnet Union to admit a destitute infant into the workhouse. The grounds of the application were, that a Polish Jewess, having no settlement in this country was brought to the asylum from the Whitechapel Union. Having no settlement, she was chargeable to the county, under the Lunatic Asylums Act.

While in the asylum, which was within the district of the Barnet Union, the woman gave birth to a child, and as the governors of the asylum had no funds at their disposal for the maintenance of the infant, and as it of course had no visible means of subsistence, they called upon the Guardians to take charge of it and maintain it. The medical officer having certified that the mother would not be able to attend to it, she being a dangerous lunatic, the Guardians had declined, but assigned no reason, but he supposed their contention would be that as the woman was sent from Whitechapel to the asylum the child should be sent to the Whitechapel Union.

Mr. Baron Huddleston said there was no statute that he knew of which made a child born in a lunatic asylum must belong to the parish, from which the Board's counsel would therefore take a rule nisi.

Evening Star – 2nd March 1888.

———◈———

1888 – BRUTAL MURDER IN WHITECHAPEL.

On Saturday the East Middlesex Coroner held an inquiry at the London Hospital, Whitechapel, touching the death of Emma Elizabeth Smith, aged 45, a widow lately living at 18, George Street, Spitalfields, who is alleged to have died from injuries received at the hands of some persons unknown who brutally assaulted her when she was returning home along Whitechapel Road on Bank Holiday night.

Mary Russell, of 18, George Street, stated that that address was a common lodging house. Deceased had been a lodger there for some months. Witness acted as deputy. Smith got her living on the streets, and when she returned home one night, she told witness that she had been thrown out of a window. When she had had a drink, she acted like madwoman.

On Bank Holiday she left the house in the evening apparently in good health. She returned home between four and five o'clock the next morning severely injured, and she said she had been shockingly treated by some men. Her face bleeding, she said that she was otherwise injured. Witness took

her at once to the hospital. On the way she pointed out the spot where she said she had been set upon and robbed. She added that she did not know the men and could not describe them. Witness believed that the woman's statements were to be relied upon. In answer to the Coroner, witness said Smith had often come home with black eyes that men had given her. When she came home on the morning in question, she was not so drunk not to know what she did.

Mr. George Haslip, house surgeon at the hospital, deposed that deceased, when admitted, was not intoxicated, though she had been drinking. She had some bruises on her head, and her right ear was torn and bleeding. She told witness that at half-past one that morning she was going by Whitechapel Church, when she saw some men coming, and she crossed the road to get out of their way, but they followed her. They assaulted her, robbed her of all the money she had, and then commenced to outrage her. She denied soliciting them. She could not say if they used a knife. She could not describe them except that one appeared to be a youth of 19. After her admission she gradually sank and died. Witness had made post-mortem, and found that the injuries had been caused by some blunt instrument, which had been used with great force. Peritonitis, a result of injuries, had caused death.

Chief-Inspector West, H Division, stated that he had made inquiries of all the constables who were near the scene of the alleged outrage, but failed to find anyone who saw it or heard of it.

The Coroner said that from the medical evidence it was clear that the woman had been barbarously murdered. Such a dastardly assault he had never heard of.

The Jury returned a verdict of "Wilful murder against some persons unknown."

Seldom, writes a lady in a London contemporary, has a more hideously sordid story of woman's career been unrolled than was that of Emma Smith. Robbed, outraged, and wounded unto death, under circumstances of exceptional brutality, by a gang of ruffians while she was staggering "home" the worse for drink down a bye-street between Whitechapel and Spitalfields after a Bank Holiday "spree," it was a terrible end to a terrible life. The "home" was a common fourpenny lodging house. She had not corresponded with, nor seen a relation for ten years. It seems scarcely possible to believe that a woman could fall to such depths of degradation, and yet she is no more than a typical example of those who patronise the foul haunts of these fearful houses, where drinking, fighting, and all other loathsome vices are the pastime of the poor wretches who can raise two shillings a week for the "accommodation" they get within their foetid walls. A woman's mission to these houses would have an awful scope of sin and misery to cope with. Are there no brave pure souls who could take up such a work?

Worcestershire Chronicle – 14th April 1888.

1888 – PICTURES OF GRIMNESS AND MISERY.

A representative of the *Central News*, who patrolled the streets and alleys of Whitechapel during last night and the early hours of this morning, writes as follows:-

"The scare which the disclosure of the fourth and most horrible of the murders occasioned in the district, has considerably subsided, and the people, having become familiar with the details of the tragedy, and being calmed by the knowledge of the active measures adopted for their protection by the police are returning to their normal condition of mind. This is plainly evidenced by the aspect which Whitechapel Road presented last night, and to an early hour of the morning, a very different one from that of the corresponding period the previous day.

On the Sunday night, the pavements were almost deserted; but 24 hours later, groups of men and women chatted, joked, and boisterously laughed upon the footpaths until long after St. Mary's clock struck one. In passing through the groups of people, the words most frequently heard in their conversation were "Leather Apron"—a term that has become already a by-word of the pavement and gutter; and one more often hears it accompanied by a vacant guffaw than whispered in a tone which would indicate any fear of the mysterious individual who is supposed to live under that soubriquet.

Whilst a large number of persons, including many members of the police force, firmly believe in the existence, and almost certain guilt, of the "aproned" one, the talk of the footways convinces the passer-by that a large number of other inhabitants of the East End are sceptical as to his personality.

It may be said that the thoroughfares last night presented their customary appearance. There was the usual percentage of gaudily-dressed, loud-mouthed, and vulgar women strutting or standing at the brightly lighted crossways; and the still larger proportion of miserable, half-fed, dejected creatures upon whom hard life, unhealthy habits, and bad spirits have too plainly set their stamp. Soon after one o'clock the better dressed members of the motley company disappeared by one's and two's, but the poor, poverty-stricken drabs, whom it would appear fortune is less kind, crawled about from lamp to lamp, from one dark alley's mouth to another, until faint signs of dawn appeared.

Off the main road, such thoroughfares as Commercial Street and Brick Lane, there was little to attract attention. Constables passed silently by the knots of homeless vagabonds, huddled in the recess of some big doorway. Other constables, whose "plain clothes" could not prevent their stalwart, well-drilled figures from betraying their calling, paraded in couples, now and again emerging from a dimly-lighted line, and passing their uniformed comrades with an air of profound ignorance.

The streets inclusively referred to by the constables on beat duty in the main thoroughfare, as "round at the back," presented a dismal appearance indeed; the dim yellow flames of the not too numerous public lamps only rendering the darkness of night more gloomy. Such passages as Edward Street, connecting Hanbury and Princes Streets. Flower and Dean Streets, between Brick Lane and Commercial Street, which in daylight only strike one as very unwholesome and dirty thoroughfares, appear unutterably forlorn and dismal in the darkness of night.

From an alley in one of these recesses, a miserable specimen of a man, hollow-chested, haggard, and dirty, shuffled hurriedly into the wider street, and, crossing to the opposite pavement, dived into another recess, and was instantly lost to view. No constable would have thought of interfering with him had he met him, nor would there have been any excuse for accosting him; and yet his ragged clothes, of some dark hue might have been saturated with the blood of a murdered victim, which would not have been visible in the depressing yellow shade of the flickering gas jets. In almost any one of these dark and filthy passages, a human being's life might be every night sacrificed with the blow dealt with the terrible suddenness and precision which evidently characterised those of the two last homicides; and a police force of double the strength of that now employed, and organised under the best possible conditions, might well be baffled in its efforts to capture the slayers.

In the immediate neighbourhood of St. Mary's Church, a wide entry presented a deep cavern of Stygian blackness. into which no lamp shone, and where, for aught a passer-by at that hour could discover, a corpse might lie, and from which, such is its position, the murderer might, if possessed of coolness, easily pass unobserved.

In a squalid thoroughfare between Hanbury Street and Whitechapel Road some houses have apparently been pulled down, the space being now waste ground, enclosed by wooden palings. This unilluminated spot is separated by a house or two from an alley which, at a point some yards from the street, turns at right angles, apparently towards the unoccupied space mentioned. Into the mouth of this passage, a slatternly woman, with her face half hidden in a shawl, which formed her only headdress, thrust her head, and in a shrill and angry voice shrieked the word "Tuppy." The cry was answered in a few seconds by the appearance of an evil-looking man, with a ragged black beard, who, in reply to an impatient question of "Where is she?" muttered, in a surly tone, "Round there," at the same time jerking his thumb backwards towards the alley. "Well, come 'long home, then; I ain't a-going to wait for her," replied the woman, who, with the dark man limping after her, soon disappeared round the corner of the street.

There was no subsequent indication of the presence of a third person. The light from the street was so dim that the features of the man and woman could not be defined; and certainly, either might have borne traces of crime, which would have attracted no attention.

Such occurrences as the above are, the police say, quite usual; and they neither have, nor wish to have authority to question any individual whose conduct may attract attention, without exciting suspicion."

Lancashire Evening Post – 11th September 1888.

1888 – ATTEMPTED STABBING.

At the Thames Police Court, on Wednesday, Charles Ludwig, a German, was brought up on remand, charged with being drunk and threatening to stab Alexander Finlay, of 51, Leman Street, Whitechapel. The evidence of the prosecutor showed that at three o'clock on the morning of Tuesday week he was standing at a coffee stall in the Whitechapel Road when Ludwig came up in a state of intoxication. The person in charge of the stall refused to serve him, Ludwig seemed much annoyed and said to the witness, "What are you looking at?" he then pulled out a long-bladed knife and threatened to stab witness with it.

Ludwig followed him around the stall and made several attempts to stab him until witness threatened to knock a dish on his head. A constable came up and he was then given into custody.

Constable 221 H said when he was called to take the prisoner into custody, he found him in a very excited condition. Witness had previously received information that Ludwig was wanted for attempting to cut a woman's throat with a razor. On the way to the station prisoner dropped a long-bladed knife which was open, and when he was searched a razor and a long pair of scissors was found on him.

Constable John Johnson, S66 City, deposed that early on the morning of Tuesday week he was on duty when he heard loud screams of "Murder" proceeding from a dark court. The court in question lead to some railway arches, and it is a well-known dangerous locality. Witness went down to the court and found the prisoner with a prostitute. The accused appeared to be under the influence of drink. Witness asked what he was doing there, and he replied, "Nothing." The woman, who appeared to be in a very agitated and frightened condition said, "Oh policeman, do take me out of this." The woman was so frightened that she could then make no further explanation. Witness got her and the accused out of the court and sent the latter off. He walked with the woman to the end of his beat, when she said, "Dear me. He frightened me very much when he pulled a big knife out." Witness said, "Why didn't you tell me that at the time?" and she replied, "I was too much frightened."

He then went to look for the prisoner, but could not find him, and, therefore warned several other constables of what he had seen, and also gave a description of the prisoner.

On the last occasion witness was unable to procure the attendance of the woman. On the application of Detective Inspector Abberline, of Scotland Yard, Mr. Saunders again remanded the accused for full inquiries to be made. He also allowed Inspector Abberline to interview the accused with the interpreter, Mr. Savage, to ascertain if he would give any information as to where he was on certain dates. The woman Ludwig was alleged to have attempted to stab has been found. She is well-known to the police and her name is Elizabeth Burne.

Illustrated Police News – 29th September 1888.

1888 – WHITECHAPEL GOSSIP.

Now that every probable theory has been suggested which may throw light on the Whitechapel murders, a stranger one than all has been sent forth to the authorities, which may be the true one, in spite of its startling novelty and the associations to which it must of necessity give rise. At any rate, the idea has been thought worthy of examination by men of experience and authority, and is likely to be taken up by Scotland Yard.

It is now argued that the mystery and silence of the crimes, added to the circumstance of the mutilations, speak at last – at the eleventh hour it may be – of the murders being possibly the work of the Nihilist conspirators, who have been arriving in great numbers lately. The publicity given by a late enactment of Russian law regarding the wide spreading of a certain Russian sect has made the public mind in Russia familiar with the idea of mutilation; the trials of the Nihilists at St. Petersburg have made the public mind in England equally familiar with the idea of the mystery and secret combinations which form part of the Nihilist doctrine, elevated as it is in our day to the dignity of a deeply studied and a most finished science.

The work done is that of the Nihilist; the manner of its execution that of the sect referred to. It is in this direction that the police authorities ought now to turn their attention. The quarter in which the murders have been committed is almost exclusively inhabited by foreign Jews. Amongst these a whole band of Russian and a German Socialists have established themselves of late, and these again are known to be interspersed with Nihilists, who have come over here to avoid the close pursuit of the Russian police.

The religious sect which first gave its name to Nihilism and to which the diabolical political association owes its birth, has altered its principles, and from original pursuit of a philosophic but wicked aim has assumed a political frenzy more wicked still. The sect has spread to a great extent of late years. Self-mutilation is one of the compulsory rules of admission to the association. The men belonging to it are mostly jewellers, the women stockbrokers and money changers. This belief in the necessity of preparing for the end of the world by preventing the advent of another generation is thought by them to be the best means of assisting the work of the Lord. The jewellers belonging to the sect are well known in the trade, and have long done business with English dealers without incurring the smallest suspicion of treason against the laws, whether of their own country or of ours. They have always been regarded as the most true and simple in all their dealings of all foreign traders, very punctual and industrious, and most reliable in the execution of the orders given them.

But few of their women have appeared in London. Some years ago, two or three of their number might be seen buying and selling stock outside the Paris Bourse, while the gaping crowd would stand amazed at the strange costume and independent bearing of the ladies as they moved to and fro, notebook in hand, among the eager jobbers and clerks who surrounded them.

Their dress was of dark blue serge, a caftan reaching to the heels, the waist confined by a broad leather belt, from which was suspended a brass-bound bag. A round fur cap formed the coiffure; from beneath it the closely-cropped hair was only seen at intervals, leaving the forehead entirely bare. The loose sleeves of the caftan held the whole paraphernalia of their trade cheque books, specimens of the various coins of Europe and America, and memoranda of their transactions taking place abroad. They remained in Paris only for a little while. The police interfered with their presence at the Bourse, and after attempting to continue their traffic in an office on the Place des Victoires they disappeared. One or two of the Paris papers gave elaborate descriptions of their style and appearance, and Jules Janin entered into exaggerated laudations of the beauty of the youngest of them, a girl of about twenty years of age, whose large blue eyes struck to his very soul as they "peered from beneath her headgear of white fox skin like gems amid the snow."

Men and women of the sect all live together in peace and harmony, sharing the same fund and partaking of the same a food – and above all joining in the same prayers, which occupy a great portion of the day. As they are convinced that the world is soon to come to an end, they believe that, the word of God having gone forth for its destruction, the generation born in the Latter Days must all be accursed and devoted to perdition. The religious motive of individual annihilation has merged into that of general destruction of all that exists, until nothing remains upon this earth, and all must be reconstituted.

Of course, the new reasoning adopted by the truth seekers in the horrible murders of Whitechapel has already found many adherents. First of all, it is remembered that the Russian Nihilists have mastered the art of conspiracy to murder as well as that of concealment of the murderer. The Russian song which extinguished the sound of all voices from the street may have been made, unknown to the singers themselves, the signal for the deed. The disappearance of the murderer, leaving no trace of his passage, is common to all Nihilist assassins in Russia, with whom every incident is prepared, every contingency foreseen. The murderer of the women may in each case have been concealed close to the spot where the act was committed. He may have been crouching in dark cellars beneath the feet of the police assembled at the sound of the whistle, or he may have retreated over the tiles, and have been lurking amid the chimneys of the roof of the very building under the walls of which the crowd had gathered, shocked and completely stupefied at the sight of the murdered woman, who had died beneath the assassin's knife without the utterance of an exclamation or a cry which could have roused the attention of the police – strained as it has been of late to its intense pitch by the horrible deeds which had previously taken place close to the spot.

As if to confirm the idea of the secrecy with which such deeds can be executed, the thieves who robbed the Aldgate Post Office had broken in through the cellars at the back of the premises, then scaled the roofs, and entered through a trap to the upper part of the building. The pulling up of a portion of the staircase by way of precaution – in order to gain admittance through the cellars – would form a very appropriate part of the programme of the Russian Nihilists.

The manual work of the Whitechapel murderer is that of a religious fanatic driven raving mad and excited to homicidal mania by the bloodthirsty counsels of those around him; but the moral intent is not the mere doing to death of one or two miserable prostitutes in the lowest quarter of London: the aim must be sought far beyond. It is the creating of hostilities between the people and the police, hatred of the Government, and determination to vent such hate and vengeance against all authority.

When the Russian Nihilists were driven out of Switzerland, they settled at Brook Green. Vera Sassovitch, the heroine of the cause, was well known in the neighbourhood. After her departure the members of the association removed to Camden Town, where they had established a printing press, whence issued all the proclamations and terrible denunciations against the Russian Government which drove the authorities to despair at their inability to discover the secret of their conveyance to Russia and their distribution throughout the country.

At one time the side streets of Camden Town displayed numerous Russian and Polish names over the shops; shoemakers and tailors, working jewellers and metal stampers, were amongst the more conspicuous. All were quiet and respectable; one or two of them well-to-do.

In a political cause all means are considered lawful, however lawless in other cases. Time presses in this instance. The crisis must be hurried on. All must be got ready for the time of the French Exhibition, meant to celebrate the destruction of monarchy in France. The hour is approaching in which England must declare herself as adhering to the League or be proclaimed *hors de loi* by the other nations. The great cataclysm which was announced even before 1848 is to be accomplished in 1889.

The letter from an East End curate which appeared some little while ago in the *Daily Telegraph* should have aroused the Government to a sense of the danger in which it stands. That letter, written by a man who mixes with the masses of whom he writes, foretells the rising "not of a few thousands cooped up in a square as hitherto, but of a million men all bent on avenging past neglect, and joining in the universal hue-and-cry against the powers who, assuming responsibility, refuse to become responsible." The writer says that foreigners are daily swarming to the East End, where they preach their doctrines unmolested, and urge the woe-begone inhabitants to prepare for the great event which is to free them all from the bondage under which they groan. This great event is the coming Exhibition, for which the Socialists of every country in Europe are preparing their arms and arguments with as much activity as is displayed by the fighting Powers of Europe in recruiting troops and storing ammunition.

England is a harder nut to crack than the rest have been, and where the Socialistic grinders have been damaged by the hard shell of common sense which envelops it; but this very resistance may have caused a desperate appeal to be made to the Nihilists, to aid, with their admission of murder as a means, their patience in constructing subterranean passages, their silence and mystery, and their trust and devotion to each other, their sacrifice of all worldly consideration, of security and comfort, of all individual advantages, their readiness to sacrifice life itself to what they consider a just and righteous cause, which render them indomitable in Russia, the land of treachery and spies, and where such supineness as displayed by our own Government officials would be punished, not with disgrace and dismissal, but with death.

Such assistance would be valuable indeed in circumventing our own honest, trusting detectives, who only begin to suspect at this very moment that the crimes cannot have been planned and executed by the same individual, and that they must have been perpetrated by a gang; and, above all, that the mysterious disappearance of the murderer cannot have been accomplished without assistance. The one comfort experienced by the hopeful is in the prospect of the destruction of the unclean nauseous slums where hundreds of our fellow creature are suffered to starve, decay, and rot without help or consolation. The pollution must be looked in the face and traced to its very source.

Amid the foul atmosphere created by all this wretchedness and misery, still may be found some spark of that redeeming love which absolves our human nature from the stain thrown upon it by the horrible disclosures made concerning our own cruelty and neglect. Where shall we seek a more touching example of Christian kindness and self-sacrifice than in the case of the landlady of the house in Hanbury Street who has kept an old lady for years – "What, out of charity?" says the astonished Coroner. The answer in the affirmative should fill with shame many a self-contented mind, satisfied with the reflection of the goodly subscription to the poor box or contributions at the church door. And the avowal of the prayer meetings held at her house, where her poor neighbours are wont to assemble to read the Bible. "What, in your workshop?" again enquired the Coroner, who had beheld its crowded state. And again, must the answer have carried reproach to the conscience of many a reader of the report, while seated in his spacious drawing room, made to serve no purpose but that of occasional display of vanity.

And then, the sister of the Berner Street victim, who, out of her pittance as trousers maker, yet found means to allow her miserable sister 2s. a week – with frequent supplements when the case became too urgent – and the poor help bestowed with words of such comfort and affection that the miserable outcast felt cheered and comforted for many hours afterwards, resolving to lead a better life, until overcome by the temptation to which all of her class succumb. Does not this specimen of the charity of the poor towards each other send a pang through the conscience of every man who hesitates in bestowing lest it should be unworthily bestowed?

And amid the trouble and consternation what are the clergy doing? The spectacle of the poor outcast women, with no shelter from the cold and wet of Monday night, crowding about the railings of the churches, as if seeking the protection which for such as they can be hoped for only there, is one of the most touching pictures ever presented to the memory.

It must be confessed that there exists some little injustice mingled with the indignation of Whitechapel against the police. This, however, is the feeling which is meant to be produced by the plotters of the fiendish schemes. The disturbance to commerce, the ruin of trade, is of course another part of the plan.

A strange proposal has been submitted to the Vigilance Committee. It has been suggested that a deputation of the fallen women of Whitechapel should proceed to the Home Office, in order to claim the same degree of protection as that bestowed some years ago upon the match girls. The project, all preposterous as it may seem, is under discussion, so 'tis said. "It is time we should show the authorities, that fallen and degraded as we may be, we are still flesh and blood, and have as good a right to protection from violence as others." The scheme, even if only publicly debated, would certainly do more to frighten Mr. Matthews into the offer of a reward for the murderer than all the reproach and argument levelled at him in the newspapers. Imagine the effect of such a procession wending its way through the City to the West End. Is there any law to prevent it, provided the women

behaved with decency? I
clerks at sight of thi~
each other, yet sisters

Birmingham ~

1888 – SLUMMING IN WHITECHAPEL BY AN AMATEUR DETECTIVE.

The following article describing a well-to-do woman's visit to Whitechapel was published over four weeks at the height of the "Autumn of Terror," and gives a fascinating insight into life in the Whitechapel slums. The articles proved so popular that they were published together in a pamphlet.

I.

Perhaps there is no locality in the United Kingdom which at the present time is so notorious as Whitechapel. The horrible tragedies so recently enacted there in such rapid succession have sent a thrill of indignant fear throughout England, whilst in the neighbourhood itself the panic still lasts, and will do so as long as the bloodthirsty monster remains unknown and uncaptured. These murders have cast a lurid sidelight on the life endured by the East End poor.

The revelations concerning the lodging houses—where no questions are asked, providing the requisite fourpence or eightpence are forthcoming, and which are the hotbeds of prostitution and crime – are sufficiently startling to ordinary decent folks; but when we also read of a wretched female who cannot get shelter till she earns the few coppers necessary to pay for her bed, and is forced to seek them after midnight by going on the streets, the question may well be asked, "What sort of a neighbourhood can this Whitechapel be, where such hideous vices can flourish darkly, but unheeded?" And this is the query that I am about to answer.

Whitechapel Road, itself, I am perfectly acquainted with, as I have frequently walked down there, and been quietly amused at the "all sorts and condition of men" and women that I have encountered. They have decidedly been a mixed, not to say job-lot, but their behaviour has been generally orderly, although their talk is louder, and the use of expletives freer than what we benighted mortals, are accustomed to. This, of course, is in reference only to Whitechapel Road,

a wide handsome thoroughfare, brilliantly
exceedingly busy. But like the majority of
table people, I had actual knowledge of the
s that branch off from the main artery of this
sely populated neighbourhood.

After the dreadful crimes so placidly perpetrated
Mitre Square and Berner Street, I conceived an
ardent desire to visit and see for myself the region of
a civilised city that seems to be given up to horrors
unmentionable. The thing that puzzled me was how
to go. Night was the best time, but it is hardly the place
where a stranger would care to be alone, and in a great
measure unprotected. I mentioned the difficulty to
a friend of mine. Inspector R., of the City police. "It
is not a nice neighbourhood," he said thoughtfully,
"and it is of no use going there unless you know your
way about, or else you stand a tidy chance of getting
knocked on your head or returning minus your
watch and chain." I looked rather glum, and he went
on to remark that "he would have been pleased to
accompany me only he was leaving town the next day
on particular business." Where do you want to go?" he
asked. "Well," I replied, "I want to go to Mitre Square,
Buck's Row, Berners Street and Hanbury Street, and
just see for myself what class of people really do live
there." "I can manage that for you," he said; "one of
our men, Mr. B., is a thoroughly efficient and highly
respectable and intelligent officer, and he can go round
with you."

I thanked the worthy inspector, who introduced
me to Mr. B., a tall, muscular, and rather handsome
man, and an arrangement was made there and then
that I should meet the officer on the next night by the
Law Courts. "Will you know me again?" I inquired.
He glanced at me sharply from a very keen pair of
blue eyes. "Yes," he answered, "I shall know you." I
felt that mentally he was taking my photograph, and
how correct my prescience was found out afterwards,
when he accurately described a ring that I wear, and
also a peculiar but trifling mannerism that I am
unconsciously guilty of.

The next evening, we met at the appointed place,
my escort looking very big and stalwart in his civilian
dress, and I, clad in the darkest and least conspicuous
clothes. It was a lovely night, clear and cold, the blue
heavens all aglow with myriads of stars. The Strand was
as busy as only the Strand can be. Hansoms flitted by
us; every now and again carriages drew up at the doors
of the brilliantly illuminated theatres, and from them
alighted gaily dressed ladies, and their cavaliers in the
regulation evening dress. Busses full inside and out
drove by; newsboys called out in stentorian accents,
"Reported harrest hof the Whitechapel murderer."
Laughing, innocent happy looking girls hurrying
along with their friends. Polite and tired policemen

were regulating the traffic, conducting nervous
ladies across the road, directing deaf old gentlemen
to various places, requesting knots of men to "move
on there please," and perfuming the various other
duties incidental to the wearing of the blue coat. The
cafes were full, and the air was noisy with the traffic,
laughter, and conversation. If a lady passed, she was
carefully escorted by some male friend. The majority
were huddled up in furs, for the wind was keen.

If vice was there, it was emphatically well-dressed,
well-fed vice, for dense as the throng was, it seemed
almost exclusively formed of warmly clad people.
I looked with measure at the lively, gay, and bright
scene; I listened to the ripple of careless laughter, the
soft, sweet, modulated voices, and the flow of silken
robes; I inhaled the fresh cold air, the perfume that was
wafted momentarily to me, from the delicate flowers
that nestled on the white bosom of some lady as she
passed me to enter a theatre, or the scent that arose
from her handkerchief, and as I looked and listened I
thought with a cold chill of that other neighbourhood,
so near, and yet so distant, where innocent joy or pure
amusements are not known.

We hailed a 'bus, and soon left the glare and bustle
of the Strand and Fleet Street far behind. At Leadenhall
Street we got down, and just at the end of that street
and Whitechapel Road is a narrow street which leads
into Mitre Square. "This is quite a respectable place,"
says Mr. B., as he glances round with a professional
eye. Although the night is light, the square seems
enveloped in gloom, and in the darkest corner,
shaded by a window, is the place where the wretched
woman was so foully murdered. Two young men and
a woman are surveying the place with a curiosity, and
the latter tells me with unctuous relish "that the blood
all congealed can still be seen down the area, where it
dripped down from the iron bars."

Slantingly opposite there is a warehouse all lit up,
and opposite is the opening from which the assassin
escaped after the completion of his ghastly work. We
stand still, the young men and the woman go away, the
lights are put out opposite, the lamp is extinguished
in the window, under which the murder took place,
and yet we remain. The square is now deserted, and it
is quite dark. We go up and stand in the shade of that
dreadful corner. The quiet is oppressive, we might be
miles away from any living being, and I catch myself
wondering if there is really a busy thoroughfare within
a few yards from where we are standing.

Presently we hear a measured tread, it comes
nearer and nearer, then dies gradually away. It is a
policeman in Mitre Street. A few moments after some
men cross the square, but we are apparently unseen
wrapped in that murderous shade, for though they
pass within half-a-dozen yards of us, they are quite

unconscious of our presence. This rather unnerves me, for I realise how comfortably a person could be murdered here.

Just then a severe voice says, "what are you doing there?" A lantern is flashed on us, and there is a bobby. He looks at me, then my companion, who he recognises immediately, explanations issue, and all is right. Still, it does not do away with the fact that we have been allowed to remain there undisturbed for fully seven to ten minutes.

Although Mitre Square is respectable, it affords facilities for crime. At night it is comparatively deserted, and, moreover, is badly lit, the corners being completely enveloped in gloom, and another thing is that there are two thoroughfares leading in and out of the square. I honestly believe that the police do their best, and I had very little idea of the difficulties they have to contend with till the night of my expedition to the east, and I could then see what an intelligent and efficient body they must be to grapple at all with the vexatious obstacles thrown in their paths.

The next place visited was Berners Street, and to get there we had to cross Whitechapel Road and go down Commercial Street. Of these places I shall have a great deal to say, but I will reserve my remarks for another article.

The bustle and noise were most grateful after the fearful hush of Mitre Square; there were quantities of men and women, but what men and women were they? As we got near to Berners Street, Mr. B. asked me "If I felt frightened?" I laughed and replied in the negative, and then he showed me with a certain amount of satisfaction that he was provided with his whistle and a thick, heavy walking stick.

In another few minutes we were in what my companion tersely described as a beastly locality. A long, ill-paved, narrow, badly lit street. The lamps are few and far between, and show a flickering, sickly, yellow light. This insufficient lighting is simply disgraceful and is an evil that demands immediate attention. After the glare of Whitechapel Road, the darkness seems trebly bad. The houses are small and squalid, and teeming with life. Late as it is, one must walk carefully for fear of falling over half naked infants, who crawl about the broken pavements. Wherever you turn you see babies—dirty, unkempt, with hardly sufficient rags to cover their nakedness. Their helplessness testifies to their infancy, but their puckered-up faces are indelibly stamped with the legacy of crime.

Conceived in vice, brought up on the streets, taught to steal and lie, good God, what can their future be? Children everywhere; but in all the scores I saw not one really childish or innocent face could I see. Little girls nursing gutter brats, and pouring over their charges such torrents of invective, such vile blasphemy, that I fairly shuddered. Girls a little older, but not yet in their teens, mauling boys as ragged, and as filthy as themselves. Girls hurrying to and from the public house and smacking their lips over the drink they had surreptitiously taken. Girls carrying infants and cursing and swearing at them like fish fags. All young, all with matted hair and dirty skins, all with precociously sharp eyes and old wizened faces; few with boots and stockings, few plump or healthy looking, few decently clad, none with their heads covered, but nearly all sporting earrings and brooches. And this, mind you, not in the daytime, but late at night, and within two miles from where I saw strong women swathed in sables and sealskins. I now stood by half naked infants crawling together as if to seek warmth, on pavements rendered disgusting by the vilest refuse. Women with their hair uncombed, and their hands folded in their aprons or skirts, stood in the doorways and shrieked to their children in harsh, shrill voices. And this was the first impression I received of Berners Street.

II.

As I have before mentioned, Berners Street is badly lit, and as we go down it, so does the gloom seem to increase. We meet a couple of policemen, and for a moment they scan us seriously under the flickering gleam of one of the few gas lamps. Evidently decently clad strangers are somewhat of a novelty in this most unsavoury neighbourhood, but my companion seems to be recognised, for a brief smile momentarily irradiates the professional stolidity which is the characteristic of our blue-coated guardians of the peace when on duty.

Soon we leave the groups of horrible children behind, and the thoroughfare looks deserted, and is so quiet that our footsteps ring out startlingly distinct on the still night air. The atmosphere Is impregnated with a cold damp mist, and now and again as doors are opened smells the reverse of agreeable are wafted to our reluctant nostrils. We cross over, and Mr. B. points out a door apparently leading into a house, but when he pushes it open, I see to my astonishment that it encloses a court or narrow alley. I peep down it, and as well as I can see in the blackness—for there is no lamp in the entry – I notice that there are houses at each side. Filthy, ramshackle cottages evidently let out in tenements, for they seem swarming with human beings.

Ragged, dirty muslin curtains are hung across the bottom of the windows, bundles of rags are stuffed in the broken panes; the wretched rooms are lit by tallow candles stuck in empty bottles. The smell is vile, the whole atmosphere seems heavy and surcharged with the foul odour of decaying animal matter. The narrow pathway is paved and broken away here and there, and down it flows a stream of abomination, which settles into little pools before it discharges itself into the gutter. A man half dressed, unshaven, and unspeakably brutal looking, emerges from one of the houses. He is short and thickset, one eye is blackened, and a strip of filthy plaster adorns his left cheek. He is clad in fustian trousers, and a ragged blue shirt, a wisp of rag is twisted round his neck, with the end of which he wipes his mouth preparatory to speaking. When he does speak it is to gently inquire in a hoarse voice, "What the b_____ h__ we ___ ___ ___ are doing?" The expletives roll easily off his tongue, and in the midst of his tirade he catches sight of my companion, who is keeping his blue eyes fixed sternly on his face. The effect is magical, for it instantly stops his eloquence, and he disappears into the interior. He evidently is familiar with the police and has no wish to voluntarily renew the acquaintanceship. In his absence we make our exit.

"You see," says Mr. B., "there are any amount of these alleys about, and while the police are patrolling the street, the Lord only knows what goes on in the courts that branch off from the main thoroughfare. For instance, we passed a couple of constables a few minutes ago, well, they are not able to visit and properly inspect every alley in Berners Street, why we should want at least a score of men for that duty alone. Look how dark the entries are. If a murder were committed in the street the murderer could easily escape observation by lurking in one of the alleys till the first hue and cry was over, and then he could mix with the crowd and get off. Of course, the place is poverty stricken, but the poverty is of the lowest and vilest description. Wait till we get you to Hanbury Street, and then you will notice that poverty and crime are so closely allied that the former is never seen without the latter. And the great friends and helpers of vice are the want of light, the almost entire absence of sanitary conveniences, and the want of proper dwelling accommodation. Old houses are rightly condemned and are pulled down, but none are erected in their stead, the consequence being that the lower and criminal classes are forced to this locality where the sexes herd indiscriminately together like animals. A lot has been written and a lot said about the East End, but as yet there has been no description strong enough to portray the actual state of things that exist here, and the newspaper that will fearlessly open its columns to a statement of unexaggerated facts will be doing a public service."

By this time, we have got to a building which Mr. B. informs me is the club rendered notorious by being so near the scene of the Berners Street tragedy, whilst

opposite is a stone block which is a board school. Next to the club is a pair of high wooden gates which open inwards into the stable yard. We go inside, first taking a hasty glance behind the gates to see if anyone is lurking there, for there is plenty of room for a hiding place, On the right is the club, the windows of which are all lit up, and further on is the side door. Opposite is three small, whitewashed cottages, the place is so narrow that if the hapless victim had made the least noise, it must have been heard, despite the singing and merriment that were going on in the club.

A girl of about fourteen, barefooted and bareheaded, with a white, frightened face and sharp furtive eyes comes out of one of the houses. She starts a little when she sees us standing, and then comes across to me. "The woman was found there," she says, with infinite gusto, smacking her lips at the chance of repeating the tale of horror to an interesting listener, "er 'ead was on that short stone post, and 'er legs was just over the iron railings, and the blood and gore was all down there," and she pointed out the various spots mentioned with great relish. "Do you live here?" we asked. "Yes, sir, in the second cottage," she answered. "And did you not hear anything?" queried Mr. B. "Not a sound, sir," says the girl, earnestly, "and nobody else down here heard nothing neither. You know sir, I think that"—. But we were fated never to hear what the girl thinks, for a voice calls out "Lizer" and she promptly vanished into the cottage.

We retrace our way back along Berners Street; we pass a public house brilliantly lit up, clean and comfortable, and affording a striking contrast to the wretched habitations we have just seen. The bar is full of men and women, many of the latter having babies suckling at their bosoms. Children are going in and coming out, carrying jugs of beer or bottles containing gin or rum. Two women standing outside, commenced quarrelling; from words they come to blows; one smacks the other's face, whereupon she rushes forward, catches hold of her assailant by the hair of her head and proceeds to shake her by it. The children stand and laugh; a knot of men smoking clay pipes encourage the combatants calling out, "Give it to her, Bess!" "Never mind, Sukey!" and so on. The shaken woman claws at the other one's face, and just as we are going to interfere, someone says, "The coppers are coming." So, the men leave off smoking, part the two furies, who are making use of choice language, and take them into the public house to "stand them a drink," the women settling their dresses and fastening up their bodices, which have got disordered in the fray. It is worthy to note that they are both in an interesting condition!

This has created a little diversion, though there seems to be a smouldering feeling of indignation amongst the onlookers that the police should have been in the neighbourhood, thus, to stop an innocent and exciting spectacle, and they clearly show that they feel injured at the performance being stopped just when it began to get Interesting.

The houses that we pass are still small and shabby, and nearly every door is propped up by either a man or woman in various stages of *dishabille*. Some of the windows are adorned with weedy-looking plants; a few have melancholy birds in wicker cages. A youth passes with his arm round a girl's waist; he is kissing her, and she is laughing. He says something, and her merriment is excessive. Then he makes a coarse jest about being "Jack the Ripper," and puts his arm round her neck and draws her head back. Her laughter ceases abruptly; she wrenches away, and, as we approach them, we observe that the colour has faded from her cheeks, and she looks white and nervous. She is shaking. "No, Jim," we heard her say, "you have upset me tonight." He apologies and evidently makes his peace, for presently they re-pass us again, and he again has his arm around her, but she is no longer laughing.

A batch of girls are coming towards us, the majority carry infants, the eldest is perhaps nineteen, and they all wear wedding rings. Men are loafing about at all corners, oily looking and desperate. At first, they seem inclined to hustle us, but directly they catch sight of my companion's face they slink away. True that he is in private clothes, but there is something about him, his walk, his calm, stern face, and his intimate knowledge of the slums, that seem to awe these loafers, who clearly recognise in him a representative of law and order. Be that as it may, we are never approached. Occasionally we meet a few brawny fellows dressed in corduroys, who peer at us curiously as they mooch along in an aimless sort of manner. Mr. B. glances at them keenly, and sometimes he smiles a little as they pass on; afterwards he tells me that they are detectives.

At length we reach Buck's Row, and I may at once admit that I was agreeably surprised in it. The street is fairly wide, well paved, and not badly lit. the houses are small, but the majority are clean and respectable-looking, and seem to be inhabited by the hard-working poor. It is quiet and orderly, and the few females that pass have their heads covered. In fact, it is a very superior locality to Berners Street. In addition to the regular beat in Buck's Row, policemen are also on duty at the top and bottom the street so that it cannot be left for more than a quarter of an hour at a time without the police being either at the top or bottom of the row. The situation is so open that it looks the very last one where an undetected murder could be committed. The actual spot of the tragedy, although rather in the shade, is still open. There is a house with green shutters; by it there is a lamp. Next to it is a pair of high wooden gates, which fall back from the road perhaps a couple of inches, and slantingly opposite is another lamp. Between the lamp by the gate, lying in the road itself, was found the barbarously mutilated body of the second victim of the four recent murders. To my mind this is the most mysterious crime of them all, for it seems impossible that so ghastly an act could be perpetrated in a comparatively well-lit, thickly populated street like this, without some trace of the assassin being found, or some clue to his whereabouts being discovered.

III.

A door is open of one of the houses in Buck's Row, and it gives us an opportunity of seeing an interior so scrupulously clean, so bright and cheerful, that the remembrance of the black deed that took place outside seems to be even yet more horrible. Two young girls, neatly but plainly dressed and looking like dressmakers, go in, and are met in the oilcloth passage by a cosy-looking old lady, resplendent in a lace cap.

We have seen all that there is to see, so passing several warehouses looking very large and dark, we leave Buck's Row on our way to Hanbury Street. There is one exceedingly disagreeable feature of all these localities that deserves mention, and yet can necessarily be only very lightly touched upon, and that is that the men and women, particularly the former, have not the least knowledge of common decency. Their ignorance or wilful defiance of the most ordinary rules of decorum is apt to prove both embarrassing and uncomfortable to ordinary mortals, who still think that modesty and decency exist even in the far East.

The sights that I saw can better be imagined than described; indeed, a description would be peculiarly offensive and I must admit that the women were nearly as great offenders as the men. Surely some means might be taken to prevent the eye being outraged by spectacles that are a deep disgrace even to the squalid quarter that we are at present in.

Hanbury Street is a very different locality to any that we have yet been in. It is long and narrow, and unevenly paved. The houses are rather high, the majority dirty, and the whole lot swarming with inhabitants. The street is light and busy; this, by-the-bye, is at the commencement for I here remarked to Mr. B. "that the place is not as bad as I thought." He tells me that we are not yet in the thick of it, and he begs me to keep close to him. I soon find out that I have been too hasty in giving an opinion, for the neighbourhood and the people are vile. So much we see, I with horror distended eyes, my companion with the placidity born of ultimate knowledge of these slums, so much that dare not be written, and can only be spoken of in whispers.

There are any number of the noisome alleys like the one in Berners Street and at first it gives me quite a start to suddenly be confronted by gaunt, grimy men, who stare with fierce wolfish eyes, and make towards us as if to clutch at our watch chains, only to find my companion's eyes fixed sternly on them, and then they draw back and noiselessly disappear in the entries. It is very ghostly, the unexpected manner in which these human birds of prey appear, and then abruptly vanish in the mist. The savage way they leer in my face, their low, brutal aspect, the expression of sullen wrath that flits across their ferocious faces as they recognise who my companion is, inspires me with a secret anger as well as a half-formed dread, and I keep very close to Mr. B.

These men are thieves, professional loafers, pickpockets, bullies living on the earnings of the prostitutes who, God knows why, live with them. They are the scum of the criminal class; they are the offspring of the foulest and most unbridled passions; they are the noxious fungi of the worst type of humanity. Yet, vicious and degraded as they are, they one and all express and have a deep abhorrence of the human devil who through his barbarous crimes is making Whitechapel a region of horrified dread. If once the assassin was caught in Hanbury Street his miserable life would not be worth ten minutes purchase, and he would suffer death from the hands of those who are also "wanted." Their ideas of morality are peculiar, for we hear one man say in reference to the mythical personage known as "Jack the Ripper," "If a man quarrels with a woman let him knock her down or give her a ____kicking, but ____ don't let him rip her up and make such a ____ mess of her." Thus, blows and kicks seem a frequent occurrence in the lives of the Hanbury Street females, for these humane remarks are with received with profound satisfaction by the men standing round.

Women pass us; I suppose we must call them women, though, truth to tell, there is nothing womanly about them. No need to be told of their unashamed calling; it is branded on them. How can they be described? The ragged, filthy finery, the pinched or bloated faces, daubed hideously over with white and red paint; the red, blearing eyes; the matted hair, with the thick fringe growing right over their eyebrows; the close, sickly smell that clings round them, the eager, watchful glances that they cast around. Ah, me! It is all too fearful.

They still appear nervous and dissipated, for they seem to go about their frightful trade with manifest dread and reluctance. Mr. B. tells me that it is only over the last few nights that these unfortunates have ventured out, and as it is, very many have sought "fields and pastures new" in the vicinity of the Strand and Drury Lane.

Some of them are quite young girls, these are mostly all half-drunk and inclined to be nosy. One woman passes us with a face so battered and bruised that there is very little expression in it. The foreign element predominates. Villainous looking Poles, ruffian Germans, starved Russians, with the scum of half a dozen other nations all live, or rather exist, about here. They speak some incomprehensible jargon but they manage to find some means of earning a livelihood. I believe that they are quiet and inoffensive if left to themselves, but it is easy to see that they are looked upon with ill-conceived aversion and distrust. I quite credit Mr B.'s statement "that if the murderer was found to be a foreigner, all the police in London would be powerless to stay the persecution that the rest would be subjected to, in fact they would be hounded out of Whitechapel."

Amongst the many foul smells that assail us, the worst, because it is the strongest, emanates from the fried fish shops. There are a number of these establishments, and they seem to do a brisk trade. The fish is cut into pieces and fried a deep brown. I should not care to hazard an opinion as to what compound the fish is cooked in, but judging from the odour, inquiries and research would probably be the reverse of gratifying. This delicacy is retailed out from a halfpenny a-piece, each piece being wrapped up in paper, which is promptly taken off and thrown into the road, which presents, in consequence, an extraordinary spectacle of torn fragments. Several baked potato cans are in the street, so a halfpenny potato and a halfpenny piece of fish makes a choice supper, which is eaten in the street. For everyone seems to eat and drink and sit and rest in these thoroughfares, as well as performing their various little toilet operations in public. There are baker shops, a few vegetable stores, and some huckster's shops, which are perfect marvels of dirt and disorder. Sometimes a wretched, hungry looking cat slinks past me, but the place is so squalid that animals shun it.

A man who has been glancing at us wolfishly darts forward to make a grab at the handkerchief I hold in my hand. "Ah, would you?" says Mr. B., and the would-be thief makes off. I laugh at the salutary effect that my companion produces. "They know me," he says; "I have walked into one of the doss houses (lodging houses) after a man, found him there amongst a score of his pals, and have marched him off quite comfortably. They have got no real pluck; why, the majority of them are miserable cowards. Besides, as they often tell me, "We're not frightened of you, but it's the clothes you wear that we are afraid of."

Sometimes they cut up a bit rough. I remember once getting into a doss house, and not being able to get out again, I blew my whistle, and fought like demon. Lor', how I laid about me; just as I was getting the worst of it, three constables came to my assistance then the scoundrels let go their hold of me, and we managed to get out whole, but I was in a pretty plight."

"Talking of doss houses," he continued, they are the worst part of a policeman's duty. I mean when we have got to inspect them. Phew, the smell, it's enough to knock you down. You cannot imagine anything like it, the rooms are generally low, and not too large, and perhaps eighteen unwashed, half drunken creatures are lying in each apartment, with windows and doors tightly shut. You can fancy how nice and pleasant the atmosphere must be. The most trying, however, are the female doss houses. I'll never forget the first time I went into one. I had not long joined the force, and was a modest lad fresh from the country, and shy of anything belonging to a petticoat. Well, there was woman "wanted," and from information we received we ascertained that she was residing in a common lodging house in _____ Street, so I was told to go and arrest her. It was late of night when I got there, and of course no such person as I wanted was there. However, I had to go in and see for myself.

The first room I went into was full of women who had precious little clothing on. The light from my lantern woke them up, and I suppose I must have looked uncomfortable, for they commenced to chaff me. I went from one room to another and in every one the confounded creatures laughed at my modesty. At last, I picked out my woman, but devil a bit of clothes had she on. She declared that she had none, whilst I felt ready to sink into the ground. I wanted some of the females to lend her some, but they were shrieking with laughter and wouldn't. I offered to purchase a couple of the most necessary articles, but no one would sell them. I dare not leave her there, so I had to force her to wrap my coat round her. I had horse's work to make her keep it on, and if I hadn't have handcuffed her, she would have had it off in the street. It was a bitter cold night, but the perspiration rolled off me in beads when I got her safe into the police station. By Jove, that walk haunted me for weeks afterwards."

We are now near the scene of the murder, there are few shops, but any number of these common lodging houses. The place is comparatively deserted, only a few unfortunates flitting by us, very likely seeking the wherewithal to pay for a night's shelter. On our left is a house with the legend, "comfortable beds," written on a board outside. Opposite is the lodging house from which the hapless victim of the Hanbury Street tragedy was turned away to meet her death, because she had not the 4d. to pay for her bed.

The night is still young, so the birds of prey have not as yet returned to their noisome nests. While we stand, we see several girls disappear down the various entries. One asks for assistance. She says that she has no money and since the last two murders she has been afraid to go out and seek it. We give her a coin, and then inquire if she has any suspicion of anyone. She glances round fearfully as if to see if there are any listeners about, and she says hurriedly, "No she doesn't know, she wishes she did, must be a _____ monster to cut up the likes of her."

These women make no secret of their calling, which they regard with callous indifference but I cannot help thinking as we watch her into the house that she and her class, if they could be persuaded to speak, could throw some light on the mysterious perpetrator of the crimes.

IV.

The mist begins to fall in a steady melancholy drizzle, and the wind blows cold and raw. I shiver involuntarily, for the chill seems to penetrate even my thick coat. The damp is surcharged with smuts, and wherever they fall they a leave a black smear. A cripple is sitting in a doorway, he looks wolfish and starved, a hunk of dry bread, rejected evidently by dogs, is lying in the gutter, and this he presently sees. He gives a low cry, and with the aid of his rough crutch he hobbles towards it, his poor maimed leg working with excitement, he clutches at that bread eagerly, drags himself back to the step and commences to gnaw and tear the crust, more like a wild animal than anything human.

His enjoyment, however, is of a short duration, for a long, yellow thieving hand, belonging to a something that bears a faint resemblance to a woman, grasps him by his frayed shirt, and with the other hand snatches the food from him, and then vanishes in the mist. First the lad curses and blasphemes, and then he gives way to a dreadful misery, he moans and cries, and the tears form grotesque little rivulets down his grimy face. "He wishes he was dead, he prays for the pluck to cut his throat, he shrieks out for the woman's heart, her vitals," he curses her with every curse, and then falls a moaning again.

Mr. B. stands behind me as I drop a coin into the poor wretch's hand. He doesn't thank me, but glares and blinks at me out of his wicked tear-stained eyes, and in low, hoarse voice says that he'll "go and get something to eat before she comes out again." I inquire if she is the person who took the bread from him? He nods his head volubly. "And who is she" I ask, "My mother," he responds laconically. I shrink back, the remembrance of the curses ringing in my ears, and I shudder. Surely instead of spending thousands of pounds annually propagating the Gospel among the

Jews, and sending missionaries abroad to reclaim the heathens, a little of that money might be better spent in the efforts to Christianise and humanise the dwellers of the East End slums.

We cross the road, there is the lodging house and there is the inevitable door that shuts in one of the usual dark courts that reek with life, and which form not only a happy hunting ground for vice, but also a convenient and safe place for murder. It was huddled up behind this door that the victim of the Hanbury Street tragedy was found, close to the house where she was wont to sleep, and within a stone's throw of the street that she had traversed in her blind despair. "After midnight," says Mr. B. "it is something dreadful to see the women congregate round the doss houses, and beg to be let in. They have generally had the price

of a night's lodging during the day, but they spend it in drink, and when it gets late and trade is bad with them, they get fair desperate at the idea of sleeping in the streets all night."

As we go along, we pass another lodging house, and there see a sight so indescribably painful that I find it difficult to realise that I am in a wealthy and humane city. It is an unfortunate, young, and as well as we can see under the dirt and paint, pretty. She has boots and stockings on and an old silk skirt, with torn velvet bodice showing the flesh through the rents. She smells strongly of spirits, and we hear her imploring the deputy to trust her a night's shelter. She offers him anything only to let her rest there that night. He refuses, she catches him by the hand, she almost kneels to him, but he is obdurate, shakes her from him, and

Fig. 22. Whitechapel Loafers

shuts the door on her. At first the poor creature seems paralysed, then she shrieks and batters at the door with her hands, then she sobs with impotent misery, and calls on Christ to assist her. She tears at her dress and falls to beating her bare breasts. She seems to take a fierce delight in torturing herself, for she strikes her head against the wall and drags out her lank hair by handfuls. It is the very personification of abandoned despair. She tears and rives at herself, she drags herself shrieking and cursing to the windows, and then another woman that she seems to know comes along, and to her she explains her plight. Oaths are interchanged, they both squat down on the curb stone, the second woman counts over her money; the result must be satisfactory, for they both go into the doss house. My companion tells me that there is an amount of clanship amongst these unfortunates; although they will nearly murder each other through jealousy. If one is down on her luck the others will help her if possible, for instance, tonight that woman will pay for the other one's lodging.

I look stealthily at my watch, and I find that it is getting late; so, we proceed to direct our footsteps towards Whitechapel Road, which is the first stage of my return journey homewards. As we go along the loafers increase in number. "These men," says Mr. B., "are professional loafers; they sleep and drink all day, and at night they come out of the alleys and courts and lurk about the dark corners to see who they can knock down and rob. Why, if I had not been with you, you would have every bit of your valuables stolen by this time. These fellows don't work because they won't; thieving pays them much better and is exciting. They know me, and they know that I know them; so that is the reason they have left us alone."

I hint a doubt as to the desirability of our detectives being so well known; but this Mr. B. laughs at. "I'm in plain clothes," he says, and the folks about here recognise me; that is, because I want them to. We are not down here on business, we are merely sightseeing, and I did not wish our pleasure to be spoiled by getting into rows which I knew we could avoid by letting my calling be clearly noticeable. You mentioned a few minutes ago that since we left Berners Street, we have met no policemen. More we have in uniform, but have kept constantly running against our men, so artfully dressed that you have seen no difference in them and the other individuals who were lounging about. The number of police that have been drafted down here is surprising. If the public only knew of the precautions that are being taken, they would cease their grumblings at Sir Charles Warren, I can tell you."

We are now in Commercial Street, and it seems to me a very paradise after the slums we have left. The mist has cleared away, and if it were not for the all-pervading and abominable smell of fried fish, the air would be delightfully fresh in comparison with Hanbury Street. In addition to the baked potato cans, the proprietors of which are calling out in stentorian tones "Hall 'ot, hall 'ot," a man is doing a thriving trade in dispensing new walnuts "ten a penny." A woman is standing in the road, by a stall on which is laid out some pallid and soft and moist objects. They seem to be in a state of mild perspiration, and do not look unlike unhealthy babyhood. They, however, appear to be a choice delicacy, for when any are sold the purchaser walks off with them in proud triumph, I ask what they are, and am told that they rejoice in the name of trotters.

A swarthy Italian is grinding away at a piano organ, and round him are a bevy of children, girls, and women. The children and the girls are dancing, some of them a sort of can-can, others kicking up their legs and whirling about like so many teetotums, whilst several girls are waltzing together slowly and gracefully. A little bare-headed ragged child, with a face like a cherub and long golden curls half-way down her back, emerges from a group of juveniles; she glides gently along, makes a deep curtsey, picks up her poor frock in one hand and dances a measure so gracefully and quaintly that we stop to see the finish of the performance. The music gets quicker and she dances faster, her eyes glow like stars, the colour mounts her delicate cheeks, and she keeps time to the music in some fantastically graceful steps. The can-can dancers are getting uproarious, they whirl their arms about, their bodies sway, and they are trying who can kick their legs up the highest. The music stops, they sink down exhausted, the waltzers' sit down on the kerb, and wipe their hot faces with their hair, and the child dancer pirouettes round, stands on one toe, kisses her hand, and rushes back to play and quarrel with her companions.

Whitechapel Road itself is a great delight to me – it is wide and noisy and presents all the appearance of a fair. Either side of the road is a long row of stalls brilliantly lit up with portable gas, and everything under the sun can be bought there. There are butcher stalls presided over by loud-voiced men, who assure the bystanders that as it is late, they are almost giving the meat away. A lean, pale woman, carrying a baby, is haggling over the price of a piece of mutton. It is a fair-sized piece and at length he agrees to take fourpence; she pays him in half-pennies, and a little boy that is clinging to her skirt claps his thin hands rapturously. There are fruit stalls, ice stalls, book stalls, and stalls where unholy-looking shellfish are being consumed with appetite that speaks for the digestive organs of the Whitechapelites. The immense greeny tinged mussels, and the coy and evading periwinkles are had with a sprinkle of pepper and salt and a soupcon of vinegar, for a half-penny a saucerful; and it is a beautiful and edifying spectacle to see how clean the saucers are left through the help of the tongue and a grimy forefinger.

There are jewellery stalls at which girls gaze lovingly, and where a brooch with a diamond rivalling the Kohinoor in size, can be bought for threepence, and there are tool stalls, where everything, from a hammer to a jemmy, can be purchased. And of course, there are fried fish stalls. I abhor and detest this delicacy; my heart is against it. I indulge in wondering as to what the fish was like before it was cooked, and marvel at the quantity that is sold without any appreciable fall in health of the population in consequence. A man on a waggon is selling a wondrous ointment, which, if he is to be believed, will not only cure all the ills that mankind is heir too, but will also remedy everything from a smoky chimney to an obnoxious mother-in-law.

The people are better (not to say well) dressed than in the other streets that we have been in. Many of the women are resplendent in plush or seal skin; these by the by are Jewesses. We pass many handsome girls. The majority wear hats, but they are noisy and self-assertive. Men lounge about here, but they give me the idea of idling after work is done, for they have very little of the raffish look of their Berners or Hanbury Street compeers. In short, the East End cannot be judged from the flourishing and busy Whitechapel Road. It is the places that branch off from it that are so vile. It is the places where the moral sewerage flows till they become hideous cesspools of vice and crime.

Fine ladies and white-handed gentlemen will do no good down here; indeed, nothing will remedy the evils while lighting is deficient, sanitary convenience is absent, and these filthy dark alleys exist. I say goodbye to Mr. B. at Aldgate Station, and thank him, as well as I may, for his courtesy and kindness, and for his presence, which has kept me from insult and robbery in what he describes as "one of the (if not *the*) worst localities in London." And as I return to my hotel, I think with a thrill of disgust at the many horrible things I have seen and heard during my night's slumming in Whitechapel.

Sheffield Weekly Telegraph – 27th October to 17th November 1888.

1888 – STARTLING DISCOVERIES.

Fresh interest has been aroused in Whitechapel in reference to the recent murders by the statement of Matthew Packer, who keeps a fruit stall near the scene of the Berner Street murder, and from whom the murderer is believed to have bought some grapes for the unfortunate woman Elizabeth Stride shortly before the murder. He says that he saw the man last Saturday night standing near his fruit stall and looking at him in a menacing manner. Packer stated that being alarmed he asked a shoeblack standing near to watch the man, who, however, then ran off and jumped on a passing tramcar, and Packer could not leave his stall to follow him. There have been renewed complaints to the police recently from women who have been accosted by a man resembling the description of the assassin.

Plain clothes officers have been watching a certain house in Kensington in connection with the Whitechapel murders, and a startling discovery has just leaked out. On Sunday night, 21st ult., a policeman found hidden, near some shrubs in the front garden of one of the houses in Harrington Gardens, a case containing a couple of huge Ghoorka knives, one much blood stained. The case is blood-stained also. A doctor says that the stains are about two months old but could not state whether the blood was human. Notwithstanding all efforts to trace the owner nothing has transpired to show whether they were stolen from one of the mansions in Kensington or belonged to the Whitechapel murderer.

Fife Free Press & Kirkcaldy Guardian – 3rd November 1888.

1888 – THE UNFORTUNATES' DEFIANCE.

The district from which the Whitechapel fiend has drawn his victims was yesterday the scene of that terrible debauchery which unfortunately character-ises that portion of London during this season of the year. The gin palaces were thronged with women reeling under the influence of drink. Police officers, who had been stationed many years at the East End of the Metropolis, declare that the terrible series of crimes which have been perpetrated during the present year has had no effect in deterring or softening the women of the unfortunate class who infest certain thoroughfares in Whitechapel. On the contrary, they appear to pursue their calling with greater callousness and brutality than ever.

Sheffield Daily Telegraph – 27th December 1888.

1889 – ALLEGED ATTEMPTED POISONING.

On Monday, at the Thames Police Court, Morris Karns, thirty--nine, a passenger agent, of Church Lane, Whitechapel, was brought up on a warrant charged with unlawfully and maliciously administering to Mark Phillips a certain poison, with intent to injure him. The case arose out of an application made at this court on Saturday by Phillips, when Mr. Lushington granted a warrant. Mr. George Hay Young defended, and Detective-Inspector Reid appeared for the police.

Prosecutor, whose evidence had to be interpreted, said that he lived at Holly's Gardens. About ten days ago he saw the prisoner, who said, "Here is a bottle. I will make you a present of it for the Passover." The accused did not say what was in the bottle. That occurred at Church Street, Whitechapel, where the prisoner lived. The prisoner gave him the bottle for helping to carry a bookcase. He took the bottle home and told his wife to save it for the holidays. The following Monday he opened the bottle and drank some of the contents. He afterwards felt a burning sensation. The bottle was corked and sealed when he received it. There was no label on the bottle to show what it contained. He drank about a tablespoonful from a glass. The liquid appeared to be wine. It was very strong, and was a red wine. He afterwards began to retch, and was taken ill. His wife fetched Dr. Kay, and he subsequently went to the London Hospital, where he remained an inmate for five days. He had had some words previous to the gift of the wine with the prisoner.

Witness had spoken to the prisoner about what he had given him. When he asked the accused, what made him give him such stuff he only laughed, and made no remark. By Mr. Lushington: He told the prisoner he had drugged the wine and that it made him ill. Prisoner only said, "Serves you right." By Mr. Young: Prisoner did not tell him he should not have stolen it. He denied that he was an escaped convict from Siberia. He knew Philip Hollander, but he was not there when he assisted in moving the bookcase. He did not assist in removing any bottles. The prisoner kept a restaurant and he saw bottles in the place. He did not help himself to one of those bottles. Hollander did not tell him not to drink

the contents of the bottle, saying, "It is not wine." He did not suggest to Hollander they should get a warrant unless the prisoner gave him money, which they would afterwards divide. Witness had not asked the accused for money. He left the hospital on Monday afternoon. The reason he did not come to the court before was that he had no money.

Mr. Henry Edward Skyrme, house physician at the London Hospital, said he first saw the prosecutor on Wednesday the 17th ult. He was brought to the receiving room and was then apparently suffering from shortness of breath. He was placed in a ward and examined. He complained of a pain in the stomach on witness examining his throat he found a slight swelling. Those symptoms were probably due to an irritant. There was no distinct evidence of anything having been swallowed. Witness received a bottle when the prosecutor was admitted. It was an ordinary wine bottle, and was nearly full of a reddish-brown liquid. There was a cork in the bottle. Witness tasted the contents, and found that it was acid, and produced intense salivation, He could not strictly say what the bottle contained, but it was an irritant poison. He treated the prosecutor medically.

Detective George Cox, H Division, said that on Saturday information was received that a man had been poisoned. He afterwards received the warrant and arrested the prisoner, who said, "The man stole the bottle. I didn't give it to him at all." The prosecutor could not speak good English.

By Mr. Young: The accused gave himself up. The man Alter who had been spoken to, was undergoing a sentence of two months' hard labour for assaulting the police. Mr. Lushington said the prisoner appeared to have been ready enough to give himself up and he should accept his recognisances to appear to answer this charge when called upon. Mr. Young said he had evidence to show that the prosecutor stole the bottle, as on that day information was given to the police about the robbery.

Illustrated Police News – 4th May 1889.

1889 – NOTHING HAS BEEN DONE.

"Nothing has been done." Such is the melancholy burden of a letter to the *Times* by Mr. Samuel A. Barnett on the "Whitechapel Horrors." When the murders of last year occurred, a large number of excellent persons awoke to the fact that there was such a place as Whitechapel, and a still larger number declared in indignant tones that its haunts of vice and misery must forthwith cease to exist. "Jack the Ripper" was hailed as a ghastly kind of reformer, since he had made it impossible for the "horrors" of the Whitechapel slums to continue.

But months have passed away and Whitechapel and its slums are as they were. "Nothing has been done." And this is all the worse since, as Mr. Barnett points out, the really horrible quarter is only "a black spot three or four acres in extent," in the midst of a district which is no more disreputable than many others that have anything but a bad character.

St. James's Gazette – 23rd July 1889.

1889 – AN INTERVIEW WITH THE "ELEPHANT MAN."

Wondering how the unfortunate so-called "Elephant Man" was faring now that he had ceased to be a nine days' wonder, a London journalist journeyed the other day on his way to the London Hospital. After a few minutes of lounging and parleying in the waiting rooms, watching all sorts of cases being brought in, from a compound fracture to a put-out thumb, the emissary gained his point and was escorted by an attendant towards the secluded part of the institution where poor Joseph Merrick makes his home.

Some time back, when the latter was abiding in one of the wards, he used to receive numbers of visits from curious impertinents, to use Cervantes' phrase; but now, though various ladies of rank, in particular, are still very kind and thoughtful in their attentions, the general public is fast forgetting the "Elephant Man."

Merrick was having a meal when the reporter entered his little room, built out on the ground floor of the ward that bears the singular name of "Blizard" (with one z). He brightened up visibly at seeing a new face, and affably motioned his visitor to take a chair, but then relapsed into his favourite attitude of resting his head upon his strangely disproportioned right hand. This he does, as he has no hesitation in telling you, to relieve the pain that he constantly feels in his head, which measures as many as 36 inches in circumference.

It would serve no good purpose to descant upon Merrick's many malformations, though, to be sure, he is willing enough to talk about himself; but it may be noted that his left hand is quite normal and gripped the newspaper man's hand in right hearty fashion, and

that he walks very lame, using a stick, and alleging that this lameness is the result of a fall in boyhood, which his family carelessly treated as of no account. He is decidedly short and rather slight and speaks in a very intelligent manner. His accent shows plainly that he is not a Cockney. As a matter of fact, Merrick was born in Leicester some 29 or 30 years back.

The disease only began to manifest itself noticeably when he was in his teens, while, unhappily, his mother, who might have looked after him, died when he was ten. There were two other children by this first marriage, but his father married again, has had a large family by his second wife, and has not set eyes upon his hapless son for 14 years. Merrick speaks with considerable bitterness of the way in which he was swindled on his tour in Belgium by his Austrian entrepreneur. In his own words he is pretty comfortable in the London Hospital, where he has been now for considerably over two years, but how can a man, whose terrible malady seems if anything to be growing worse, be as cheerful as a cricket or as blithe as a lark. His little room is hung round with pictures and decked out with knick-knacks.

Joseph Merrick spends a good deal of his time in making cardboard models, but his chief relaxation and solace is reading. He has some shelves filled with books of various kinds and loves nothing better than to plunge into some exciting, sensational novel or book of travel. He says that he is apt to imagine himself as actually in the position of the hero of these tales; and without this comfort, indeed, he might possibly turn melancholy.

Kentish Independent – 18th May 1889.

1889 – "LYNCH HIM!"

On Friday night, last week, the cries of a woman in East Aldgate created some excitement. The woman had been seen approaching a dark portion of the thoroughfare near the Aldgate East Station, Whitechapel, with a sailor, and they had not been long at the corner before the woman was heard to cry, "No, I won't." The man thereupon seized her and dragged her a short distance along the ground. He held her by the hair with one hand, and with the other produced a knife or dagger, with which he commenced to cut the woman. Her screams soon attracted attention, the crowds of men and women ran from all directions to the spot. The woman was struggling with her assailant, and was covered with blood.

Several members of the Local Vigilance Association were among the first to arrive, and they pursued the man, who had attempted to escape. He was seized, and a dreadful struggle ensued. It was seen that the man had a long knife in his hand, and it was some time before he could be deprived of it. It was eventually taken from him, but even then, his fight for liberty was determined, and in the fray the woman crawled away. Police whistles were heard in all directions, and soon a great number of officers, both of the City and Metropolitan force, were on the scene, where a crowd of about six hundred persons had assembled.

When the police came up the man was cut and bleeding profusely from wounds inflicted by the mob, who had raised the cry of "Lynch him," and were throwing all kinds of missiles at the prisoner. Under a strong escort of police, he was got to the Commercial Street Police Station. When asked if he had anything to say, he replied, "The woman robbed me." He was asked why he drew the dagger, and he replied, "In self-defence." He said he was a sailor, gave a Scotch name, and said

he arrived from South Shields about a week before. He could not say where he was on the morning of the 17th inst. He did not know where he had stayed whilst in London. On being searched a smaller knife was found in his possession, together with a seaman's discharge.

Mr. Albert Backert, of 13, Newnham Street, Whitechapel, one of the Vigilance Committee, who seized the knife, and whose clothes were blood stained, has made the following statement, "At twenty minutes to ten this evening I was standing at the corner of Goulstone Street, near Castle Alley, when I saw a, woman standing under the lamp post at the corner of Goulstone Street and Wentworth Street. She was fair, and wore a red bodice, with a white apron. She had no hat or jacket on. A dark man with a slouch hat came up and spoke to her. He was about five feet eight inches tall, and about forty years of age. They walked towards Aldgate together. I followed them. When they got near Aldgate East Station, I heard her say, "No, I won't." With that he caught hold of her, and struggled with her. She screamed, and he dragged her to the kerb, opposite Wood's, the butcher's, where he

Fig. 23. Accosting the Assailant (Illustrated Police News)

threw her down. She screamed, "Jack the Ripper," and I rushed at him. I saw then that he had drawn a long knife or dagger from his sleeve, or pocket, and was holding it in his hand. He held her hair in the right hand and the knife in the left. He made an attempt, or did stab her, when I closed with him. He struggled violently, but I got the knife from him. Others came up in response to my cries for help, and he was held till the police arrived. He struggled hard to get away. There was a crowd of about six or seven hundred people there. A large number of City and Metropolitan police came up and surrounded the prisoner, who was cut and bleeding. The crowd became very violet, and tried to lynch him, and threw all kinds of missiles at him. The police got him to the station, where he presented a sorry appearance, cut and exhausted. I detailed what I had seen, and handed the knife to the Inspector. I noticed that the prisoner wore a belt round his waist, with a leather sheath attached. I have blood on my cuffs, shirt, and tie; but I am not cut. The knife is a formidable weapon, with a black I handle. It has a broad blade, about seven or eight inches long, which comes up to a point. I did not see the woman while I was in the struggle, but the police were looking for her."

Illustrated Police News – 27th July 1889.

1889 – ANOTHER WHITECHAPEL MURDER.

Whitechapel has again been the scene of another of those revolting murders which, during the last eighteen months, have shocked the country and spread consternation in the East End of London. The scene of the last atrocity is within a comparatively short distance of the localities where previous victims of "Jack the Ripper" have met their death, and contiguous to Dorset Street, Spitalfields, where, on the 9th of November last, Mary Jane Kelly was killed and mutilated. Mitre Square, Berner Street, and Buck's Row, each with its tragic record, are all near at hand, and, indeed, it may be said that all the eight murders committed in this neighbourhood were perpetrated within the radius of less than half a mile.

Castle Alley, where the latest crime has been committed, is a turning off Wentworth Street, Commercial Road, situated in the midst of a district consisting of a labyrinth of narrow side streets, alleys, and courts, the particular alley in question is probably about a hundred and fifty yards in length, with a breadth varying from a few feet to some twenty or thirty feet it its widest parts. It is a turning just past Aldgate East Station, and from there runs through into Wentworth Street, Spitalfields. From the Aldgate end it is approached by a narrow-covered passage,

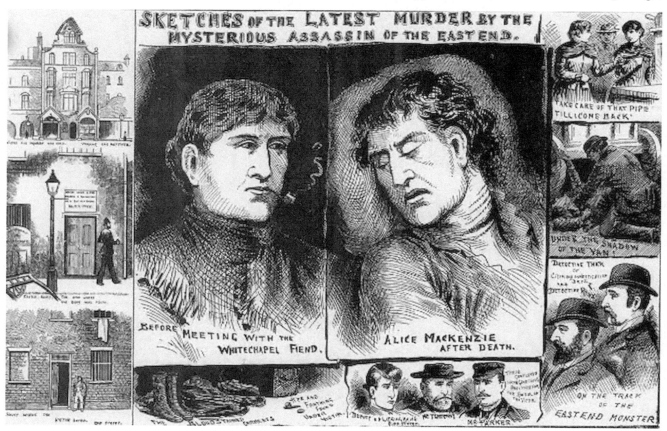

Fig. 24. The Mysterious Assassin of the East End (Illustrated Police News)

along which it would be impossible for two persons to walk, and beyond this passage the alley widens out considerably. This portion of the alley certainly has sufficient width to enable two large vehicles to pass each other at the same time with ease. At the time of the outrage, however, this open space was crowded with waggons, vans, trucks, and other vehicles, and afforded ample cover and darkness for the stealthy perpetration of a crime.

A few minutes before one o'clock on Wednesday morning Police Constable Andrews, while going about his beat round Castle Alley, saw a woman lying stretched on the pavement underneath a lamp post dead and lying in a pool of blood. Blood was still flowing in a stream from a deep stab in the neck. Her clothes were disarranged so that the lower limbs were exposed, and the constable found a severe wound on the abdomen, which had evidently been caused by an extremely sharp instrument. No portions of the body, however, have been removed as in some previous cases, and with this wound the mutilation ceased. It is surmised from the latter circumstance that the murderer was interrupted and had to seek safety in immediate flight. The constable, Andrews, at

once raised an alarm, and other policemen hastened to the spot, but not a trace could be found of the miscreant. The body was warm when found by the constable, and death could only have occurred just before he appeared upon the scene. It is remarkable that although three or four policemen were on duty around the alley, the murderer should have got away without either being seen or leaving one solitary clue as to his identity or course of flight.

Mr. Wynne Baxter, coroner for the south-east division of the county of London, opened the inquest at the Working Lads' Institute, Whitechapel Road, on Wednesday.

Mr. McCormack said, "I live at a common lodging house, 54, Gun Street, Spitalfields. I am a porter. I have seen the body in the mortuary, and recognise it as Alice MacKenzie. She was about forty years old, and had been living with me as my wife for about six years. I recognise her by the thumb on the right hand, which had been crushed at the tip. She also had a scar on the forehead. I know the clothes she wore, and recognise them. She said she came from Peterborough. I do not know whether she ever had any children. She worked very hard as a washerwoman and charwoman for the

Fig. 25. H Division Police Station

125

Jews. I last saw her alive between three and four o'clock on Tuesday afternoon. She left me in bed at the time to go and pay a night's rent, which was eightpence. In addition to that I gave her another shilling to do what she liked with, I did not see her again until the time when I saw the body in the mortuary. The deputy told me my "old woman" was lying dead in the mortuary, and I went there. She was always at home until last night. Yesterday I had a few words with her, and that upset her. She did not say she was going to walk the streets. I went down to the deputy and asked whether she had paid the money. That was about half-past ten or eleven o'clock, when I found she had not returned. The deputy told me she had not paid the rent. I said to the deputy, "What am I to do? Am I to walk the streets too?" She said "No." I immediately went upstairs and went to bed. I got up the next morning at my usual time. She was a great smoker."

Elizabeth Rider, the lodging house deputy, corroborated McCormack's statement. Witness added that MacKenzie was not a woman to be out late at night, and she did not think she got money on the streets. At nine o'clock witness saw her go out. She was then in drink. Witness often saw her smoke a short clay pipe. Never saw her with any man but McCormack.

Police Constable Joseph Allen, 423 H, stated that he entered Castle Alley from High Street, at fifteen minutes past midnight, and stood right under the lamp, where the body was found, to have something to eat. He then walked out at the other end into Wentworth Street, having been in the alley five minutes without seeing MacKemzie.

Police Constable Andrews, 272 H, said, "At ten minutes to one on Wednesday morning I saw Sergeant Baddam at the corner of Old Castle Street, leading into Castle Alley. He said, "All right?" I replied, "All right." We then proceeded through the alley, and while trying the doors on the west side, in the middle I saw a woman lying on the pavement. Her head was lying westwards, nearly resting on the edge of the kerb; she was close to a lamp about two feet away directly in front of a wheelwright's. There were two waggons in the roadway – one was a brewer's dray and the other a scavenger's cart. The vehicles would hide the view of a person's body from the opposite windows. Her clothes were thrown up to her chin, and exposed the lower part of the body. Blood was running from the left side and from the neck. I felt her hand, and it was quite warm. I blew my whistle, and Sergeant Baddam came up and gave orders not to touch the body until Dr. Phillips arrived. After I saw the body lying on the pavement, I heard a footstep. The next minute I saw a young man named Isaac Lewis Jacobs, living close by. He came back with me. At about 12.23 or 12.25 I went through the alley, but nobody was there

Fig. 26. 25 H. Division, Whitechapel

then. I met Police Constable Allen at that time. I went down one side of the alley and up the other. I looked in the vans, and saw nothing there. I then went into Goldstone Street, walked round into High Street, through Middlesex Street, and then into Wentworth Street, where I met the sergeant. No one in High Street specially attracted my attention.

By the position in which I found the deceased I should think she was murdered on the spot. I have been on that beat before. Whenever anyone was found sleeping in the vans, we turned them out. Altogether there were six or eight vans in the alley, besides several barrows, left there at night. The Three Crowns was open when I passed at twenty-five past twelve.

Isaac Lewis Jacobs, bootmaker, and Police Sergeant Baddam, 31 H, gave confirmatory evidence.

Police Constable Neve, 101 H, said he had seen deceased talking to men, and in his opinion, she was a bad character. Sometimes she was the worse for drink. Never saw her after eleven o'clock at night.

Mrs. Charlotte Smith, whose bedroom window looks into the alley, said she went to bed between quarter and half-past twelve, and was reading when she was called up and told of the murder. She had heard a sound.

The inquiry was adjourned.

On Thursday the inquiry was resumed. Inspector Reid, who was called to the scene of the tragedy about five minutes past one o'clock, said that after the body had been examined by the doctor it was lifted on to the police ambulance. Underneath the body was found a short clay pipe, saturated with blood and broken. There was also a farthing by the side of it. During the whole time, from the finding of the body to its removal, it was only seen by one person except the police. On searching the deceased at the mortuary, he found her clothing in a filthy condition, and he thought her one of the worst type of women to be found in the streets of Whitechapel.

By the Foreman: Do you consider the locality was well or sufficiently lighted? The Witness: I should think it sufficiently lighted. Was not a similar coin found in some of the other cases? Yes; two farthings were found in one case.

Mr. G.B. Phillips, of Spital Square, surgeon of police for the H Division, deposed, "On Wednesday I received a call at one in the morning. I immediately went to Castle Alley, arriving there in less than ten minutes. At the back premises of the wash houses, lying on the pavement, two and a half feet from the wall, lay the body of a woman. Her head was turned eastward, and her feet in a straight line in a contrary direction. She was about six yards from a gas lamp, which was lighted, her feet towards the lamp. Later on, I made a post-mortem examination. The body

was still warm in the region of the abdomen. When I saw the body first in Castle Alley the parts exposed to the air were cold. Below the left collar bone was a well-marked bruise about the size of a shilling, and on the right side was a larger, well-defined recent bruise. These both were the result of injury during life. Seven inches below the right nipple was an external wound seven inches long. It only divided the skin and not any muscular structure, and therefore did not injure any internal cavity. There were seven scored wounds running upwards from the larger wound, and seven more running downwards. It was apparent that the woman had suffered from an old disease. There was a wound in the neck reaching from the left ear to the fore part of the neck. Taking the wound as made it must have taken a somewhat upward direction, and judging by smaller wounds the worst incision seems to have been interrupted by the prominence of the lower jaw. There was a second incision, which was begun from behind, immediately below the first, and leaving a tongue of slain about three-quarters of an inch long. This second incision joined the former incision in its deepest part, which was immediately over the carotid vessels which were entirely severed down to the vertebra of the spinal column. There is not the slightest doubt that the cause of death was syncope from loss of blood through the divided vessels, and that such death was probably almost instantaneous. There was not any division of any portion of the air passage."

This concluded the medical evidence for the present, the Coroner permitting the witness to reserve several points till the next hearing. Two or three women, who knew the deceased, having given some unimportant evidence, the inquiry was adjourned to Wednesday August 14th.

Absolutely nothing has been discovered which is in the least degree likely to lead to the capture of the murderer. Several arrests have been made, but none of them have been of the slightest importance, and all the men have been set at liberty again. Plenty of "theories" are being circulated, but the police are no nearer to the discovery of the murderer now than they were when the first of these eight horrible crimes were committed.

McCormack told an interviewer on Thursday that he first knew the deceased woman in London about seven years age. She had not a friend in this city, but he believed she had one son, probably in America. Before he became acquainted with her, she lived with a blind man who played a concertina in the streets for a living. McCormack "took up" with her because she was homeless, and appeared to be a hardworking woman. He had heard her say she was the last of her family, and had often heard her speak of her father, who was a postman in Liverpool. McCormack never saw any of her relations. For several years he served in the army, and took part in the Crimean War, after which he was invalided, and received a pension for eighteen months.

On Saturday, before Mr. Lushington, at the Thames Police Court, William Wallace Brodie, thirty-three, having no occupation, and no settled abode, was charged with being a wandering lunatic. He was farther charged, on his own confession, with having murdered Alice MacKenzie in Castle Alley, Whitechapel, on the 17th ult. Detective-Inspectors Moore (Scotland Yard) and E. Reid (H Division) watched the case on behalf of the Criminal Investigation Department.

On the evening of Thursday week, the prisoner, who is a tall, powerfully built man, went to the Leman Street Police Station and stated to Inspector Pinhorn that he wished to give himself up for the murder of the woman on Tuesday night, but declined to say anything about "the other eight or nine." The prisoner afterwards repeated his confession to Detective-Inspector Moore, to whom he also made a long statement of a rambling and singular character. In it, Brodie stated he walked to Land's End and back in half an hour or three quarters of an hour, and on his return went into Whitechapel through an avenue of trees. It was 16.00 or 17.00 o'clock when he spoke to the woman, who was attired in a bright red dress. Having got her down, he whipped a knife out of his pocket and cut her throat. He described the knife as a white-handled one, and added it was specially made for the purpose at Sheffield. Brodie also added he could feel a worm crawling about in his head.

Inspector Moore said he had made inquiries into the case. Prisoner was discharged in August, 1888, and was only here ten days when he started for the Cape. On August 31st Mary Ann Nicholls was murdered in Buck's Row. When at the Cape the prisoner gave himself up as the Whitechapel murderer. He worked his passage home from the Cape on the 15th inst., and there was no doubt he was in bed at Harvey's buildings on the night of the murder. On the 17th he was charged at the Mansion House with annoying his brother, and was bound over to keep the peace. Mr. Lushington said he had a letter from the doctor of his time in prison stating that when he was admitted he was not responsible for his actions. He was sane now. The prisoner, who deserved to be punished for what he had done, would now be discharged. The prisoner was immediately rearrested by Inspector Moore on a charge of fraud, and conveyed to Clerkenwell, in which district the alleged fraud took place.

Illustrated Police News – 27th July 1889.

1889 – SHOCKING OUTRAGE IN WHITECHAPEL.

Another shocking outrage was discovered in Whitechapel on Tuesday morning. As on almost all previous occasions the victim is reported to be

Fig. 27. 26 Edmund Reid and H. Division

a woman of the unfortunate class, while, from the atrocious method in which her end was brought about, there is no reason to doubt the assassin is the same miscreant who has kept the East End of London, and, indeed, the whole Metropolis, in a state of alarm during the last two years.

It was not until nearly half-past five on Tuesday morning that this latest addition to the long roll of Whitechapel horrors was discovered. Our representative has been able to gather the following particulars:—

At about 20 minutes past five Police Constable Pennett, 239 H, who had been on this beat the whole of the night, was proceeding along Pinchin Street, a poor neighbourhood close to Leman Street Station on the Great Eastern Railway, within three minutes' walk of the Police Station, when, the morning being fairly light, he noticed the body of a female under one of the numerous railway arches with which this neighbourhood abounds. This arch is used for breaking stones by the Whitechapel Board of Works, and there are a few boards nailed up against it; but the apertures are sufficiently wide to enable a man to get through, and Pennett, who had been round the spot a short time previously without noticing the female, went inside with the view of seeing who she was. On coming close to the body, the constable was horrified to find evidence of another brutal murder, the head of the woman being severed from the body, and the legs missing.

The policeman hastily summoned assistance from the Leman Street Police Station, and while a number of constables were conveying an ambulance to the spot, Inspector Pinhorn arrived and directed the police operations.

The body was at once conveyed to St. George's Mortuary, and Dr. Clark, the partner of Dr. Phillips, the Police Divisional Surgeon, was very soon in attendance, and commenced to make a minute examination of the remains.

Telegrams were sent in all directions to the police stations, and soon after seven o'clock Mr. Monro, the Chief Commissioner, was on the spot, followed by Colonel Monsell, the Chief Constable of the Division. Superintendent Arnold, of the H Division, had been earlier on the scene.

By order of Mr. Monro, a cordon of police was drawn round the neighbourhood, and detectives were soon on the spot investigating the circumstances. Quite an alarm was created in the immediate locality, and Pinchin Street was impassable soon after the news spread.

From later inquiries we learn that the murder seems to have been committed two or three days ago, there being certain signs on the body of the beginning of decomposition. The remains were apparently those of a woman of 5ft. 3in. in height, and probably 40 years of age. The trunk was almost nude, with the exception of the fragments of an old chemise, which had been torn up and spread over the remains. These strips of calico were covered with bloodstains. The woman to whom the trunk belonged had been well nourished, and the hands did not appear to have been employed in hard work. The complexion of the skin was that of a brunette, the hair being dark brown. The head and the legs were missing, the former having been cut from the body, while the lower limbs were severed from the hip joints. The body had been cut open, and the intestines could be seen through the aperture thus made; but the mutilation of the trunk extended no further.

The police have been making the most minute inquiries in every direction, particularly in the immediate neighbourhood of the spot, as they surmise, and with some show of reason, that owing to the crowded state of the district, and the risk that must necessarily have been run in removing the body any great distance, the murder was perpetrated somewhere adjacent to the spot where the body was found. Not only the scene of the discovery, but also the neighbourhoods of the Leman Street Police stations and that of the mortuary in which the body is deposited, are surrounded by small crowds. The Coroner for the district, Mr. Baxter, has been communicated with by the police.

Dr. Clark having completed his examination of the body, left the mortuary shortly before ten o'clock, without communicating to the police any opinion of his as to the weapon with which the mutilation had been carried out, or as to the time the woman, had been dead. Until such opinions have been arrived at, together with details as to the condition of the trunk, the police will be unable to make any minute inquiries with a view to the identification of the remains. Dr. Clark will not be able immediately to furnish the officers with a full report, his other professional duties having taken him away from his residence in Spital Square.

At the mortuary there have been the usual number of callers, women particularly desiring to see the body with a view to ascertaining if it is that of any of their acquaintances; but of course, no opinion could be formed without the head, a diligent search for which is now being carried out in the various arches and secluded spots with which the locality abounds.

Our representative has had an interview with a person who had a good opportunity of examining the remains, and he asserts that the woman must have been dead at least three or four days, basing his opinion on the offensive odour which arose from the trunk. He judges that the Deceased was about five feet three inches high, and forty years of age. The work of severing the head and cutting off the legs was quite cleanly executed, thus proving that a very sharp instrument was employed. On the right arm, just above the wrist, there are two cuts as if the unfortunate victim had a struggle with her assailant. There are also several bruises on the arms.

As Constable Pennett is confident the body was not under the arch on the last occasion he went round his beat before the discovery, it is quite clear the murderer must have carried his ghastly burden to the spot where it was found at an hour when several people were about, and the police are actively instituting inquiries with a view to ascertaining if anyone met a man so encumbered.

The police officials in charge of the investigations being prosecuted in this district are Inspector Pinhorn, of the Leman Street Division, and Inspectors M'Naughten and Iwanson of Scotland Yard. These officers have examined the neighbourhood of the railway arches and stone yard near where the body was found, with a view of ascertaining whether any indication could be obtained as to the place from which the body was carried to the particular archway in which the discovery was made, but so far without success. The inference, therefore, is that the person carrying the headless and legless trunk entered the archway from Pinchin Street, which is immediately adjacent, and having emptied the body from the sack or other covering in which it must have been conveyed along the neighbouring thoroughfares, threw over it the strips of calico found upon it, and at once decamped. There can be no doubt that the body had not been deposited in the place where it was found more than a few minutes, as the police on that particular beat pass the spot regularly ever quarter of an hour or twenty minutes and must have seen it had it been there on either of the rounds made by them previous to the discovery. There are no blood stains at the place where the corpse was found. From the length and bulk of what remains of the body the murdered woman was probably from nine to ten stone in weight.

Up to the present moment there has been no report of anyone missing from the locality whose description would answer that of the corpse now lying at the mortuary. There is a marked difference between the mutilations effected in this case as compared with those that have accompanied the performances attributed to the notorious Whitechapel murderer; hence some people have inferred that if one set of murders are attributable to one individual, and another to a second person, the crime which is now horrifying the East End of London was perpetrated rather by the man who consummated the murders of Rainham and Battersea than by him who is responsible for the fiendish work done by the so- called "Jack the Ripper."

One of the first things discovered by the police when a thorough search was made was three sailors sleeping in a railway arch adjoining that in which the remains were found. They were detained and closely examined at the police station, but it was evident they knew nothing of the murder, or of depositing the remains on the spot They had neither seen nor heard anything and were accordingly discharged.

Mr. Albert Backert, chairman of the Whitechapel Vigilance Committee, writes as follows:—

"As chairman of the last-formed Whitechapel Vigilance Committee, I have been questioned by a large number of people about Tuesday's discovery. From the time our committee was formed, my colleagues and myself have done all in our power to discover the Whitechapel murderer. Night after night I have been out watching and making inquiries; but when the dock labourer's strike commenced, the interest in the murders seemed to cool down, and thus several of my supporters relaxed the energy they had hitherto displayed.

From inquiries, I am confident that the murderer is a Whitechapel person, or at any rate, he is well acquainted with the back streets. It is a curious fact that in all places where these murders have occurred, the houses are such that any person can enter by pulling a string which lifts the latch. My opinion is that the murderer knows this, and the moment he has committed a murder he enters one of these houses. I firmly believe that if the police had searched the houses in the vicinity the moment the murder was discovered, the murderer would have been discovered."

The examination of the abdomen by Dr. Phillips's assistant, who was summoned to the scene, showed that nothing had been removed from the intestines or any other part of the stomach. The motive for the crime is less apparent in this case than in several which have preceded.

It was on Tuesday morning deemed advisable that Detective-Inspector Tonbridge, who conducted the investigations in the recent Thames mystery, should be called in. Accordingly, in company with the Chief Constable, Colonel Monsell, he visited the place where the discovery was made, and subsequently viewed the remains. Those are at present at the mortuary in Cable Street, St. Georges, awaiting an inquest.

The extra men who have been stationed in the district for some months past had not been withdrawn, but on the contrary, their members had been reinforced in consequence of the dock

1. The House on the North-East Coast of Anglesey occupied by the Boys
2. The Arrival: Kit-bags and Tent-poles
3. A Sail in a Fishing-boat
4. Launching the Boat
5. A Boy Falls Overboard, but is Rescued as he had learned to Swim
6. Fiddling and Dancing in the Evening
7. The Kitchen, where the Whitechapel Boys learned to do Simple Cooking
8. "Hallo! What's the matter with you?" "Only fallen down an old Shaft, Sir"
9. Ghost Stories at Night
10. A kindly Clergyman Entertains the Party

"WHITECHAPEL IN WALES"

Fig. 28.   Graphic – 5th October 1889.

strike. About the time the trunk was supposed to be deposited under the arch, some hundreds of constables were on their way from all parts of the metropolis through the neighbourhood en route to Leman Street Police Station, where they are assembled to relieve the men who have done duty throughout the night.

The Star- 12th September 1889.

1889 – WHITECHAPEL IN WALES.

Mr. Wilfred Grenfell, of the London Hospital, sends us the following interesting letter:-

"With forty-seven boys we again spent a fortnight in camp, in our rocky bay in Anglesey, this August. Our expeditions were of a more ambitious character than before, and included a three days' outing. We journeyed in our sailing boats to Beaumaris; thence walked to Menai Bridge, Bethesda, and along the Nant Francon Pass up the Glider Fawr. Two boats did not reach home till the fourth day. That no money should go in hotel expenses was insured by arranging with friends to lay out their stables with straw, or lend us their barns to sleep in and they almost always kindly provided a breakfast as well – an arrangement we can heartily commend. An account, illustrated by sketches if possible, from a series of photographs taken by one of the boys, with a camera of his own make, will shortly be forwarded to all subscribers. We shall be only too glad to send it also, with an audited balance sheet, to anyone interested in the work. In thanking those who helped us, we may mention that three other companies imitated our example this summer, and enjoyed the same period of absolute happiness. One party came to our abode the day we left, and saved any waste by arranging with us for our surplus stores.

On the lads themselves the result has been most encouraging. An increased knowledge of Nature, has led many to an increased love for it, and for its and his Maker. I beg to acknowledge here the following anonymous subscriptions From Royston, 7s. 6d. from Edinburgh, 3s.; from "M.M.," Kensington, 3s. from Dublin, "Ardent Sympathiser," 3/. Total, 3/. 13s. 6d."

1889 – FATAL FIGHT IN WHITECHAPEL.

At the Thames Police Court, on Friday, James Donovan, fifty-eight, a labourer, of 6, Upper Well Alley, Whitechapel, was charged with feloniously killing Edward Arthur Careless, a labourer, in a fight.

Sophia Careless, of 6, Pearl Street, who appeared deeply affected while giving her evidence, said that between three and four o'clock on Tuesday afternoon her husband came home with a cut on his forehead. He said it had been caused through falling down. After he washed the wound, he said he had been fighting with a man, and went out again. He returned home soon afterwards, and went to bed, which he did not again leave alive.

At ten minutes to seven on Thursday morning she found her husband lying dead in bed. On Tuesday she noticed a bruise on the face of the deceased, and it was now much more distinct. She did not think the deceased knew he was so near death No doctor saw him alive. Deceased told her he had been blinded with blood, but witness did not notice if his clothes were dirty. He was not tipsy when he came home. Witness did not know the prisoner.

John Hooper, a labourer, of 28, New Gravel Lane, said shortly after two o'clock on Tuesday afternoon he was in the Ship and Dolphin beer shop, New Gravel Lane. The prisoner came in, and at that time the deceased man was there. Donovan started talking about work, when Careless told him "to hold his row." Donovan refused, and called Careless a bad name. Deceased then struck Donovan a blow on the jaw with his fist. Prisoner told the deceased to go outside and he would fight him. They went out of the house and went to Coleman Street. They took off their coats and commenced fighting. They struck one another and wrestled, when both fell to the ground, the prisoner being underneath. Careless struck his head on the ground, cutting it. They got up and again fought. Donovan struck the deceased man a blow between the eyes, and they again struggled. Careless said, "Let go of me and I'll have another go." They sparred up, when Careless said, "I'm blind."

Witness and some more men took him away and wiped the blood from his eyes. They afterwards bathed his head. Donovan then came up and wanted to fight witness. The prisoner was quite sober, but Careless had been drinking. Detective-Sergeant George Glenister, H Division, said he arrested the prisoner on the previous night. On telling him the charge said, "I didn't have any row. I did have a go, but I did not hit him." My daughter cut my head open, where you see the plaster, the same night with a cup."

The doctor said the cause of death was erysipelas, consequent on the wound.

Mr. Lushington remanded the accused.

Illustrated Police News – 30th November 1889.

1890 – THE MISERIES OF EAST END TAILORS.

A mass meeting of East End tailors and assistants was held on Saturday night, at Whitechapel, for the purpose of calling public attention to what they describe as the utter failure of the Parliamentary Sweating Commission to alleviate the miseries of the sweated East End tailors, to point out how the provisions of the Factory Acts are evaded by the master sweaters, and, in consequence, to declare a strike, and for that purpose both in London and the provinces, to empower a strike committee to fix a date which the strike is to begin, and to take all other necessary steps for successfully carrying on the strike.

Mr. Lewis Lyons occupied the chair, and said he would shame the Government, for he would telegraph to the Berlin Conference the fact that "the East End tailors are dying in great numbers from consumption because of the insanitary condition of the dens in which they are compelled to work." Resolutions in sympathy with the objects of the meeting were unanimously passed.

Preston Herald – 6th March 1890.

1890 – FREE DINNER FOR POOR CHILDREN.

In "Uncle Tom's Cabin," Mrs. Beecher Stowe has given a forcible illustration of the difference between the abstract and philosophical, and the concrete and practical ways of looking at a troublesome question. An honest and conscientious Congressman, after careful study of the Fugitive Slave Law, has come to the conclusion that if men are legally entitled to own slaves, they are also entitled to recover their human property should it stray away. But when this Congressman is brought face to face with a poor, footsore, hungry, trembling, fugitive, he forgets all his fine theories, and aids and abets the escapee to get across the border into Canada.

The same remark may be made about the Free Dinner Question. Many a worthy citizen, especially when his own dinner has rendered him genially talkative and argumentative, will utter solemn warnings against the pauperisation of the lower classes by the transference to the shoulders of charitable strangers of the burden which the parents ought to bear. But introduce this worthy citizen to such a scene as is here delineated by Mr. Barnes's pencil, and, ten to one, his politico-economical doctrines, which are nevertheless perfectly sound, will melt away. He will say – perhaps not aloud, but at all events to himself – "We cannot wait until the problem of parental responsibility is solved; these poor, pale-faced children are hungry – they rarely get what I should call a good square meal – so hang political economy! let us feed them first, and moralise afterwards."

In this manner the heart is wont to conquer the head, but it does not follow that the heart is always wise in its conclusions. There can be no doubt that, while conferring a temporary benefit on the children, we may, by our well-meant charity, only succeed in confirming the parents in habits of unthrift. The problem is a very difficult one to solve, and we will say no more about it now.

Mr. Barnes's sketches were made at the King Edward's Mission, Whitechapel. The small engraving affords an admirable study of boy-nature. The lads, having finished their dinner, were experiencing a pleasant and, it is to be feared, unusual, sense of repletion, when they suddenly discovered that they were being "took" by the artist. He has skilfully seized their various expressions.

1890 – DEATH OF THE "ELEPHANT MAN."

The inquest on the body of Joseph Merrick, better known as the "Elephant Man," was held yesterday at the London Hospital by Mr. Baxter.

Charles Merrick, of Church Gate, Leicester, a hairdresser, identified the body as that of his nephew. He was 29 years of age and had followed no occupation. From birth he had been deformed, but he got much worse of late. He had been in the hospital for four or five years. His parents were in no way afflicted, and the father, an engine driver, is alive now.

Mr. Ashe, house surgeon, said he was called to Merrick at 3.30 p.m. on Friday, and found him dead. It was expected that he would die suddenly. There were no marks of violence, and the death was quite

Fig. 29.   Free Dinners to poor at the King Edwards's mission, Whitechapel – "Before" (Graphic)

Fig. 30.   Free Dinners to poor at the King Edwards's mission, Whitechapel – "After" (Graphic)

natural. The man had great overgrowth of skin and bone, but he did not complain of anything. Witness believed that the exact cause of death was asphyxia, the back of his head being greatly deformed; and while the patient was taking a natural sleep, the weight of the head overcame him, and so suffocated him.

Mr. Hodges, another house surgeon, stated that on Friday last he went to visit Merrick, and found him lying across the bed dead. He was in a ward specially set apart for him. Witness did not touch him.

Nurse Ireland said that Merrick was in her charge. She saw him on Friday morning, when he appeared in his usual health. His midday meal was taken into him, but he did not touch it.

The Coroner, in summing up, said there could be no doubt that death was quite in accordance with the theory put forward by the doctor.

The Jury accepted this view and returned a verdict to the effect that death was due to suffocation from the weight of the head pressing on the windpipe.

Morning Post – 16th April 1890.

1890 – TERRIBLE STORY OF AN OUTCAST.

The following sympathetic account of the wretched outcast, "The Elephant Man," whose death was recorded in the *South Wales Echo* last week, is taken from the current number of the *Speaker*:—

Fig. 31. A portrait of Joseph Merrick by Adam Skutt

We can remember no invented tale that speaks so to the heart at once of the cruelty of life, and the beauty of human compassion, as the true story closed this week by a sentence in the newspapers, announcing that Joseph Merrick, the "Elephant Man," was dead. Imagine a human soul clothed in a body so unspeakably frightful that, seeing it, men turned sick with loathing, and women fainted; a being who had to be conveyed from place to place in secret; who hardly dared to venture abroad even by night; who, finding his fellow-creatures run from him, grew terrified by the terror he created, and shuddered in dark corners like a hunted beast. Imagine him driven by starvation to accept a showman's offer and be exhibited to the most brutal of audiences, that commonly enough shrieked and ran pell-mell from the tent as soon as the curtain was drawn.

Early in 1886, Mr. Frederick Treves, one of the surgeons of the London Hospital, found Merrick in a penny show, in a room off the Whitechapel Road, crouching behind an old curtain and trying to warm himself over a brick that was heated by a gas jet. Mr. Treves went up to him not only without fear or loathing, but with sympathy. For the first time in his life of twenty-four years Merrick heard a kind word and was spoken to like a man. The effect was curious. It made him afraid at first. He shrank as an ordinary man would from something uncanny. Then as he began to realise the truth, he broke into sobs of gratitude. Days and even weeks passed, however, before he recovered from the shock of hearing a compassionate word. The police prohibited his show on the ground of public decency.

So, he went to Belgium, where again the police interfered, and where an agent decamped with his money. Merrick was left destitute and starving in the streets of a foreign town, where the ignorant mob thought him a fiend.

He came back to London—how, no one quite knows. At every station and landing place crowds dogged him. Steamers refused to have him on board. But he came back to London because in London lived the only man who had ever given him a kind word. He made his way to the London Hospital, found Mr. Treves, who had him lodged for a time in an attic in the hospital, and determined to find a permanent shelter for him. But now it was found that no institution would receive him. The Royal Hospital for Incurables and the British Home for Incurables alike declined to take him in unless sufficient funds were forthcoming to pay for his maintenance for life. He himself begged that he might be placed in a Blind Hospital. It is hard to match the pathos of this plea.

Then in November 1886, Mr Carr Gomm, the Chairman of the London Hospital, wrote to the *Times*, asking help for this case, and the British public responded. A room was built for Merrick on the ground floor in a remote wing of the hospital, and there, surrounded with books, flowers, and a hundred tokens of the kindness that is really quick in the public heart, he has lived until this last week.

He had found many friends – the Prince and Princess of Wales, Mr. Gladstone, Mrs. Kendall, and others. To Mrs. Kendall is due the happy suggestion that Merrick should be taken to see the Christmas Pantomime at Drury Lane. She engaged the Royal box; she had him brought to the theatre and took every precaution that no strange eye should see him. Hidden from the house, behind the curtains of the box, the "Elephant Man" tasted an hour or two of intoxicating happiness. It was all real to him—the fairies, the splendour, and the jewels.

Merrick, in spite of his hideous exterior and terrible experiences, was in his way a gentle sentimentalist, and gushed forth at times, under the happy conditions of his life at the hospital, in verse modelled on the hymns of Dr. Watts, in which he gave utterance to feelings of gratitude, the sincerity of which none ever questioned. It was a tender heart that was beating beneath a mask more hideous than that of Orson. Above all it was a heart that was filled with love for the man who was literally his saviour, who first spoke kindly to him, who rescued him from a fate a thousand times worse than death, and to the end was both his doctor and his friend.

Recently it was only Mr. Treves who could thoroughly understand the poor creature's maimed utterances and to Mr Treves he clung to the last with the wistful trust and affection, of a dumb animal. It is difficult to speak of this man's case without emotion. But luckily it is harder still to hear of it and believe that the struggle-for-lifers have grasped the true secret of life, or even a half of it.

South Wales Echo – 22nd April 1890.

1890 – A "RIPPER" HOAX?"

Mr. Albert Backert, chairman of the Whitechapel Vigilance Committee, has written the following letter from Newnham Street, Whitechapel, dated Friday, to the *Daily Chronicle*:-

"In connection with the late Whitechapel murders the most remarkable and sensational statement was made to me this morning at my place. At eleven o'clock a very respectable middle-aged woman called at my house and wished to see me. She was asked in, and then made the following statement to me, which she declared was all quite true. About two years ago, she said, she was living in the model dwellings close by here and had a bedroom to let furnished. A young man called and engaged the room. After living for some time with her he stated that he had been to sea, and that at the present time he was receiving £1 a week from his father, and was also receiving an allowance from his brother, who was a doctor, and that he did not work himself. She also noticed that he had plenty of clothes, including hunting breeches, revolvers, guns, and many other articles which an ordinary working man would not have.

He had the door key and could go out and in at all hours of the night and used generally to get up at about five p.m., but she could not say what time he arrived home at night. On several occasions she noticed that his towels were very bloodstained, for which he accounted by saying that he was fond of painting and had wiped his brush on them. She also stated that she knew he had sent the liver, because one afternoon she happened to go to his room and saw him with several pieces of liver on a newspaper, which he stated he had got from a New Zealand boat, as he knew a friend who was on board a frozen mutton boat. She saw him pack it in a box and address it to the chairman of the then Vigilance Committee. He also put some pieces into different envelopes, which he intended sending to the Central News and the Press Association, and the police, but he forgot them, and she threw them into the dustbin.

She noticed also that he had several brass wedding rings on the mantelshelf, and on one or two occasions he brought home a white apron bloodstained, and gave them to her, which she has at the present time. He always seemed to have plenty of money, and on the morning of the last murder (the Castle Alley) he left and has never returned. He left a pair of silent shoes, several bags, which she says are bloodstained, and a long overcoat, which is also bloodstained. I asked her if she had been to the police, and she said she had not, as she was afraid of getting into trouble for not having given information before. She said she could hold the secret no longer, and she feels convinced that the man she had lodging with her was the real "Jack the Ripper" and Whitechapel murderer.

I feel sure that she was in earnest about this statement, and she appeared very nervous, and did not wish her name to be published. I have no doubt that the police will make inquiries into this statement at once, and I directed her to go to Leman Street and give all particulars. I may add that there was another person present when this statement was made this morning."

Respecting this strange story, the *Globe* have made inquiries in Whitechapel. Our contemporary states that the woman is hiding, as she is afraid the man she

suspects will do her bodily injury. "So careful has she been that the police have not yet succeeded in finding her or obtaining the following further details of her story. It appears that while living at the top floor of a block of model dwellings in the neighbourhood of Aldgate the man engaged, on the floor below, a bedroom, with lumber room adjoining, and paid her to keep the former clean, her occupation being that of an office cleaner. The lumber room, which contained a sink, was always kept locked, and although she did a portion of his washing, it was evident he did much of it himself.

She describes him as young, of middle height, well-built, with a small fair moustache and light brown hair, although she had frequently remarked that he had means by which he made his moustache and eyebrows much darker on some occasions than others. His movements during the time the murders were occurring were very mysterious. He had not the appearance of a working man, and admitted that his parents, although in a good position, would have nothing to do with him, as he had been a scapegrace. His brother, who she understood was a doctor, visited him on two occasions, and appeared much older than he. She has no doubt he is English, but he spoke with a nasal twang, which he evidently affected, and used the word 'Boss' very frequently in ordinary conversation. He usually rose at two in the afternoon, and would go out about five o'clock, invariably wearing a tall hat and dressed very respectably, but as he had a large number of suits of clothes he often dressed differently, or, as she puts it, "He was a man who could so alter his appearance that if you met him in the street once you would not know him again."

His clothes were mostly of the best quality, and included dress, shooting, and morning suits. On one occasion he gave the woman a dark-coloured overcoat to sell, and she offered it to the wife of a working man. The latter, however, pointed out that it was so stained with blood that she would not let her husband wear it. The patches, which were of a dull brown, were thought by the woman to be paint, but when she returned it to the mysterious lodger with an intimation that she could not sell it because of the blood, he laughed lightly, saying the stains were nothing. Nevertheless, he burnt the coat, for she subsequently discovered the remains, together with the horn buttons, in the grate.

As the murders were committed her suspicions were increased, but she did not communicate them to anyone until the day following the discovery of the body in Pinchin Street. She went to clean the bedroom as usual, when she found upon the three mats footmarks of blood and upon one a large clot of the same substance. She then spoke of her suspicions to a person, who advised her to say nothing of the matter.

As time went on, and the murders continued, she saw in his room many articles which were bloodstained, although he never would allow her to enter the room alone but remained with her while she performed her work. The lumber room she never entered, for he kept the key, and at times when she wished to enter it for various purposes, he always told her to go upstairs to her own apartments.

With regard to the 'Jack the Ripper' postcards, the man always wrote his letters in red ink, of which he had a large bottle on the mantelshelf. Upon the same shelf, too, she first noticed one brass wedding ring, but the number was afterwards increased until there were five, and these he left when he suddenly disappeared.

On another occasion she found a piece of dirty rag screwed up and concealed behind a chest of drawers. This she discovered to be a portion apparently torn from a woman's print apron, and on taking it upstairs she saw that it was bloodstained. She washed it and had it still in her possession. The pattern of the apron may form an important clue.

The most remarkable fact, however, is that on the night of each of the murders he was absent and returned at early morning. On the morning of the Castle Alley murder he disappeared, having previously sold the whole of his belongings. The woman afterwards removed, but a few days ago she again saw him near Aldgate, and this fact, combined with the letters recently published in the press, led her to lay the facts before Mr. Backert."

It is stated that there is no truth in the sensational reports published about extra police measures in the East End in connection with what is called the "Jack the Ripper" scare. The police precautions have not been relaxed, and are still in force, and they are wholly independent of the letters lately received. In the opinion of the responsible authorities all these letters have been attempts to hoax the police and the public, and no importance is attached to them at Scotland Yard.

Illustrated Police News – 18th October 1890.

1890 – CHILDREN'S HOLIDAY HOME AT SHANKLIN.

Among the benevolent efforts to help the poor, there are none more praiseworthy than those which are directed to succour the sick children of the "slums" who are too often left uncared for and unaided in their fight for life.

The benefit conferred upon the poor of the East End by such an institution as the London Hospital

Fig. 32. Children Convalescing in Shanklin (ILN)

is incalculable; but many of the gutter children, who are there rescued from death, return to their squalid and poverty-stricken homes in more or less weak and debilitated condition.

A small cottage home has lately been established at Shanklin, in the Isle of Wight, for the reception of East End children after leaving the hospital. The children sent down are of the poorest class, and few of them have ever been outside the slums in which they live. They are all convalescent after more or less serious illness, and they remain at the seaside for a month. With unstinted food, fresh air, and kind treatment they are benefited both in body and mind, and after their month's holiday they are placed once more in a fit condition to renew their struggle for existence.

Thirty children have been sent down since the summer; and next year it is hoped to double the number if the necessary funds can be obtained. £150 will accomplish this, including the railway fares of the children.

Donations and subscriptions for the Children's Holiday Home, Greengrounds, Shanklin, will be gratefully received and acknowledged by Miss Constance Francis, Luccombe Chine, near Shanklin, Isle of Wight.

Illustrated London News – 20th December 1890.

⎯⎯◦◉◦⎯⎯

1891 – POVERTY IN THE EAST END.

The prolonged severe wintry weather during the last December and first January weeks must have caused much suffering to the very poor, some of whom are "always with us;" for the want of fuel and warm clothing, as well as of nourishing food, is cruel destitution in cold weather. There are doubtless, at this season, in different parts of London—in the crowded district between Lincoln's Inn fields and St. Martin's Lane, in the bye-streets of Westminster and Chelsea, in Clerkenwell, and in Lambeth and Southwark, as well as in East London—many persons and families in real distress.

The present total amount of such helpless poverty is believed, on the safest reports and computations,

Fig. 33. Whitechapel Family Making Cheap Wire Implements (ILN)

not at all to exceed the average at this time of the year. There is apparently less difficulty than in former years of finding employment for unskilled able-bodied labourers, for some of the suburban vestries—that of Hampstead for instance—could hardly get five or six men together for the work of clearing the roads of snow; and at the Victoria and Albert Docks, which have seldom been fuller of ships, the men hired to unload corn for Canadian steamers, earning at the rate of twelve shillings and sixpence a day, struck for higher wages.

It is the aged and infirm, the forlorn women, too often deserted wives, the feeble persons cast adrift by the wreck of homes, perhaps far off in the country, and permitted by careless neighbours to come to London in quest of relatives or friends whom they fail to find, or who cannot assist them—it is these classes of people who mostly suffer. They are not seen much in the streets, but they starve, or at best live wretchedly by ill-paid and precarious work, if they know how to get it, which few strangers to London can know; and only the "district visitors," the ministers of religion, or the agents of well-organised systematic charity, acquainted with the locality and its inhabitants, can discover these cases, or can test the reality of their needs.

Our Artist, under trustworthy guidance, has gone his rounds in Whitechapel and the neighbourhood:

the subjects of his Sketches are such as we have generally described. Here is a decent old couple who make such cheap wire articles toasting forks, gridirons, and the like, carrying them about in the evening for sale in the streets. They may bring home a shilling or two, but it is a poor livelihood; their meals are nothing but a piece of bread and some weak tea; their companion is a stray cat. It is long since either the old man or his old wife could buy any clothes, and his boots are so unsound that he has wet feet at his first step in the miry snow.

There is a family, a mason's labourer, his sick wife, son and daughter, who came up from Lancashire on Christmas Eve. It is a pity that they, and hundreds monthly who are like them, should ever be encouraged to come to London. Of course, he can get no work here; nobody knows him; and he pays fourpence a night for his own bed in a lodging house, while the room occupied by his wife and children costs a shilling a night.

The cost of lodging or apartments in London is alone sufficient reason why the poor all over England should not think of seeking to better their condition by removing to this overburdened Metropolis without assured employment. This mistaken practice is really the main cause of nearly all the extreme poverty, beyond that occasioned by accident or

Fig. 34. Lancashire Family in Whitechapel (ILN)

by personal misconduct, that is to be deplored in London life.

Illustrated London News – 10th January 1891.

1891 – SALVATION ARMY SOCIAL SCHEME.

The British nation is just now in a serious mood, and inclined to consider its social problems. Of all the schemes for their solution which are urging their claims upon both the public attention and the public purse, the plan propounded in "Darkest England" has had the greatest success of late.

With the scheme as a whole it is not here my purpose to deal. The object of this Sketch is to present only one side of it—its City colony, the particular function of which is to provide for that most difficult class, the homeless and destitute. For the needs of the majority of these there has hitherto been only the relief offered by the charitable institutions, the whole of which, although doing good work, are quite inadequate, I personally am inclined to think, to meet the demand made upon them. It is estimated that there are, at least, 10,000 destitutes within the metropolitan area, and this ever-present evil holds so tenaciously to life, and the difficulties in dealing with it are so great, that a large portion of the community has become inured to its presence. The homeless poor, in fact, have come to be accepted as one of the unavoidable features of our civilisation.

Fig. 35. Sketch in the Women's Shelter (Illustrated London News)

To deal with this class the operations of the social reform wing of the Salvation Army has been specially directed, and, as a first step, shelters have been opened from time to time, until at the present moment five are in operation, four for men and one exclusively for women. The particular intention of this article is to deal with that shelter specially reserved for women and the Industrial Workshops for destitute men.

Hanbury Street, Whitechapel, is a notorious locality. Squalid and shut away in one of the darkest recesses of the Metropolis, it has a history peculiarly of its own. If its past is unsavoury, its present is certainly hopeful. Always a locality of doubtful reputation, respectable society gave it a wide berth, until latterly, when, by reason of the Salvation Army work here described, it has been visited by large numbers of earnest, not to say critical, people, and from being the theatre of some gruesome crimes it has become a centre of active Samaritanism.

It was during the season of horror which followed the Whitechapel murders that the old baths came into the hands of the Salvation Army, and were at once transformed into a night shelter for the accommodation of homeless women. The interior arrangements are marked by two valuable characteristics—cheerfulness and cleanliness. When full, there are assembled within its walls upwards of two hundred and fifty of London's human wrecks. The floors and seats have been scrubbed to almost a perfect whiteness, and the bright colours of the walls, as well as the furniture,

seem to have a counterpart in the cheering influences exercised by the officers in attendance. Each afternoon at three the doors are opened, and from that hour until midnight there gather types of every grade of womanhood, all, however, bearing more or less the stamp and impress of the seamy side of London life. Many of these are regular attendants, who, before the shelter was opened, alternated between the common lodging house, the railway arches, and the casual ward. To them the shelter has become home, while they eke out a bare existence by working in the neighbouring markets or in doing odd jobs in the households of their Hebrew neighbours.

To the majority of the residents of the shelter, however, work is more a memory than an experience. To watch them assembling is a sight that creates a feeling of indescribable sadness and hopelessness. One sighs over the despairing, broken women, many of whom, from a variety of causes, have drifted down from comfortable and useful walks of life. Here can be traced the not yet wholly obliterated indications of early refinement; there we see those who, youthful in years, are yet old in sin, although they are tractable enough while under the influence of the shelter. Occasionally there is a newcomer, who, fresh from a country home, has fallen into one or other of the snares of the great city, and is at length piloted to the shelter by some friendly policeman, and to such it has often proved the opportunity for the beginning of a new life of usefulness.

Fig. 36. Sleeping Arrangements in the Whitechapel Women's Shelter (Graphic, 1892)

Once past the entrance, the women proceed to the reception room, where they may sit and rest or occupy their time in mending their garments. The entire building is heated with steam pipes placed round the lower portion of the walls, and is kept at a very comfortable temperature. Hot water is also provided, with the necessary laundry accommodation for those who desire the luxury of a clean garment. It is at these times that the Salvation lasses are able to accomplish their most efficient work. By their kindly sisterly attentions, the heart-winning is here accomplished, and foundations laid for the friendly interest that may lead to a reconstruction of habits and character.

To the most casual observer the untiring devotion of these good women exhibits sacrifice of a very high order, and cannot but exert the best influence upon their charges. It is in this direction, far more than in fervid exhortation, that we have the secret of the success of Salvationism among these outcasts. The payment of threepence entitles all comers to a bed, and, in addition, a meal night and morning. All the food is of the plainest, consisting of a pint mug of tea (which is the favourite beverage) or cocoa, with large piece of bread, generally with the addition of butter or jam, according to the generosity of the visitors, who most frequently leave as a memento of their visit the wherewith to provide such little luxuries. After the serving of the evening meal, a meeting of about one hour's duration is held. It consists of music and song, interspersed with short prayers and exhortations. In these meetings as many of the shelter women as are

able take part, and for a short time at least the old-time softness seems to steal into the most hardened and careworn faces, reviving memories of days when many of them sang and prayed in different surroundings.

It is now time (between nine and ten o'clock) to take possession of the dormitory. It is constructed of what was once the large swimming bath, and has a gallery running all round. On the floors, everywhere, ranged in rows side by side, are the box-like arrangements for sleeping, the end of each being a raised sloping shelf which, when covered by the American cloth mattress, forms the pillow. This, with a leather covering, forms the equipment, and, by the time the clock strikes ten, the majority the inmates are forgetting their toils and sorrows in slumber.

Since the opening of this shelter, in March 1889, upwards of 100,000 homeless women have been accommodated, not few of whom have been assisted into respectable and useful walks of life.

Crossing the road from the shelter above described, we find another department of Salvation Army endeavour—namely, the industrial workshops opened some six months ago, being once the germ and embryo of that portion of the "Darkest England" scheme designated the "City Colony." The object of these workshops is to provide food and shelter for homeless and destitute men, in exchange for work done by them, until such time as they are able to procure work for themselves, or until it has been procured for them through the agency of the Labour Bureau of the Salvation Army.

Fig. 37. Mat Making Shed (ILN)

Fig. 38. Mat Making, Hanbury Street (ILN)

The plan of operations is as follows:-

All those applying for assistance are placed in what is termed the first class. They must be willing to do any kind of work allotted to them. While they remain in the first class, they are entitled to three meals a day and shelter for the night, and are expected, in return, cheerfully to perform the work allotted to them.

Promotions are made from this first class to the second class of all those considered eligible by the Labour Directors. They, in addition to the food and shelter above mentioned, receive sums of money up to five shillings at the end of the week, for the purpose of assisting them to provide themselves with tools to get work outside.

Third class workers are arranged for, who receive such further sums as are mutually agreed upon from time to time. Hours of work: 7 a.m. to 8.30 a.m., then breakfast; 9 a.m. to 12.30 p.m., then follows a meeting, and the dinner hour; 2 p.m. to 5.30 p.m., at which time the workshops close. The doors are closed five minutes after 7, 9 and 2 p.m. Each meal is supposed to have been earned before it is given, and the men are encouraged to feel that all they receive is the result of their own exertion. There is, so to speak, a squaring-up each mealtime, each man entering on the understanding that he must expect

Fig. 39. Sergeant of Mat Makers (ILN)

Fig. 40. Sergeant of Wood Shed (ILN)

nothing beyond his food and shelter, and such clothing as the generosity of friends may enable the officials to provide for him. If, however, at the end of the week the conduct and industry has been satisfactory, the value of the man's work is compared with the cost of his maintenance, and out of the excess of value, if any, a sum of money is handed to the worker as a gratuity for his encouragement. In some cases, indeed, men have risen in the third class until they have received wages nearly equal to those paid in the ordinary labour market. In these cases, the men no longer use the shelter or are supplied with food or clothing, they being in a position to provide for their own needs.

As far as possible the produce of the workshops is disposed of among the members and supporters of the Army, as it is, of course, most desirable that goods manufactured here should not come in competition with goods of a like character in the open market. At present this economic question presents little difficulty,

but when the Farm Colony is in working order the wisdom of administration will be shown in as far as possible producing only those articles required there, and by the various other branches of the social scheme.

Within the walls of the workshop there were engaged in December last between 140 and 150 men per day. These were placed at such work as was considered most suitable to their ability and previous avocations. Seven distinct departments are in active operation, the industries represented consisting of wood chopping, sack, mat, and shoemaking, brush manufacturing, carpentering, and an ingenious method for producing leather shoelaces.

One very pleasing result of the workshop operations is that, out of the large number of men who have passed through those who have either refused to work or who by reason of their bad conduct have had to be dismissed would not amount in all to a dozen in the six months during which the scheme has been in operation.

Fig. 41. Wood Cutting Shed (ILN)

There can be no doubt that this Salvation Army departure from what has been termed purely spiritual work has done much to inspire hope as to the possible solution of the difficult question, "What shall we do with our destitute classes?" Whether it really does present a possible solution, one thing is certain—it is a more humanising effort than that put forth by the Poor Law system, and, whatever may be the ultimate proportions to which the "Darkest England" scheme may develop, it is quite evident that the experiences of the Hanbury Street ventures will have a considerable effect. It will surely assist in the laying of foundations upon which, let us hope, some superstructure may be raised, not only to be a help to those sitting in the dark regions of poverty and destitution, but also be a source of untold happiness and prosperity to posterity at large.

That there are many difficulties to be faced cannot be doubted; but if business lines are adhered to, and the interests of the scheme and of the poor are considered above and before all other interests, the earnestness of the workers of the Salvation Army, both officers and soldiers, can be relied upon to overcome, them, if there is a possibility of doing so.

Illustrated London News – 17th January 1891.

—◦◦◦—

1891 – THE GENERAL BOOTH ONSLAUGHT.

This morning there is a general chorus of condemnation of "General" Booth's scheme and of his methods of working, from men who have a right to speak. One by one the veteran workers of the East End have spoken — the Bishop of Colchester, the vicars of Mile End, Barking, and other East End parishes, Mr. Archibald Brown, of Stepney, Mr. Cuff, of Shoreditch, Dr. Barnardo among others, and these are now joined by Mr. Kitto, who, before he was appointed to St. Martin's-in-the Fields, was one of the most indefatigable of workers, first at Poplar and afterwards at Stepney and Whitechapel.

Mr. Kitto says of the Salvation Army at the East End, which was its roman birthplace, that "while as an advertising agency it was evident enough, its religious influences upon the masses of the poor were of the feeblest kind. In the homes of the outcast in the Whitechapel slums and lodging houses it was virtually unknown."

Sir Edmund Hay Currie is a man with equally wide East End experience, who has devoted a large part of his life to the service of the poor, and declares that he is surprised, "that anyone in the least acquainted with the conditions of the poor who live in our great cities should receive seriously any attempt to deal with the misfortunes of the lowest poor by a universal scheme."

Among others who have now pronounced an adverse opinion on the scheme are the Bishop of Carlisle, the vicar of St. Matthias, Stoke Newington, and that conspicuous leader of the Evangelical Party in the Church, the Rev. H.W. Webb-Peploe, who at first was sympathetic towards Mr. Booth, but having failed to obtain from him such satisfactory pledges as any reasonable man might readily give, regretfully withdraws his support.

We apprehend that not a few other impulsive gentlemen, whose names have helped to starve existing useful agencies and to fill the Salvation Amy war chest, now have serious misgivings as to the wisdom of their conduct.

Nevertheless, the "General" is unmoved. He tells Mr. Webb-Peploe and his friends, in reply to their modest request, that he should appoint three or four well-known public men as co-trustees, that if they cannot trust him and his unknown successor absolutely, he will do without their assistance, and yet he goes to the City Temple and says that one of his difficulties is that he had asked for too little money, and that he is puzzled to know how to make £100,000 go round, so that he could properly try the scheme in its entirety. Yet in his book he says — "We have carefully calculated that with £100,000 the scheme can be successfully set in motion, and that it can be kept going on an annual income of £30,000. . . . and our judgment is based not on mere imaginings, but upon the actual results of the experiments made."

Even the annual £30,000 was not to be permanently required, for he says in the same chapter that, once fairly afloat, there is good reason to believe that in all its branches the scheme will be self-supporting. Miscalculations at the outset are bad enough, but on almost all the chief points with which he deals Mr. Booth's ignorance is simply stupendous. He declares in his book that 870,000 persons are in receipt of out-door relief; the Rev. R.H. Hadden points out that the latest returns show 592,000. He declared in his speech yesterday that we spend £20,000,000 annually in charity and Poor-law-relief, "yet there is no diminution in the number of people, who are under the dark sea," and this in face of the fact that the inmates of our local prisons have diminished from 20,800 in 1878, to 13,300 in 1890, and in convict prisons from 10,500 to less than 5,890.

But the most amazing statement of all is that, "in England there are fifteen millions of acres now lying idle capable of producing remunerative crops, and to every man in the land he would allot five acres of land." Now let us come to the facts taken from official statistics. The total area of land in England and Wales is 32,597,398 015. acres; the total cultivated area is 24,991, The uncultivated area, which includes all the mountain and heath land, is 7,606,383 acres. But we will give Mr. Booth the whole area of the country, including towns and rivers, and all land built upon, and then he has only 37,324,000 acres of land out of which to find his fifteen millions of acres of waste that would produce remunerative crops. The man who deals in this wild way with facts and figures not only asks for money, but refuses to allow any other person to have any voice in its expenditure.

Mr. Frank Smith, the ex-Commissioner of the social wing of the Army, has published a lengthy explanation, the substance of which is that he found that the social wing was continually short of money, and that not till he flung up his task, because he could not obtain a complete separation of the social and general work of the Army, did the autocrat of the scheme make full and sufficient preparations for the separate working. Mr. Smith's temperate letter amply proves that Mr. Booth is as disingenuous as the judges found him, and that unlimited despotism is the most unsafe base of operations in this country.

Royal Cornwall Gazette – 8th January 1891.

escape suspicion. But for the confession of a dissolute sailor see how much would have been made of the possession of a second hat by the poor wretch last assassinated. In a moment the cry was not that a woman had always been believed to be the murderer, as if these victims would be likely to be enticed into dark corners by one of their own sex. But the simple statement of the boozy Sadler reduced this false scent to ridicule. Even on this theory much nonsense is written. "No woman, " it is said, "would be strong enough to commit these murders." After what Mrs. Pearcey did with Mrs. Hogg this argument has had the bottom knocked out of it.

As to the bloodhounds, they have not been used not because the police are negligent, nor because they have run away, but because, fairly tested in the country, they were proved to have lost their instincts of following the track of a blood-stained garment. The suggestion that slum sisters should be employed to obtain confessions is absurd. After the manner in which the emission of the Tunbridge Wells youth who was hanged for murder was at once used to bring him to justice there will be no more confidences of that description.

Gravesend Reporter, North Kent and South Essex Advertiser – 21st February 1891.

1891 – NUMBER TEN.

Another Whitechapel murder—the tenth of a mysterious series—has naturally in London revived the public feeling of sickening bewilderment that we experienced in the year 1888 to an especial degree, and again in 1889. Assuming that these butcheries were all committed by the same hand—and surely it is not possible that there can be more than one such fiend on the face of the earth—the intervals between the crimes ought to be very closely studied in searching for a clue.

We had murders during the late summer of 1888, and then the monster was quiet. Then he re-appeared again in about the same period in 1889. Last year he was again lying low. Now he comes with early spring. All this looks as if the man were a traveller. The police, however, have at last become fully alive to the danger of giving any information to the Press. The papers, with their modern system of private detectives, and conversion of offices into amateur police courts, are a hindrance rather than an assistance to justice, and a clever villain has only to read them to know how to

1891 – THE PRESS AND WHITECHAPEL.

We yesterday published a letter, alleged to have been written by the man Sadler now under arrest charged with the latest murder in Whitechapel, which is of some public interest. Whether the letter be authentic or not – and we see no reason to doubt its authenticity – it aptly expresses the truth about the terrible position in which a poor man in prison under a charge of murder is placed. Public sympathy with an accused suspect of such butchery as that in Whitechapel is not to be readily excited. The very horror aroused by the brutality of the deed prevents most people from remembering that to be accused is not necessarily to be convicted, and that large numbers of men have been charged with these Whitechapel atrocities against whom, as it proved in the sequel, there was no evidence worthy of consideration. Sadler in the letter to which we have referred writes as follows:-

"The police will hurry my case to suit their own ends. Anything turning up in my favour will be squashed. All the money and sense in Scotland Yard will be used to hurry me to a finish. What a godsend my case will be to them if they can only conduct me, innocent as I am, to the bitter end! The whole detective system of Scotland Yard will be whitewashed in the sight of the whole world."

Without at all endorsing this grave charge against the police, we may point out that there is an unpleasant truth in the above sentences. This man is a prisoner cooped up in a cell without money and without friends. He has against him all the skill and resources of the London police, which are being diligently devoted to the task of discovering evidence against him. Any evidence in his favour which may turn up will not, we hope, be, as he says, suppressed.

That were a crime quite as horrible as that with which he is charged. But it is too often the custom of the police when they have a man in custody to apply their energies not to find the author of the crime, but to find evidence which will connect the accused with it, and in this case the heated state of public opinion, as well as the natural anger and professional spleen of the police at their previous failures, all tend towards the formation of a judgment which may be erroneous.

These considerations lend a pathetic interest to this wail from the police cells by a man charged with a capital crime, and who complains that he is friendless. "My mother is too old, and I have no brother or sisters or public house pal worth a ___" If Sadler be convicted, he will be tried by Jury and have a fair trial according to the evidence. But here again there are influences at work which are seriously prejudicing his case.

Attention was called in the House of Commons the other night to the nature of the statements published in a portion of the press concerning the prisoner, statements which Mr. Howorth suggested amounted to contempt of court and the Home Secretary regarded as "seriously interfering with the administration of justice." We frankly confess that champions as we are of the freedom of the press, we believe that it is being abused in this matter most recklessly.

Take one specific instance. Several London and provincial newspapers yesterday and on Thursday published an alleged interview with the wife of the prisoner, almost every line of which was damaging to his character, and indeed the whole tendency of which is to associate with the prisoner not only the murder with which he is charged but the other Whitechapel murders with which he is not so much as charged.

Sadler, it seems, was married fifteen years ago, and his wife has borne five children. His wife, if she be correctly reported, stated to the interviewer that she "was married on a Thursday, and knew by the Sunday that it was a mistake." He knew, we are also informed on her authority, "every nook and corner of London," and once worked at a factory in Bucks Row, the scene of one of the Whitechapel murders! He used to leave her, and not inform her of his movements. She met him by appointment and did not know him. "He seemed to have disguised himself." He drank, "but if he were as tight as a maniac at two o'clock and had to commence work at six, he would be at his post." "He can pretend to be very ignorant," said Mrs. Sadler, "but he's sharp enough in all that's no-good."

Then there is the following: "When living in Poplar he had a long-bladed double-edged sort of dagger knife. She got possession of it and hid it away from her husband. On the day she met him in Fenchurch Street they walked along the streets together till, coming to a rather dark place, he said, 'I can take you up that place and show you where somebody was killed.' She replied, 'It doesn't interest me; I don't want to see such places.' It was a dark court; but she did not know what part of Whitechapel it was in. He afterwards said, 'Don't you think he must have been artful. I wonder where the bobby could have been when such a thing occurred,' or words to that effect."

In this interview there are in fact fathered on the accused many of the strange characteristics which the imagination naturally associates with the author of all the Whitechapel murders. He, like Sadler, is probably "strong as an elephant and with wrists like iron." It is an abuse of the Press to prostitute it to the dissemination of those damaging and unsupported allegations against a man who is entitled by English law and by universal justice to be treated as innocent till he is proved to be guilty. There are hundreds of men of Sadler's class in London whose wives might give an account of them exactly similar to that reported to have been given of him. But they not being charged with murder, the accounts are not forthcoming, and if they were the Press would not print them.

It is because Sadler is charged with murder that there is this reckless raking into his past life. The motive of the publication may be no worse than a desire to benefit by a sensation. But it is not the less an injustice and an outrage.

Northern Echo – 21st February 1891.

1891 – CHILDREN AT PRAYER.

The Church Schools in Osborne Street, Whitechapel, also receive a great number of children within their gates. The children are well housed and well looked after and are possibly not quite erogenous a community as at the crowded Board Schools a little further away. It is an impressive scene to witness the girls at prayers before being dismissed for the day.

Graphic – 9th April 1891.

———◦◉◦———

1891 – A COMMOTION IN WHITECHAPEL.

A sensation was caused in the notorious Buck's Row, Whitechapel, early yesterday morning, when a gentleman drove up in a cab, and alighted at the corner of Queen Anne Street. He opened a conversation with a woman standing nearby, and the woman, resenting the intrusion, called him "Jack the Ripper." He immediately became excited, drew a six-chambered revolver, and threatened to fire indiscriminately upon the crowd which rapidly gathered. A police Inspector and sergeant who were near at hand immediately arrested him, and he was taken to Bethnall Green

Police Station. Upon being searched a large-bladed knife was found upon him.

At Worship Street yesterday, Percy Greathead, 29, who was described as a "gentleman" on the police sheet, living at Wood's Hotel, Furnival's Inn, Holborn, was charged with presenting a loaded revolver at Margaret Sweeny, "supposed with intent to shoot her," in Queen Anne Street, Whitechapel, at 2.30 yesterday morning. There was a good deal of excitement in court, owing to a report having been spread that "Jack the Ripper" had been captured.

The evidence showed that the accused went for a walk down Buck's Row, Whitechapel, to see the scene of the Whitechapel crimes. He had taken a cab to Whitechapel and left the vehicle whilst he went down the street so painfully celebrated. He had in his possession a revolver, and passed the woman Margaret Sweeney, who stood at a door in a by-street. A man came towards him, and made some remark to Sweeney, who retorted, "Now, then, big head, go home. Its time you were in bed." "Big head" suggested "Greathead'" (the prisoner's name) and caused him to think the woman was insulting him. He turned to her and she seems to have remarked, "Here's Jack the Ripper." The prisoner produced his revolver, and immediately there was a scene.

One or two men, being on the spot, raised an alarm, whilst the prisoner said they also alarmed him, and was the cause of his producing the weapon. A constable appeared and took him to the station,

Fig. 42. Osborne Street School – Whitechapel (Graphic)

149

where, to Inspector Wells, he gave up a six-chambered revolver, fully loaded. The Manager of Woods Hotel said he had known the prisoner fourteen years, and he had travelled a great deal. He always found him quiet.

Mr. Montagu Williams remanded the prisoner and refused an application for bail made by Mr. Morris.

Reynolds's Newspaper – 23rd August 1891.

1892 – MY VISIT TO THE OPIUM DEN.

It had for a long time been my wish to see for myself the slums of London. And at last, an opportunity arose which gave me a great chance of seeing Whitechapel and the environs under the best conditions. I was to go with a sergeant of the detective force, who undertook to show me all about the place.

The day came and having had an early dinner I put myself into the underground railway and reached Aldgate Station. The Three Nuns public house was the rendezvous, and there sure enough was my friend waiting for me.

After having had a drink, we start, and walk down to Fenchurch Street Station. As is usual when one particularly wishes to catch a train, we miss it, and I have to try to keep patient for a space of 15 minutes. At last, however, our train starts, and after some ten minutes stops at a station called the "East India Docks." Here we alight and walk about 300 yards to No. __, of __Street.

A Chinaman comes to us and asks our business, and after a few words with my friend admits us to his house with many bows and salaams, not to speak of cigars proffered. After staying in the shop for about two minutes we are shown the way upstairs to a room about 15 feet long by about 12 feet broad. This room is entirely devoid of furniture, except some divans, which are arranged all round the room, and on which some 10 Chinamen are lying about, all intent on smoking this drug and on playing a sort of game like draughts, but on which they were gambling like anything.

My next move was to try a pipe of opium, and I use the word "try" advisedly, as I was utterly unable to make my pipe draw properly, which occasioned the derisive laughter of all the habitues of the place. The taste, to one unaccustomed to the drug as I am, was excessively nasty, and I own I was very glad when my pipe went out in order to have an excuse for stopping. Had I gone on I should undoubtedly have "shot the cat."

And now to describe the method used in smoking this drug. The opium was a thin black liquid, something like very thin black paint, and was in a round tin about 3 or 4 inches in height, and about 1½ inches in diameter. A wire is produced and placed in the opium and held over the flame of a small lamp till it crackles and swells with the heat. It is then put into the pipe by means of this wire, and then lighted.

The pipe is about two feet long with an excrescence in the form of a circle, about three-quarters of the way down it. This is the bowl of the pipe, and it contains three or four small holes, each about the size of the head of a pin, and in communication with the tube of the pipe.

The smoker having filled his pipe and lighted it, lies back and draws all the smoke into his lungs. This can be done in one long breath. He then blows out the smoke through his nostrils and recommences the work of filling his pipe. They smoke on an average from ten to twelve pipes each in the course of a day, and the effect is truly dreadful.

I saw many sights that night horrible and appalling, but none to compare with this. The men themselves who had fallen into this habit are conscious of the effects produced by it, and no one who has seen it and them will ever in the future deny that to smoke opium is as bad and worse than to take to drink. A fearful thing either, but the signs of the opium smoker are almost worse, if possible, than those of the drunkard.

The men I saw (all confirmed opium smokers) were hardly to be called men. Their hands and all their bodies were shaking like aspen leaves, their faces literally yellow, their appetites gone, whether for food or drink, and the signs of approaching dissolution horribly and most plainly palpable.

But can anything be done for this? No, most emphatically No. The drunkard will drink, and the opium smoker will smoke, though both know in their sane moments that they are only to quote an expression, "clinging to the hand which smites them." A very near relation of mine who had been in India, who was for 30 years in charge of a large opium district, was only a few days ago saying how absurd it was for a few men to try to stop it, or even for the Government.

As we all know well, our Indian Government make some three million a year from this traffic alone, and it is under the strictest possible regulations. But were we to forbid the growth of poppies in India there are quite enough States in the same country who are entirely independent, and whom we could not stop from growing poppies. Besides, it is a necessary drug when used in moderation. It would thus be inadvisable to stop this traffic, even were it possible, as we should not only have endless trouble with the smuggling of opium but take away at one swoop three million from the revenue of our Indian dependency, and with the rupee at an already fearful discount, manage to bring our "brightest jewel in the Crown" to the verge of, if not to, absolute bankruptcy.

Lisburn Herald and Antrim and Down Advertiser – 7th May 1892.

1892 – THE COURAGE OF WILLIE FLOOD.

A poem in a picture! Look at the touching sketch of the little cripple hero, Willie Flood, who wheeled Alice Noble all the way from Whitechapel to Epping Forest, and avow that it was worthwhile for this one act of sweet humanity itself to have set on foot the noble mission which is to give thousands on thousands of town little ones one bright country holiday during the summer months. Gallant Willie Flood on Monday last did as brave and as kindly an act as the wee hero of Mr. G. R. Sims's ballad of "Billy's Rose" did. His patient devotion struck a sympathetic chord in the breast of the P.I.P. Artist, who has, we feel certain, earned the thanks of our readers by delineating this good young Samaritan of Whitechapel.

But what a pity Willie Flood did not happen to know that Mr. C. Arthur Pearson has started in *Pearson's Weekly* the very "Fresh Air Fund" which is to benefit the "Tiny Tims" and" Blades o' Grass" of London! This happened to be the opening excursion of the season organised by Mr. Pearson in conjunction with Mr. John Kirk, the indefatigable secretary of the Ragged School Union. A merry band of some two hundred poor children enjoyed a delightful, renovating holiday in pure country air at Snaresbrook,

Fig. 43. The Country Treat (Penny Illustrated Paper)

Epping Forest—one of those vernal haunts likely to fill the minds of the little ones with brightest recollections when the weather becomes sultry in their squalid courts and alleys.

With the gracious consideration that has characterised the Common Council of the City of London in its beneficent action in Epping Forest, a free site has been granted the Ragged School Union for the "Country Retreat" at Snaresbrook. Here it was that Mr. Pearson and Mr. Kirk, Mr. Clement Scott, and the P.I.P. Artist had the supreme gratification of seeing the host of children enjoying themselves jubilantly, feasting amply, indulging in invigorating games, and taking in a stock of exhilarating fresh air to cheer them for many a day in London.

May these benevolent excursions continue! Mr. Pearson, who is duly portrayed as founder of the feast, says in *Pearson's Weekly*:-

"Now, what we have set our hearts on is to raise enough money to enable us to send a party of 200 children away for a day's outing every weekday between Monday, June 13, and Saturday, Sept. 17. A large sum will be needed for this, but surely it can be raised among our hundreds of thousands of readers."

All who wish to help forward this good work should make haste to send their mites to swell the "Fresh Air Fund" at the offices of *Pearson's Weekly*, Temple Chambers, E.C.

Penny Illustrated Paper – 18ᵗʰ June 1892.

1892 – A SAD POISONING CASE.

On Tuesday morning, shortly after nine o'clock, a shocking tragedy was discovered to have taken place at No. 9, Lambeth Street, Whitechapel. The house in question has been tenanted for some time past by a Mr. Frederick Kopinski, a Polish Jew, his wife, Sofia Kopinski, and their three children—Bessie, aged ten; Frederick, aged eight; and Antonio, aged five years. Monday morning Mr. Kopinski had occasion to go out to attend a case at the Thames Police Court, and during his absence the boy Frederick (Bessie being away from home) saw his mother put on her hat and cloak and go out with little Antonio. She went to a workshop, and poisoned herself and child.

From the position of the bodies, it would seem though Mrs. Kopinski stood on the table with the child in her arms, poured some poison down its throat, and then drank some herself. After this she appears to have reeled over and fallen, still clasping the child, which

was partly under her. Mrs. Kopinski was twenty-six years of age, and had been married eleven years. She had always appeared to live happily with her husband and family. Her father is a photographer, and it is conjectured that she managed to get the poison from his place.

Penny Illustrated Paper – 1ˢᵗ July 1892.

1892 – GHASTLY DISCOVERY IN WHITECHAPEL.

The Press Association is informed that at a late hour last night, a parcel containing human remains was found on the premises now undergoing alterations in Flower and Dean Streets, Whitechapel. The discovery was made by a watchman going about his rounds, and he at once communicated with the police.

The parcel was taken by them to the nearest house for examination by the Divisional Surgeon, and detectives were told off to make inquiries into the affair. The police are reticent regarding the discovery but elated that the remains are those of an adult person, though the sex is unknown.

The Press Association says, "Later information confirms the discovery of human remains at Whitechapel, and at present points strongly in the direction of a series of crimes committed many years ago. As stated, the discovery was made in Flower and Dean Street, Spitalfields, a thoroughfare some years ago one of the most notorious in the East End of London as a resort of criminals and bad characters. The street runs from Commercial Road to Brick Lane, and at the former end is a plot of land which has been vacant for some ten years, since the demolition in connection with the East End improvements commenced.

There were many old cellars and cesspools on this site, but they were untouched until recently, when a firm of engineers took the site for building purposes. In the course of yesterday two labourers came upon a wooden box in no way resembling a coffin at about nine feet from the surface. When opened it was found to contain human remains in a good state of preservation. The contractor at once communicated with the police, who took charge of the remains, which were those of three persons fully grown, but of what sex it is not yet known. There were three skulls and the bones of various limbs, but they were so thrown together by the unearthing of the box that it was impossible to tell the position in which they had lain.

All the circumstances point to a crime committed at a remote period."

The remains are at present at the police station. but the Coroner for the district has been communicated with, and no doubt an inquest will be held. The discovery has naturally created considerable excitement in the district.

A telegram today says, "With regard to the discovery of three skeletons during the course of excavations on some unoccupied ground in Whitechapel, it appears that the first was found on Thursday night, and was considerably damaged in the darkness. The following morning, during the course of further excavations, a coffin containing two skeletons was found a little way below the other, but not in any way connected with it. When exposed to the air the coffin, which was of the ordinary length but abnormally wide, dropped to pieces, and the remains, which were placed side by side but in reversed positions, were not extricated without damage. The skull of the uppermost skeleton was battered in, but it is uncertain whether this was caused by the workmen's pick or foul play.

Flower and Dean Streets, where the discovery was made, was—before the low lodging houses congregated there were demolished—the rendezvous of thieves and criminals. The ground was known to possess many ancient cesspits and cellars, the remains of the former tenements, and it is supposed that in one of the former the record of two ghastly crimes had been hidden. The spot had remained undisturbed for over ten years, but the police theory is that the crime is of a much older date than this. The skeletons were those of adults and were in a good state of preservation. The remains await careful expert examination.

Hartlepool Northern Daily Mail – 8th October 1892.

1892 – WAS IT "JACK THE RIPPER?"

The "Jack the Ripper" scare has been revived in all its old intensity so far as Scotland Yard is concerned. Three days ago (says the *Morning*) a most extraordinary communication was made to the officials of the Criminal Investigation Department. A young girl of the unfortunate class, named Emily Edith Smith, alias Norton, of 3, Bingfield Street, Caledonian Road, made a deposition to the effect that she had narrowly escaped murder in Whitechapel at the hands of a man whom she met in Cheapside.

Her story itself is a remarkable one, but it would not have arrested the attention of Scotland Yard in the marked degree it has, had it not been for certain characteristics which it bore to the outrages perpetrated by the notorious miscreant for whom the police authorities have never ceased to watch. She returned her age as 18 years last July, and was, when she first went to business, a dressmaker. Subsequently she posed as an artists' model, and a year ago lived with a man called Norton, whose real name she did not know, but whom she thought was a German. She then with some diffidence admitted that she had led "a gay life."

Though there was a large family, she has no surviving sisters or brothers, and was given a fairly good education. In height she is five feet three inches. She has a petite figure, a florid complexion, soft blue eyes, a small mouth, and a rather short nose. Her hair is a light brown, and her apparel particularly quiet.

On the evening of Saturday, November 5th (Guy Fawkes Day), the girl Smith, shabbily dressed, and wearing an old black hat, was walking down Cheapside towards St. Paul's Churchyard. A tall man accosted her, remarking, "Goodnight, Nellie." She made no reply, and continued her walk, but at the corner of Friday Street, the man who had addressed her was by her side again, and proffered an invitation to have "a cup of tea," which the girl, after some hesitancy, accepted. The couple then walked up Cheapside. He talked incessantly of where he had been during the last 18 months, stating that he had paid lengthened visits to the Continent, and had only recently returned to England.

The man then hailed an omnibus and drove with the girl along High Street, Whitechapel, to the corner of Commercial Road. She was unacquainted with the locality, and asked "Where they were now?" The man replied, "This is Whitechapel." The girl answered, "Oh! then, this is where the girls were murdered." "Pshaw, not girls," said the man deprecatingly, "old women, you mean. They were better out the way."

It ought to be mentioned that the man's talk showed him to be thoroughly familiar with the locality. Before entering the tram car, he pointed towards Leman Street, saying, "That is where Jack the Ripper is best known."

In the beer house, where the man asked for a small soda for himself, because, as he stated, he never drank anything stronger, the girl, for the first time, closely observed her companion.

He was tall and thin, looking like a consumptive, with high cheek bones, his face being pale. He stood over 5ft. 9in. His forehead seemed rather square, and though speaking English well, he struck her as being a foreigner.

Leaving the beer house in Sutton Street, the man and the girl walked towards the further end of it. The time was then about 20 minutes past six o'clock. The street, which is usually black and deserted, was, by reason of the fog, almost in darkness. One hundred yards down they passed under a railway arch, and turning to the right entered a long narrow passage known as Station Place, which, save for a few yards at the entrance, was enveloped in complete gloom. A new railway platform to the Whitechapel line of the Metropolitan Railway is in process of construction at one part of the passage, and a hoarding has been raised round a portion of the works. The girl said she would not venture further and that she did not like the appearance of the place. The man urged that his offices were at the end of the lane.

But the young woman would not advance with him. They were standing then in the gloom opposite an angle in the hoarding which, even had there been no fog, would have completely prevented any chance of their being seen. A street lamp some few feet away, projecting from the opposite wall, shed but the faintest glimmer of light.

"Let us go on a bit further," said the man. "I will not," replied the girl. "Then I'll settle you now," answered the man quietly. He caught the girl by the back of the collar of her dress, and dragged her into the dark angle of the hoarding. They were face to face. He made to twist her round so that her back might be to him, and at that moment the girl saw a knife in his hand. Where he got it from, she cannot say, nor can she explain how he opened it. But she has described, and drawn, as well as she can, the blade of the knife. It was, she said at Scotland Yard, about 9in. long, and curved to a point, but not a sharp point. The authorities have put it down as something like a gardener's pruning knife.

The girl gave "one big scream," and raising her right knee with all the power she could command dealt the man a violent blow in the abdomen. The man released his hold, and exclaimed, "Oh! my God," then made a dive at the girl with the knife, but missing her stumbled forward. The girl, screaming loudly, rushed into Sutton Street, where two women endeavoured to ascertain from her what had happened. The man was not seen again.

What gives the girl Smith's story the strongest interest is that her description of the man who accompanied her is almost word for word identical with that which the police authorities have always held to be the description of the appearance of the criminal for whose arrest they sought so eagerly two years ago. Another point of significance is that this case, as in all the Whitechapel outrages, the passage into which the woman was lured has both an entrance and an exit.

A telegram this morning says the mother of the girl Smith was interviewed by a reporter this morning, when she expressed her full belief in her daughter's narrative.

Yorkshire Evening Post – 22nd November 1892.

1892 – OUTRAGE IN WHITECHAPEL.

An atrocious outrage was committed, about ten o'clock on Friday night in a house of ill fame in Pearl Street, which forms a crescent at the back of Commercial Street, the two entrances in the main thoroughfare being separated by the Cambridge Music Hall. The street, which is badly lighted, is frequented by girls and young women.

It seems that one of these "unfortunates" had accompanied a young man from Commercial Street to a house is Pearl Street, and after an interval of some minutes the man was seen to emerge from the doorway, which is on a level with the pavement, and run hurriedly in the direction of Commercial Street, He was closely followed by the woman, who shouted out that her throat was cut, and who was seen to be bleeding somewhat profusely. The cry was taken up by several others, and the fugitive was stopped in Commercial Road by two men. He struggled violently until a constable stepped across the road and took him in charge. The police station is only a few yards off, and thither the victim, as well as her assailant, was conducted. The Divisional Surgeon was quickly in attendance, and although he found that the young woman had received a nasty curved gash across the throat it was not of such a character as to give any real ground for alarm or to necessitate her immediate removal to the hospital. The woman's name is Johnson.

On Saturday, at the Worship Street Police Court, Albert Edward Hawthorne, stated to be twenty-one years of age, but looking older, a barman, who gave the address of his mother, at 13, Gibraltar Walk, Bethnal Green, was charged with feloniously cutting and wounding Mary Ann Johnson. Mr. T.W. Moore appeared for the prisoner.

The prosecutrix, who was described on the police sheet as a prostitute, is twenty-nine years of age. When brought into court she had a bandage under her chin, passing over her head, and her left hand was also bandaged. The evidence she gave was in reply to questions put to her. She said she was accosted by the prisoner in Commercial Street about half past nine

Fig. 44.   *Girl Stabbed by a Youth (Illustrated Police News)*

Fig. 45.

Fig. 46.

on Friday night, and at his request she took him to her home at 26, Pearl Street. He attacked her in her room. She was lying down, and felt something sharp at her throat. On putting her hand up she found she was bleeding. She screamed out "police" twice. The prisoner tried to cut her neck again, and then she began struggling with him for the knife. In the struggle her left hand was cut. She thought the knife fell out of his hand, and she had just time to rush out of the door and get to the police station, when she lost her senses. In being questioned by Mr. Moore her deafness ceased her to give several contrary answers. She admitted having received from the prisoner all she asked him for but denied having accosted him. She said she had not robbed him in the room. She did not know if he had a stick, she did not see one, and had not taken a silk handkerchief from him. They had not quarrelled, and she did not know why he had attacked her. They were only together three or four minutes. What she thought a knife was a razor, (a broken razor was produced), but she had not opened the razor nor taken the case out of his pocket. It was found in his pocket at the station.

Mr. Percy J. Clark, surgeon and assistant to Mr. Bagster Phillips, Divisional Surgeon of police, 2, Spital Square, deposed to dressing the wounds of the woman. There were two injuries in the neck, one under the chin running inwards and downwards; the other a small incised wound just through the chin, half an inch in length. The former wound left a flap of skin hanging, and a third cut was across the left thumb, inner side. Witness had attended to two wounds on the prisoner's left hand, cuts from a sharp instrument. The razor produced would cause all the wounds,

Police Constable Jacobs, 77 H, said at 9.40 he heard cries of "Stop him," and saw the prisoner held by two or three men. At the station when charged he made no answer. After being placed in a cell witness was watching him, and the prisoner said, "I intended doing it; I put the razor into my pocket this morning. She is always following me about of a night when I come from places of amusement. I have been on the spree for a fortnight."

Mr. Moore said the latter statement took him by surprise. The prisoner had given him no account of the matter, but denied having been "on the spree." His friends said he was a quiet, inoffensive man.

Inspector Beck, HHH Division, said there were other witnesses, and he asked for a remand, and that the Magistrate would certify for legal aid. Mr. Bushby granted a remand, and marked the charge sheet that he thought the Treasury should afford legal aid to the police.

The prisoner in appearance is a quiet, respectable looking young man. He made no remark during the hearing or when remanded. With respect to the suggestion made in cross-examination that the woman robbed the prisoner, it was stated by him that the prosecutrix put her hands into his coat pockets, that his silk handkerchief was stolen, and that three women rushed into the room to rob him. As to his reported statement to the constable that he had been "on the spree" for a fortnight, it is somewhat confirmed by the fact that that period had elapsed since the prisoner left his last situation as barman at the Dudley Arms, Harrow Road, Paddington. Prosecutrix has parents in Tarville Street, Bethnal Green, and her father was in court.

Illustrated Police News – 10th December 1892.

1893 – A FRENCH CRITIC IN WHITECHAPEL SLUMS.

A Paris correspondent of the London *"Daily News"* writes:-

Mr. Francisque Sarcey, the great French theatrical critic, has returned to Paris, and gives us his impressions on the East End of London. It was quite an affair, his visit there.

"People had spoken to us of a visit to Whitechapel as a very exciting curiosity. It was at Whitechapel that Jack the Ripper murdered his victims. There are hidden the most infamous lairs of robbery, the most dismal dens of misery and vice. Everybody said to me "You must see it." I was unwilling. I con- fess I do not care to see ignoble sights or to breathe sickening smells. But they took me at my weak point. "Are there any theatres?" "Theatres! There are twopenny theatres, with a public in rags which swarms, laughs, sings, and fights." "That's another case," said I. "This belongs to theatrical criticism." "In order to see the Whitechapel slums," said my new friend, "you must have a policeman with you."

The policeman turned up after dinner – a big and burly fellow. He would have knocked down an ox, and he had a smattering of French "We must, be off," he said, "and home again early. When my wife knows I am going to Whitechapel, she waits for me, and only goes to sleep after my return."

We looked at one another in silence. The party left in three cabs, and alighted at the Pavilion Theatre. Reynaud went to the office window, and suddenly turned back amazed. "What is the matter? Do you know what they want for a box?" "A guinea and a half." We looked astonished at our Colossus. He did not stir. He stood upright, motionless and dumb. Reynaud took eighteen-penny seats. They placed us right up "in the gods." It was just like the theatre of Belleville or Monmatre – a crowd in Sunday clothes (it was Saturday). The house was full except the boxes. On the stage a sailor was telling a story which must have been very funny, as the house burst out laughing every minute. "Parbleu," said I to my companion, "these people are enjoying themselves thoroughly. But we don't come to Whitechapel for this sort of thing. We have seen enough."

"The weather outside was most pleasant. A gentle breeze blew down the street, which was wide and airy; the shops were open, and along the sidewalks a lively, noisy, laughing crowd moved, reminding us of the Grande Rue de Belleville on a fete day. Was this Whitechapel? Our interpreter was directed to tell the giant that we came to see slums, and intended to see some. He bowed, and took us down a back street, motioning us to keep elbow to elbow. Our hearts began to beat. He stopped, and, pointing to a flag on the pavement said, "It was here that one of Jack the Ripper's victims perished." We stared. It was a street like any other one, very neat and clean. On both sides, honest English houses, with a look of calm and virtue. The nightmare that had weighed upon our imagination began to vanish, and we began to laugh and be merry. The giant remained stolid; he waved his hand towards a house in which Jack the Ripper had cut the throat of a victim. We started off on foot; and reached the fatal house. The Colossus stooped to enter the room on the ground floor, said something in English to the host, and invited us to follow. It was a poor room, but very habitable. "You'll see," remarked the policeman, "the bloodstain is still on the wall." The man lifted up a lantern, and, with a trembling hand, pointed to a red stain behind the bed. After which he put out his hand, and each of us gave him a few coppers. Once in the street, we all laughed at one another for our gullibility. All these stories about Whitechapel are a vast hoax."

The big guide then took them to a night refuge. To their surprise they found there "gentlemen in threadbare or soiled clothes, but of respectable air, and who washed themselves, when they entered, in nicely-arranged basins." The French visitors then stepped into the "grillroom." M. Busson, scenting the pleasant aroma of the meat which was being cooked, was sorry he could not come there to dine. He was tired of the food he was provided with at restaurants and hotels, and, as M. Sarcey says, to understand what English cookery is one should first try it. The casuals' refuge seemed to the Frenchmen a palace of philanthropy.

They next went to a Salvation Army service. The "barrack" in Paris is a thing to laugh at and Parisian "blague" seems to taint it with its mocking levity. But in Whitechapel every Salvationist was as serious as a Pope. Faces wore a "wrapped up" expression, and voices were hard and tuneless. Nobody noticed the Frenchmen until the collection was being made, but the practical English then came down on them, and, dropping pence into the begging bag, they made their way out by an alley, and uttered a cry of admiring surprise on finding themselves in the High Street of Whitechapel.

The flush of life there was prodigious. An immense crowd circulated on the wide footway, in which there was no end of comely and well-dressed women. Children were so plentiful that one might have said they had been falling from the skies all day instead of rain. Everyone was jolly and ready for fun, and a happier population there never was. A little girl fell, and M. Sarcey, picking her up, was thanked in French. He felt as if he had been at Belleville on the 14th of July. Never had he seen such outdoor gaiety before in London. Gas flared everywhere, and everyone was boisterously happy.

At last, one of the strangers realised that it was growing late, and asked the Goliath whether his wife might not be uneasy. He treated the suggestion with calm contempt, and the excursion went on. When it came to an end, they asked their purser, M. Reynaud, what the policeman who guided them might expect. The best course would be to ask him plump, and M. Reynaud, going up to him, conversed with him beneath his ordinary tone of voice. M. Sarcey, cutting in, proposed to invite "Goliath" to supper. It would be an opportunity to drink champagne. But M. Reynaud, looking down in the mouth, said, "The terms, he says, are a pound for each. The deuce take him! A hundred francs in all!" All burst out laughing. M. Sarcey wanted to give him what was asked, for the fun of the thing. But his friends said, "No, he'll think us fools if we do." Then, turning round to "Goliath," he explained that they were French journalists. On hearing this the giant laughed too. They might give him what they pleased, as he was proud and happy to have taken them – without so much as a scratch befalling them – through the worst part of London.

When all was settled, M. Sarcey wanted to end the evening at the theatre, but the others would not hear of this, and so he did not see "Diplomacy" at the Garrick. He learned one lesson, however. It was to reject legends and to turn a deaf ear whenever the horrors of Whitechapel may be talked of to him.

Western Mail – 28th June 1893.

1893 – TRAGEDY IN WHITECHAPEL.

On Saturday night Whitechapel and the surrounding districts were thrown into a state of the greatest excitement by a tragedy which occurred in James Street, Cannon Street Road, Commercial Road. The throughfare where the tragedy was enacted is a narrow street close to the scene of one of the Jack the Ripper murders.

In a three-storey tenement a man named Edward Johnstone, who is described as an unemployed tailor, lived with his wife and three young children, the eldest not ten years of age. Johnstone is said to have been out of work for some time, the home being kept together by his wife, who earned a scanty living by charing. On Saturday night about six o'clock Johnstone came home, it is said, in an intoxicated condition, and proceeded to his rooms on the third floor. Then, according to the narrative of a neighbour, he was heard quarrelling with his wife, but no notice was taken. The word "money" was frequently mentioned, and in a few minutes all was still.

The other lodgers in the house thought that the quarrel was ended, and nothing else happened until Mrs. Johnstone's father called for the purpose of seeing his daughter. He opened the door of the room and found her lying on the floor, and at once asked his son-in-law what was the matter. At that time, he was sitting on a chair and made no reply. The father was then alarmed by the crying of the children, and on endeavouring to raise the wife found to his consternation that she was dead. He immediately made a rush at Johnstone, who, however, managed to elude his father-in-law, and opening the window, before it was possible to stop him, threw himself into the street, a distance of about forty feet. The alarm was raised and information promptly sent to the Inspector on duty at Leman Street Police Station.

He, with a force of constables, was quickly on the scene, and an ambulance arriving the man was conveyed to the London Hospital, where the house surgeon discovered that he was suffering from concussion of the brain, and was in a dangerous condition. In the meantime, the Divisional Surgeon of police was summoned, and after examining the woman pronounced life to be extinct, death having resulted from a blow evidently just above the heart.

From statements made by the children it appears that as soon as Johnstone entered the room he began quarrelling with his wife and struck her several times. At the last blow she fell to the ground and lay still. The husband then began to kiss his wife, and finding that she was dead, sat on a chair until the arrival of his father-in-law. The general opinion expressed by those who know the man Johnstone is that the fatal blow was unintentional.

Illustrated Police News – 12th August 1893.

1893 – THE EMIL GOTH TRAGEDY.

As sketched by another P.I.P. Artist, poor Emil August Goth, aged eleven, third son of Mr. Goth, a traveller, residing at 13, Cannon Street Road, St. George's-in-the-East, came to a terrible end on Monday evening week.

Owing to hot weather, the people in the neighbourhood flocked in great numbers to the Jubilee Public Baths, in Betts Street, and the officials were taxed to their utmost to meet the demands.

Little Goth, who was an expert swimmer, able to accomplish twelve lengths of the bath with ease, was engaged to take tickets at the door. At half-past nine, the bathers having left the bath, the water was being run off, preparatory to refilling the bath. Goth assisted to turn the valve to let the water out, and the grid over the outflow pipe was removed to allow the accumulated rubbish at the bottom of the bath to be carried away without interfering with the flow. When the bath, which holds 62,000 gallons, was half empty, Goth slipped off his clothes, and it is said threw a towel into the bath, and at once dived after it. The force of the water was so great that instead of rising where he anticipated he was carried to the outflow pipe and dragged into it.

Although the diameter of the pipe is only 9in., so great was the force of the water that he was carried down to the bend in the pipe, where his knee rested and impeded his course. It was not until after eleven o'clock that the body was got out.

The greatest sympathy is felt for the family throughout the district.

Penny Illustrated Paper – 26th August 1893.

1893 – FIRE IN WHITECHAPEL.

A disastrous fire, involving the loss of no fewer than five lives, and recalling in many respects the recent

Fig. 47.   Sucked into the Pipe (Penny Illustrated Paper)

terrible fatality in Fulham Palace Road occurred last Tuesday morning in High Street, Whitechapel.

The scene of the disaster was No. 99, High Street, Whitechapel, in the occupation of Mr. Joseph Hermann, Baker and Confectioner, and when the occupants of the premises retired to rest shortly before midnight on Monday night six people were in the place. These were Joseph Hermann, aged twenty-six, the proprietor of the shop; Mrs. Hillsworth, aged about fifty years; Miss Hillsworth, aged about fourteen years; Miss Jennings and Miss Ransley, each aged about twenty years; and Frederick Mark, aged eighteen. It was he who discovered the fire. He was sleeping in the back room on the top floor, and woke up to find the room full of smoke. He ran down and aroused his master, and then appears to have run downstairs, in order to go and call the fireman. He succeeded in getting out into the street, and is the only survivor.

Hermann, it is supposed, went upstairs to awaken his lodgers, and the door left open by Mark must have sent the flames up the staircase with such terrific force that none of the other inmates could make their way downstairs. Some of them were seen for a few moments at the top window piteously appealing for help, and then they disappeared. The upper part of the place presented the appearance of a veritable furnace when the first body of firemen arrived from the Commercial Road East station.

Fig. 48.   Fire at the Bakers (Penny Illustrated Paper)

Superintendent G. Smith was one of the first to arrive at the scene. The top floor was blazing furiously. With hydrant in hand the members of the Brigade searched the lower floors rapidly, but effectively, and made certain that no one was there. Gradually the firemen worked their way up the staircase, playing on the flames as they went, and at last made their way to the top floor. A shocking spectacle here presented itself, for the whole of the five bodies, fearfully charred, were found close together among the debris. Further examination of the premises showed that the fire had broken out in the back room on the second floor, and had then attacked the staircase. It had run up by means of the staircase to the third floor, and so had involved the whole of the floor. The remains were carefully placed in shells and removed to the mortuary to await an inquest.

Penny Illustrated Paper – 23rd September 1893.

contiguous courts. Squalor was, moreover, existent in the West End as well as the East, and he had seen sweating dens, slums, and overcrowded dwellings in the purlieus of Covent Garden, within a few yards of the palatial mansions of Piccadilly, and near the wealthy shops of Bond Street.

M. Zola also saw the rookeries inhabited by the Polish Jews, the Old Commodore Tavern, and other places. Nothing, however, came up to the theatrical ideas which many Frenchmen entertained about London. He was greatly struck by the crowds of children in the streets.

Drink had a good deal to do with whatever misery and squalor existed, but as far as he could make out men were drinking less in London than formerly, while women were drinking more."

Shields Daily Gazette – 2nd October 1893.

1893 – ZOLA'S IMPRESSIONS OF LONDON.

Interviewed yesterday by the Paris correspondent of the *Daily Telegraph* as to his first impressions of London, Zola said, "I came away from London with a profound admiration of its wealth, grandeur, and immensity. Each bridge is a Cyclopean structure. We have nothing in France to equal such things, nothing to be compared to the port of London, that wonderous gathering of masts and funnels which eclipses anything of the sort in Bordeaux, Havre, or Marseilles. It is in fact a city, as my wife said, made for me, and I hope to have leisure to study it better someday.

The conversation next turned to Whitechapel, which every Frenchman visiting London is expected to see. The novelist gladly prolonged the talk for a few moments in order to speak of the district which in later times has been identified with the terrible deeds of "Jack the Ripper." M. Zola visited some of the places where "Jacques L'Eventreur" carried out his exploits, and what most struck him was the tendency to efface and forget these crimes exhibited by the inhabitants.

Whitechapel, he considered, had been much belied, and he referred to the fact that many of his fellow countrymen had come away from it with preposterous stories of murder and misery. Whitechapel, as he saw it, was a thriving, prosperous place, with its wide, busy, well-lit central artery, and all the wretchedness and squalor were buried in

1893 – A WHITECHAPEL PAUPER IN TROUBLE.

At the Worship Street Police Court on Wednesday, John West, 41, described as a collier, who, however, having only one leg, explained, in a broad Lancashire dialect, that he "couldna' go down th' pits noo," was charged with breaking a pane of glass at the Whitechapel Infirmary, the property of the Guardians.

Evidence was given by Walter Williams, gate porter, of the prisoner wilfully smashing the glass, his grievance being that his two children were not admitted to the workhouse. The prisoner's wife had been taken into the infirmary on her application, as she was on the eve of her confinement; and then the prisoner wanted his two children taken in as well. The prisoner was offered the workhouse with the children, but refused to go in himself. He explained that the children were only five and three years old, that he had only the shelter of a lodging house at 10d. a night for the lot, and as the mother was away, he could not take care of the children. He only wanted them taken care of till the mother got about again, and would then have removed them.

Mr. Rose: But why should the ratepayer keep your children for three or four weeks? The expenses attending your wife's trouble falls on them, and you take advantage of it, and, in addition, want your children kept for a month?

Prisoner said he had no home.

Mr. Rose: Yes; you pay 10d. a night to a lodging house. That is 5s. 10d. a week, but you might have a comfortable apartment for less if you are the steady, independent man you want to make out. You break the window to force the Guardians to lock you up, and you got what you want—your children taken into the workhouse. So, what you can't get by fair means you obtain by foul.

The prisoner was fined 6d., and 5s. damage, or three days.

East London Observer – 14th October 1893.

1893 – AN EMPLOYMENT EXPERIMENT.

With the winter upon us in earnest, the question of what to do with the unemployed assumes very pressing importance. In this respect the Whitechapel Guardians are making a new and bold experiment. They intend to employ a certain number men on farms in Essex for a season, and when they have discovered by trial which of them are willing to take to agricultural work permanently, to try to establish them there.

This will be a very interesting experiment, and will be well made in the eastern counties, from whence come such melancholy accounts of farms going out of cultivation. But, on the other hand, we have heard a great deal about agricultural labourers being turned off by the hundred, on account of the prevailing depression. If the Whitechapel pauper is introduced to a new kind of work only to find that he cannot get employment at it, his last state will be no better than the first.

Western Mercury – 9th December 1893.

1895 – AN IMPUDENT ATTEMPT TO DECEIVE.

At the Whitechapel County Court, before Judge Bacon, Mrs. Rebecca Stachell, the tenant of some premises at 22, Philpot Street, St. George's-in-the-East, was to have appeared on an ejectment summons.

Henry Benabo, the landlord's agent, stated that this case had been adjourned because defendant's husband had died in the workhouse. Whenever a notice was served upon this woman she went to bed and declared that she could not be moved.

Judge Bacon: But I have a medical certificate here from a doctor in the Commercial Road that the woman had a miscarriage yesterday, and is suffering from exhaustion and cannot attend the court.

Witness: We are up to that trick of hers. We know her too well. We got another doctor to examine her, and this is what he says:_

Judge Bacon, amid roars of laughter in court, read the following certificate:- "This is to certify that I have this morning examined Mrs. Stachell. She stated that she had a miscarriage yesterday but I find no traces of it, and believe it to be untrue. She produced something to me, which I found upon examination to be a newly-born kitten, or some other small animal, with which, she had managed to deceive her own doctor."

Judge Bacon: This a barefaced impudent attempt to impose upon the court. Possession will be given forthwith.

Illustrated Police News – 30th March 1895.

1896 – EXCITING CHASE ON THE HOUSE TOPS.

A terrible double murder, the circumstances surrounding which somewhat resemble those of the Muswell Hill tragedy, was perpetrated on Saturday afternoon in Whitechapel, London.

The victims were an old gentleman named Levi, reported to be possessed of considerable wealth, and his female servant, Annie Gale. The former, a Jew, was 74 years of age, and the latter, a married woman, is stated to have been between 30 and 35.

The scene of the murder was the house where the two resided, No. 31, Turner Street, a thoroughfare chiefly inhabited by Jews. Mr. Levi was a retired umbrella case manufacturer, and since the death of his wife, nine months ago, had been the sole occupant, with his servant, of the house. He had gained the reputation of being a miser, and was rarely seen out of doors. His servant was well-known to the neighbours and is said to have been a very respectable and kindly disposed woman.

The first intimation of anything amiss at the house was received shortly before 1 o'clock. About that time a person who was accustomed to supply coal to Mr. Levi was seen by the neighbours to be knocking at the side door in Varden Street. The knocking went on for some time, but no answer could be obtained, and ultimately, after a crowd had gathered together, the police were called. The front door was broken in, and a constable entered the house.

He had only been in the house a few minutes when he rushed out to the street and called on some of the neighbours to come into the house, as a tragedy had occurred. Two men at once volunteered to render assistance.

The constable informed them that a murder had been committed and that he had suspicions that the murderer was in the house. Acting on this suspicion, one of the men went to the door at the end of the hall leading into the yard ready to interrupt anyone's flight in that direction, while the other kept guard at the front door.

The constable then proceeded to a lavatory situated in the basement of the house, and there discovered the dead body of Mr. Levi lying on the floor. His head was doubled up underneath him, and to all appearances, he had been strangled. There was a quantity of blood about the floor, but no weapon of any kind. The constable at once searched the rooms on the ground floor for any traces of the perpetrator of the deed, and lying on the sofa in the front parlour he discovered an overcoat which seems to have been hastily thrown off, and a leather knife sheath.

Locking all the doors on the ground floor the policeman ascended the stairs to the first floor. In the front room all the drawers of a sideboard had been forced and the contents strewn about the place. Ornaments were smashed and the lids forced off two boxes; in the back room there were similar signs of confusion.

On the second floor the front bedroom was topsy-turvy, and lying on the ground beside the bed was the mangled body of the woman Gale, who was fully dressed. There was blood all over the head, and the throat was cut from ear to ear. The top of the skull was smashed in and the fingers on both hands were gashed in a terrible manner, indicating that the unfortunate woman had endeavoured to shield herself with her hands. Life was extinct, although the body was quite warm. The apartment bore all the appearance of a desperate struggle having taken place, the bed clothes and carpet being be-spattered with blood.

After acquainting those below with his discovery and giving instructions for a doctor to be summoned, the constable set to work again to find the murderer. After searching the other room on the second floor and finding nothing, he noticed a large hole in the ceiling of the apartment where the woman was found. It was some three feet in diameter and the plaster seemed to have been freshly broken away. The man who had been on guard at the street door was called upstairs, and climbing on to his shoulders, the

constable armed with a poker, and by the light of a candle, climbed through the aperture in the ceiling into the space between the latter and the roof. He then observed that there was a hole corresponding to the one in the ceiling through the slates.

Wragg followed the constable, and the two commenced to search the roof. This is "V" shaped, and to guard against the possible escape of anyone who might be hiding among the numerous chimney stacks each went different ways.

Their operations were watched by a crowd of several thousand people who had assembled in the street after the first alarm had been given. Great excitement prevailed and the windows of the houses facing Mr. Levi's were crowded with persons anxious to catch a glimpse of the scene.

Hardly had the search been commenced before it was announced from the street that someone could be seen behind one of the chimneys, and the next moment, amid the shrieks of the onlookers, a man, apparently of middle age and with red whiskers and a beard was seen to rise from the hiding place behind the chimneys and rush past the constable. Wragg made a clutch at his clothing, and managed to get hold of his coat, but wrenching himself free, the man ran along the roof towards the gutter and jumped headlong among the people in the street. He alighted on a little girl named Leah Hymans, who was standing on the edge of the pavement, and then fell to the ground.

He was at once seized by the police, a number of whom had by this time arrived from the Arbour Lane Station, and taken in an ambulance to the London Hospital; he was at the time unconscious, and on being examined at the hospital was found to have sustained a fractured shoulder and other injuries in his fall. In view of the fact that the roof of the house is some 70ft. from the ground and only the roadway where he fell is covered with stones, it is remarkable that he was not killed.

At the hospital he remained unconscious. While the constable and Wragg continued their search of the roof, detectives from Scotland Yard had arrived and took charge of the house. Dr. Ambrose, the Divisional Surgeon, was also in attendance, and after examining the bodies of Mr. Levi and the woman Gale gave instructions for their removal to the mortuary

Mr. James Bell, the landlord of the Pincher Tavern, Turner Street, stated in the course of an interview that the man who jumped from the roof and was captured had of late been a regular customer at his establishment. The man was an Englishman and a bricklayer by trade. He was known as "Long Bill" by the few who knew him locally, and he was generally accompanied by a strongly-built, thick set man, whose clothing seemed to indicate that his trade was that of a general labourer. Both men had been in the house that day, but stayed only a few minutes and left hurriedly. He (Mr. Bell) did not see anything more of him until attracted to the scene of the murder by the shouting of the crowd that had collected in the street. He then saw "Long Bill" on the top of the roof, crouching near to the coping stone.

Later inquiries go to show that a quantity of jewellery and money was found upon the man now in custody and lying in an unconscious condition at the London Hospital. His name has not transpired, although entered in the hospital books as George Crawley, and he is described as a man of powerful build and of repulsive features.

The Coroner's inquiry was opened on Easter Monday at the Mile End Vestry Hall. Evidence as to the identification was given, and it proved that Gale was not a widow, but had been living for ten years separate from her husband.

A little boy named Whittaker, who had been sent to the house on the day of the murder on an errand, but failed to obtain entrance, stated that he saw a man look over the garden wall and then disappear. He also saw another man jump off the roof into the street, where he was captured by the police. The man who looked over the wall was not the one who jumped off the roof.

William Schaffer, a tailor, who lived next door to the scene of the murder, said he looked over the partition wall when the alarm had been given, and saw a man moving about in Mr. Levi's house. It was not Mr. Levi, but was the same man who afterwards jumped from the roof.

Two police witnesses described the finding of the bodies and the pursuit of the man who jumped from the roof, and who is now in custody at the hospital.

Medical evidence was given to the effect that Mr. Levi's death was due to a wound in the throat and fracture of the skull and ribs, and the woman's to similar injuries.

It was stated that a quantity of jewellery had been found on the prisoner, part of which was identified as having belonged to Mr. Levi and Mrs. Gale.

The inquest was adjourned until the 16th ult.

Levi was reputed to be a miser, and no less than three attempts at burglary had been previously made upon his premises. William Seaman, (for that is his real name) who is described as powerfully built, was well known to the police as a burglar, and was at the time of the murder out on ticket-of-leave. He resided in one of the numerous alleys at Millwall Docks, and when his rooms were searched incriminatory matter was disclosed.

At his trial he pleaded not guilty, and declined an offer of counsel to defend him, and when called upon for his defence he said he had no statement to make and no witnesses to call. The Jury, without leaving the box, found the prisoner guilty, and Justice Hawkins passed sentence of death upon him. The prisoner, as he was leaving the dock, said, "I hope the Lord will have more mercy on my soul than I have had upon my body."

It was stated that Seaman was assisted in his crime by another person who escaped by jumping on a tramcar and, passing among the passengers, made his exit at the opposite end, and so eluded his pursuers. Seaman was executed at Newgate.

Cornish and Devon Post – 11th April 1896.

———◆———

1896 – WHITECHAPEL ROAD.

"Whitechapel," says Strype, "is a spacious fair street for entrance into the City eastward and somewhat long, reckoning from the lay stall east, unto the bars, west. It is a great thoroughfare, being the Essex road, and well resorted onto, which occasions it to be the better inhabited, and accommodated with good inns for the reception of travellers, and for horses, coaches, carts, and waggons."

It will be seen from the above view that the pathway on the left is almost as wide as an ordinary road. The tram starts at Aldgate, and goes direct to Stratford Church, whence one may take another car to the confines of Epping Forrest or to Ilford, on the way to Romford.

The stranger in London, on noticing the immense width of the Whitechapel Road, is apt to inquire after the whereabouts of the slums of which he has heard so much. He need not, however, go very far from the spot depicted in this view to find some of the very worst localities in all Europe – notably those that figured so prominently in that appalling series of crimes known as the Whitechapel Murders.

On the right-hand side, we see the London Hospital, which well merits the description of "The Great General Hospital for East London." This great institution was founded in 1740, and the first buildings were erected in 1752, form the designs of Mr. B. Mainwaring. There were originally only 35 wards and 439 beds. The London Hospital now contains about 900 beds and its expenses are about £55,000 a year. The additional buildings, which were founded by the Duke of Cambridge in 1890, and opened by

Fig. 49. The Whitechapel Road

His Royal Highness a year later, include a fine portico entrance from the street, a comfortable reception room, a new operating theatre, a clinical theatre, and a suitable chapel.

Bookplate from *The Queen's Empire*, 1896.

1896 – JOHN ANDERSON.

A little while back the Ipswich papers announced that a man who had confessed himself to be the long-wanted East End murderer had died in Iquique, South America. The informant was a Mr. James Brame, who had been a shipmate with the man, and he has called at Lloyd's and given a detailed account of the circumstances which led him to believe that "Jack the Ripper" has gone to his account.

Mr. Brame left Shields as cook in the *Annie Speer*, a barque bound for Caldera, South America, in October, 1890. Amongst the crew, was one man who particularly attracted attention by his strange behaviour soon after the voyage commenced. He answered to the name of John Anderson, was apparently about thirty-eight years old, and was a fine, well set-up man with a bearing almost military.

His complexion was fair, his hair being red; he wore a moustache and a slight beard, and his face was much pitted with smallpox.

Anderson, who obtained a knowledge of surgery in the United States Navy through acting as a hospital assistant, said he had been robbed and almost ruined by a low woman in London. He brooded on this, and at length resolved to be revenged as far as he could on the whole class. He had shipped in the weekly boats running between Rotterdam and London, but when he determined to carry out his vengeance, he left these, and, having a little money, took lodgings at a quiet farm-like house near Bromley, where he passed as a ship's watchman engaged at night work in the docks. He would leave his lodgings in the evening and make his way to the Whitechapel district, where he committed the terrible deeds as he found opportunity.

He had found a confederate in his awful work, and it was this fact that enabled him to evade capture. The confederate would wait at a spot appointed with a clean smock, which Anderson at once drew over his blood-stained garments, so avoiding his suspicious appearance.

Illustrated Police News – 24th October 1896.

1896 – A FASTING MAN'S MISERIES.

At the Whitechapel County Court on Wednesday, Professor Alexandre Jacques claimed £15 salary from Wonderland Company of Whitechapel.

Plaintiff said he was engaged to fast at Wonderland at a salary of £5 a week. Plaintiff started fasting on September 21, and continued fasting till October 21. He was allowed to partake of lemonade and a secret powder and smoke cigarettes. The Plaintiff, called and examined, described Wonderland as a "sixpenny show." He admitted that there was a counter claim for £1 8s. 6d. against him for cigarettes.

Judge Bacon: What is the defence? Surely you don't suggest that a fasting man should abstain from his salary? (Laughter.)

I had no refreshments except lemonade.

Mr. Morris: An unknown, an American, competed with you?

Plaintiff: Yes.

Mr. Morris: Yes; and then you got no more sugar and lemonade. (Laughter.)

For the defence, Mr. Moods stated that the defendant had agreed to fast, but didn't. When the American, or the unknown, came on the scene defendant had to give in because he was likely to die. Then the plaintiff had lemonade.

Mr. Wolff, manager of Wonderland, said that the fasting was not real.

Judge Bacon: I supposed not. You connived at the fraud and now you don't want to pay. Did the Committee connive at this eating and drinking?

Defendant: They did not see it.

Judge Bacon: What a useful Committee!

Mr Longstaffe: Didn't Mr. Wolff get a testimonial from the plaintiff for his cigarettes?

Judge Bacon: What on earth does 3s. 6d. for a supper mean?

Defendant: It was when he commenced to fast. (Laughter.)

Judge Bacon: There will be judgment for the plaintiff for his salary, but he must pay for the sugar and lemonade.

Reynolds's Newspaper – 15th November 1896.

1897 – SALVATION ARMY PROCESSION DOWN THE WHITECHAPEL ROAD.

There is probably no part of the British Empire in which the great organisation founded by "General Booth," and known as the Salvation Army, is unknown. A detachment of the Army is here shown in the streets of London. The "Hallelujah lads and lasses," preceded

Fig. 50. The Salvation Army Procession

by a band playing the famous Salvation Army tunes, is passing down the Whitechapel Road, one of the principal thoroughfares of the East End. Conviction, earnestness, and self-sacrifice compel respect in every land peopled by men of English speech; and, despite what some may consider its extravagance and mistakes, the Salvation Army has undoubtedly deserved and won widespread sympathy.

Bookplate from *The Queen's Empire*, 1897.

1897 – LONDON WATER FAMINE.

The London Water Famine has become serious during the recent hot weather. Blocks of houses in the vicinity of Whitechapel Road inhabited by hundreds—in some cases thousands—of the poorer classes, have been cut off altogether from the prime necessary of life. Surely our legislators are shamefully apathetic respecting the great question of the Water Supply of London. If the subject is much longer neglected it may lead to a terrible outbreak of disease.

A benevolent worker on behalf of the suffering poor, the Rev. J.E. Hand, curate of St. Jude's, Whitechapel, has made a statement of his investigations, showing a deplorable state of things. Poor, hard-working women, who obtain with difficulty an occasional pail of water, have to carry it eighty-two steps to the rooms they occupy. As to other sanitary arrangements, they are too dreadful to contemplate. Something must be done and soon. A kind-hearted statesman, the Right Hon. Henry Chaplin, M.P., President of the Local Government Board, should see to this.

Penny Illustrated Paper – 7th August 1897.

Fig. 51. Courageous Woman Fights off Ruffians

1897 – RUFFIANS MEET THEIR MATCH.

Annie Tofler is not an easy woman to rob, as two Whitechapel ruffians named James Cronin and William Downes have found to their cost. They were each sentenced at the Old Bailey to twelve months' hard labour, and ordered to receive twelve strokes from the "cat," for robbing the young woman in Cable Street in broad daylight. Downes snatched the purse she was carrying, but she seized him by the collar and held him until she recovered it.

In the course of the struggle Downes struck her repeatedly in the face. Cronin and other companions of Downes appeared on the scene, and they compelled her by force to release her hold. The prosecutrix was commended for her courageous conduct, and a reward of £1 was given her.

Illustrated Police News – 6th November 1897.

1898 – EAST END WATER FAMINE.

Considerable distress still prevails in the densely populated districts of the East End owing to the inadequate supply of water. The rain which fell on the early days of the week did some good in flushing the drains, but the actual supply of water is not visibly increased. Poplar, Hackney, Whitechapel, and Forest Gate are still in a sad plight, and local medical men begin to look aghast at the prospect if the East London Waterworks Company does not bestir itself to relieve the distress. Instead of this, further curtailment is threatened.

The prospect is certainly none of the brightest, for the reservoirs are very low. At the same time, scarce as the supply is, it must be admitted that it is not economised as it ought to be. When our Artist visited the East End, he saw the carts on their rounds delivering the daily supply. He also saw examples of lavish outlay such as he has pictured in our Illustrations. All along the line, it would seem, "someone has blundered."

Illustrated London News – 3rd September 1898.

1898 – IN THE SAME PLACE.

Dorset Street, Whitechapel, has been once more the scene of a murderous crime. A little more than ten years ago—November 9th, 1888—just as Lord Mayor Whitehead was preparing for his journey to the Law Courts, the crowds waiting for the civic procession were startled and horrified by the hoarse cries of the street paper hawkers announcing the perpetration of another terrible murder in Whitechapel.

This was the seventh, and in some respects the most horrible, of the series connected with the name of "Jack the Ripper," the victim being a woman named Mary Kelly, who was a tenant in the lower room in the house known as No. 2, Miller's Court, a squalid cul-de-sac, which forms one of several running out of Dorset Street, and inhabited by the poorest of the poor.

London has not yet forgotten the sensation which was produced when the full particulars of the ghastly crime were given to the world, and it was shown that the wretched woman had just been murdered and afterwards mutilated in an indescribable manner. It was, as we have said, the seventh of a series of fiendish atrocities, the perpetrator of which has up to this day remained a mystery.

It was natural that the earlier rumours connected with the occurrence which took place on Sunday morning should have been to the effect that the "Ripper" had reappeared. The locality, the fact that it had taken place in the same building though not in the same room as that in which Mary Kelly met her death, gave credence to such an assertion. But fortunately for the peace of the public mind it was not the case.

Stated in bald facts the affair resolves itself into one of a very sordid and by no means unusual nature. So far as can be ascertained the principal actors in the latest tragedy of East End life are three in number. One is a man named Roberts, described as a labourer, who occupies apartments on the first floor; the second is, or rather was, Elisabeth Roberts, his wife, aged thirty-six; and the third, her sister, named Kate Marshall, forty-four years of age, who appears to have been staying in the same apartments, and who is alleged to have been recently released on license after serving five years for murderous assault.

Just how the occurrence took place cannot be stated with certainty until the inquest is held, but a little after midnight the two women appear to have had a serious altercation which threatened to lead to blows. The man Roberts, who had retired to rest in the little bedroom adjoining came out and endeavoured to make peace. Having as he thought succeeded, he returned to bed, but almost directly afterwards the quarrel would seem to have been renewed, and the next that is known is that the house was alarmed by

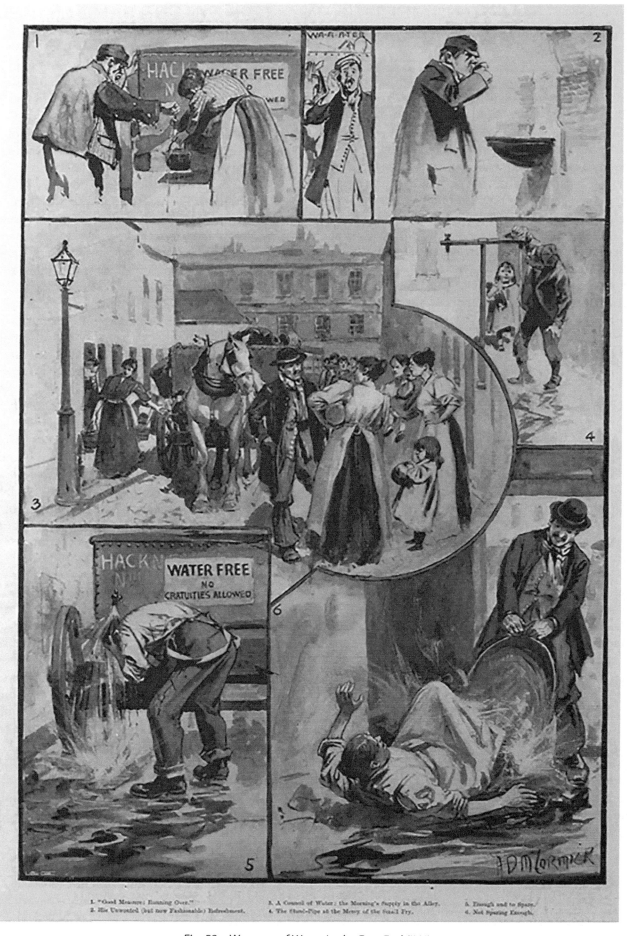

Fig. 52.   *Wastage of Water in the East End (ILN)*

piercing shrieks and the body of Mrs. Roberts was found lying on the landing outside the door of the room, blood issuing in streams from wounds in her breast.

A doctor and the police were sent for at once, but the unfortunate woman was found to be dead, having received several stabs in the region of the heart and other wounds on the arm. A large carving knife was discovered on the floor covered with blood, and this is evidently the weapon by which the wounds were inflicted. Both Roberts and Kate Marshall ware taken to Commercial Street Police Station, which is close by, with the result that Marshall was detained in custody.

Dorset Street was fairly alive with curious folk, who stared with morbid interest at the narrow court and the grimy buildings. In the course of an interview with a reporter, David Roberts, a painter and decorator, and the husband of the murdered woman gave a graphic account of the struggle which led to the death of his wife, whose age was thirty-six. She was the mother of eight children, but only three survived. A little boy, aged three, was present during the interview, and a pathetic incident occurred. The little fellow kept crying, "Where's mummy—is mummy coming?" and those present had to tell him that his mother would be there presently. Roberts alleged that both women had been drinking. They quarrelled, and he got out of bed two or three times to separate them. The last time his wife complained that she had been stabbed,

and in Marshall's hand Roberts said he found an old shoemaker's knife which was very sharp.

Blackburn Standard – 3rd December 1898.

1898 – RENTS IN WHITECHAPEL.

High rents have long formed a subject of deep grievance in Whitechapel and district, and full expression was given to this feeling at a crowded and enthusiastic meeting which was held last night in the baths at Aldgate. In the absence of Lord Rothschild through the death of Baron Ferdinand Rothschild. Sir S. Montagu, Bart., M.P., presided.

Sir Samuel much regretted has lordship's absence, because he had done more to delay the raising of rents in Whitechapel than any other man. Has lordship had founded a 4 percent Industrial Dwellings Company and built several blocks of houses in Whitechapel and at Stepney. Sir Samuel hoped that a 3 percent Industrial Company would be started, because not more than 3 percent, ought to be taken from the rents paid by working classes. He denounced the practices of those landlords in Whitechapel who were nothing more nor less than bloodsuckers of the working classes,

Fig. 53. The Poor of Whitechapel

and pictured the flagrant misery they caused. There were some half-dozen of them who were members of the Jewish community. He considered them to be enemies of that community. Them landlords ought to be ousted from every honourable position, and the existing law brought to bear upon them by a Tenants' Defence Committee.

There was a great congestion of population in Whitechapel, and it demanded early attention. As he had announced his intention to surrender his political connection with the constituency, he had resolved to give, as a parting gift, twenty-six acres of land at Edmonton to the London County Council for the erection of 700 houses, which would be capable of accommodating between 3,000 and 4,000 people, the conditions being that the County Council should simply take ordinary interest on their outlay, and that preference should be given to those persons who had resided in Whitechapel for over three years.

The Chief Rabbi moved a resolution strongly protesting against the practice of exacting unduly high rents for working class dwellings, which caused misery, overcrowding, and eviction, and declaring that means should be taken for obtaining for the tenant's security of tenure and fair terms. Pointing out that rents were being terribly increased, with consequent manifold hardships, he urged that it was the duty of the Legislature to step in and prevent these grasping practices on the part of landlords. These practices were not confined to Jewish landlords. There were many others transgressing the sacred commands of humanity. If these men would only reflect upon the cruelty they practised, try to live nobler ideals, and refuse to live upon the blood and sweat of the poor, Whitechapel would not contain as many cases where money had been wrung from the tenants by cruel and dishonest means.

Mr. Stuart M. Samuel, seconding the resolution, advised the tenants to resist unjust rents. Although Jews were law-abiding citizens, an organised effort should be made by which one individual representing the bulk of the inhabitants could bring the question to a test. As it was, the present dishonest practices of landlords in Whitechapel were simply placing thrift at a discount.

Mr. Lawson, L.C.C., in supporting the resolution, lamented the cause of Lord Rothschild's absence. The late baron was a man of genuine benevolence, cultivated mind, and distinguished character. The overcrowding, not only of Whitechapel but of the whole of the East End, was the gravest and most pressing problem confronting today. Denunciation of extortionate landlords was in itself no remedy. The Jewish community, like every other, had its black sheep, but unjust men were to be found everywhere. If moral pressure could be brought to bear upon these people, who were forgetful of their own principles and their own laws, all well and good, but for an adequate and permanent remedy they must trust the common action of the municipal authorities for common ends.

Bethnal Green was as bad as Whitechapel. The rebuilding of London was a cruel process for the industrial classes. The clearing of slums did not provide houses for the slum dwellers. Business premises took the place of tenement dwellings, and in many areas in Whitechapel the population was 350 to the acre, and 50 percent of them were below the line of poverty. The County Council must increase facilities for locomotion and communication with the outer and suburban districts. Better air would be obtained in such areas as Sir Samuel Montagu had munificently offered to the people. They must also pursue a housing policy free from some of the restrictions and conditions of the past, and resolve to change the condition of East London for the better.

The Rev. S. Singer looked to the London County Council and private effort for a change in the housing of the working classes. It was abundantly clear from what they saw in Whitechapel that no class of the community paid more proportionately for bad accommodation than the working classes.

Mr. Seager, L.C.C., moved: "That it is desirable to form a committee called "The Tenants' Defence Committee," Mr. J. Harris (chairman of the Board of Works) seconded it, Mr. H. Lewis supported it, and it was agreed to with loud cheering.

Daily Telegraph & Courier (London) – 20th December 1898.

1899 – MYSTERY BOOTS.

At the Whitechapel County Court, before His Honour Judge Bacon, an action was brought by Messrs. L.I. Rosenthal, shoe manufacturers, against Messrs. J. and E. Reynolds, of Chesham, Bucks, for payment for goods supplied.

Defendant denied liability and said that the boots were not made of leather but of "compo."

A pair of the boots were produced in court. They had been taken to pieces in order that his Honour could examine them. They were handed to the Bench, and his Honour immediately took out a slip of paper-like material from between the sole and the upper.

Plaintiff said that was Austrian pulp (Laughter.)

His Honour: Does that make the boots squeak? (Laughter.)

Plaintiff: That is better for the boots, and the customers like it.

His Honour: You must leave the customers alone. You are taking advantage of my ignorance. (Laughter.) the poor little kidlings' feet would suffer, I should think.

Witness: They take their chance.

His Honour: I am afraid that they do.

Pulling out a blue-coloured slip of material and holding it up, His Honour asked, "What that?"

Witness; That's rather a mystery.

His Honour: Isn't that paper? (Laughter.) I suppose that is to make the boot softer. (Renewed laughter.)

Judgment for the defendants.

Illustrated Police Budget – 18th February 1899.

———※◎※———

1900 – THE FATAL FIRE IN WHITECHAPEL.

The adjourned inquest upon the bodies of the five children— Polly, eleven; Annie, eight; Harry, six; Jane and Dora Krasnapolsky (twins)— who were burned to death in the fire which occurred at St. Georges Street, E., on the night of December 11, was resumed yesterday, by Mr. Wynne Baxter, the Coroner, at the Vestry Hall, Cable Street, E.

The Coroner said the main object of adjourning the former inquiry was to secure the presence of the brother of the victims, Israel, who was the last person in the room and the only one who could give any definite information as to the cause of the fire. He was seriously burned, and the doctor had told him the day previously that the young man could not leave the hospital for at least three weeks. He also had received a doctor's certificate to say that the mother, whose evidence was material, was unable to be present.

Simon Krasnapolskv, the eldest brother of the deceased, stated that he assisted his father as manager of a provision shop in Gravel Lane. On the night of December 11, he was at the latter address, when he heard that his father's house was on fire, and went there at once. He asked about the children, and was told they were safe. His brother Israel was badly burned, and when he arrived was in a butcher's shop opposite. All the people told Witness the children were safe, but he did not get nearer to the house than the opposite side of the road. He told the firemen about the children, and one of them went in and found them.

Sarah Krates, wife of a neighbour, stated that the fire broke out at a quarter to ten, and she rushed to the fire call in the vicinity, broke the glass, and started the alarm. She then saw no flames from where the children were. The side door was open, and she saw flames through it in the yard. The children upstairs were saved some time before the fire escape came. After raising the alarm, she returned, and saw the lad Israel in the road, looking like a bundle of rags. She saw a man break the window of the kitchen, and flames came out. That was the room in which the children were lying. There might have been a shutter, but the flames came out at the top.

Daniel Regan, a coal porter, said he was in a neighbouring beer shop just before ten o'clock, when the alarm was given. A girl came in and said a man was alight in the middle of the road. He rushed out, and saw a man (Israel) with his legs alight. He took off his coat, and beat the flames out. There were other people who helped. He cut the man's burning trousers off with a knife. There were children screaming in the upper window, and he went to their assistance. By that time there was a crowd. A meat van was handy, and he and others backed it against the burning house, and persuaded the inmates to hand the children upstairs out of the window. He got on the window ledge to facilitate that operation.

George Crow, a carman, stated that about a quarter to ten he saw the fire break out. There were flames in the passage, and a man was jumping about in the middle of them. He stepped in, and pulled the man out. The young man was alight, and ran down the street. Witness ran after him, and pulled off his jacket and waistcoat. The bottom of his trousers were alight. He returned to the fire, and pulled a woman out of the shop, which was on fire. Then he heard children crying in the upper part, and, with the assistance of Regan, rescued them by means of the meat van. A ladder was then brought, and a man came down it on to the top of the trolley.

The Coroner: You acted very cleverly in the matter. Witness added that the fire burned so rapidly and strongly that he thought there must have been oil. The floor of the passage looked as if oil had been spilt om it. It was alight, and the oil was running towards the kitchen door. The lad he pulled out took down a red petticoat, with red flowers, from behind the kitchen door, and began to beat the blaze on the floor. So far as he could see, the flames then were only in the passage. The first child dropped out of the upper floor was not two years old.

By the Jury: If he had known of the five children, he could certainly have saved some of them. At that time, he could have got into the room.

Corroborative evidence was given by other Witnesses, who also spoke to the recovery of the charred remains of the five children after the fire had been extinguished.

The Jury returned a verdict to the effect that the deaths of the deceased were accidental, that the evidence of the family was unsatisfactory, and they commended George Crow and Daniel Regan, by whose efforts several lives were probably saved.

The Jurors gave 1s. each out of their fees to be divided between these two men.

London Evening Standard – 10th January 1900.

1900 – A NARROW ESCAPE.

A number of workmen who were engaged repairing two small unoccupied shops at 463 and 465 Commercial Road, E., narrowly escaped being buried alive on Monday.

Shortly before noon the premises began to show signs of giving way, and the workmen had hardly left the building when the whole fabric collapsed. A large portion of the debris was thrown into the street, blocking the pavement and a portion of the roadway. Fears are entertained that the building either side may also collapse.

The usual big crowd collected. Fortunately, nobody was injured.

Tower Hamlets Independent and East End Local Advertiser – 3rd March 1900.

1900 – A GRISLY DISCOVERY.

Mr. Wynne E. Baxter (the Coroner for East London) has been informed of the discovery of three skeletons, believed to be those of a man, woman, and a fairly well-grown child, at 189, Whitechapel Road, a house which has latterly been used as a Jewish Club, but which is now in process of demolition.

On Wednesday afternoon a workman, engaged in reducing the front part of the house, found the remains embedded in the soil, about three feet beneath an iron grating in the pavement. The bones are dislocated and crumbling with age, and half disintegrated by the action of the earth in which they have been buried for many years — as many as fifty according to the surgeon who examined them at the mortuary.

Although the above account is a fairly reliable conjecture, the sex and age of the remains can be a matter for speculation only. The remains lie in the mortuary awaiting an inquest.

Leeds Chronicle – 5th May 1900.

1900 – ADAM AND EVE IN WHITECHAPEL.

A curious baptismal story in real life was unfolded, says the *Daily Telegraph*, before the Deputy-Coroner for East London during an inquest, which he held in his court at Whitechapel, on two infants—a boy and a girl who only lived a few minutes after birth. The father did not wish them to appear on the depositions as anonymous, and asked the Coroner to mark them down as Adam and Eve. This strange request caused some amusement in court, one of the Jurors gravely remarking that if the first bearers of these names had died at as early an age it would have been a serious matter for the race, while another hazarded the reflection that the little ones were disappointed at finding themselves in Whitechapel instead of in the Garden of Eden.

Pall Mall Gazette – 6th July 1900.

1900 – JUDGE BACON ON SCHOOL TEACHING.

In giving judgment in an action at the Whitechapel County Court, his Honour Judge Bacon, referring to the evidence of a boy about ten years old, said that the boy had been brought to the court to tell deliberate lies, after being well coached by his mother. To try and destroy his idea of truth and its value was most disgraceful and wicked. In that end of London people seemed to prefer lies to the truth. A good general education was given at the schools, but no moral instruction. If children were only taught to be honest folk, it would do far more good than cramming them with many things they were taught. If left to the mercy of some parents it was not very promising for the next generation.

East Anglian Daily Times – 20th November 1900.

1900 – AT A SCIENCE LECTURE IN WHITECHAPEL.

A number of well-disposed and wealthy residents of the West End of London started some classes for the purpose of giving instruction in elementary science to their less fortunate fellows who lived in the neighbourhood of Whitechapel.

One evening quite a small crowd came together, ostensibly to hear a discourse on "Air," which was to be delivered by a gentleman who had the misfortune to be extremely bald headed.

The lecturer was furnished with a good supply of interesting diagrams, with which he used every means to make his address instructive. In fact, he soon flattered himself that he had thoroughly succeeded, for even the youngsters seemed to pay great attention to what he had to say.

When his peroration was in full swing, he oracularly remarked, "It is quite impossible for any person to live without air."

The lecturer's collapse was, however, very speedy when a sharp wilted urchin shouted, "'Ow about yerself, guv'ner?"

Sheffield Telegraph – 1st December 1900.

1900 – SHOCKING MURDER OF A CONSTABLE IN WHITECHAPEL.

London was startled on Saturday by the murder of a policeman in Whitechapel. A Jew has been arrested. At the Thames Police Court on Saturday Barnet Abrahams, aged forty-one, a cigar maker, an English Jew, residing at 50, Newark Street, Whitechapel, was charged with feloniously killing and slaying Police constable Ernest Thompson by stabbing him in the neck with a knife while in the execution of his duty.

Mr. Deakin, instructed by Mr. Ben Cooper, of the Cigar Makers' Union, of which body the accused is a member, defended.

The prisoner is a man of small stature with prominent cheek bones. He was observed to be suffering from two black eyes, a broken nose, and a burst ear, and told his solicitor there were bruises all over his body.

Mr. Deakin said it was impossible to adequately go into the matter that day, and he, therefore, suggested that only short evidence should be taken.

Constable Alfred Timms, 100 H, deposed at twenty minutes past one he was on duty in Commercial Road, when he heard the blowing of police whistles. He ran in the direction of the sound, and at the corner of Union Street he saw Constable Thompson holding

Fig. 54. Shocking Murder of a Constable in Whitechapel

the prisoner on the ground. The officer was bleeding terribly from a wound in the neck. With the assistance of other constables Thompson was got into a cab and taken to the London Hospital. On the way he breathed frequently, but when within about fifty yards of the hospital he gave one long breath, and on arriving at that institution he was, examined by Dr. Hilyard, who pronounced life extinct.

Detective-inspector T. Divall, H division, said when he charged the prisoner he first said, "Do you understand English?" and the accused replied, "Well." Witness then said, "I am an inspector of police, and am going to charge you with feloniously killing and slaying Constable Thompson by stabbing him in the neck with this knife," at the same time pointing to a long pocket-knife covered with blood. Prisoner then said, "Then I am charged with maliciously killing?" Witness answered, "You are charged with feloniously killing." Abrahams said, "It is quite possible. I don't remember anything about it. I had no cause to do an injury to anyone."

Mr. Frayling, from the Treasury, who happened to be present in another case, said on the next occasion his department would take charge of it.

Inspector Divall was prepared to call seven or eight other witnesses, but Mr. Deakin, the prisoner's counsel, pointed out that it would be in the interests of the prisoner as well as in the interests of justice that the further hearing should be postponed till after the inquest. The police raised no objection to this course, and the magistrate concurring, the case was adjourned till Friday next, at two p.m., the prisoner being formally remanded till that date.

Another account says, "Of late there has been an alarming recrudescence of Hooliganism in London. Harmless pedestrians have been brutally assaulted by lawless and savage ruffians, and crime has followed crime in rapid succession, the latest being the murder in the East-end of a policeman who -was engaged in the discharge of his duties. There is little divergence in the many narratives of the occurrence, and briefly the facts appear to be these. Police constable Thompson, an officer attached to the Leman Street Station, had, as a part of his beat, the junction between Union Road, Whitechapel, and Commercial Road. Soon after one o'clock on Saturday morning sounds of disturbance attracted him to this spot. There, it is said, he discovered several men and woman quarrelling; after some persuasion the party moved a little distance away, where, however, the altercation was renewed. Once more the officer interposed, and shortly afterwards loud shouts were heard, followed by the violent blowing of a police whistle. This speedily brought Police constable Brooke, 190 H; to the spot. He found his comrade lying on the ground and obviously suffering from grievous injury. Covered with blood he was struggling with a man, who is alleged to be Barnet Abrahams, a cigar maker, residing at Whitechapel. This person was promptly arrested, and, later in the day, remanded at the Thames Police Court on the charge of having murdered the constable. An examination disclosed that Thompson was in a critical condition – indeed, it was at once apparent that there was little chance of saving his life. Already he had lost consciousness by reason of loss of blood from two terrible wounds in his throat.

While awaiting the arrival of a cab, everything possible was done in the way of first aid, but all was unavailing, for when this latest victim was conveyed to the London Hospital life was pronounced to be extinct. Thereupon the body was placed in the mortuary, close to the scene?"

In the course of conversation with a Press representative, the keeper of a coffee stall near the scene of the murder stated that the quarrel commenced first in Gower's Walk, a narrow alley opposite to Union Street, in which thoroughfare it was later continued. Owing to his position he could not see the termination of the affair. He heard sounds of an altercation in Gower's Walk, but paid no particular attention to them as rows were of frequent occurrence, and it was dangerous to interfere. Five minutes afterwards he saw a little knot of men, six or eight in number, cross Commercial Road from Gower's Walk into Union Street, where they stopped, and recommenced quarrelling. He heard nothing more until about ten minutes after, when a police inspector and a sergeant passed his stall and walked across to Union Street. It was then that he heard the whistle blown. The summons was an urgent one, as he gathered from the frequent repetition of the blasts, and he sent his assistant over to ascertain the nature of the alarm. Several policemen answered the call of the whistle, running past his stall, and he then heard from his assistant that a policeman had had his throat cut. The murdered constable, he said, was a kindly man, and had never rendered himself unpopular or distasteful in any way. Another eye-witness states that he was passing, about half past one o'clock, when he saw a crowd of roughs' surrounding a policeman. Other officers rushed up, and then he observed that the murdered constable was struggling with a man on the ground. Thompson, he says, exclaimed, "Hold on, I am done."

A married woman living near made the following statement on Saturday to a reporter, "I was lying half awake and half asleep when I heard some 'jangling'. But, bless you, that's nothing. There is frequently a row going on here, so I just took no notice. There was then a scuffling of feet on the pavement and shouting, but

I did not take much notice of that. When the houses close there always is a row somewhere. Not, perhaps, people coming from the place quite near here, but people on their way home. Next, I heard a policeman's whistle, but we are used to that too, so I did not get up. However, it kept on for a long time, and then I got up. The whistles were blown very loudly indeed. I looked out into the darkness, and could see a lot of people on the pavement and in the road. I saw three policemen. The crowd got round them and hemmed them in so; that they all appeared to be mixed up. I heard a cry, and I saw a scuffle take place, and the policeman, whom I now know as a very peaceful good-natured sort of man, fell forward. In the noise I could not hear what was said, but I saw the crowd fall back a bit. Underneath the policeman was a man on the pavement. Two other policemen came and lifted their comrade up, and grappled with the man who was underneath. There was now a big crowd, and I could see nothing distinctly; besides, they all began to move off."

The scene of the murder has an unenviable reparation. It is notorious for affrays and disturbances, and, indeed, it is due to this fact that Thompson had been instructed to give special supervision to the district. The deceased officer, whose home was at Stepney Green, leaves a widow and four children. His connection with the force dates back some eleven years, and it is recalled that he was the discoverer of the "Ripper's" last murder in Swallow Gardens, Royal Mint Street. On that occasion he was commended for the smartness he had displayed. He was extremely popular with his colleagues, and, while known to be courageous, was commonly regarded as a man of kindly and inoffensive disposition. It is not improbable that a subscription will be raised for the widow; who is prostrated with grief.

On Monday night Mr. Wynne E. Baxter, the East London Coroner, opened his inquiry at the London Hospital into the circumstances surrounding the death of Ernest Thompson, a police-constable (240), late attached to the H division, who was murdered in Commercial Road, Whitechapel, on the early morning of Saturday last. Barnett Abrahams, forty-one, a cigar maker, of 50, Newark Street, Mile End, who was arrested immediately after the crime, stands remanded from the Thames Police Court on a charge of killing the deceased. The accused man was present in court in the custody of two warders, and still bore a number of marks of violence about his face.

He was represented by Mr. C. Deacon, solicitor. The Chief Commissioner of Police was represented by Chief Inspector Divall, of the H division. None but those immediately interested in the inquiry were allowed to remain in court.

The first witness called was Albert Thompson, residing at 41, Deverell Street, New Kent Road, who said he was a police constable, 246 N. The deceased was his brother and resided at 1, Prince's Street, Mile End Old Town, and was thirty-two years of age. He had been in the force about twelve years. The witness last saw him alive on Thursday week, when he was in the best of health and spirits.

Dr. Francis Hilliard, house-surgeon, deposed that the deceased was brought to the hospital, at 1.35 a.m. on Saturday morning last. The witness examined the body, and found life extinct. He had a punctured wound on the left side of the neck. The witness had since made a post mortem examination of the body, by the coroner's order, and externally found an old scar on the chin and also a recent graze. There was the punctured wound on the left side of the neck, already mentioned, about three-quarters of an inch long, and the tissues of the neck were infiltrated with blood. The wound was downwards and inwards, and the weapon passing deeply had transfixed the internal jugular vein and the common carotid artery was severed. The haemorrhage had been very extensive. Death was due to the injuries described.

The Coroner (showing the witness a long-bladed penknife): Do you think the injuries could have been caused by this? The Witness: Yes, certainly. By a Juror: There was only one wound inflicted. A shorter man than the deceased could have inflicted that without difficulty had the deceased been in a standing position. The Coroner said that was all the evidence he proposed to take, and the inquiry was adjourned.

In the presence of a very large gathering, the funeral of the late officer took place at Bow Cemetery. The cortege left the house of the deceased officer in Princess Street, Stepney, shortly before one o'clock, and, headed by the band of the division to which deceased had been attached, and which played the "Dead March" in "Saul," proceeded on its melancholy journey. Behind the carriages containing the relatives and friends of deceased, considerably over 3,000 officers and men of the Metropolitan Police followed. All along the line of route the streets were densely packed with sympathising spectators. The blinds of the houses were drawn, and in some cases the shop keepers closed their establishments entirely whilst the procession proceeded solemnly along. At the cemetery an impressive service was held. Hundreds of beautiful wreaths were sent to the residence and the coffin was covered with costly emblems.

Barnett Abrahams, who stands charged with the murder of Police constable Thompson in Whitechapel was brought up on Friday on remand at the Thames Police Court. The only new features were the statements that the immediate neighbourhood of the

Fig. 55. Funeral of the Late Police Constable Thompson

murder was "light as day," and that when Thompson was brought into the hospital his truncheon was in the place in which it was usually carried at night, that the officer's lantern was uninjured, and that his whistle was inside his tunic. From this it was to be inferred, said Mr. Simms, that the officer had not struck the prisoner with his truncheon.

Mr. Francis Porteous Tyrrell Hilliard, house surgeon at the London Hospital, told the court that Thompson was dead when brought to the hospital. The wound from which Thompson had died was about three quarters of an inch long, about one inch below the angle of the jaw. It was nearly two and a half inches deep. The instrument with which the wound was inflicted had had its sharp edge uppermost. The jugular vein was very nearly severed, and the artery almost cut through. The wound might have been inflicted with the blood-stained clasp knife which was produced. "Do you think it feasible that after the blow was struck the constable blew his whistle?" asked Mr. Deakin for the defence. "Yes; it was possible within an absolute limit of two minutes."

"Stand up," said Mr. Deakin to the prisoner, who stood up immediately with an almost automatic precision. "Hold up your hand," continued the solicitor. Abrahams did so. "Now, do you think that the prisoner could have struck that blow without jumping up to the deceased, considering his height, the doctor, scanning the prisoner carefully, said very slowly, "Yes," and clinched his answer with a shake of his head.

The ex-warder repeated the story he told at the inquest, and the accused was remanded for another week.

At the Limehouse Coroner's Court on Monday Mr. Wynne E. Baster concluded the inquest on the body of Policeman Ernest Thompson. Barnet Abrahams, who stands charged with the crime, was again present. A police surgeon was the next witness. He said that he examined Abrahams at the station after his arrest. His injuries might have been caused by blows from a fist, and some by a truncheon. The face and the clothing were smothered with blood, but not from his own injuries. The accused was perfectly sober, and in the witness's opinion he was not suffering mentally as a result of his injuries.

Evidence was next given by Lewis Michaels and Emanuel Cohen, both members of the Netherlands Choral and Dramatic Club in Bell Lane, of which the accused was also a member. They both saw the accused on the Friday night and averred that he was sober. They also gave Abrahams the character of being a hard-working and inoffensive, man. Neither of them had ever seen him in possession of such a knife as the one produced. The accused was the principal support of his aged mother and two orphan nieces.

Lyon Hartz, cashier of the Netherlands Club, said that the accused was in the habit of borrowing a penknife from him. The last occasion he did so was in the early part of the week on which the crime was committed. The witness had suggested that he should buy a knife, but Abrahams said he had no reason to do so when he could always borrow one. The witness had never seen the knife produced, and it would be absolutely useless to cigar makers. The accused returned him his knife after he had used it.

The Coroner asked if Abrahams wished to make any statement on oath.

Deakin: No, sir; acting under my advice he will not.

After a very brief deliberation the jury returned a verdict of "Wilful murder" against Abrahams, who was committed to take his trial on the coroner's warrant. The jury expressed their satisfaction at the manner in which the police had performed their duties and given evidence.

At the Central Criminal Court last evening Barnet Abrahams (41), cigar maker, charged with the murder by stabbing of Police Constable Thompson in the East End of London, on December 1st, was found guilty of manslaughter and was sentenced to penal servitude for 20 years.

Illustrated Police News – 8th December 1900.

and children were compelled to clamber out on to the parapet of the lofty building.

Thick, suffocating smoke was rolling out in dense clouds, and the terror-stricken party could hear the fire roaring beneath them. The crowd below shouted to not jump, as they seemed likely to do, for the firemen were coming, and just in the nick of time the horsed escape from the Commercial Road East Fire Station dashed up. The firemen ran the escape off its van, got into position against the burning place, and then proceeded with the difficult work of rescue. They succeeded in bringing the six people safely to the ground. There was no trouble with the children, but the women were so terror-stricken, and clutched at anything and everything so frantically, that the work was rendered doubly hazardous. Hardly were the people out of the building when the whole place burst into flames from top to bottom.

Nottingham Journal – 13th December 1900.

1900 – ALARMING FIRE IN WHITECHAPEL.

Just before four o'clock on Tuesday morning it was discovered that premises at 96, Whitechapel High Street. E., were on fire. The lower part of the place was used as a boot and shoe factory firm named Lazarus, while in the upper floors lodged a Mr. S.E. Brown, his wife, mother-in-law, and three children. The fire broke out in the ground floor, and had obtained a very strong hold of the big shop when it was first discovered. Brown was not aware of the outbreak till he saw the flames leap to the window. At once he roused the household, and essayed to escape by the staircase with the children, but to their extreme terror they found the stairs were enveloped in fire. The intense heat drove them higher and higher, and at last the man, women,

"THE AUTUMN OF TERROR AND BEYOND"

Much has been written, argued and debated about the crimes of "Jack of the Ripper," but one point is undeniable – his reign of terror sold newspapers. The public could not get enough of *the graphic* descriptions and illustrations sensationalised by the press.

This section is a selection of news articles from the time covering the "canonical five" murders as well as some of those debated to have been committed by "Jack the Ripper."

"Jack" was never caught and there have been many theories and arguments that still rage today concerning his identity – a mystery never likely to be solved!

1888 – POSSIBLE "RIPPER" VICTIM?

About 10 minutes to five o'clock on Tuesday morning a man, who lives at 47, George Yard buildings, Whitechapel, was coming downstairs to go to work, when he discovered the body of a woman lying in a pool of blood on the first-floor landing. Reeves at once called in Constable Barrett, 26 H, who was on his beat in the vicinity of George Yard, and Dr. Keleene, of Brick Lane, was communicated with and promptly

arrived. He made an examination of the woman, and pronounced life extinct, giving it as his opinion that she had been brutally murdered, there being knife wounds on her breast, stomach, and abdomen. There were 39 wounds in various parts of the body, which was that of a woman apparently between 35 and 40 years of age, about 5ft. 3in. in height, complexion and hair dark; with a dark green skirt, a brown petticoat, a long black jacket, and a black bonnet. The woman was not known to any of the occupants of the tenements on the landing on which the deceased was found, and no disturbance of any kind was heard during the night. The body was removed to Whitechapel mortuary.

Mr. George Collier opened an inquest on the body on Thursday at the Working Lads' institute, Whitechapel. She was stated to be Martha Turner, aged 38, a single woman, lately living at 4, Star Place, Commercial Road, but previous to calling the first witness the Coroner said that the body had been identified that morning, but he had just been informed that two other persons also identified it as quite a different person, and under these circumstances be thought the question of identity had better be left till the last.

Elizabeth, Mahony, of 47, George Yard buildings, Whitechapel, the wife of a carman, stated that on the night of Bank holiday she was out with some friends. She returned shortly before two in the morning with her husband, and afterwards left the house to try and get some supper at the chandler's shop. The stairs were then perfectly clear of any obstacle, and were the same on her return. She and her husband heard no noise during the night, but at 10 o'clock she was told that a murder had been committed in the building. There

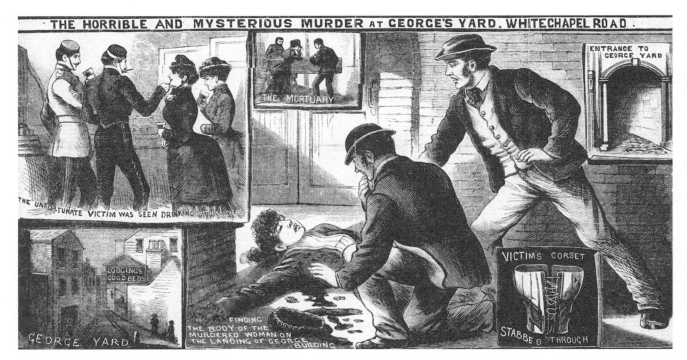

Fig. 56. Scenes from the Murder (Illustrated Police News)

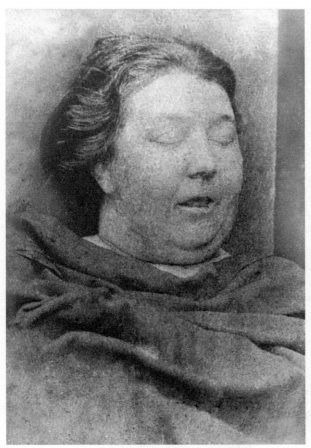

Fig. 57. Mortuary Photo of Martha Tabram (Turner) (Possible "Ripper" victim)

was no light on the staircase. The spot where the body was found had been pointed out to her. She was sure it was not there at two o'clock as she went in, as it was in the wide part of the stairs, and quite in the dark.

Alfred George Crow, a cabdriver, of 35, George Yard buildings, deposed that on Tuesday morning he returned home from work at half-past three. On his way up the stairs, he saw somebody lying on the first landing. It was not an unusual thing to see, so he passed on and went to bed. He did not know whether the person was dead or alive when he passed.

John Saunders Reeves, 37, George Yard buildings, a waterside labourer, deposed that on Tuesday morning he left home at five o'clock to go in search of work. On the first floor landing he saw a female lying in a pool of blood. She lay on her back, and seemed dead. He at once gave notice to the police. The woman was a perfect stranger to the witness. Her clothes were all disarranged, as if she had had a struggle with someone. The witness did not notice any instrument lying about.

Police Constable Barrett, 226 H, deposed to being called by the last witness to view the body of the deceased. She was lying on her back, and before she was moved a doctor was sent for, and on arrival pronounced life extinct. The woman's hands were clenched, but did not contain anything. Her clothes were disarranged.

Dr. Timothy Robert Keleene, 28, Brick Lane, stated that he was called to the deceased and found her dead. He examined the body and found 39 punctured wounds. There were no less than nine in the throat and 17 in the breast. She appeared to have been dead three hours. The body was well nourished. He had since made a post-mortem examination, and found the left lung penetrated in five places, and the right lung in two places. The heart had been penetrated, but only in one place, otherwise it was quite healthy. The liver was healthy, but penetrated in five places, and the spleen was penetrated in two places. The stomach was penetrated in six places. In the witness's opinion the wounds were not inflicted with the same instrument, there being a deep wound in the breast from some long, strong instrument, while most of the others were done apparently with a penknife. The large wound could have been caused by a sword bayonet or dagger. It was impossible for the whole of the wounds to be self-inflicted. Death was due to the loss of blood consequent on the injuries. At the conclusion of this witnesses evidence the inquiry was adjourned.

The case is in certain respects one of a very puzzling character, owing to the fact that so many stab wounds were inflicted, and that no cries were heard, although the poor woman was on some stone steps, close to the doors of small rooms wherein several separate families resided. It now appears that on the night of Bank holiday there were several soldiers in the neighbourhood, some of whom were seen drinking in the Princess Alice – two minutes' walk from George Yard buildings – and other taverns near. With these soldiers were the deceased and another woman, the latter being known in the district as "Mogg" and "Pearly Poll." One of these men was a private, the other a corporal. It has been ascertained that only corporals and sergeants are allowed to wear side arms when on leave. This fact, of course, narrows the issue as to the possible identity of the assailant – presuming he was a soldier.

Inquiries were at once set on foot by the police and military authorities, with the result that it is stated two soldiers have been placed under military arrest at the Tower. The authorities decline to give their names unless some definite charge is formulated. The two soldiers are said to belong to the Guards.

A perplexing feature in connection with the outrage is the number of injuries on the young woman's body. That the stabs were from a weapon shaped like a bayonet is almost established beyond doubt. The wound over the heart was alone sufficient to kill, and death must have occurred as soon as that was inflicted. Unless the perpetrator was a madman, or suffering to an unusual extent from drink delirium no tangible explanation can be given

Fig. 58. Discovery of the Body

of the reason for inflicting the other 38 injuries, some of which almost seem as if they were due to thrusts and cuts from a penknife. On the other hand, if the lesser wounds were given before the one fatal injury the cries of the deceased must have been heard by those who, at the time of the outrage; were sleeping within a few yards of the spot where the deed was committed.

The difficulty of identification erose out of the brutal treatment to which the deceased was manifestly subjected, she being throttled while held down, and the face and head so swollen and distorted in consequence that her real features are not discernible. There is little doubt, although she has been variously identified as a Mrs. Withers, and a Mary Bryan, that she is a woman known as Martha Turner.

Mrs. Bousfeld, in whose house she lived till three weeks back, states that she had resided in her house for two months with Turner. The deceased had told her that her real name was either Staples or Stapleton. and that she had left her husband 13 years, and had taken up with Turner. Both she and this man got their living by selling trinkets in the streets, such as studs, links, chains, and menthol cones. She used to stand in Cheapside and various places, whilst Turner occupied other ground. Turner left her some few weeks ago, and then the deceased, who paid 2s. per week for her room, got two weeks in arrear, and as she could not pay, she suddenly left.

In addition to being identified by Mrs. Bousfield, the deceased has already been identified by one or two other women, who saw her in the company of some soldiers at neighbouring public houses. There was a dispute, and one of the soldiers struck the companion of the deceased a blow. This was just by George Yard, a long, dark thoroughfare, and it is believed that the deceased was forcibly dragged up to the place where she was found so brutally ill-treated and so fearfully wounded. The police have a description of the two soldiers who, as before stated, are believed to be in the Guards.

Lloyd's Weekly Newspaper – 12th August 1888.

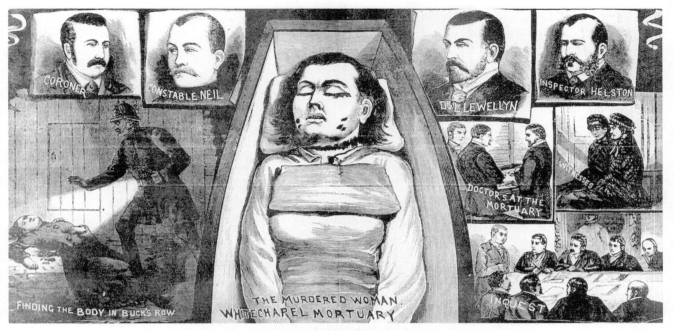

Fig. 59. Sketches from the Illustrated Police News

1888 – MARY ANN NICHOLS.

The sensation caused by the discovery of a murdered woman in Whitechapel a short time ago has scarcely abated when another discovery is made which, for the brutality exercised on the victim is even more shocking. As Constable John Neil was walking down Buck's Row, Thomas Street Whitechapel, about a quarter to four o'clock this morning he discovered a woman between thirty-five and forty years of age lying at the side of the street with her throat cut and bleeding profusely. She was immediately conveyed to the Whitechapel mortuary, where it was found that besides the wound in the throat the body had been ripped open, evidently with a large knife. The hands are bruised, and bear evidence of there having been a severe struggle. Some of the front teeth have also been knocked out, and the face is bruised on both cheeks, and very much discoloured. The clothes are torn and cut up in several places, bearing evidence of the ferocity with which the murder was committed.

The greatest excitement prevails in the district. Several persons in the neighbourhood state that there was some disturbance shortly after midnight, but no screams were heard, nor anything beyond what might have been considered evidence of an ordinary brawl.

St. James's Gazette – 31ˢᵗ August 1888.

1888 – INQUEST OF MARY ANN NICHOLS.

The able Coroner for South East Middlesex, Mr. Wynne E. Baxter, last Saturday brought to a close the inquiry into the death of Mary Ann Nichols, the discovery of whose dead body in a Whitechapel street was depicted in *The Penny Illustrated Paper* of Sept. 8.

Coming to a consideration of the perpetrator of the murder, the shrewd Coroner said, "It seems astonishing at first thought that the culprit should have escaped detection, for there must surely have been marks of blood about his person. If, however, blood was principally on his hands, the presence of so many slaughter houses in the neighbourhood would make the frequenters of this spot familiar with blood-stained clothes and hands, and his appearance might in that way have failed to attract attention while he passed from Buck's Row in the twilight into Whitechapel Road, and was lost sight of in the morning's market traffic. We cannot altogether leave unnoticed the fact that the death that you have been investigating is one of four presenting many points of similarity, all of which have occurred within the space of about five months, and all within a very short distance of the place where we are sitting.

All four victims were women of middle age, all were married, and had lived apart from their husbands in consequence of intemperate habits, and were at the time of their death leading an irregular life, and eking out a miserable and precarious existence in common lodging houses.

Fig. 60. Mary Ann Nichols Discovered in Buck's Row

Fig. 61. Buck's Row – Arrow pointing to where body was found

In each case there were abdominal as well as other injuries. In each case the injuries were inflicted after midnight, and in places of public resort, where it would appear impossible but that almost immediate detection should follow the crime; and in each case the inhuman and dastardly criminals are at large in society.

Emma Elizabeth Smith, who received her injuries in Osborn Street on the early morning of Easter Tuesday, April 3, survived in the London Hospital for upwards of twenty-four hours, and was able to state that she had been followed by some men, robbed and mutilated, and even to describe imperfectly one of them.

Martha Tabram was found at three a.m. on Tuesday, Aug. 7, on the first-floor landing of George Yard Buildings, Wentworth Street, with thirty-nine punctured wounds on her body. In addition to these, and the case under your consideration, there is the case of Annie Chapman, still in the hands of another Jury. The instruments used in the two earlier cases are dissimilar. In the first it was a blunt instrument, such as a walking stick; in the second, some of the wounds were thought to have been made by a dagger; but in the two recent cases the instruments suggested by the medical witnesses are not so different.

Dr. Llewellyn says the injuries on Nichols could have been produced by a strong-bladed instrument, moderately sharp. Dr. Phillips is of the opinion that those on Chapman were by a very sharp knife, probably with a thin, narrow blade, at least six to eight inches in length, probably longer. The similarity of the injuries in the two cases is considerable. There are bruises about the face in both cases; the head is nearly severed from the body in both cases; there are other dreadful injuries in both cases; and those injuries, again, have in each case been performed with anatomical knowledge.

Dr. Llewellyn seems to incline to the opinion that the abdominal injuries were first, and caused instantaneous death; but, if so, it seems difficult to understand the object of such desperate injuries to the throat, or how it comes about that there was little bleeding from the several arteries that the clothing on the upper surface was not stained, and, indeed, very much less bleeding from the abdomen than from the neck. Surely it may well be that, as in the case of Chapman, the dreadful wounds to the throat were inflicted first and the others afterwards.

This is a matter of some importance when we come to consider what possible motive there can for all this ferocity. Robbery is out of the question; and there is nothing to suggest jealousy; there could not have been any quarrel, or it would have been heard. I suggest to you as a possibility that these two women may have been murdered by the same man with the same object, and that in the case of Nichols the wretch was disturbed before he had accomplished his object; and having failed in the open street he tries again, within a week of his failure, in a more secluded place. If this should be correct, the audacity and daring are equal to its maniacal fanaticism and abhorrent wickedness. But this surmise may or may not be correct, the suggested motive may be the wrong one; but one thing is very clear— that a murder of a most atrocious character has been committed."

The Jury, after a short consultation, returned a verdict of wilful murder against some person or persons unknown in the case of Mary Ann Nichols. A rider was added expressing the full coincidence of the Jury with some remarks made by the Coroner as to the need of a mortuary for Whitechapel.

The *Penny Illustrated Paper* – 29th September 1888.

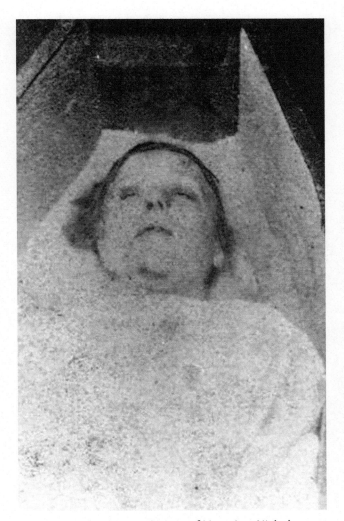

Fig. 62. Mortuary Picture of Mary Ann Nichols

1888 – ANOTHER BARBAROUS MURDER IN WHITECHAPEL.

Saturday morning, at a quarter-past six, the neighbourhood of Whitechapel was horrified to a degree bordering on panic by the discovery of another barbarous murder of a woman at 29, Hanbury Street (late Brown Lane), Spitalfields.

Hanbury Street is a thoroughfare running between Commercial Street and Whitechapel Road, the occupants of which are poor, for the most part of Jewish extraction. The circumstances of the murder are of such a revolting character as to point to the conclusion that it has been perpetrated by the same hand as committed that in Buck's Row and the two previous murders, all of which have occurred within a stone's throw of each other.

The murdered woman, who appears to have been respectably connected, was known in the neighbourhood by women of the unfortunate class as Annie Sivvy, but her real name was Annie Chapman. When her body was found it was respectably clad. She wore no head covering, but simply a skirt and bodice and two light petticoats. A search being made in her pockets, nothing was found but an envelope stamped "The Sussex Regiment."

The house in Hanbury Street in the yard of which the crime was committed is occupied by a woman named Richardson, who employs several men in the rough packing line. There is a small shop in front at the basement of the house, which is utilised for the purposes of a cat's meat shop. From the upper end of the house there is a passage with a door at either end leading to a small yard, some 13ft. or 14ft. square, separated from the adjoining houses by a slight wooden fence. There is no outlet at the back, and any person who gains access must of necessity make his exit from the same end as his entry. In the yard there were recently some packing cases, which had been sent up from the basement of the dwelling, but just behind the lower door there was a clear space left, wherein the murder was undoubtedly committed.

The theory primarily formed was that the unfortunate victim had been first murdered and afterwards dragged through the entry into the back yard; but from inspection made later in the day it appears that the murder was actually committed in the corner of the yard, which the back door, when open, places in obscurity. There were on Saturday some marks of blood observable in the passage, but it is now known that these were caused during the work of removal of some packing cases, the edges of which accidentally came in contact with the blood which remained upon the spot from which the unhappy victim was removed.

The evidence shows that the murder was committed shortly before 5.30 o'clock in the morning. Albert Cadosch, who lodges next door, had occasion to go into the adjoining yard at the back at 5.25, and states that he heard a conversation on the other side of the palings as if between two people. He caught the word "No," and fancied he subsequently heard a slight scuffle with the noise of falling against the palings, but thinking that his neighbours might probably be out in the yard he took no further notice and went to his work.

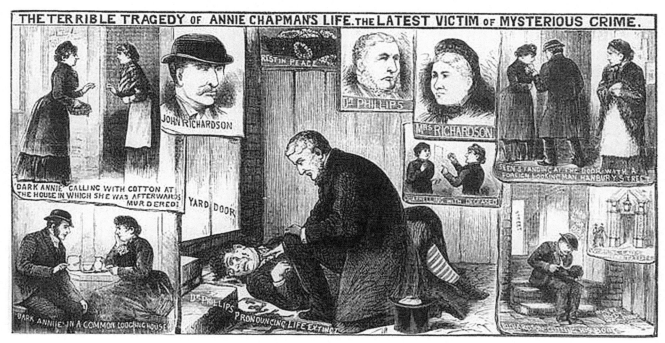

Fig. 63. The Terrible Tragedy

Nothing farther can be traced of the dreadful tragedy until shortly before six o'clock, when the man Davies, passing into the yard at the back of 29, Hanbury Street, observed a mutilated mass which caused him to go shrieking in affright into the street.

In the house the back premises of which happened to become the scene of this hideous crime no fewer than six separate families reside. One of the occupants of the house is the man named John Davies, a porter in the Spitalfields Market. When he discovered the body in the yard, he made no attempt to ascertain the condition of the deceased, but immediately alarmed the other inmates of the house, and then proceeded to acquaint the police at the Commercial Street Station of what had occurred. In the meantime, Mrs. Richardson, the principal occupier of the premises, together with a young woman named Eliza Cooksley, sleeping on the second floor, were aroused, and under the notion that the building was on fire ran to the back bedroom window, whence they were enabled to see the murdered woman lying on the paved yard, horribly mutilated.

When the police arrived, they found that the woman had been murdered in a terribly brutal fashion. It was obvious both from the marks upon the body and of the splashes of blood upon the palings which separate the dwellings one from the other that the woman, while lying down, had her throat first cut, and then was ripped open and disembowelled. The perpetrator of the ghastly deed undoubtedly occupied some considerable time in doing his victim to death, inasmuch as it appears that he, with fiendish resolve

not only killed the object of his caprice or passion, but afterwards mutilated her body in a terrible manner, leaving the heart and liver lying by the shoulder.

There is on every hand one opinion prevailing that the Whitechapel murders have been all enacted by the same person. The body is already in a shell, and the autopsy having been made by Dr. Phillips and assistants, the portions of flesh and entrails removed by the fiendish hands of the murderer have been so far as possible replaced in their natural positions, and there is little else observable beyond the usual post-mortem indications. The body is that of a fairly nourished woman, but bears traces of rough usage.

Mrs. Richardson, the landlady at 29, Hanbury Street, the house where the body of the deceased was found, in the course of an interview said, "I have lived at this house 15 years, and lodgers are poor but hard-working people. Some have lodged with me as long as 12 years. They mostly work at the fish market or the Spitalfields Market. Some of the carmen in the fish market go out to work as early as 1 a.m., while others go out at four and five, so that the place is open all night, and anyone can get in.

It is certain that the deceased came voluntarily into the yard, as if there had been any struggle it must have been heard. Several lodgers sleep at the back of the house, and some had their windows open, but no noise was heard from the yard. Just before six o'clock, when Mr. Davis, another of my lodgers, came down, he found the deceased lying in the corner of the yard, close to the house, and by the side of the step. The lower part of her body was uncovered. There was not

Fig. 64. Entrance to the Yard of 29 Hanbury Street

the slightest sign of a struggle, and the pool of blood which flowed from the throat after it was cut was close to the step where she lay. She does not appear to have moved an inch after the fiend struck her with the knife. She must have died instantly. The murderer must have gone away from the spot covered with blood. There was an earthenware pan containing water in the yard; but this was not discoloured, and could not, therefore, have been used by the murderer. The only possible clue that I can think of is that Mr. Thompson's wife met a man about a month ago lying on the stairs. This was about four o'clock in the morning. He looked like a Jew, and spoke with a foreign accent."

The deputy of a lodging house at 30, Dorset Street, stated that Annie Chapman used to lodge there about two years ago with a man called Jack Sivvy, a sieve maker: hence her nickname Annie Sivvy. She appeared to be a quiet woman, and not given to drinking; in fact, she was quite surprised to hear that she had been seen drinking the night before her murder. The woman had two children to his knowledge—a boy who was a cripple, and who he believed was at some charitable school, and a daughter who was somewhere in France.

Timothy Donovan, the deputy at the lodging house, 35, Dorset Street, where the deceased frequently stayed, stated that the deceased stayed there on Sunday night last. She had been in the habit of coming there for the past four months. She was a quiet woman, and gave no trouble. He had heard her say she wished she was as well off as her relations, but she never told him who her friends were or where they lived. A pensioner or a soldier usually came to the lodging house with her on Saturday nights, and generally stayed until the Monday morning. He

Fig. 65. 29 Hanbury Street – Entrance to Courtyard Under the House Number

would be able to identify the man instantly if he saw him. After the man left on Monday deceased would usually keep in the room for some days longer, the charge being 8d. per night. This man stayed at the home from Saturday to Monday last, and when he went the deceased went with him. She was not seen at the house again until Friday night about half-past eleven o'clock when she passed the doorway, and Donovan, calling out, asked her where she had been since Monday, and why she had not slept there, and she replied, "I have been in the Infirmary." Then she went on her way in the direction of Bishopsgate Street. About 1.40 a.m. on Saturday morning, she came again to the lodging house, and asked for a bed. The message was brought upstairs for him and he sent downstairs to ask for the money. The woman replied, "I haven't enough now, but keep a bed for me. I shan't be long." She was the worse for drink at the time, and was eating some baked potatoes.

On being asked whether he knew the man called "Leather Apron," Donovan said he knew him well. He came to the lodging house about twelve months ago, a woman being his companion. In the early hours of the morning the woman commenced screaming "murder," and it seems that "Leather Apron" had knocked her down and torn her hair and clothes. "Leather Apron" said the woman was trying to rob him, but (Donovan) did not believe him, and turned him out of the house. The man had come there several times since for lodging, but they would not admit him.

About ten o'clock on Saturday morning a woman named Amelia Farmer gave important information that she had seen a fellow lodger with the deceased, and had known her for some considerable time. She stated that the deceased woman was Annie Chapman, the wife of a veterinary surgeon, who had died at Windsor about eighteen months ago. She was accordingly taken to the mortuary at half-past eleven o'clock and immediately recognised her friend, apparently being much touched at the dreadful spectacle.

Later she made a statement of what she knew of the history of the murdered woman. Annie Chapman had for a time been separated from her husband, a veterinary surgeon at Windsor, by mutual agreement, and had been allowed 10s. a week from him for her maintenance. The money had been sent by Post Office order, made payable at the Commercial Street Post Office, and had always come regularly. About eighteen months ago the instalments suddenly ceased, and upon inquiry being made, it was found that the husband had died.

Last Monday Chapman had intimated her intention of communicating with her sister, saying, "If I can get a pair of boots from my sister, I shall go hop picking." Another relation, a brother-in-law of the deceased, lived somewhat in or near Oxford Street. Farmer asserted that her murdered friend was apparently a sober, steady-going kind of woman, and one who seldom took any drink. For some time past she had been living occasionally with a man named Ted Stanley, who had been in the militia, but was now working at some neighbouring brewery. Ted Stanley was a good-tempered man, rather tall, about 5ft. 10in., fair, and of florid complexion. He was the last man in the world to have quarrelled with Chapman, nor would he have injured her in any way.

At the beginning of the week the deceased had been rather severely knocked about in the breast and face by another woman of the locality, through jealousy in connection with Ted Stanley, and had been obliged to go the casual ward. As a regular means of livelihood, she had not been in the habit of frequenting the streets, but had made antimacassars for sale. Sometimes she would buy flowers or matches, with which to pick up a living.

Great weight is attached to the statement to the rings which were on the murdered woman's hand before the murder was committed, but which had been wrenched off by the wretch before he made good his escape. On Saturday evening a further and still more important clue had been gained. It was ascertained that a pawnbroker in Mile End Road had detained rings which had been presented to him for pledge, but which on being tested had not been found genuine. Should these rings prove to be those taken from Annie Chapman, and should Amelia Farmer be able to identify them, a solid trace of the bloodthirsty and cruel murderer will be obtained which may lead to his capture.

Mrs. Elizabeth Bell, of Hanbury Street, states, "I have been living here some time, and wish I had never come. Such a terrible sight is enough to shock any woman with the hardest heart. The house is open all night next door, and this poor creature was taken into the yard and butchered, no doubt, by the same man who committed the others. We were all roused at six o'clock this morning by Adam Osborne calling out, "For God's sake get up, here's a woman murdered." We all got up and huddled on our clothes, and on going into the yard saw the poor creature lying by the steps in the next yard, with her clothes torn and her body gashed in a dreadful manner. The people in the house next door were all asleep, I believe, and knew nothing of the matter until the police came and roused them up. The passage is open all night, and anyone can get in, and no doubt that is what happened."

All the other tenants of the house gave the same opinion, and those in the house of Mr. Richardson, at 29, where the murder occurred, state that they heard no cries of "Murder" or "Help," nor anything unusual during the night.

John Davis, who was the first to make the shocking discovery, says, "Having had a cup of tea this morning at about six o'clock. I went downstairs. When I got to the end of the passage, I saw a female lying down, her clothing up to her knees, and her face covered with blood. What was lying beside her I cannot describe — it was part of her body. I had heard no noise, nor had my missus. I saw Mr. Bailey's men waiting at the back of the Black Swan ready to go into their work—making packing cases. I said to them, "Here's a sight; a woman must have been murdered." I then ran to the Police Station in Commercial Road, and I told them there what I had seen, and some constables came back with me. I did not examine the woman when I saw her—I was too frightened at the dreadful sight. Our front door at 29, Hanbury Street, is never bolted, and any one has only to push it open and walk through to the gate at the back yard. Immoral women have at times gone there, and Mrs. Richardson, our landlady, had occasion to keep a closet locked there, but no lock has ever been placed on the front door; at least, I have never seen one. It is only a fortnight ago that I came to lodge there. I have known people open the passage door and walk through into the yard when they had no right there. There are about fifteen altogether living in the house."

Mrs. Davis has made the following statement. "The bell was ringing for six o'clock, and that is how I know the time that my husband went downstairs. He then said to me, "Old woman, I must now go down, for it is time I was off to work." He went down, but did not return, as he tells me that when he saw the deceased, and the shocking state in which she was, he at once ran off for the police. We never heard any screams, either in the night or this morning. I went down myself shortly after, and nearly fainted at what I saw. The poor woman's throat was cut, and the inside of her body was lying beside her. Someone beside me then remarked that the murder was just like the one committed in Buck's Row. The other one could not have been such a dreadful sight as this, for the poor woman found this morning was quite ripped open. She was lying in a corner of the yard, on her back, with her legs drawn up. It was just in such a spot that no one could see from the outside, and thus the dead creature might have been lying there for some time."

Two young men, named Simpson and Stevens, living in Dorset Street, who know the deceased as residing at that address, state that her name is Annie Chapman. She returned thither about 12 o'clock, stating that she had been to see some friends at Vauxhall. It is also stated that the murdered woman has two children—one of them, a girl aged 14, is at present performing in a circus travelling in France. The other is a boy between four and five years of age. He is now at school at Windsor, the native place of the woman Chapman.

At 10 o'clock on Saturday night it was found upon inquiry that a man had been detained on suspicion of the Whitechapel murder, at Limehouse Police Station.

Last night Hanbury Street, Whitechapel, was in all but an impassable state owing to the crowds which had assembled in the neighbourhood of the scene of the tragedy. That the public are anxious to second the efforts of the police is testified by the presence on record at the Commercial Street Police Station of no fewer than 50 personal statements made with the object of assisting in the work of identification.

A special representative, in pursuing his investigations last night, heard, in the presence of the police, a statement which perhaps ought not to be altogether dismissed as unworthy of notice. The informant was a young woman named Lyons, of the class commonly known as "unfortunates." She stated that at three o'clock that afternoon she met a strange man in Flower and Dean Street, one of the worst streets in the East End of London. He asked her to go to the Queen's Head public house at half-past six, and drink with him. Having obtained from the young woman a promise that she would do so, he disappeared, but was at the house at the appointed time.

While they were conversing, Lyons noticed a large knife in the man's right hand trousers pocket and called another woman's attention to the fact. A moment later Lyons was startled by a remark which the stranger addressed to her, "You're about the same style of woman as one that's murdered," he said. "What do you know about her," asked the woman? to which the man replied, "You are beginning to smell a rat. Foxes hunt geese, but they don't always find them." Having uttered these words, the man hurriedly left. Lyons followed until near Spitalfield's Church, and turning round at this spot, and noticing that the woman was behind him, the stranger ran at a swift pace into Church Street, and was at once lost to view.

One noteworthy fact in this story is that the description of the man's appearance is in all material points identical with the published description of the unknown, and up to the present undiscovered "Leather Apron."

Over two hundred common lodging houses have been visited by the police, in the hope of finding some trace of the mysterious and much talked of person, but he has succeeded in evading arrest. The police have reason for suspecting that he is employed in one of the London sweating dens as a slipper maker, and that it is usual to supply food and lodging in many of those houses he is virtually in hiding. Though "Leather Apron" was a figure well known to many of the policemen in the Whitechapel district prior to the murder of Mrs. Nicholls in Bucks Row, the man has kept himself out of the way since, and this is regarded as a significant circumstance.

The generally accepted theory is that the whole series of murders are the work of one, but medical opinion is that the knife wounds on the woman found in August in George Yard may after all have been self-inflicted. Whether this was so or not, the wounds were not of the kind inflicted on later victims.

Telegraphing at midnight the Press Association says, "The man arrested at Deptford has not up to the present been brought to Commercial Street Police Station for the purpose of identification, and no farther particulars concerning him can be obtained. Inspector Chandler has been to Deptford to see the prisoner, but what the result of his inquiries is is kept secret, but it is understood that not so much importance is attached to the arrest as was the case in the first place."

At five minutes after ten o'clock on Saturday forenoon a man suddenly attacked a woman in Spitalfields Market while she was passing through. After felling her to the ground with a blow he began kicking her and pulled out a knife. Some women who had collected, having the horrible tragedy that brought them there still fresh in their minds, seeing the knife, raised such piercing shrieks of "Murder!" that they reached the enormous crowds in Hanbury Street. There was at once a rush for Commercial Street, where the markets are situated, as it was declared by some that there was another murder, and others that the murderer had been arrested.

Seeing the immense crowd swarming around him, the man who was the cause of the alarm made more furious attempts to reach the woman, from whom he had been separated by some persons who interfered on her behalf. He, however, threw these on one side, fell upon the woman, knife in hand, and inflicted various stabs on her head, cut her forehead, neck, and fingers before he was again pulled off. When he was again pulled off the woman lay motionless— the immense crowd took up the cry of "Murder," and the people who were on the streets raised cries of "Lynch him!"

At this juncture the police arrived, arrested the man, and after a while had the woman conveyed on a stretcher to the police station in Commercial Street, where she was examined by the Divisional Surgeon. She was found to be suffering from several wounds, but none of them were considered dangerous. She was subsequently removed to the London Hospital, where she was detained as an in-patient. Her assailant is described as a blind man, who sells lace in the streets, and whom she led about from place to place. The blind man is described as having a most ungovernable temper, and he was seen whilst the woman was leading him along, to stab her several times in the neck. Blood flowed quickly, and it was at first thought that another terrible murder had been committed. The affair occurred midway between Buck's Row and Hanbury Street, where the last two horrible murders have been committed.

Sheffield Independent – 10th September 1888.

1888 – A SUSPICIOUS-LOOKING CHARACTER.

The only clue of any value found up to yesterday was that furnished by Mrs. Fiddymont, wife of the proprietor of the Prince Albert public house, half a mile from the scene of the murder.

Mrs. Fiddymont states that at seven o'clock in the morning she was standing in the bar talking with another woman, a friend, in the first compartment. Suddenly there came into the middle compartment a man whose rough appearance frightened her. He had on a brown stiff hat, dark coat, and no waistcoat. He came in with his hat down over his eyes, and with his face partly concealed, and asked for half a pint of four ale. She drew the ale, and meanwhile looked at him through the mirror at the back of the bar. As soon as he saw the woman in the other compartment watching him, he turned his back, and got the partition between himself and her.

The thing that struck Mrs. Fiddymont particularly was the fact that there were blood spots on the back of his right hand. This, taken in connection with his appearance, caused her uneasiness. She also noticed that his shirt was torn. As soon as he had drunk the ale, which he swallowed at a gulp, he went out. Her friend went out also to watch him. Her friend is Mrs. Mary Chappell, who lives in Stewart Street, nearby. Her story corroborates Mrs. Fiddymont's and is more particular. When the man came in the expression of his eyes caught her attention; his look was so startling and terrifying, it frightened Mrs Fiddymont, so that she requested her to stay. He wore a light blue check shirt, which was torn badly—into rag's, in fact, on the right shoulder. There was a narrow streak of blood under his right ear, parallel with the edge of his shirt. There was also dried blood between the fingers of his hand.

When he went out, she slipped out at the other door, and watched him as he went towards Bishopsgate Street. She called Joseph Taylor's attention to him, and Joseph Taylor followed him.

Joseph Taylor, a builder in Stewart Street, states that as soon as his attention was attracted to the man, he followed him. He walked rapidly, and came alongside him, but did not speak to him. The man was rather thin, about 5 ft. 8 in. high, and apparently between 40 and 50 years of age. He had a shabby-genteel look, pepper and salt trousers which fitted badly, and a dark coat. When Taylor came alongside him the man glanced at him, and Taylor's description of the look was, "His eyes were as wild as a hawk's." Taylor is a perfectly reliable man, well known throughout the neighbourhood. The man walked, he says, holding his coat together at the top. He had a nervous and frightened way about him. He wore a ginger-coloured moustache and had short sandy hair. Taylor ceased to follow him, but watched him as far as Halfmoon Street, where he became lost from view.

Dundee Evening Telegraph – 10th September 1888.

1888 – INQUEST OF ANNIE CHAPMAN.

The inquest on the body of Annie Chapman the victim of the latest Whitechapel tragedy, was resumed yesterday at the Working Lads' Institute, Whitechapel, before Mr. Wynne Baxter, the District Coroner.

Inspector Chandler described the position in which he found Chapman's body when called in on Saturday morning, confirming the statements of previous witnesses as to the state of the clothing, and adding that a portion of the intestines still connected with the body was lying over the left shoulder, while some pieces of skin were lying near the head. After the removal of the body, he found lying near where the feet had been a piece of muslin, a tooth comb, and a pocket comb, while near was part of an envelope containing pills. On the flap of the envelope were embossed the words "Sussex Regiment," an on the front were written the letters "M" and "Sp," the rest of the words being "London, August, 1888." A wet leather apron was also lying nearby. There were no indications of a struggle, and none of the palings were broken, though they bore bloodstains, as did the ground in the immediate neighbourhood of the body, none, however, being traceable outside the void. Most of the clothes were more or less soiled with blood. Richardson informed the police early on Saturday that the body was not there at five o'clock, but anyone who only went to the top of the steps might have failed to see it.

The foreman of the Jury asked whether any steps had been taken to produce Ted Stanley, who was said to have been much in deceased's company, as he was a pensioner, and the envelope which was found bore a regimental name. It was especially desirable that he should be forthcoming.

Witness replied that the police had not been able to find Stanley.

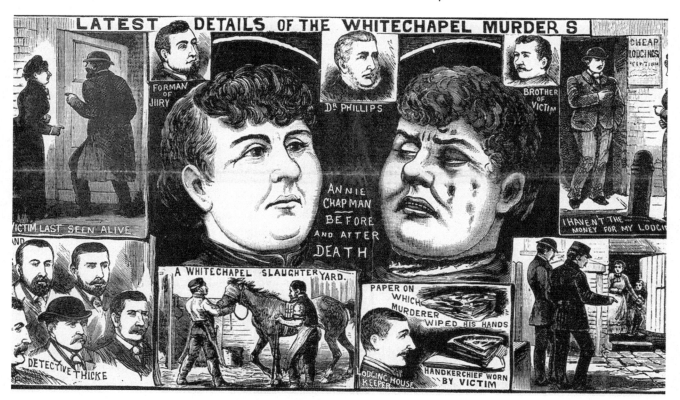

Fig. 66. Annie Chapman (Illustrated Police News)

The Coroner observed that if he was well advised he would come forward. Adverting to a farther remark from the Jury as to the desirability of offering a reward, the Coroner said he believed the Government had given up making such offers.

Dr. Phillips, Divisional Police Surgeon, corroborated Chandler's evidence as to the position in which the body laid when he was called in. He added that the face and tongue were much swollen, and that a portion of the small intestines and of the abdomen was lying on the ground over the right shoulder, but still attached to the body. Two other parts of the wall of the belly were lying in a pool of blood above the left shoulder. There was still warmth in parts of the body, but rigor mortis was setting in. The throat was severed by a jagged cut extending all round the neck. On the ring finger were marks of rings, the removal of which had caused abrasions. The throat had been cut from the left with such force as to separate all the muscular structures, and to notch the vertebrae, which an attempt had apparently been made to divide. There were other mutilations, evidently inflicted after death, which were of such a nature that he preferred, if possible, not to describe them. For cutting the throat and for mutilating the body a sharp, thin, narrow blade, six to eight inches long, must have been used. A slaughterman's knife well ground down would inflict similar injuries. The knives used in the leather trade would not be long enough. The manner of the employment of the knife indicated

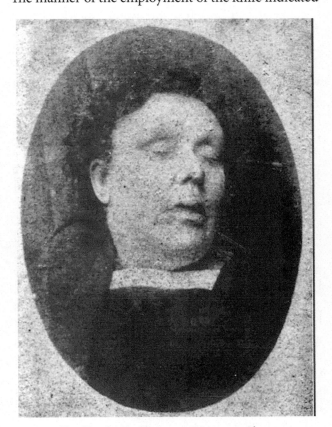

Fig. 67. Annie Chapman Mortuary Photo

anatomical knowledge, which was perhaps not more fully displayed in consequence of haste. Some portion of the abdomen had been removed. Death had taken place at least two hours, probably more, when he saw the body at 6.30, The back yard showed traces of a struggle, but there were no marks of any sort in the passage.

After further evidence the inquest was adjourned until Wednesday next.

The police, we learn, have received some important information as to the hour at which the crime was committed, and the possible neighbourhood of the murderer. A woman named Burrell has communicated with the authorities in reference to these points. She originally made a statement to the effect that at about half-past five o'clock on the morning of the murder of Mrs. Chapman she saw a man and woman conversing outside No. 29, Hanbury Street, the scene of the murder, and that they disappeared very suddenly. She was taken to the mortuary yesterday, and there she identified the body of Chapman as that of the woman whom she saw in Hanbury Street. If this identification can be relied upon, it is obviously an important piece of evidence, as it fixes with precision the time at which the crime was committed, and corroborates the statement of John Richardson, who went into the yard at a quarter to five, and has consistently and persistently declared that the body was not then on the premises.

Davis, the man who first saw the corpse, went into the yard shortly after six o'clock. Assuming, therefore that the various witnesses have spoken the truth—which there is not the slightest reason to doubt—the murder must have been committed between half-past five and six o'clock, and the murderer must have walked through the streets in almost broad daylight without attracting attention, although he must have been at the time more or less stained with blood. This seems incredible, and it has certainly strengthened the belief of many of those engaged in the case that the murderer had not far to go to reach his lodgings.

The inquest into the circumstances connected with the death of Annie Chapman was resumed and concluded yesterday at Whitechapel, before Mr Baxter. The evidence having been closed at the last sitting, the Coroner proceeded to sum up.

He came to the conclusion that no unskilled person could have carried out the operations, and that someone accustomed to the post-mortem room must have committed the deed. The desire to possess the missing abdominal organ seemed overwhelming. It was abhorrent to their feelings to conclude that a life should be taken for so slight an object, but he quoted evidence to show that there was a market for that part of the anatomy, as stated by an official of the Pathological Museum. He doubted the theory of lunacy, and was of opinion that the country was confronted with murder of no ordinary character, committed, not from jealousy, revenge, or robbery, but from motives less adequate than the many which still disgraced our civilisation.

The Jury, without retiring, returned a verdict of wilful murder against some person or persons unknown.

The Central News understands that a man giving the name of John Fitzgerald gave himself up at Wandsworth Police Station last night, and made a statement to the inspector on duty to the effect that he committed the murder in Hanbury Street. He was afterwards conveyed to Leman Street Police station, where he is now detained.

Telegraphing at noon today a London correspondent says, "The man Fitzgerald, who accused himself to the police at Wandsworth last night of being the Whitechapel murderer, is a bricklayer's labourer, he says he has been wandering about the country, and appears to have been under the influence of drink. His statements are somewhat incoherent, and his appearance does not tally with the descriptions given at the inquest. The authorities disincline to attach importance to the matter. A companion of Fitzgerald, named John Locus, has made a statement to the effect that Fitzgerald entered a public house in Wandsworth last evening and commenced talking about the Whitechapel murder. He produced a knife with which he illustrated a theory as to how the murder was committed. He then left, saying he had no home. He will be charged at the Thames Police Court.

Eastern Evening News – 14th September 1888.

1888 – FUNERAL OF ANNIE CHAPMAN.

The funeral of Annie Chapman, the last victim of the Whitechapel murderer, took place early this morning. The utmost secrecy was observed in the arrangements, and none but the undertaker, the police, and the relatives of the deceased knew anything about it. Shortly after seven o'clock a hearse drew up outside the mortuary in Montagu Street and the body was quickly removed. At nine clock a start was made for Manor Park Cemetery, the place selected by the friends of the deceased for the interment, but no coaches followed, as it was desired that public attention should not be attracted. Mr. Smith and other relatives met the body

at the cemetery, and the service was duly performed in the ordinary manner. The remains of the deceased were enclosed in a black covered elm coffin, which bore the words, "Annie Chapman, died September 8, 1888, aged 48 years."

Globe – 14th September 1888.

1888 – A TOPIC OF CONVERSATION.

The almost exclusive topic of conversation in London during the past the week has been the murders at the East End. London always makes the most of a good murder within its own boundaries. If poor Annie Chapman had been slaughtered in Sheffield or Leicester, even as one of a series of victims done to death apparently by the same hand, the London papers would have dismissed the affair with a brief paragraph. But a familiar quarter in London having been the scene of the tragedy, it has been exploited with the fullest energy of the London Press, the minutest details being enlarged upon and a good many invented.

One peculiarly striking result of this intense journalistic energy was the creation of the great bogey, "Leather Apron." A half-penny evening paper, anxious to go further and faster than its fellows, seized upon some idle gossip overheard in the street, and created a being, half fiend, half shoemaker, who, armed with a knife, and clad in a leather apron, prowled by night through the streets of Whitechapel, a terror to unfortunate women. The "*London Journal*" in its palmiest days never equalled this feat, and though the narrative lacked the literary finish of De Quincey's picture of John Williams, the hero of the Ratcliffe highway murders, it was fully as circumstantial and bloodcurdling.

On Wednesday the redoubtable "Leather Apron" appeared in the box at the Coroner's inquest, and the carefully built fabric of his ghoulish reputation crumbled into the dust. "Leather Apron" is a poor little underdone half-fed Jew shoemaker, who, guarded by his uncles, his cousins, and his aunts, has been crouching in terror in his humble abode lest an angry people should rend him in pieces. The police, compelled in the state of public opinion to take notice of the newspaper romance, arrested "Leather Apron"—surnamed Piser—and a thorough investigation of his doings on the night of the murder established his absolute innocence.

So poor "Leather Apron" gratefully crawled down from the bad eminence on which he had unwittingly been thrust, and got him back to his cellar and his boots and shoes. This myth disposed of, the police are left blindly groping for the criminal, not without an uneasy feeling that he may make himself heard of again by some fresh deed of blood.

The librarian at one of the big clubs in Pall Mall tells me that since Saturday afternoon, when this new horror in Whitechapel was announced, there has been an incessant run upon the volumes of De Quincey's miscellaneous essays, including the famous one on "Murder as a Fine Art." It is in a so-called postscript to this quaint essay that De Quincey, with a graphic power that leaves the modern newspaper hopelessly in the rear, describes the murder committed in Ratcliffe Highway in the winter of 1812.

Another book also coming into sudden demand is Edgar Poe's prose works, which contained the weird story of the murder in the Rue Morgue. A hundred newspapers have by this time pointed out the points of similarity between the Whitechapel murders and the exploits of John Williams in Ratcliffe Highway in the early years of the Century. Poe's masterpiece of Newgate Calendering resembles the Whitechapel murders only in respect of the peculiar atrocity of the crime and the mystery which surrounded the identity of the murderer. In the Rue Morgue a woman was found slain under circumstances of peculiar atrocity. It was evident that robbery was not the object of the attack, and there was no evidence of existence of other ordinary inducement to the crime. No sound of struggle had been heard, and the murderer had escaped without leaving any trace as far as the police could discover. Poe introduces on the scene an amateur detective, who, with infinite ingenuity, perseverance, and skill, traces the tragedy step by step till he brings the murder home to an escaped and infuriated orangutang.

Northampton Mercury – 15th September 1888.

1888 – OUTCRY AGAINST THE POLICE.

The *Standard* says — It is needless to inquire what motive underlies the attacks which have been made on Mr. Matthews and Sir Charles Warren. The matter was grave enough, one would have thought, to suggest reserve even to professional manufacturers of melodramatic sensation. But there is no accounting for fancy. If say serious purpose were entertained of prejudicing either the Home Secretary or the Chief Commissioner in the eyes of their countryman, the method employed has been too gross to succeed. The writers who demand the instant dismissal of a group of officials have absolutely nothing to back their ultimatum with except the circumstances that, as yet, the Whitechapel murderer has not been discovered. We are all sorry for that indisputable fact; but the community has not, on that account, lost all control of its senses, and called for vengeance on this or that functionary. Those who have been pandering to the feeling of unreasoning discontent which they hoped could be blown into a flame have had a severe disappointment.

There is nothing at all in the facts of the case which would tend to make ordinary people lose their heads. A very natural feeling of horror has been produced by the series of outrages. But if there was abundant reason for horror, there was none for consternation.

Even in Whitechapel there is no "Terror." The reason is obvious. No decent person, who keeps to the ordinary thoroughfares, has anything to fear. The murderer, whoever he may be, has, in each case, succeeded in finding a victim only among those whose haunts are out-of-the-way spots—someone who was willing to go where the guarantees for security were reduced to zero. In fact, he has been able to select the place and the time, as well as to fix the method of murder. He dealt the fatal wound only when he was assured that all the conditions were favourable to his escape. His "extraordinary recklessness," when it comes to be analysed, will be found to be simply cold-blooded reliance on the fact that the ready consent of his wretched victims almost assured the success of his arrangements.

Meanwhile, it is an absolute fact that no honest, self-respecting woman, however companionless she may be, however irregular may be the hours she may have to keep, has any additional reason to anticipate murderous outrage in the streets. The old dangers remain, but they have not been aggravated, unless it be by the demoralisation produced by the senseless outcry against the police.

Bradford Daily Telegraph – 5th October 1888.

1888 – DOUBLE MURDER.

The alarming facts that Burglary is rife in London, and that in the small hours of Sunday morning last, two additional murders of a sadly familiar type were committed in the neighbourhood of the Hanbury Street atrocity, are terribly eloquent proofs that a stronger and more energetic government is needed for London. A veritable Reign of Terror prevails in the populous East End of London; and it has been abundantly shown that the police force of the Metropolis should be largely increased in every branch.

The first of the two murders in point of time took place not long after midnight last Saturday in Berner Street, a narrow, badly lighted, but tolerably respectable street, turning out of the Commercial Road, a short distance down on the right-hand side going from Aldgate. It is a street mainly consisting of

small houses, but which has lately been brightened and embellished by one of the fine new buildings of the London School Board. Just opposite this is an "International and Educational Club," domiciled in a private house, standing at the corner of a gateway leading into a yard in which are small manufacturing premises and four small houses occupied by Jewish families. The yard gates are usually closed at night, a wicket affording admission to the lodgers and others residing in the houses. Friday or Saturday, however, brought round the close of the Jewish holiday season, and down in this part of London, where the people are largely composed of foreign Jews, some departure from regular habits was more or less general. The International and Educational Club was on Saturday evening winding up the holidays by a lecture on "Judaism and Socialism." A discussion followed, which carried on proceedings to about half-past twelve, and then followed a sing-song and a general jollification,

Fig. 68. Scenes from the Murders (Penny Illustrated Paper)

Fig. 69. Discovery of the body of Elizabeth Stride (Illustrated Police News)

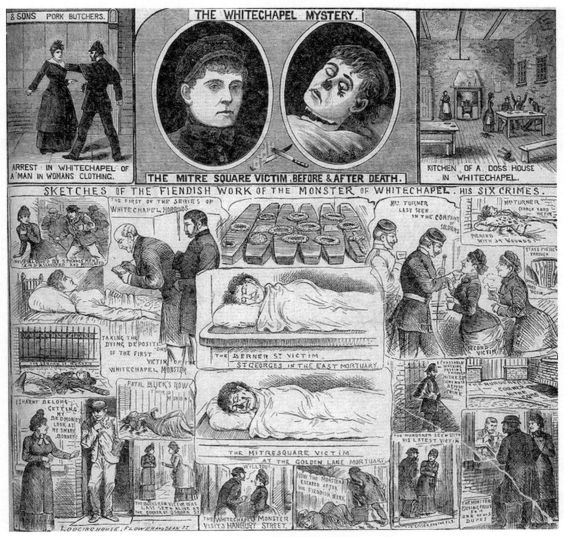

Fig. 70. Sketches from the Illustrated Police News

accompanied, as the neighbours say, by noise that would effectually have prevented any cries for help being heard by those around.

The hilarious mirth, however, was brought to a sudden and dreadful stop. The steward of the club, Lewis Diemschitz, who lives in one of the small houses in the yard, and had been out with some sort of a market cart, returned home just before one. He turned into the gateway, when he observed some object lying in his way under the wall of the club, and without getting down first prodded it with his whip. Unable to see clearly what it was, he struck a match and found it was a woman. He thought at first, she was drunk, and went into the club. Some of the members went out with him and struck another light, and were horrified to find the woman's head nearly severed from her body and blood streaming down the gutter.

The police were summoned, and amid the intense excitement of the few who were out and about at this unhallowed hour, the poor creature was borne to St. George's dead house.

On Sunday it was stated that the corpse was identified as that of a woman who had been living in a common lodging house in Flower and Dean Street, and had been in the habit of frequenting this neighbourhood, where it appears she was known as "Long Lizzie." It subsequently was asserted that her name was Elizabeth Stride and she had a sister living somewhere in Holborn, and that her husband, from whom she had been separated some years was living at Bath. But the Coroner declared on Monday that the body had not been fully identified. The body when found was quite warm. In one hand was clutched a box of sweets and at her breast were pinned two dahlias. She was respectably dressed for her class, and appears to be about thirty-five years of age, about 5 ft. in. in height, and of dark complexion. The theory of the police is—and it is generally endorsed by those who have inquired into the matter on the spot—that precisely the same thing was attempted as in the case of the Hanbury Street murder, and that but for interruption the same ghastly mutilation would have been perpetrated. In some way, however, the fiendish assailant was disturbed, as it is assumed the same individual was disturbed in Buck's Row. It is supposed that, finding he had not time to complete what he had intended without running the risk of capture, he left his victim, very possibly, as it would seem, with little or none of her blood upon him. He may simply have seized her by the pink scarf round her neck, pulled her head hard, and given one horrible gash across the throat from behind, severing the windpipe, and thus at once putting it out of power of his victim to cry for help, though, as we have seen, even though she had cried out, it is quite possible that no one could have heard it, as dancing and singing were going on in the adjacent club.

It was shortly before two o'clock last Sunday morning that the next horrible discovery was made by the police. It appears that Police Constable Watkins

Fig. 71. Finding the Mutilated body of Catherine Eddowes in Mitre Square (Illustrated Police News)

(No. 881), of the City police, was going round his beat when, turning his lantern upon the darkest corner of Mitre Square (near Aldgate and Leadenhall Street) he saw the body of a woman, apparently lifeless, in a pool of blood. He at once blew his whistle, and several persons being attracted to the spot, he despatched messengers for medical and police aid.

Inspector Collard, who was in command at the time at Bishopsgate Police Station, but a short distance off, quickly arrived, followed a few moments after by Mr. G.W. Sequeira, surgeon, of 34, Jewry Street, and Dr. Gordon Brown, the Divisional Police Doctor of Finsbury circus. The scene then disclosed was a horrible one. The woman, who was apparently about forty years of age, was lying on her back, quite dead, although the body was still warm. Her head was inclined to the left side, her left leg being extended, whilst the right was bent. Both arms were extended. The throat was cut halfway round, revealing a dreadful wound, from which blood had flowed in great quantity, staining the pavement for some distance around. Across the right cheek to the nose was another gash, and a part of the right ear had been cut off.

Following the plan in the Whitechapel murders, the miscreant was not content with merely killing his victim. The poor woman had been completely disembowelled, and part of the intestines had been laid on her neck. After careful notice had been taken of the position of the body when found, it was conveyed to the city mortuary in Golden Lane. Here, a more extended examination was made.

The murdered woman was apparently about forty years of age, and 5 ft., in height, and evidently belonged to that unfortunate class of which the women done to death in Whitechapel were members. Indeed, one of the policemen who saw the body expressed his confident opinion that he had seen the woman several times walking in the neighbourhood of Aldgate High Street. She was of dark complexion, with auburn hair and hazel eyes, and was dressed in shabby dark clothes. She wore a black cloth jacket with imitation fur collar and three large metal buttons. Her dress was made of green chintz, the pattern consisting of Michaelmas daisies. In addition, she had on a thin white vest, light drab lindsey skirt, a very old dark green alpaca petticoat, brown ribbed stockings (mended at the feet

Fig. 72. 70 Catherine Eddowes

with white material), black straw bonnet, trimmed with black beads and grey and black velvet, and a large white handkerchief round the neck.

In the pockets of the dress a peculiar collection of articles was found. Besides a small packet containing tea and other articles which people who frequent the common lodging houses are accustomed to carry, the police found upon the body a white pocket handkerchief, a blunt bone-handled table knife, a short clay pipe, and a red cigarette case with white metal fittings. The knife bore no traces of blood, so could have no connection with the crime.

When the news of this additional murder became known the excitement in the crowded district of Aldgate was intense. Usually a busy place on Sunday morning, Houndsditch and connecting streets presented a particularly animated appearance, men with barrows vending fruit and vegetables doing a brisk trade. Crowds flocked to the entrance of the square where the body had been discovered, but the police refused admittance to all but a privileged few.

Sir Charles Warren visited the spot at a particularly early hour, and made himself thoroughly conversant with the neighbourhood and the details of the affair. Major Smith (Acting Superintendent of the City Police), Superintendent Foster, Detective-Inspector M'William (Chief of the City Detective Department), Detective-Sergeants Downes and Outram also attended during Sunday morning.

A little while after the finding of the body all traces of blood had been washed away by direction of the authorities, and there was little to indicate the terrible crime which had taken place.

Before proceeding further, it may be convenient to describe the scene of the murder.

Mitre Square is an enclosed space in the rear of St. Katharine Cree Church, Leadenhall Street. It has three entrances, the principal one—and the only one having a carriage way—is at the southern end, leading into Mitre Street, a turning out of Aldgate High Street. There is a narrow court in the north-east corner leading into Duke Street, and another one at the north-west, by which foot passengers can reach St. James's Square, otherwise known as the Orange Market. Mitre Square contains but two dwelling houses, in one of which, singularly enough, a City policeman lives, whilst the other is uninhabited. The other buildings, of which there are only three, are large warehouses. In the south-east corner, and near to the entrance from Mitre Street, is the backyard of some premises in Aldgate, but the railings are closely boarded. It was just under these that the woman was found, quite hidden from sight by the shadow cast by the corner of the adjoining house. The officer who found the body is positive that it could not have been there more than a quarter of an hour before he discovered it.

The police theory is that whilst the woman lay on the ground her throat was cut, causing instant death. The murderer then hurriedly proceeded to mutilate the body; for the wounds, though so ghastly, do not appear to have been caused so skilfully and deliberately as in the case of the murder of Annie Chapman, in Hanbury Street. Five minutes, some of the doctors think, would have sufficed for the completion of the murderer's work; and he was thus enabled to leave the ground before the return of the policeman on duty.

Fig. 73. The Fatal Spot in Mitre Square

The murderer probably avoided much blood-staining on account of the woman being on her back at the time of the outrage; and leaving the square by either of the courts he would be able to pass quickly away through the many narrow thoroughfares without exciting observation. But one of the most extraordinary incidents in connection with the crime is that not the slightest scream or noise was heard. A watchman is employed at one of the warehouses in the square, and in a direct line, but a few yards away, on the other side of the square, a City policeman was sleeping.

All day Sunday crowds thronged the streets leading to Mitre Square, discussing the crime, and the police in the neighbourhood of the square, under Inspector Izzard and Sergeants Dudman and Phelps, and other officers, were fully occupied in keeping back the excited and curious people.

The post-mortem examination of the body, which took place at the mortuary, Golden Lane, and was conducted by Dr. Phillips, Dr. Gordon Brown, and Mr. G.W. Sequeira, occupied nearly four hours.

Penny Illustrated Paper – 6th October 1888.

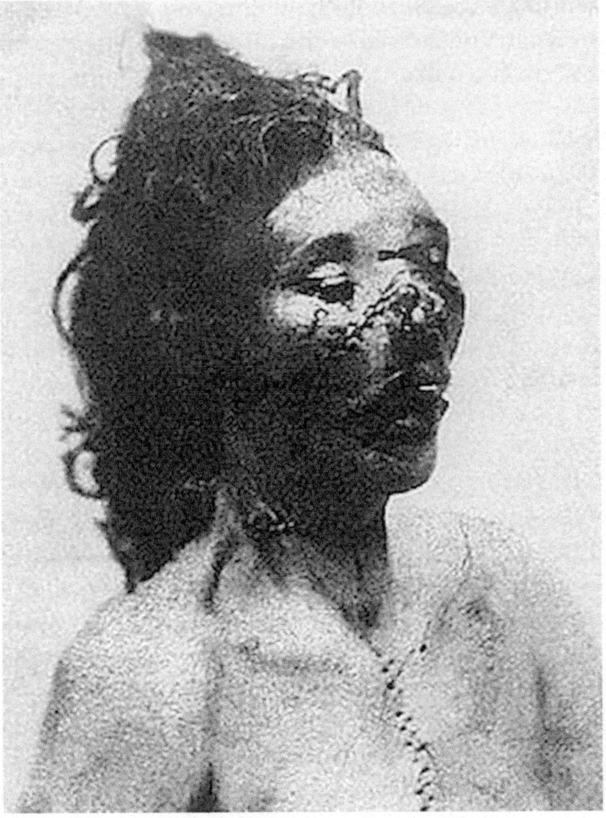

Fig. 74. Catherine Eddowes Mortuary Photo

1888 – WHAT PANIC?

A special London representative has visited the scene of the Whitechapel murders, and he telegraphs that the reports of panic existing in the East End are greatly exaggerated. The people are buying and selling, marrying and giving in marriage, apparently quite undismayed by the atrocities. Groups of people were gathered opposite the spot in Berner Street where the fifth murder took, place, quietly talking of the occurrence, and it needed only a solitary police constable to keep order. In Mitre Square, on the contrary, there was present a strong posse of police, who vigorously keep visitors moving on.

The occupants of the offices in the square, which is by no means a "slum," were loud in their protest against the morbid curiosity of the crowd. Several young men took their sweethearts to see the spot, which, being very centrally situated, is easily accessible, and their merry laughter and giddy conversation jarred painfully on the ear as out of place.

Even ladies from the West End condescended to drive to the square in cabs to gratify their curiosity. But the discovery at Westminster within a stone's throw of the House of Commons is now exciting the greatest interest, especially since it has been announced that the victim there did not belong to the poorer class.

Somerset County Gazette – 6th October 1888.

1888 – AN EXTRAORDINARY LETTER.

The Central News says:—

On Thursday last the following letter hearing the E.C. postmark, and directed in red ink was delivered to this agency:-

25th September 1888.
"Dear Boss,

I keep on hearing the police have me, but they won't fix me just yet. I have laughed when they look so clever and talk about being on the right track. That joke about Leather Apron gave me real fits. I am down on _____s and I shan't quit ripping them till I do get buckled. Grand work the last job was. I gave the lady no time to squeal. How can they catch me now? I love my work, and I want to start again. You will soon hear of me with my funny little games. I saved some of the proper red stuff in a ginger beer bottle over the last job to write with, but it went thick, and I can't use It. Red ink is fit enough, I hope. Ha! Ha! The next job I do I shall clip the ladies' ears off and send to the police officers just for folly. Wouldn't you? Keep this letter back till I do a bit more work. Then give It out straight. My knife's so nice and sharp, I want to get a chance. Good luck."

Yours truly, "JACK THE RIPPER."

"Don't mind me giving the trade name. Wasn't good enough to post this before I got all the red ink off my hands. Curse It. No luck yet. They say I am doctor now."

The whole of this extraordinary epistle (says the Central News) is written in red ink in a free, bold, clerkly hand. It was, of course, treated as the work of a practical joker; but it is singular to note that the latest murders have been committed within a few days of the receipt of the letter, and apparently in the case of his last victim the murderer made an attempt to cut off the ears, and he actually did mutilate the face in a manner which he has never before attempted. The letter is now in the hands of the Scotland Yard authorities.

ANOTHER EXTRAORDINARY LETTER.

A postcard bearing the stamp "London, E., Oct. 1" was received on Monday morning, addressed to the Central News Office, the address and subject matter being written in red, and undoubtedly by the name person from whom the sensational letter already published was received on Thursday last. Like the previous missive this also has references to the horrible tragedies in East London, forming, indeed, a sequel to the first letter. It runs as follows:—

"I was not codding, dear old boss, when I gave you the tip. You'll hear about Saucy Jacky's work tomorrow. Double event this time—number one squealed a bit; couldn't finish straight off. Had not time to get ears for the police. Thanks for keeping the last letter back till I get to work again."

"Jack the Ripper."

The card is smeared on both sides with blood, which has evidently been impressed thereon by the thumb or finger of the writer, the corrugated surface of the skin being plainly shown upon the back of the card. Some words were nearly obliterated by a bloody smear. It is not necessarily assumed that this has been the work of the murderer, the idea that naturally occurred being that the whole thing is a practical joke. At the same time the writing of the previous letter, immediately before the commission of the murders of Sunday, was so singular a coincidence, that it does not seem unreasonable to suppose that the cool, calculating villain who is responsible for the crimes has chosen to make the post a medium through which to convey to the Press his grimly diabolical humour.

REWARD OF £500 OFFERED.

The Lord Mayor of London on Monday offered a reward of £500 on behalf of the Corporation for the detection of the miscreant. The editor of the *Financial News* wrote to the Home Secretary forwarding £300, on behalf of a number of the readers of the paper, to be offered as a Government reward. The Home Secretary replied on Monday night, returning the money, and stating that had he conceived such a measure likely to produce useful results he would have at once made the offer himself, but he was not of that opinion.

THE CORONER'S RIDICULOUS THEORY AS TO THE FORMER MURDERS.

The eminent surgeon, Sir J.R. Bennett, in a letter to the *Times*, indignantly repudiates the suggestion of the Coroner that part of the body of the Whitechapel victim was wanted for any quasi-scientific publication, or any other more or less legitimate purpose. "To say nothing," he says, "of the utterly absurd notion of the part or organ being preserved in a particular way to accompany each copy of an intended publication, the facilities for obtaining such objects for any purpose of legitimate research in any number, either here or in America, without having recourse to crime of any kind, are such as to render the suggestion made entirely untenable."

THE POLICE STILL WITHOUT ANY CLUE.

Up to the present the police have been unsuccessful in their search for the perpetrator of the Aldgate and Whitechapel horrors. Several arrests have been made, but the men have all been discharged. The police have issued the description of a person who was seen in company with the Berner Street victim on Saturday evening. The woman murdered in Mitre Square has not yet been identified.

THE PROPOSAL TO EMPLOY BLOODHOUNDS.

Mr Percy Lindley, in a letter to the *Times*, says, "With regard to the suggestion that bloodhounds might assist in tracking the East End murderer, as a breeder of bloodhounds, and knowing their power, I have little doubt that, had a hound been put upon the scent of the murderer while fresh, it might have done what the police have failed in. But now, when all trace of the scene has been trodden out, it would be quite useless. Meanwhile, as no means of detection should be left untried, it would be well if a couple or so of trained bloodhounds—unless trained they are worthless – were kept for a time at one of the police headquarters, ready for immediate use in case their services should be called for. There are, doubtless, owners of bloodhounds willing to lend them, if any of our police, which I fear, is improbable, know how to use them."

Fife News – 6th October 1888.

1888 – A CLUE LOST.

A startling fact has just come to light in reference to the recent Whitechapel murders, which goes somewhat towards clearing up the mystery with which the crimes have been surrounded. After killing Catherine Eddowes in Mitre Square, the murderer, it is now known, walked to Goulstone Street, where he threw away the piece of the deceased woman's apron, upon which he had wiped his bloody hands and knife. Within a few feet of this spot, he had written upon the wall, "The Jews shall not be blamed for nothing." One of the police officers gave orders for this writing to be immediately sponged out, probably with a view of stifling the morbid curiosity which it would certainly have aroused. But in so doing a very important link was destroyed, for had the writing been photographed a certain clue would have been in the hands of the authorities.

The witnesses who saw the writing, however, state that it was similar in character to the letters signed "Jack the Ripper;" and though it would have been far better to have clearly demonstrated this by photography, there is now every reason to believe that the writer of the letters (facsimiles of which are now to be seen outside every police station) is the actual murderer. The police consequently are very anxious that any citizen who can identify the handwriting, should without delay communicate with the authorities.

The Central News, since the original letter and postcard of "Jack the Ripper" was published, has received from 30 to 40 communications daily signed "Jack the Ripper," evidently the concoction of silly notoriety hunters. A third communication, however, has been received from the writer of the original "Jack the Ripper" letter and postcard, which, acting upon official advice, it has been deemed prudent to withhold for the present. It may be stated, however, that, although the miscreant avows his intention of

committing further crimes shortly, it is only against prostitutes that his threats are directed, his desire being to respect and protect honest women.

Tavistock Gazette – 12th October 1888.

1888 – OUTCASTS OF THE EAST END.

The repeated horrible murders and mutilations of the dead, perpetrated in the dark nooks and corners of a wretched quarter in the vicinity of Whitechapel and Spitalfields, with the failure of the police either to detect the criminal or to guard against the commission of these atrocities, have excited much alarm. Various suggestions have been offered in the correspondence of the daily newspapers, or submitted to Sir Charles Warren, the Chief Commissioner of Police; and it has even been proposed that the keen scent of bloodhounds should be employed to track the retreating path of the murderer.

A local "Vigilance Committee" has been formed to watch the neighbourhood of low lodging houses, and the lonely courts and alleys, where the miserable female victims of the indescribable cruelties that have shocked the public mind are stated to have been accustomed nightly to resort.

One of our Artists, having accompanied such exploration of the dismal haunts of a degraded class of the city population, amongst whom, it may be charitably hoped, not a few are comparatively innocent of crime or vice, presents Sketches of the figures and groups that he has seen, which, in any case, must appeal to humane feelings of regret and earnest desire to check the downward course of so many of our fellow creatures in the foul places of great and mighty London.

llustrated London News – 13th October 1888

1888 – INQUEST OF ELIZABETH STRIDE.

It may be humiliating to acknowledge, but, nevertheless, it is the plain truth, that the police are just as far off any clue as to the perpetrator of the atrocious crimes in Whitechapel, as they were weeks ago.

Fig. 75.   Sleeping Rough in a Stable (Illustrated London News)

Fig. 76.   Local Vigilance Committee (Illustrated London News)

The Coroner's inquiry into the death of Elizabeth Stride, who was murdered at Barner Street, Whitechapel, on Sunday morning, the 30th ult., was concluded on Tuesday, at the Vestry Hall, Cable Street, before Mr. E. Wynne Baxter, Coroner for East Middlesex, and a Jury.

At the previous sitting, evidence was given by Mrs. Malcolm to the effect that deceased was her sister and she was married to Mr. Watts, son of a wine merchant of Bath, but had lately led a dissipated life, and that she had regularly contributed to her support up to the week of the murder. She added that she had had a presentiment of the crime because while lying in bed at the hour of the occurrence she felt a peculiar pressure.

On Tuesday, Mrs. Watts herself appeared and flatly contradicted the statements of her sister. It was further shown that the murdered woman was the widow of a carpenter.

Mr. E. Reid, Inspector of Police, deposed, "Since the last sitting I have made inquiries and examined the Sick Asylum, Bromley, and find therein an entry of the death of John Thomas Stride carpenter, of Poplar, on the 24th October, 1884. The nephew of Stride is here to give evidence. I have also seen Elizabeth Watts, whose sister is now married and resides at Tottenham. She informed me that the whole of Mrs. Malcolm's statement is false; that she had not seen her sister on the Monday before the murder. I have directed her to appear here as a witness today, and she promised to attend."

Police Constable Walter Stride said, "I recognise the photograph of the deceased as that of the person who married my uncle J.T. Stride, in 1872 or 1873. He was a carpenter, and the last time we saw him he lived in East India Dock Road, Poplar.

Elizabeth Stokes, 5, Charles Street, Tottenham, wife of Joseph Stokes, brickmaker, said, "I was formerly married to Mr. Watts, wine merchant, Bath. The Coroner: "He is dead?" Witness: "I have a letter which I wish to show you." (Witness was much agitated and said that the case had excited her greatly.) "Mrs. Mary Malcolm, of Eagle Street, Red Lion Street, Holborn, is my sister."

The Coroner, having read the letter handed to him, said it purported to have been written by "W.Y.Z." on board ship, and stated that the woman's husband was alive. To Witness: "Are you on friendly terms with your sister?" "I have not seen her for years. She has given me a dreadful character, and said I was the curse of the family. I have not received a penny from her." "Her evidence is false?" "All false. I can tell you the names of all of us. There were Matilda, Thomas, James, Mary and Elizabeth. I am positively sure that Mrs. Malcolm is my sister, who has given these cruel statements."

A Juror: "That must have been a mistake. Instead of referring to you she must have referred to some

Fig. 77. Scenes from the East End (Illustrated Police News)

Fig. 78. 78 Sketches from the Elizabeth Stride Inquest (Penny Illustrated Paper)

other person." Another Juror: "She referred to a sister with a crippled foot." Witness: "It was I that kept a coffee shop and was a disgrace to the family. It is infamy and lies, and I am truly sorry to think I have a sister in my family that has given me such a terrible and dreadful character." The Coroner: "You have contradicted the statements." Witness: "It has put me to dreadful trouble. I am only a poor woman, and my husband, who is a cripple, is now outside. Why should my sister be allowed to tell such terrible falsehoods?"

A Juror: "We did not know at the time they were falsehoods." Witness: "You can see" Coroner: "We can see now." Witness "I hope you will allow me my expenses." The Coroner: "Is Mrs. Malcolm here?" Officer: "No, sir."

The Coroner, in summing up, remarked upon the coincidence between the habits of the murdered woman and those described by Mrs. Malcolm. If her evidence was correct, there were points of resemblance which almost reminded one of "The Comedy of Errors." Both had been courted by policemen; they have the same Christian name, and were of the same age; both lived with sailors; both at one time kept coffee houses at Poplar; both were nicknamed "Long Liz;" both were said to have children in charge of their husband's friends; both were given to drink; both lived in common East End lodging houses; both had been charged with drunkenness at the Thames Police Court; both had escaped punishment on the ground

that they were subject to epileptic fits, although the friends of both are certain that this was a fraud; both had lost their front teeth; and both were leading very questionable lives.

Fig. 79. Elizabeth Stride Mortuary Photo

The murdered woman, it appears, was born in Sweden, in 1848, but having resided in England for twenty-five years could speak English fluently with a slight foreign accent. At the time of her death, she could have had a few pence in her pocket. It was shown that the man with whom she was seen shortly before was about five feet seven inches in height and wore dark clothes, including an overcoat which reached nearly to his heels. There was no one among her associates to whom any suspicion was attached, and it was not shown that she recently had a quarrel with anyone.

The ordinary motives of murder – revenge, jealousy, theft, and passion – appeared to be absent from this case, while it was clear from the accounts of all who saw her that night, as well as from the post mortem examination, that she was not otherwise than sober.

In conclusion, the Coroner, while expressing regret the time and care bestowed on the inquiry had not eventuated in a result which would be a perceptible relief to the metropolis – the detection of the criminal – was bound to acknowledge the great attention which Inspector Reid and the police had given to the case.

The Jury found a verdict of wilful murder against some person or persons unknown, and that the murdered woman was the widow of John Stride.

Sir Charles Warren recently took occasion to point out that the mere fact that detectives engaged in connection with the Whitechapel murders were following up clues without the circumstances coming to the knowledge of the public showed that they were doing their works in a proper fashion. Scotland Yard is, in fact, on the alert night and day, making as little noise as possible. Every day the authorities receive "information" which is never regarded as too trivial to be passed over without consideration.

The facility for manufacturing nonsense signed "Jack the Ripper" has landed in Sir Charles Warren's office several communications bearing the appearance of childish jokes, but now and then there comes a statement which is carefully investigated.

The horrible incident of the box containing a portion of a kidney sent to Mr. Lusk, of the Whitechapel Vigilance Committee, is not generally regarded as a practical joke in view of the opinion given by two medical gentleman, Dr. Openshaw and Dr. Reed. The box and its contents were taken from Leman Street to the City Police Office in Old Jewry, for Dr. Gordon Brown, police surgeon to examine and make a report in due course.

A reporter had an interview with the curator of the Pathological Museum at the London Hospital. In the course of the conversation that gentleman stated with regard to the small parcel received by Mr. Lusk that his microscopic examination of the contents proved it to be the anterior of the left human kidney. It had been preserved, in his opinion, in spirit for about ten days. Until the portion of the kidney had undergone a more minute examination it is almost impossible to say whether it has been extracted from the body of a male or female.

A statement which may possibly give a clue as to the sender of the strange package received by Mr. Lusk was made on, the 20th ult., by Miss Emily Marsh, whose father carries on business in the leather trade at 218 Jubilee Street, Mile End Road. In Mr. Marsh's absence, Miss Marsh was in the front shop, shortly after one o'clock on the 15th Ult., when a stranger, dressed in clerical costume, entered and referring to the reward bill in the window, asked for the address of Mr. Lusk, described therein as the President of the Vigilance Committee. Miss Marsh at once referred the man to Mr. Aarons, the, treasurer of the Committee, who resides at the corner of Jubilee Street and Mile End Road, a distance of about thirty yards. The man, however, said he did not wish to go there, and Miss Marsh thereupon produced a newspaper in which Mr. Lusk's address was given as Alderney Road, Glebe Road, no number being mentioned.

She requested the stranger to read the address, but he declined, saying, "Read it out," and proceeded to write something in his pocket book keeping his head down meanwhile. He subsequently left the shop after thanking the young lady for the information, but not before Miss Marsh, alarmed by the man's appearance, had sent the shop boy, John Cormack, to see that all was right. The lad, as well as Miss Marsh gave a full description of the man, while Mr. Marsh, who happened to come along at the time, also encountered him on the pavement outside. The stranger is described as a man of some forty-five years of age, fully six feet in height, and slimly built. He wore a soft felt black hat, drawn over his forehead, a stand-up collar, and a very long black single-breasted overcoat, with a Prussian or clerical collar partly turned up. His face was of a sallow type; and he had a dark beard and moustache. The man spoke with what was taken to be an Irish accent.

No importance was attached to the incident until Miss Marsh read of the receipt by Mr. Lusk of a strange parcel, and then it occurred to her that the stranger might be the person who had despatched it. His inquiry was made at one o'clock on the 15th ult., and Mr. Lusk received the package at 3 p.m. the next day. The address on the package, curiously enough, gives no number in Alderney Road, a piece of information which Miss Marsh could not supply. It appears that on leaving the shop the man went right by Mr. Aaron's house, but did not call.

Mr. Lusk has been Informed of the circumstances, and states that no person answering the description has called on him, nor does he know anyone at all like the man in question.

Illustrated Police News – 3rd November 1888.

1888 – FUNERAL OF CATHERINE EDDOWES.

The funeral of Catherine Eddowes, the victim of the Mitre Square murder, took place on Monday afternoon. The body was removed from the City mortuary in Golden Lane at a quarter past 1 o'clock for interment in the City of London cemetery at Ilford. There were dense crowds in the vicinity of Golden Lane, and the junction of Osborn and Commercial Streets the people were so numerous that a large force of police had to direct the traffic. The body was conveyed in an open hearse, a wreath being placed on either side of the coffin. Following the remains were two mourning coaches, and in the rear of these was a large waggon crowded with women, the majority of whom were attired in a style not at all befitting the occasion.

Warminster and Westbury Journal, and Wilts County Advertiser – 13th October 1888.

1888 – PORTRAIT OF THE SUPPOSED MURDERER.

The sketches are presented (says the *Daily Telegraph*) not, of course, as authentic portraits, but as a likeness which an important witness has identified as that of a man who was seen talking to the murdered woman in Berner Street and its vicinity until within a quarter of an hour of the time when she was killed last Sunday morning.

Three men, William Marshall, James Brown, both labourers, and Police Constable Smith, have stated before the Coroner that a man and woman did stand in Fairclough Street, at the corner of Berner Street, for some time – that is, from a quarter to twelve o'clock, as stated by Marshall, to quarter before one a.m., the hour mentioned by Brown. The policeman appears to have seen the same pair in Berner Street at half past twelve.

The evidence of another witness has yet to be taken, and this man seems to have had a better opportunity of observing the appearance of the stranger than any other individual, for it was at his shop that the grapes which other witnesses saw near the body were bought. This witness, Mathew Packer, has furnished Information to the Scotland authorities, and it was so important that he was examined in the presence of Sir Charles Warren himself. He has also identified the body of Elizabeth Stride as that of the woman who accompanied the man who came to his shop not long before midnight on Saturday.

In accordance with the general description furnished to the police by Packer and others, a number of sketches were prepared, portraying men of different nationalities, ages, and ranks of life. These were submitted to Packer, who unhesitatingly selected one of these here reproduced—the portrait of the man without the moustache, and the soft felt American hat. Further, in order to remove all doubt, and, if possible, to obtain a still better visible guidance, Packer was shown a considerable collection of photographs and these, after careful inspection, he picked out one which corresponded in all important respects to the sketch. It was noticed that Packer, as also another important witness presently to be mentioned, at once rejected the faces of men of purely sensual type, and that they thus threw aside the portraits of several noted American criminals. Both witnesses inclined to the belief that the man's age was not more than thirty, in which estimate they were supported by the police constable, who guessed him to be twenty-eight. If the impressions of two men, who, it may be supposed, have actually conversed with the alleged murderer, be correct, and their recollection of his features can be relied upon, then, in their opinion, at all events, the above sketches furnish a reasonably accurate representation of his general appearance described and adapted by them.

A man like the one without the moustache, and wearing the soft black felt deerstalker hat, as drawn, was seen by Mathew Packer, of 44 Berner Street, two doors from the scene of the murder, late on Saturday night, and Packer, as above stated, attests the general accuracy of the likeness given. He describes the incident which brought the man to his notice as follows:-

On Saturday night, about half-past eleven o'clock, this man and the woman identified as the deceased came to the fruiterer's shop which he keeps. It was not necessary for them to enter it as customers usually stand upon the pavement, and make their purchases through the window, which is not a shop front of the ordinary kind. Packer is certain that the woman, who wore a dark jacket and a bonnet with some crepe stuff in it, was playing with a white flower which she carried. The man was square-built, about 5 feet 7 inches in height, 30 years of age, full in the face, dark complexioned, without moustache, and alert looking. His hair was black. He wore a long black coat and soft felt hat. It seemed to Packer that he was a clerk, and not a working man. He spoke in a quick, sharp manner, and stood in front of the window. The man purchased half a pound of black grapes, which were given to him in a paper bag, and he paid threepence in coppers. The couple then stood near the gateway of the club for a minute or so, and afterwards crossed the road and remained talking by the Board School for some time. They were still there when Packer had had supper and when he went to bed; and Mrs. Packer remarked it as strange that they should remain, for rain was falling at the time.

It is a remarkable circumstance – much more than an ordinary coincidence – that the description of the supposed murderer, given by Packer was on Sunday confirmed by another man who without being aware of the fact, also chose from the sketches the one which had previously been already selected by Packer. Search for an individual answering to

the description above detailed, but having a small moustache and wearing a black deerstalker felt hat, instead of a soft one, has been made by the police in Whitechapel ever since Saturday, September 1st, the day following the Buck's Row tragedy. Information was tendered at the King David's Lane Police Station at about that time by a dairyman who has a place of business in Little Turner Street, Commercial Road.

It will be recollected that on Saturday, September 1st, a desperate assault was reported to have been committed near to the music hall in Cambridge Heath Road, a man having seized a woman by the throat and dragged her down a court, where he was joined by a gang, one of whom laid a knife across the woman's throat, remarking, "we will serve you as we did the others."

The particulars of this affair were subsequently stated to be untrue; but the milkman has reason to suppose that the outrage was actually perpetrated, and he suspects that the murderer of Mary Ann Nicholls in Buck's Row had something to do with it. At any rate, upon that Saturday night, at five minutes to eleven o'clock, a man, corresponding with the description given by Packer of the individual who purchased the grapes in Berner Street, called at the shop, which is on the left of a covered yard, usually occupied by barrows, which are let out on hire. He

Fig. 80. Sketches of the Supposed Murderer

was in a hurry and asked for a pennyworth of milk, with which he was served, and he drank it down at a gulp. Asking permission to go into the yard or shed, he went there, but the dairyman caught a glimpse of something white, and, having suspicions he rejoined the man in the shed, and was surprised to observe that he had covered up his trousers with a pair of white overalls, such as engineers wear. The man had a staring look, and appeared greatly agitated. He made a movement forward, and the brim of his hard felt hat struck the dairyman, who is therefore sure of the kind that he was wearing. In a hurried manner the stranger took out of a black shiny bag which was on the ground, a white jacket and rapidly put it on, completely hiding his cutaway black coat, remarking meanwhile, "It's a dreadful murder isn't it?" although the subject had not been previously mentioned. Without making a pause, the suspicious person caught up his bag, which was still open, and rushed into the street towards Shadwell, saying, "I think I've got a clue!"

The matter was reported to the police, and although a strict watch has been maintained for the reappearance of the man, he has not been seen in the street since. He is said to have had a dark complexion such as a seafaring man acquires. The style of collar that he was was then wearing was that of a turn down pattern. He had no marked American accent, and his general appearance was that of a clerk or student whose beard had been allowed three days growth. His hair was dark, and his eyes large and staring. The portrait gives, according to the statement of the witness, a good approximate idea of his look. The bag carried by the young man, whose age the dairyman places at 28, is stated to have been provided with a lock at the top, near the handle, and was made, as stated, of a black glistening material.

Dundee Weekly News – 13th October 1888.

1888 – MARY JANE KELLY.

On Friday another addition was made to the series of horrible crimes that has created a panic in the East End of London for many weeks past, and has sent a thrill of horror through the country at large.

As in the previous cases, the scene of the tragedy lies in the district of Whitechapel, within almost a stone's throw of Hanbury Street, where the unfortunate woman Nicholls was so brutally put to death. The victim was another of the unfortunate class, who occupied a miserably furnished room in a court off Dorset Street, a narrow thoroughfare out of Commercial Street, not far removed from the police station. She had lived in the court for some little time, and was known as Mary Jane Kelly, alias "Ginger." She

Fig. 81. The Murder of Mary Jane Kelly (Illustrated Police News)

was a Welsh woman, and it is believed was married, but separated from her husband.

Recently she had lived with a man who was known in the neighbourhood as Dan, but the couple parted a few days ago. Since that time the murdered woman had been seen several times walking about the locality, and on more than one occasion has been in the company of men. It is supposed that she met the man who was to be her murderer at a late hour on Thursday night and that he induced her to allow him to accompany her home. Though there is good reason to believe that the murderer was in the house the whole of the night, he did not carry out his terrible purpose until a period later than half-past eight o'clock on Friday morning. At that time the deceased was seen walking along Dorset Street, and it is supposed that she left the house for the purpose of purchasing provisions for breakfast. She is then said to have appeared cheerful and looking bright and well. Some two hours from this time the unfortunate woman was found lying dead and frightfully mutilated. At half-past eleven o'clock a man went to the room to collect the rent, and failing to gain any answer to his knocking at the door, he looked through the window. It was then seen that the woman was lying naked and bleeding on the bed, and an alarm was at once given.

A policeman was summoned, and he at once took possession of the room and refused to allow anyone to enter until a medical man had been brought to the pot. When this had been done, a scene more terrible than any of the others that have preceded it was disclosed. Such a shocking state of things was there as has probably never been equalled in the annals of crime. The throat had been cut right across with a knife, nearly severing the head from the body. The abdomen had been ripped partially open, and both of the breasts had been cut from the body. The left arm, like the head, hung to the body by the skin only. The nose had been cut off, the forehead skinned, and the thighs down to the feet, stripped of the flesh. The abdomen had been slashed across and downwards, and the liver and entrails wrenched away. The entrails and the other portions of the frame were missing, but the liver, &c., it is said, were found placed between the feet of this poor victim. The flesh from the thighs and legs, together with the breasts and nose, had been placed by the murderer on the table, and one of the hands of the dead woman had been pushed into her stomach.

Inspector Beck took charge of the case, and, having sent out all the constables that could be spared to

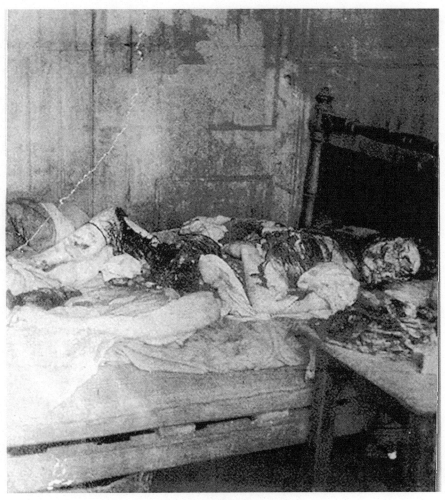

Fig. 82. The Mutilated Body

make inquiries, he repaired to Dorset Street, where he established a kind of blockade at Miller's Court, refusing either egress of ingress to the inhabitants. The traffic in Dorset Street was also regulated, and the immense crowds which the news of the murder had attracted thither were prevented from entering the street. The refusal of the police to allow anyone to enter or to leave Miller's Court was connected with an intention to put the bloodhounds on the track of the murderer, and it was feared that the scent would be seriously interfered with, if not completely destroyed. If indiscriminate traffic were allowed. The bloodhounds were asked for immediately the discovery was made, but they could not be found.

The victim of the monstrous outrage belonged to the very lowest class. She occupied a cheerless and dismal looking room on the ground floor of No. 26, Dorset Street. The entrance to her room, however, is from the passage between the houses No. 26 and 28, leading into Miller's Court. The room, which was at the back of the house, was very scantily furnished. It contained little besides a bed, a table and a couple of chairs. Both Nos. 26 and 28 are in the occupation of a Mrs. M'Carthy, who carries on the business of a provision dealer at No. 28. It was the son of the

landlady who first discovered the murder and gave information to the police. The landlady adheres strictly to the principle of "ready" cash in dealing with the lodgers. It is usually her practise to call on them in the course of the morning, and receive each day's rent in advance.

Dr. Dukes; Dr. Phillips, of Spital Square; Dr. J.R. Gabe, of Mecklenburg Square; and Dr. Bond, of Westminster Hospital, all saw the body, of which a photograph had been taken, shortly before two o'clock. As it lay on the bed it presented a ghastly spectacle, and so complete had been the mutilation, that it was difficult to tell whether it was that of a man or woman. It lay on its back, with the legs outspread. The face had been so cut and hacked that the features could not be discerned at all. The conclusion was arrived at that the woman's throat had first been cut, causing her instant death, and preventing the possibility of cries.

The body was placed in a plain coffin and removed, shortly before four o'clock, to the mortuary in Shoreditch, in a spring van, followed by a crowd.

A Mrs. Pannler, a young woman who sells roasted chestnuts at the corner of Widegate Street, a narrow thoroughfare, about two minutes' walk from the scene of the murder, told a reporter a remarkable story.

Fig. 83. Discovering the Body of Mary Jane Kelly

She says that about twelve o'clock (noon on Friday,) a man dressed like a gentleman, came to her and said, "I suppose you have heard about the murder in Dorset Street." She replied that she had, and the man grinned and said, "I know more about it than you." He then stared into her face, and went away down Sanden Row, another narrow thoroughfare off Widegate Street. When he had got some way off, however, he looked back as if to see whether she was watching him, and then vanished.

Mr. Pannler says that the man had a black moustache, was about five feet six inches high, and wore a black silk hat, a black coat, and speckled trousers. He carried a black shiny bag about a foot in depth, and a foot and a half in length. Mrs. Pannler states further that the same man accosted three young unfortunates in Dorset Street on Thursday night, and they chaffed him, and asked what was in the bag, and he replied, "Something that the ladies don't like." Mrs. Pannler told her story with every appearance of truthfulness.

Maurice Lewis, a tailor, living in Dorset Street, stated that he had known the deceased woman for the last five years. Her name was Mary Jane Kelly. She was short, stout, and dark; and stood about five feet three inches. He saw her on the previous (Thursday) night, between ten and eleven, at the Horn of Plenty in Dorset Street. She was drinking with some women and also "Dan," a man selling oranges in Billingsgate and Spitalfields markets with whom she lived up till as recently as a fortnight ago. He knew her as a woman of the town. One of the women whom he saw with her was known as Julia. To his knowledge, she went home overnight with a man. He seemed to be respectably dressed. Whether or not the man remained all night he could not say.

Soon after ten o'clock in the morning, he was playing with others at pitch and toss in M'Carthy's Court, when he heard a lad call out "Copper," and he and his companions rushed away and entered a beer house at the corner of Dorset Street, known as Ringer's. He was positive that on going in he saw Mary Jane Kelly drinking with some other people, but is not certain whether there was a man amongst them. He went home to Dorset Street on leaving the house, and about half an hour afterwards heard that Kelly had been found in her room murdered. It would then be close upon eleven o'clock.

Dr. J.R. Gabe, of Mecklenburg Square, saw the body, but in reply to a question put to him, he declined to give any details. He merely said that he had seen a great deal in dissecting rooms, but that he had never, in all his life, seen such a horrible sight as the murdered woman presents. In addition to the mutilations already named, it was afterwards ascertained that the forehead and even the cheeks were skinned.

John M'Carthy, who resides at 27, Dorset Street, informed a reporter that Mary Jane Kelly, the murdered woman, was a person about twenty-five years of age. She was an unfortunate. The last that he heard of her was at one o'clock on Friday morning, when she was singing in her room and appeared to be very happy. At eleven o'clock on Thursday night she was seen in the Britannia public house, which is situated at the corner of this thoroughfare, with a young man with a dark moustache. She was then intoxicated. The young man appeared to be very respectable and well dressed.

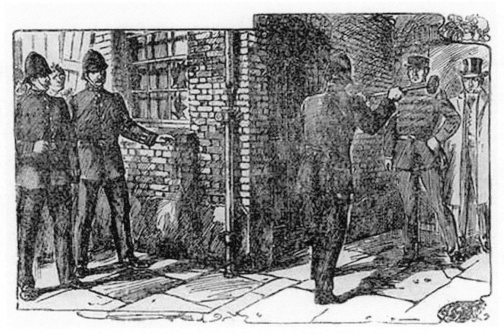

Fig. 84. Police Breaking down the door of 13 Miller's Court

With respect to the discovery of the appalling crime, M'Carthy said, "About half-past ten this (Friday) morning I saw a man named Henry Bower go to Mary Jane Kelly and ask for the rent she owed. Bower went to the house, but got no answer to his knocks. He peered through one of windows and saw the woman lying cut up on the bed. The bed was saturated with blood. Bower called out, telling me what he had seen, and we went and looked through the window. I cannot fully describe her injuries, for the sight was too much for him. She was quite naked. I noticed that both breasts were cut off, and that she was ripped up. The intestines were laid on the table, both ears were cut off, as was also the nose. The legs of the deceased were cut to such an extent that the bones could be seen. Her face was one mass of cuts. We ran to the Commercial Street Police Station and told them of it. In answer to questions as to whether the woman was married, M'Carthy said deceased's husband was a fish porter employed in Billingsgate, but in consequence of a quarrel between them four nights ago the man left her, and went to lodge at Mr. Buller's boarding house in Bishopsgate Street.

Dorset Street, the scene of the murder, runs off Commercial Street, and is almost opposite St. Stephens Church, Spitalfields. It is a narrow thoroughfare, with barely sufficient room for two vehicles to pass one another. There are several lodging houses in the street, and there is hardly a house that does not give shelter to lodgers, many of whom come at night and disappear in the morning. The courts leading out of the street are full of lodging houses. Miller's Court, leading at right angles out of Dorset Street, is a miserable alley, forming a cul-de-sac. It is known in the locality as M'Carthy's Court, on account of being owned by the keeper of the chandler's shop. There are three or four houses of the meanest description, with whitewashed fronts, and approached by a narrow-arched passage, not more than a yard and a half wide. The surrounding district is very rough. It is in close proximity to Spitalfields Market, and within a hundred yards or so of Toynbee Hall.

The most curious item in the entire surroundings is a large placard posted on the walls of the next house to one where the murder was committed offering, in the name of the *Illustrated Police News*, a reward of £100 for the discovery of the diabolical assassin. This is shown by our illustration, together with a plan of the locality. The precise spot where each crime was committed is indicated by a dagger and a numeral.

1. Emma Elizabeth Smith, forty-five, stabbed near Osborne Street, Whitechapel, April 3rd.
2. Martha Tabram, thirty-five, stabbed in thirty-nine places, at George Yard buildings, Commercial Street, August 7th.
3. Mary Ann Nicholls, forty-seven, had her throat cut and body mutilated, in Buck's Row, Whitechapel, August 31st.
4. Annie Chapman, forty-seven, her throat cut and body mutilated, in Hanbury Street, Spitalfields, September 8th.

Fig. 85. Dorset Street, Whitechapel

5. Elizabeth Stride, throat cut in Berner Street, Whitechapel, on Sunday, September 30th.
6. Catherine Eddowes, alias Conway, alias Kelly, mutilated in Mitre Square, Aldgate, also on September 30th.
7. Mary Jeanette Kelly, mutilated in Miller's Court, Whitechapel, November 9th.

There was no appearance of a struggle having taken place, and, although a careful search of the room was made, no knife or instrument of any kind was found. Dr. Phillips, on his arrival, carefully examined the body of the dead woman, and later on made a second examination in company with Dr. Bond, from Westminster; Dr. Gordon Brown, from the City; Dr. Duke, from Spitalfields; and Dr. Phillips's assistant, Mr. Anderson, the new Commissioner of Police, Detective-Inspectors Reid and Abberline (Scotland Yard), Chief-Inspector West, H Division, and other officers were quickly on the spot. After the examination of the body, it was placed in a shell which was put in a van and conveyed to the Shoreditch mortuary to await an inquest.

From inquiries made among the persons living in the house adjoining the Court, and also those residing in rooms in No. 26, it appears clear that no noise of any kind was heard. No suspicious or strange-looking man was seen to enter or leave the murdered woman's room, and up to the present time the occurrence is enveloped in as much mystery as were the previous murders. The man Kelly was quickly found, and his statement ascertained to be correct. After the examination the windows were boarded up and the door padlocked by direction of the police, who had considerable difficulty in keeping the street clear.

Another account says that she had a little boy, aged about six or seven years, living with her, and latterly she had been in narrow straits, so much so that she is reported to have stated to a companion that one would make away with herself, as she could not bear to see her boy starving.

There are conflicting statements as to when the woman was last seen alive. One of them is that of a young woman, who states that at about half-past ten o'clock on Thursday night, at the corner of Dorset Street, she met the murdered woman, who said to her that she had no money, and if she could not get any would never go out any more, but would do away with herself. Soon after they parted, and a man who is described as respectably dressed, came up and spoke to the murdered woman Kelly, and offered her some money. The man then accompanied the woman home to her lodgings, and the little boy was removed from the room and taken to a neighbour's house. Nothing

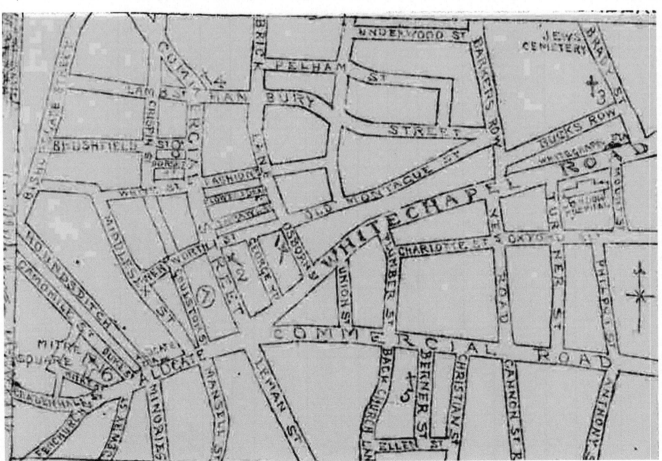

Fig. 86. Localities of the Seven Murders

more was seen of the woman until Friday morning, when, it is stated, the little boy was sent back into the house, and subsequently dispatched on an errand by the man who was in the house with his mother.

Another statement is to the effect that Kelly was seen in a public house known as the Ringers, at the corner of Dorset Street and Commercial Street, about ten o'clock on Friday morning, and that she there met her paramour, Barnatt, and had a glass of beer with him.

If the following statement can be confirmed, it has a very important bearing upon the question, "who is the murderer?" because it fixes approximately the time at which the murder was committed. But so many stories have been invented for the sake of gain by people who live in the locality since these murders became the sensation in the newspapers, that it is difficult to ascertain at once whether they are accurate or otherwise. However, it is the latest statement, and it is given on the authority of the *Central News.* Mrs. Maxwell, the wife of the deputy of the lodging house is Dorset Street, situated just opposite the court where Mary Kelly lived, said to a *Central News* reporter, "I assist my husband in his duties, but we live next door, at No. 26, Dorset Street. We had to stay up all night, and yesterday morning, as I was going home carrying my lantern and other things with me, I saw the woman Kelly standing at the entrance to the court. It was then about half-past eight, and as it was unusual for her to be seen about at that hour, I said to her, "Hallo, what are you doing up so early?" She said, "Oh, I'm very bad this morning. I have had the horrors. I have been drinking too much lately." I said to her, "Why don't you go and have half a pint of beer? It will put you right." She replied, "I have just had one, but I am bad as I am unable to keep it down." I didn't know then that she had separated from the man she had been living with, and I thought he had been "paying" her. I then went out in the direction of Bishopsgate to do some errands, and on my return, I saw Kelly standing outside the public house talking to a man. That was the last I saw of her. Who he was I don't know. He was a short, stout man, of about fifty years of age. I did not notice what he had on, but I saw that he wore a king of plaid coat. I then went indoors to go to bed, as I had been "on duty" all night. Mary Jane (I only know her by that name) was a pleasant little woman, rather stout, fair complexion, and rather pale."

Although rumours were current on Friday that the woman had been seen in the morning, they could not be authenticated, and the opinion of the police was that the woman had been murdered during the

Fig. 87. Removing the Body

night by a man whom she took home to her lodgings. Mrs. Maxwell, however, who knew the deceased well by sight, is emphatic both as to the two occasions she saw the deceased on Friday morning, and also as to the conversation reported above. At half-past nine on Friday morning, therefore, the deceased was alive, and, according to her own statement, suffering from a drinking bout. Presumably, between half-past eight and half-past nine she had been drinking with the man who afterwards butchered her, for at the latter hour she was seen talking to a man outside a public house. At a quarter to eleven the body was discovered in the room which served as lodgings, the remains being open to the view of anyone who chose to look through the window facing the court. Therefore, assuming Mrs. Maxwell's story to be accurate, the murderer must have walked from the public house to the victim's lodgings, and in broad daylight killed the woman and performed the most horrific barbarities. He must have removed from himself any traces of the crime and walked away from the spot unnoticed. But, having seen the man in broad daylight, Mrs. Maxwell ought to be able to give a description upon which the police can work; and if it be true that murderer and victim were drinking together in the public house between nine o'clock and half-past nine, then the people at the house should be able to partially corroborate Mrs. Maxwell's story and description.

On Sunday the excitement created by the murder in Whitechapel had not abated to any appreciable extent, and the streets of the district were crowded, Dorset Square, the scene of the tragedy, being in the afternoon and evening in a practically congested condition. The crowds which extended even into Commercial Street rendered the locomotion all but impossible. Vendors of pamphlets descriptive of the Whitechapel crimes, advertised their wares in shrill tones which could be heard even above the cries of the proprietors of fruit barrows and confectionary boxes, who appeared to be doing a thriving trade.

Fig. 88.   Sketch of Mary Kelly

Two police constables guarded the entrance to Miller's Court, where, of course, the crowd was thickest, and the adjacent shop of the landlord of the house in which the body of the murdered woman had been found was besieged with people anxious to glean further particulars regarding the crime. A very short distance away an itinerant street preacher sought to improve the occasion. The assemblage within and about Dorset Street comprised men and women of various classes, and now and then vehicles drove up containing persons impelled by curiosity to visit the scene of the tragedy.

Great excitement was caused shortly before ten o'clock on Sunday night, in the East End, by the arrest of a man with a blackened face, who publicly proclaimed himself to be "Jack the Ripper." This was at the corner of Wentworth Street, Commercial Road, near the scene of the latest crime. Two young men, one a discharged soldier, seized him, and the crowds, which always on Sunday night parade this neighbourhood, raised a cry of "Lynch him!" sticks were raised, and the man was furiously attacked, and, but for the timely arrival of the police, he would have been seriously injured. The police took him to Leman Street Station. He refused to give any name but asserted that he was a doctor at St. George's Hospital. His age is about thirty-five years, height five feet seven inches, complexion dark, and dark moustache, and he was wearing spectacles. He wore no waistcoat, but had an ordinary jersey worn beneath his coat. In

his pocket he had a double-peaked light check cap, and at the time of his arrest he was bare headed. It took four constables and four civilians to take him to the station and protect him from the infuriated crowd. He is detained in custody, and it seems that the police attach importance to the arrest, as the man's appearance answers to the police description of the man who is wanted.

The excitement in the neighbourhood of Dorset Street is intense and some of the low women, with whom the street abounds, appear more like fiends than human beings. The police have naturally great trouble to preserve order, and, one constable who is alleged to have struck an onlooker, was so mobbed and hooted that he had to beat a retreat to Commercial Street Police Station, whither he was followed by a large crowd, who were only kept at bay by the presence of about half a dozen stalwart constables, who stood at the door and prevented anyone from entering.

Mrs. Kennedy, who was on the day of the murder staying with her parents at a house facing the room where the mutilated body was found has made an important statement. She says that about three o'clock on Friday morning she entered Dorset Street on her way to the house of her parents, which is situated immediately opposite that in which the murder was committed. She noticed three persons at the corner of the street near the Britannia. There was a man – a young man, respectably dressed, and with a dark moustache – talking to a woman whom she did not

Fig. 89. 13 Miller's Court the Day of the Murder

know, and also a female poorly clad, and without any head gear. The man and woman appeared to be the worse for liquor, and she heard the man say, "Are you coming?" whereupon the woman, who appeared to be obstinate, turned in an opposite direction to which the man apparently wished her to go in.

Mrs. Kennedy went on her way, and nothing unusual occurred until about half an hour later. She states that she did not retire to rest immediately after she reached her parent's abode, but sat up, and between half-past three and a quarter to four she heard a cry of "Murder!" in a woman's voice proceed from the direction in which Mary Kelly's room was situated. As the cry was not repeated, she took no further notice of the circumstance until the morning, when she found the police in possession of the place, preventing all egress to the occupants of the small houses in the court. When questioned by the police

as to what she had heard throughout the night, she made a statement to the above effect. She has since supplemented that statement by the following:- "On Wednesday evening, about eight o'clock, I and my sister were in the neighbourhood of Bethnal Green Road, when we were accosted by a very suspicious looking man about forty years of age. He was about five foot seven inches high, wore a short jacket, over which he had a long top coat and wore a billy cock hat. He invited us to accompany him into a lonely spot, as he was known about there, and there was a policeman looking at him." She asserts that no policeman was in sight. He made several strange remarks and appeared to be agitated. He was very white in the face, and made every endeavour to prevent us looking him straight in the face. He carried a black bag. He avoided walking with them, and led the way into a dark thoroughfare at the back of the workhouse, inviting them to follow,

Fig. 90. The Miller's Court Murder (Penny Illustrated Paper)

which they did. He then pushed open a small door in a pair of large gates and requested one of them to follow him remarking, "I only want one of you," whereupon the women became suspicious. He acted in a very strange and suspicious manner, and refused to leave his bag in possession of one of the females. Both women became alarmed at his actions, and escaped, at the same time raising the alarm of "Jack the Ripper."

A gentleman who was passing is stated to have intercepted the man while the women made their escape. Mrs Kennedy asserts that the man that she saw on Friday morning with the women at the corner of Dorset Street resembled very closely the individual who caused such alarm on the night in question, and that she would recognise him again if confronted with him. There is no cause to doubt this woman's statement.

The following notice was posted in Dorset Street, and at all the police stations in the Metropolis on Saturday:-

Murder – Pardon – Whereas, on November 8th or 9th in Miller's Court, Dorset Street, Spitalfields, Mary Jane Kelly was murdered by some person or persons unknown, the Secretary of State will advise the grant of her Majesty's gracious Pardon to any accomplice not being a person who contrived or actually committed the murder, who shall give information and evidence as shall lead to the discovery and conviction of the person or persons who committed the murder. (Signed) – Charles Warren, the Commissioner of Police of the Metropolis, Metropolitan Police Office, Whitehall Place, November 10th, 1888."

Illustrated Police News – 17th November 1888.

1888 – PERFECTION OF WICKEDNESS.

For the seventh time the Metropolis has been thrilled by the sensational deeds of the Whitechapel murderer, and the gaiety of the Lord Mayor's Day crowd converted into horror and despair.

The slaughter of the latest victim, Mary Jane Kelly, presents no novel features, and only differs from the preceding outrage in the sickening minuteness of barbarity with which it has been accomplished. Anything more ghastly than the details have never been conceived even in the wild ravings of Edgar Allan Poe or the gruesome mysteries of Gaborieau and the realistic school of literature.

The murderer evidently chose his opportunity with a ghoulish delight in the sensation which his act would cause when made known among the holiday folk crowding the streets to enjoy the historical procession. Above all he must have been well aware that whilst the police battalions, horse and foot, were being mustered in Trafalgar Square, and a whole army of constables tailed off to conduct the Lord Mayor through the streets, the purlieus of Whitechapel and Spitalfields, which have been so closely watched during the period since his last act of murder was committed, would be comparatively free of police supervision.

Then again, he had less cause to fear detection, inasmuch as the labours of the innumerable amateur detectives, and vigilant committees, after the first excitement of their self-imposed task had worn away, were beginning to relax their efforts. Of these facts he was cognisant, and he has again, to all appearances, succeeded in baffling the pursuit of justice.

The columns of all the newspapers as in the former cases teem with revolting detail, and again the theorists are hard at work rolling their Sisyphoean stones of conjecture. These constantly repeated acts of violence cannot but have a completely demoralizing effect on all who are brought into close communication with the inner life of our lower classes in the great centres of the kingdom. There is an old saying that crime begets crime; and though the truism of the remark can only be upheld in a very restricted sense, yet it is certain that the example and punishment of crime amongst the lowest orders of our civilization acts rather as an incentive than a deterrent. The dread of justice is a remote and remoter preventative of crime, as the immunity of murderer after murderer becomes an undeniable fact.

That brute instinct, which hyde-like underlies all human nature, and which finds a vent where the restraints of education and morality are but imperfectly developed, only too surely manifests its hideous existence in deeds of the kind which during this memorable autumn have become familiar to us. What, then, is specially to be apprehended from these continued murders, with all their sordid and miserable surroundings, is that the disease may spread, and we may be subjected to a curse even more awful than the horrors which disgraced the later Roman Empire and the days of the French Revolution.

Meantime, we have to face the fact that there is among us a criminal class of which this monster fiend of diabolical ingenuity and truculence is the leading spirit and perfection of wickedness. There is one remarkable similarity about the series of his seven atrocities commenced by the violent death of an unknown woman in Whitechapel last Christmas. They have all been committed towards the end of the week; and it has been suggested that the assassin is only an occasional visitant to the locality where the crimes have been perpetrated.

Now, it is well known that there is a great shifting population upon the Thames, who come and go in the course of their trade between England and the Continent. Among the number is a guild of butchers trading between Antwerp and the City, whose advent in the river is usually at the end of the week. The coincidence of time and the nature of detail in each case may form an important clue in the eventual discovery of the murderer, for all along it has been clear that he is possessed of considerable anatomical skill, which enables him to carry out his barbarities with a precision that can only be the result of a certain knowledge in dealing with physiological subjects.

Of all the thousand theories put forward, this strikes us as the most remarkable and most hopeful to lead to discovery. The police are apparently no nearer the object of their search than in the previous cases; and there is the same total absence of any definite clue to guide—therefore we must be content to wait, how long who shall say.

Fife News – 17th November 1888.

1888 – INQUEST OF MARY JANE KELLY.

The inquest on the body of Mary Jane Kelly, the victim of the Dorset Street tragedy, was opened on Monday at the Shoreditch Town Hall, before Dr. Macdonald, M.P., Coroner for North East Middlesex.

Great interest was taken in the proceedings, but the room in which the enquiry was held barely sufficed to accommodate the Jury and the many representatives of the Press who attended. The first witness called was Joseph Barnett, who said, "I am a labourer. I lived a year and eight months with the deceased. She told me her name was Marie Jeanette Kelly. I have seen the body, and from the hair and eyes recognise it to be her. I lived with her in Miller Court about eight months. I separated from her on the 30th of this month, because she took in another woman out of compassion on her, and I objected to it. I saw her last alive between half-past seven and a quarter to eight on the night before she was murdered. I called on her and stayed for a quarter of an hour. We were on friendly terms. She has been drunk several times in my presence. She told

me she was born in Limerick, but went to Wales very young. She said her father's name was John Kelly, and that he was gaffer in an iron works in Caernarvonshire or Carmarthenshire. She said she had been married in Wales to a collier named Davies, who was killed in an explosion. She lived a bad life in Cardiff, and afterwards in the West End of London. She went to France for a short time, and she then came to the East End. She lived with a man named Morganstone, near the Stepney Gasworks, and afterwards stayed at another house, where she was visited by a man named Joseph Kelly, who lived in Bethnal Green Road. She used to ask me to read to her about the Whitechapel murders, and I did so."

At this point the Coroner said Dr. Phillips had written asking whether his attendance would be required. He (the Coroner) thought that Dr. Phillips should attend to give formal evidence as to cause of death.

Henry Bowyer said, "About a quarter to 11 on Friday morning I was sent by my master, Mr. McCarthy, to ask Mary Jane Kelly for the rent. I knocked and got no answer, so I put my hand through the broken window, moved the curtain, and saw flesh on the table and the body on the bed. I told Mr. McCarthy, and we fetched the police."

John McCarthy said, "I am a grocer and lodging house keeper, in Dorset Street. About a quarter to 11 I sent the last witness to the deceased for the rent. He came back and said he knocked at the door, and, getting no answer, looked through the window and saw the blood. I went and looked myself, and saw the body of a woman and went to the police station and reported to Inspector Beck. I often saw the deceased drunk. When sober she was a very quiet woman."

Mary Ann Cox, residing in Miller's Court, said, "I last saw deceased on Thursday night. She was very drunk. She was going up the Court with a short, stout man, shabbily dressed. He wore a long dark coat and a billy-cock hut, and had a pot of ale in his hind. He had a blotchy face, and a full, carotty moustache. I heard deceased singing "A violet I plucked from my mother's grave." I went out again at one o'clock, and she was still singing. At three I returned, the light was out, and all was quiet. I did not sleep a wink that night. I heard someone go out at a quarter past six, but I do not know from what house. I should think the man I saw with Kelly was about five or six and thirty. If there had been a cry of murder, I should have heard it."

Elizabeth Jones said, "I live in a room over deceased. I went home about half-past one on Friday morning. About half-past three my kitten came across my face, and just as I pushed it away, I heard a suppressed cry, "Oh, murder." Being accustomed to such cries I took no notice of it."

Caroline Maxwell, who was cautioned by the Coroner as to her evidence, said, "I saw the deceased standing at the entrance to the court on Friday morning about half-past eight o'clock. I asked her why she was up so early. She said she was so bad. I asked her to have a drink, and she said, "I have just had half a pint of ale and brought it up again." I went to Bishopsgate, and on returning, saw her standing outside the Britannia public house talking to a man. He seemed to be a short, stout man, and I believe be wore a plaid coat."

Lewis Laundress said, "I saw a man waiting outside Miller's Court, about half-past two on Friday morning. I remained in the Court all night, and about four heard a woman cry murder. On Wednesday night I was with a female, when a well-dressed man carrying a black bag asked us to come down a passage. We were afraid and ran away. He had a black moustache and was very pale. On Friday morning as I was going to Miller's Court, I met the same man with a female in Commercial Street."

Dr. George Baxter Phillips deposed, "I am surgeon to the H Division of the Metropolitan Police. I cannot give the whole of my evidence now. On Friday morning, about 11 o'clock, I proceeded to Miller's Court, and in a room, there found the mutilated remains of a woman lying two-thirds over towards the edge of the bed nearest the door. Subsequent to the injury which caused death, the body had been removed from the opposite side of the bed which was nearest the wooden partition. The presence of a quantity of blood on and under the bed lead me to the conclusion that the severance of the carotid artery, which was the immediate cause of death, was indicted while deceased was lying at the right side of the bedstead, and her head and neck in the right-hand corner. That is as far as I propose to carry with the evidence now."

The Coroner said he proposed to continue taking evidence for another hour. The Jury expressed a wish to adjourn for some time. The Coroner replied he would resume in quarter of an hour. On resuming, Julia Yenturney said, "I am a charwoman, and live at Miller's Court. Deceased told me she liked another man other than Joe Burnett, and he often came to see her. I was at home during Thursday night, and had there been any noises I should have heard them."

Maria Harvey, laundress, said, "I have slept with the deceased on several occasions, and never heard her express a fear of anyone."

Inspector Beck, H Division, said, "I accompanied Dr. Phillips to the house. Do not know that deceased was known to the police."

Inspector Abberline, Scotland Yard, deposed, "I went to Miller's Court at 11.30 on Friday. When there I received intimation that bloodhounds were on the way. I waited till 1.30 when Superintendent Arnold arrived, and said the order for bloodhounds had been countermanded. The door was then forced. In the grate were traces of the woman's clothing having been burnt. The opinion is they were burnt to give sufficient light for the murderer to do his work."

The Coroner said this concluded the evidence offered at present. The question was whether the Jury had not already heard sufficient testimony to enable them to determine the cause of death. His own opinion was they might conclude and leave the case to the police.

The Jury, after a few moments' consultation, returned a verdict of "Wilful murder against some person or persons unknown."

The Press Association states that the police have received information which not only establishes a clue to the perpetrator of the Dorset Street murder, but places the authorities in possession of an accurate description of the person seen in company of the murdered woman shortly before her death. It appears that a man, apparently of the labouring class, with a military appearance, who knew the deceased woman, Monday evening lodged with the police a detailed account of the appearance of the incident which attracted his attention on the morning of the murder, and although his story has been sifted and the narrator cross-examined, he adheres to it rigidly. For this reason, the police believe the clue a new and important one.

The informant stated that on the morning of the 9th he saw the deceased woman, Mary Jeanette Kelly, in Commercial Street, Spitalfields, in the vicinity of where the murder was committed, in the company of a man of respectable appearance. The man was about five feet six inches in height, and thirty-four or five years of age, with dark complexion and dark moustache curled upwards at the ends. He wore a long dark coat, trimmed with astrachan, a white collar, with black necktie, in which was affixed a horseshoe. He wore a pair of dark gaiters over button boots, and displayed from his waistcoat a massive gold chain. The highly respectable appearance of the man was in such contrast to the appearance of the woman that few could have failed to notice them at that hour of the morning.

This description, which agrees with that given of the person seen with the deceased by others, is much fuller in detail than has yet been in the possession of the police, and the importance which they attach to it may be estimated from the fact that immediately it was taken a special messenger was sent to the headquarters of H Division, where Detectives Aberline, Nairn, and Moore started an investigation.

Wrexham Advertiser – 16th November 1888.

1888 – FUNERAL OF MARIE KELLY.

The funeral of Marie Jeannette Kelly the victim of the latest Spitalfields murder, took place today at Leytonstone Cemetery, Essex, in the presence of a large number of people. An hour before the remains left the Shoreditch mortuary many hundreds of onlookers assembled in the vicinity and watched while the final arrangements were being made. The coffin was placed upon an open hearse, drawn by two horses, and followed by two morning carriages containing the man, Joseph Barnes, who had lived with the deceased, and several of the unfortunate woman's associates, who gave evidence at the inquest.

The coffin bore the following inscription, "Marie Jeannette Kelly, died November 9th, 1888, aged 25 years," and on it were placed two crosses, and a cross made of heartsease and white flowers.

The whole of the funeral expenses was borne by Mr. Wilton, sexton of St. Leonard's Church, Shoreditch, who for many years has shown practical sympathy for the poorer classes.

Belfast Telegraph – 19th November 1888.

1888 – TAKEN FOR "JACK THE RIPPER."

The following is the letter to which we referred in a Note yesterday upon the new danger of carrying a black bag in the East End:—

(To the Editor of the *Globe*.)
Sir,

The record of an afternoon's experience in Shoreditch may possibly be of use as a warning to such of your readers as are in the habit of carrying about with them that sinister article of luggage — a shiny black bag. It is hardly necessary to say that mine was the most innocent imaginable, and the contents consisting, as they did, exclusively of papers, would not at the highest calculation have been worth more than eightpence to anybody but myself. Had I imagined when I got out of the train at Shoreditch station the trouble it would cause, I would certainly have left it in the carriage as booty for the next dishonest passenger.

For a time, I was so much amused by the large crowd which had gathered for the obsequies of Mary Jane Kelly, that I never dreamt of being myself an object of attention, especially as I have not hitherto had reason to think that I possessed a particularly murderous looking face. Yet it occurred to me once or twice that very likely the assassin might be so fascinated by the funeral as to be there in disguise to see the close of his work. He would have been mad, indeed, however, if he had come with the very bag he is supposed to carry. It dawned on me, by degrees, that I was an object of suspicion. At the door of a public house, which, like all the other establishments of the kind in the vicinity, was chockful of women of all ages, from 17 to 70, a paralytic old crone dropped her gin in terror as I passed, and the light girls in the street glanced suspiciously at my bag out of the corners of their eyes. Even the poet who was selling his funeral lay for the modest price of a half-penny to the "ladies," whom he assured "they would find nothing there that would hurt a babby," seemed to scruple about taking a copper from me.

Some time had passed before I paid much attention to these small indications. In the centre of the road, however, where the crowd had stopped the traffic, and a gang of roughs had invaded a cart on which they had mounted to view the scene, the cause of all this attention was explained. A ragged rascal who was smoking a short clay pipe remarked in a distorted spirit of fun. " There's Jack the Ripper." That did not alarm me in the slightest. On the contrary, I considered it a harmless joke, and in one sense it was convenient. The impulse of those even who did not believe it was to get out of my way, and I had only to move to find a lane through any part of the crowd. If I had been a leper, they would not have avoided me more carefully. What was a jest in the centre where it originated was dead earnest before it reached the outskirts of the crowd.

A little respite occurred when the hearse drove up, and the dissipated females who in the public houses had been diluting their beer and gin with maudlin tears, thronged out. Everything else was forgotten in admiration of the coffin, which, covered with immortals, could be seen through the glass sides of the conveyance. Look why don't you look! Splendid! Ain't it lovely! I told you the body was short! were the cries of the female mourners, about 90 per cent of whom had babies in their arms.

Had I gone away then; returned, for instance, to Shoreditch Station, I would have been all right; but I was anxious to see how far the crowd extended, and for that purpose walked in advance of the cortege along Hackney Road. It was with difficulty that the policemen could make a way for it. But they were all mere sightseers, and nowhere did I find the slightest trace of mourning, or even of awe. Those who write as though the people of Whitechapel were as sentimental and sensitive as the scholars at a young ladies' boarding school have little idea of the callousness which results from the life they lead. Mr. Barnett does well to have nearly all the pictures in St. Jude's Church calculated to impress the mystery and solemnity of death, for nowhere is it treated with less respect; in spite of the fear they have inspired, I do not believe that this long series of crimes have impressed, or even greatly shocked, the population.

However, that is a digression. After getting past Cambridge Heath Station the driver of the hearse quickened his pace, and soon passed out of view; so, after following at a sharp pace for a length of time, I began to look for some means of returning to the City. The locality was a poor one, and, as I seemed to be at the head of a crowd all hurrying after the funeral, I thought it would be as well to diverge from the main street and look about for a cab, an omnibus, a railway train, or some other means of conveyance. But to get off the route was impossible; at least, so I began to think, for it always appeared as though I were in front of the crowd of squalid mourners.

Until then I had never been directly molested, though I had an uncomfortable and inexplicable sense of being regarded as a suspicious personage. When the fact became apparent that I and not the hearse was being followed, I simply walked quietly on my way, hoping against hope either that the crowd would see their folly, or that a cab or a station would turn up. At last, I did see an omnibus, and hailed the driver, but though it was empty he would not take me in, and I did not wonder at it on looking round at my following, who now began to hoot and cry "Jack the Ripper" as loud as they could. Still my equanimity was not disturbed, though there was one woman with a cancer-eaten nose, whom — well, I certainly would not like to hear of another crime, but if there must be a victim, I would not be sorry if she were the victim. She hounded the others on, and when after vainly attempting to get some information about a mode of exit from a passer-by, I was surrounded, and in acute danger of being lynched, she seemed by far the most active of the mob.

Evidently, she was a thorough coward too, for when I opened the bag in the hope of making one or two friends by showing the innocent contents, she shrank away in fright and continued to egg on the others. At this very critical moment a policeman, who had seen the crowd break away from the funeral, hurried up; and never was a policeman more welcome. I could have embraced him like a brother, but the crowd put a different interpretation on the business, and thought Jack the Ripper was caught at last. "How well he carries it off," they said, as I laughed at the danger attendant upon the possession of a black bag, in the vain hope of

disabusing their minds of error. The guardian of order asked me to go into a public house till he dispersed the crowd; but his efforts seemed only to increase the excitement, and, finally, I was marched down to the station — the railway station — my entrance being greeted by a storm of yells and hooting.

However, the railway people kept the doors shut, and I was saved — though ever since, the feeling has hung about me that I am a suspicious character; and I cannot meet a knot of people in the street without watching whether they eye me or not. I have given that bag away. I may add that about a score of the roughs came into the station with tickets back to Bishopsgate, and were quite eager to enter into conversation about the adventure. They peered into the bag with greatest curiosity, and were obviously disappointed with the perfectly innocent nature of its contents. Upon my representing to them that it was somewhat inconvenient to set upon a harmless pedestrian in the way they had done, they defended themselves with much spirit and ingenuity, alleging that they needed to be vigilant on account of the cleverness and treachery of the assassin, and not denying that their efforts had been stimulated by the hope of reward. It was the greatest shock of all to find that I had been taken, not in jest, but in reality, for a murderer. "Not that we were sure," explained the spokesman of the band, apologetically, "but we thought it might come off, and if it didn't, we could get the train back again."

I enclose my name and address, not for publication, but to let you know that I am

Not Jack the Ripper.

The Star – 24th November 1888.

1888 – "JACK THE RIPPER'S" PAL.

The appended letter has been received by Mr. Thomas Porter, of Hucknall Torkard, who immediately handed it over to the county police. The writer is supposed to be a man who was formerly in the employ of Mr. Porter, when that gentleman was in business as a saddler at Hucknall, and who went out to Colorado. The letter bore the "E.C." postmark, November, London, E.C.

Sir,

I now take the liberty of writing to you hoping I am not taking a liberty in doing so. I have no doubt you will be surprised to hear it is me and a pal of mine doing this work in Whitechapel; but I feel I cannot continue much longer – shall have to give it up – cannot reign much longer. Have been in America some years, and since leaving Colorado have been carrying on a "deadly" (word omitted here) in the East of London. I feel at this moment as if I could burn or blow all those dens down, and all those filthy low women in them. When I go to bed at night, I can see all my past life before me, can see everything I have done wrong, and thousands of rats; it is dreadful, and when I lie awake in the morning, I fancy I've been dreaming I am not that man. It is too true; I am the right one. Oh, I do wish I had gone to Nottingham when I left Colorado, it makes me feel miserable.

Most people think there is only one in the affair but allow me to tell you – I guess there are two, and that is him who learnt me how to do it, a scamp, but I am as bad as him now, if not worse, for I never feel frightened in cutting a woman up now, felt at times I never should get caught, am just like a maniac. Oh, how I wish I could do without any more of this sort of life I have been leading of late – must go on or my pal would do for me – I guess it is a sworn thing between us.

When I am talking to a woman, I can see the very Devil, would give my life any time if I could just speak to some of my old friends. Do feel bad just now, hope the Lord will forgive me all the sins I have committed – always feel better in the afternoon when we go to a public house and hear someone reading about the Whitechapel affairs, have many a laugh as if I could not help it, when it is getting dark, I do feel funny – my pal is a wild wretch, he has learned me how to do all this. I am a native of Notts but lived in Hucknell some years ago. My pal is a Bavarian. We met on board a steamship, and I swore you I was mesmerised when I had found out his hideous calling which had been concealed from me for some time. I had become so intimate with him, and he cast a sort of spell over me.

Myself and my pal are just what they call "Jack the Ripper," we are not the cause of all the nonsense about that letter writing and that writing on the wall, we have never done anything of the sort. You must not allow any hope to exist in your body, I really feel miserable, and scarcely know what to do with myself at this moment, expect we shall pop off another or two, when I guess we go back to Colorado never to return.

Yours goodbye,

"JACK THE RIPPERS PAL."

Tower Hamlets Independent and East End Local Advertiser – 1st December 1888.

1888 – "JACK THE RIPPER" A RUSSIAN?

A Russian newspaper, in an article on the Whitechapel murders, expresses the belief that the perpetrator of these dreadful crimes is a Russian named Nicolai Vassilyeff, of whose past career it gives the following details.

Vassilyeff, who was born as Tiraspol in 1847, was a student at the Odessa University, and having become a fanatical Anarchist, he migrated to Paris in the seventies, when he shortly afterwards became insane and was placed under restraint. Before being lodged in an asylum, however, Vassilyeff, whose mania appears to have been that fallen women could only atone for their sins and obtain redemption by being killed, murdered several unfortunates in Paris under conditions somewhat similar to those of the Whitechapel crimes, and on his arrest, his insanity having been proved, he was placed in a criminal lunatic asylum.

This happened 16 years ago, and Vassilyeff, or the mad Russian as he was called, remained in the Paris asylum until shortly before the first Whitechapel outrage, when he was dismissed as cured. He is then said to have proceeded to London, where for some time he lived with the lower class of his fellow countrymen. After the first Whitechapel murder, however, Vassilyeff was lost sight of, and the Russian residents in London believe that their insane countryman is no other than the murderer.

Tower Hamlets Independent and East End Local Advertiser – 1st December 1888.

1889 – THE SPIRIT POWER.

Some time ago, says a London correspondent, a woman of a village of Lorraine was convicted of the wilful murder of her mother-in-law. She had been fairly tried, the crime was duly proved, and yet the Jury acquitted her, with the expressed opinion of her having been the victim of somebody possessing willpower over her of sufficient potency to force her to obedience even though the hypnotiser were residing at a distance, and could never have been seen by the subject of his experiment.

The total absence of motive for the murder, the utter oblivion of the act, the surprise and consternation of the woman when arrested with the hatchet with which the deed had been accomplished still grasped in her hand, were all brought forward as proof of her subjection to some power of will greater than her own by which she had been impelled to commit the crime.

The theory has penetrated Whitechapel, and the terror inspired in some minds belonging to the upper classes of that low quarter by the idea of supernatural possession is beyond description. That the murder of the miserable victims of "Jack the Ripper" has been accomplished by "the spirits" has become the general belief, and a consequent reaction in favour of the police has taken place among the population. Recklessness has replaced indignation. What is the use of resistance to the Evil One? "How shall we escape?" has become the theme of street-corner gossip and public house whispering.

Norfolk Chronicle – 7th August 1889.

1889 – INTRIGUING CONJECTURE.

A report having been current that a man has been found who is quite convinced that "Jack the Ripper" occupied rooms in his house, and that he had communicated his suspicions in the first instance to Dr. Forbes Winslow, together with detailed particulars, a reporter had an interview with the doctor on Thursday afternoon on the subject. "Here are Jack the Ripper's boots," said the doctor, at the same time taking a large pair of boots from under his table. "The tops of these boots are composed of ordinary cloth material, while the soles are made of India rubber. The tops have great bloodstains on them." The reporter put the boots on, and found they were completely noiseless. Besides these noiseless coverings the doctor says he has the "Ripper's" ordinary walking boots, which are very dirty, and the man's coat, which is also bloodstained.

Proceeding, Dr. Winslow said that on the morning of August 30th a woman, with whom he was in communication, was spoken to by a man in Worship Street, Finsbury. He asked her to come down a certain court with him, offering her £1. This she refused, and he then doubled the amount, which she also declined. He next asked her where the court led to and shortly afterwards left. She told some neighbours, and the party followed the man for some distance. Apparently, he did not know that he was being followed, but when he and the party had reached the open street, he turned round, raised his hat, and with an air of bravado said, "I know what you have been doing. Good morning!" The woman then watched the man go into a certain house, the situation of which the doctor would not describe. She had previously noticed the man because

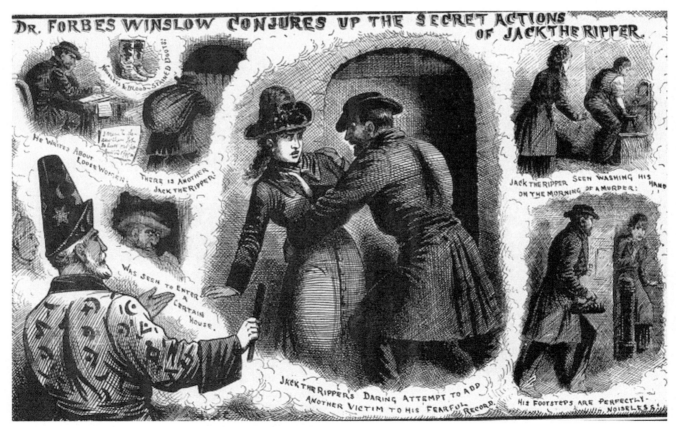

Fig. 91. 91 The Conjecture of Dr. Forbes Winslow

of his strange manner, and on the morning on which the woman Mackenzie was murdered (July 17th) she saw him washing his hands in the yard of the house referred to. He was in his shirtsleeves at the time and had a very peculiar look upon his face. This was about four o'clock in the morning. The doctor said he was now waiting for a certain telegram, which was the only obstacle to his effecting the man's arrest.

The supposed assassin lived with a friend of Dr. Forbes Winslow's, and this gentleman himself told the doctor that he had noticed the man's strange behaviour. He would at times sit down and write fifty or sixty sheets of manuscript about low women, for whom he professed to have a great hatred. Shortly before the body was found in Pinchin Street the other day the man disappeared, leaving behind him the articles already mentioned, together with a packet of manuscript, which the doctor said was in exactly the same handwriting as the Jack the Ripper letters which were sent to the police. He had stated previously that he was going abroad, but a very few days before the body was discovered (September 10th) he was seen in the neighbourhood of Pinchin Street.

The doctor is certain that this man is the Whitechapel murderer, and says that two days at the utmost will see him in custody. He could give a reason for the head and legs of the last murdered woman being missing. The man, he thinks, cut the body up, and then commenced to burn it. He had consumed the head and legs when his fit of the terrible mania passed, and he was horrified to find what he had done. "I know for a fact," said the doctor, "that this man is suffering from a violent form of religious mania, which attacks him and passes off at intervals. I am certain that there is another man in it besides the one I am after, but my reasons for that I cannot state. The police will have nothing to do with the capture. I am making arrangements to station six men round the spot where I know my man is, and he will be trapped."

The public had laughed at him, the doctor went on to say, but on the Tuesday before the last body was discovered he had received information that a murder would be committed in two or three days.

In conclusion Dr. Winslow remarked, "I am as certain that I have the murderer as I am of being here."

The chairman of the Whitechapel Vigilance Committee, Mr. Albert Backert, stated that the police at Leman Street Station, having received a letter stating that it has been ascertained that a tall, strong woman has for some time been working at different slaughterhouses, attired as a man, searching inquiries have been made at the slaughterhouses in Aldgate and Whitechapel by the police. It is presumed that this has something to do with the recent Whitechapel murders, and it has given rise to a theory that the victims may have been murdered by a woman. It is remarked that in each case there is no evidence of a man being seen in the vicinity at the time of the murder.

Illustrated Police News – 28th September 1889.

———————

1889 – ANOTHER LETTER FROM "JACK THE RIPPER."

The Press Association says:—

Mr. Albert Backert, Chairman of the Whitechapel Vigilance Committee, on Saturday received the following letter:—

"Whitechapel, 9th October 1889.

Dear Boss,

I write you these few lines to let you know, as you are the boss of the Vigilant Society, that the last job wasn't me, for I shouldn't have made such a botch of it. Never mind, young men, you can keep your lamps open for the 18th October. I am on the job again. There's no blood knocking about, or I would let you see some. Never mind, look out, old man. You're a brave sort. You thought you had me once. Don't forget the 18th.

Yours, in haste, Jack the R.—"

The envelope bears the East London postmark, and was posted on Saturday. The writing corresponds with that in letters previously received by Mr. Backert.

Western Times – 14th October 1889.

———————

1890 – IN MURDERLAND.

It is announced that "the police are taking extra precautions in Whitechapel this week." For such precautions, says the *Pall Mall Gazette*, there is plenty of room. It is now just two years ago since "Jack the Ripper" was busy with his devil's work in Whitechapel, but next to nothing has yet been done in any one instance to prevent another murder taking place tonight, on any one of the self-same spots which a mutilated corpse once lay. Again, although at the time of, and for some weeks after the murders, nearly every other person that one ran against in Whitechapel was either uniformed or a plain clothes policeman, their numbers were gradually reduced with the subsidence of the scare, until the force stationed in Whitechapel today is just about the same in point of numbers when the assassin's knife first commenced its deadly work, and in point of efficiency, probably even worse.

There are strong and even startling statements to make, but they are supported by close personal investigation which has been undertaken on behalf of the *Pall Mall Gazette* throughout the length and breadth of Murderland. The results of the investigation are recorded in an article, from which the following are extracts:-

"I went first to the scene of the very first murder—the landing of the common lodging house in George Yard, where Martha Tabram's dead body, shockingly mutilated, was found on the morning after Bank Holiday. It is true that, on the recommendation of the Coroner's Jury who investigated the circumstances of her death, a lamp was fixed there, and it is true also that it exists at the present time. But then, lamps can't be alight all night in common lodging houses—so the landlords say—and, if what some of the tenants say be true, after 11 or 12 o'clock at night the lamp is turned out, and in every essential respect the landing assumes the appearance it bore when Martha Tabram was done to death there. Yet it was between two and three o'clock in the morning when she was murdered. Policemen seldom if ever visit that landing now as it is no part of their beat, and the only contingency to be faced by any would-be murderer who should take his victim there after midnight would be the arrival of one of the occupants of the upstairs tenements. And even that contingency is a very improbable one, for the occupants are nearly all of them unskilled labourers, the exigencies of whose work leave them no opportunity for midnight dissipations.

Then, take next, that blank wall in Bucks Row, where the next victim was butchered. Nothing whatever in the way of change of any kind has taken place there. The wall is just as blank, the light at night is just as indistinct, and the row at midnight is just as denuded of civilians and policemen as when the unfortunate woman Nichols was stabbed and mutilated there. The unfortunates have forgotten the fate of their "pal," the police patrol has been withdrawn, and passers-by at night are rarer than ever. It might, perhaps, be a slight exaggeration to say that the murderer of Mary Ann Nichols would find it just as easy to repeat his hellish work tonight, for a police "point" has been established a little nearer Buck's Row than formerly; but this at all events can be safely said—that the operation would be attended with but the merest fraction of increased difficulty.

Mitre Square—the scene of probably the worst butchery of all—is undoubtedly better patrolled than it used to be; the beats have been shortened, the policeman's bullseye flashes its light all round the square far too frequently to allow of such deliberate and cold-blooded butchery as occurred there before. But then the Metropolitan Police Force can take no credit for that. The credit, if any, belongs to the very much better organised and much more adequate City Police. The self-same Sunday morn that heralded the discovery of the Mitre Square victim was the one that found another unfortunate lying in the gateway in Berner Street, St. George's East, with her throat cut. It is true that since that time the gateway has been religiously closed after the last van has entered it. But then the vans are sometimes very late in arriving, and what is there to prevent a murderer decoying another victim there? When you push open the gates it is as dark as Erebus; when the gate is pushed back there is an effectual screen from any prying passer-by, although passers-by, who are constituted very largely of the foreigners who reside in the locality, are far too scared to ever peep inside that gate with its terrible history; and, dually, there is always singing or some other form of entertainment going on at the International Club next door to effectually drown a faint shriek.

But what about the policeman on the beat, you say? The police on that beat have got so tired of opening that gate and finding nothing there since the murder that they have long ago despaired of ever finding anything, and consequently pass it now with the most complete indifference. And, even should, by the most remote possibility, the murderer be disturbed by anybody opening the gate from the street entrance, he is by no means caught in a trap, for there are plenty of backyards that can scaled, and a great many courts and passages, leading to Berner and other streets, to be easily reached. On the whole, then, that gateway in Berner Street would form a very safe place for any operations of the Ripper just now.

Next, there is that mysterious house in Hanbury Street at which the world looked in askance when the evidence given at the inquest on the disembowelled body found in its backyard revealed the fact that unfortunates, somehow or another, seemed to possess a right of way through the passage, and so into the yard. One would have thought that after such a revelation that some steps would at least have been taken to put a stop to such a scandal. But no. After midnight there is nothing whatever to prevent anybody from lifting the latch of the door and proceeding, by way of the passage, to the very spot where the Ripper in a paroxysm of fury plucked out the entrails of another victim. The reason is obvious. The premises are nothing more than a "doss" house on a small scale; its residents change nearly every day, and nobody would presume to question the right of anyone to pass through the passage and so into the fateful yard, where, as before, a murder could be committed now with comparative impunity. And yet, what outburst of popular indignation there would be if another butchery occurred on the self-same spot that reeked before with the blood of a murdered woman! What is true of the house in Hanbury Street is true also, though in a lesser degree perhaps, of the lodging house in the court off Dorset Street, where the discovery of another mutilated victim cast gloom on the Lord Mayor's festivities of two years ago. It was the boldest stroke of all when the Whitechapel fiend decoyed his victim there. And what boldness—or rather absolute wantonness—accomplished before, it can doubtless accomplish again.

There is some prospect at last of the vile hole known as Castle Alley, where the last murder occurred, being swept off the face of the earth, for the Whitechapel Board of Works have lately decided to convert it into a public thoroughfare. But the archway in Pinchin Street remains in precisely the same condition in which it appeared when the sackful of human remains was found beneath it. That archway, it may be remembered, forms but one of several, some, of which are partially boarded up from the street, and which form, at the present time, an acknowledged resort of unfortunates, who ply, almost undisturbed, their degraded trade there.

"But are the conditions precisely the same for the perpetration of murders as was the case two years ago—are intended victims to be decoyed as easily as then?" some sceptical reader may ask. The personal investigations of the writer have convinced him that, should the Whitechapel terror appear in our midst again, bent on the same murderous mission, he would find the conditions precisely the same as before, and his victims just as easily decoyed and just as numerous. The unfortunate class in Whitechapel and St. George's, or rather, the lower unfortunate class, from whom the victims were chiefly recruited—for there are distinctions even in degradation—is just as numerous as ever it was. They form the very dregs of humanity. Better conditions of trade and better conditions of labour affect their numbers not at all. They drift down through a life of shame until they become veritable pariahs even among the unfortunates in other parts of London; until the streets of Whitechapel become their only home, and immorality, in its very worst form, their only resource. The very worst of disorderly houses will seldom open their doors to them, and the practising of their vile trade in the courts and alleys and archways of the district constitute their only resource against absolute starvation. Prowling through this district for the greater part of nearly every night,

and sleeping for the rest of the night in one or other of these plague spots, they have the locality of each at their fingers' ends, and long experience has made them equally well acquainted with the exact time at which the policeman on beat passes each of these places. What need of decoying these creatures? The very exigencies of their degraded calling make them accessories to their own murder. God help them when they get in a would-be murderer's hands."

Portsmouth Evening News – 3rd October 1890.

1891 – TERROR IN WHITECHAPEL.

The perpetration of another murder in the neighbourhood of Leman Street has naturally revived the excitement caused by the series of similar atrocities committed in that unhappily notorious locality. As regards the character of the victim and the circumstances under which the assassin did his work there is a close, though by no means a complete, resemblance to the previous crimes. The facts, so far as they have been ascertained, may be put into the briefest compass. The district which is bounded on the North by the Whitechapel Road, and is separated from the River on the South by the Mint, St. Katharine's and the London Docks, is, emphatically, a region of slums. Leman Street, running roughly, from North to South connects the line of the Whitechapel Road with the immediate vicinity of the Docks. Through the heart of the quarter passes the Great Eastern Railway, which is carried on its dingy brick viaduct towards the East. A little to the west of Leman Street, one of the arches affords a passage to the comparatively open thoroughfare of Royal Mint Street, from squalid court which, no doubt, commemorates by its name, Swallow Gardens, the time when it was a green space in the rear of cottages. The roadway below the line was but dimly lit by the lamps at each end of the arch, but it was not absolutely dark. A portion of it, however, was boarded off as a builder's yard. Nevertheless, it was, as a probable place for the resort of bad characters, by no means likely to escape the close observation of the constable on his round.

It is unnecessary to add that the most elaborate precautions were made for strict supervision throughout the whole area, under stress of the horror caused by the long series of undetected murders; nor is there any reason to suppose that the length of time — nearly a year and a half— which has elapsed since the last outrage has led to any serious relaxation of police vigilance.

Yesterday morning, at about two o'clock, the officer on patrol duty visited the place in due course; and, though it may be presumed that had there been anything unusual, he would have observed it, he appears to have passed on. Returning, however, less than a quarter of an hour later, he saw a body lying in the middle of the passage. On examination, it proved to be that of a dying woman. There was a long deep gash in the throat, and, though the body was still warm, only the faint beating of the pulse indicated that she was not yet dead. As the Divisional Surgeon arrived in time to take careful note of the precise condition of the body, the character of the injury, the posture, and other details of the kind, there will be no deficiency of evidence on this score, should anyone be made amenable to justice. But at present there is nothing that deserves to be called a clue.

The sad life of the poor creature who figures as the last of the Whitechapel victims ended before preparations could be made for removing her. All that can be confidently asserted is that she belonged to that wretched class of women from whom the earlier victims were taken. She was known by sight as one of the many who in this locality earn a miserable living by immorality. The surmise is inevitable that she met the murderer and was induced to accompany him to the scene of the crime. Her dress denoted poverty; but the only feature that can be regarded as of the slightest significance is that, besides a shabby crepe hat which lay on the ground near her, another was found half thrust into the pocket of her dress.

Those who feel a morbid satisfaction in speculating as to the authorship of this and the other mysterious crimes will find material enough to suggest half-a-dozen inconsistent hypotheses, and yet not sufficient to give the slightest colour of genuine probability to any one of them. The discovery of two shillings concealed behind a pipe under the arch may have nothing whatever to do with the fatal incident which prompted the search. Some persons have come forward to say that earlier in the morning they had observed a man and a woman in talk near the place of the outrage. The suggestion is, of course, that these were the assassin and the victim; but there is no reasonable warrant for presuming that any other persons were about at the time. The discovery of the

Fig. 92. FRANCES COLE – A Victim of "Jack the Ripper?" (Illustrated Police News)

second hat will give a momentary colour to the theory started in connection with the previous crimes, that the miscreant, or the maniac, was a woman. But it is at least as likely that the poor creature picked it up with a vague idea of adding it to her scanty wardrobe.

The whole complexion of the affair denotes deliberation on the part of the murderer, and almost superhuman coolness. It was certainly not the result of a sudden quarrel. The police authorities are, of course, bound to neglect no clue, however trivial and, on the surface, unpromising, and to follow up every scent on the remote chance that, somehow or other, by exhausting every available resource, they may at last light upon the track of the criminal. It was, no doubt, in this spirit that a search was made yesterday on board various ships, and in a number of lodging houses, and that some persons were detained, not so much "on suspicion" as to give them an opportunity of conclusively proving their innocence. The result is that, so far, no ground has been apparent for keeping any one in custody.

Had the criminal left behind him anything likely, however indirectly, to betray his awful secret, the terrible fascination which these repeated horrors have for the public mind would lose much of its force. The mystery in which the atrocity is veiled is as much an element in the tragic effect as the barbarous brutality of the deed. The one thing certain is that within the space of, perhaps, ten minutes, in the thick of a populous quarter, and almost under the shadow of a police station, some savage ruffian finds the means of inflicting death, in its most frightful form, and then, having left the body of the poor wretch whom he has marked out for doom as the sole evidence of the crime, disappears into the impenetrable obscurity from which he emerged.

It is only natural that popular feeling, both in the locality and in that larger world to which tidings of this fresh atrocity has been flashed, should attribute it to the same hands that are already believed to be stained with the blood of nine preceding victims. It would be useless to argue against an impression which has rooted itself so firmly in the imagination as the assumption that the Whitechapel murders have been the work of one person. Even the most sceptical of philosophers might admit that it was almost a moral necessity to personify the spirit of those repeated horrors in some name of terror. As far as we know, the prevailing theory rests mainly on the fact that several of the crimes have, in a way, coincided with warnings sent in letters signed with the same signature. The fact that warnings similarly given have not been fulfilled is, by the common weakness of popular logic, ignored; while the circumstance that the various outrages, if they had points of resemblance, had still more

striking points of difference is similarly left out of account. The Swallow gardens murder has a strong likeness to the others; but the absence of mutilation distinguishes it. Not that this is conclusive, since the murderer may have feared that delay might lead to his apprehension. Conjecture in one direction or another is, however, for the present vain. The material fact is that within a limited area, ten atrocious murders have been committed with absolute impunity. Leman Street Police Station is almost the centre round which the spots rendered infamous by these successive enormities are grouped.

Yet not in a single instance has there been the slightest approach to the detection of the criminal. Less than three years have elapsed since the first of these cold-blooded outrages startled the people on the spot, and with each ensuing tragedy the sense of horror has grown. It would be preposterous to disparage the acumen of our detectives because their diligence has not sufficed to solve the fearful problem. But we cannot, on the other hand, affect surprise that, in many minds, the failure of justice to track the villain has produced a state of excitement amounting almost to panic. So far as the impression takes the form of apprehension for personal safety, nothing can be more irrational than the fear which has from time to time possessed sections of the Whitechapel folk. No decent, self-respecting woman runs the slightest risk of being affronted, much less injured and, indeed, the tendency of the whole chapter of horrors would rather be to free the neighbourhood from the least desirable class of residents. But terror is deaf to reason; and we can only hope that, whether or not all the crimes referred to have been committed by the same person, the culprit in this instance may be brought to justice.

London Evening Standard – 14th February 1891.

1892 – A FAR-FETCHED THEORY.

The Star (Darlington) yesterday commenting on the attempt to connect the man Williams with the Jack the Ripper murder, says:—

It will be remembered that the theory most favoured by the police was that the Whitechapel murderer invariably managed to get away on board some vessel trading from London. Bilbao was believed to be his destination, and vessels from that port were closely watched. It was apparently not considered necessary, however, to keep a similar watch over ships bound to and from ports in our own country, and to this circumstance "Jack the Ripper" may have owed his escape. Between London and the Tyne, for instance, a regular traffic by sea is carried on, and it would be a simple matter for anyone wishing to get out of the metropolis speedily to ship on board a Tyne-bound vessel.

Lending colour to this theory, a curious story was current in South Shields last year. A young man who had "come down in the world" became a lounger near the docks and attracted the attention of some of the frequenters of the public houses by his strange behaviour. He was often heard muttering to himself, and his morose manner made him the object of suspicion. Little heed was paid to him amid the bustle of the port, but it was noticed that on several occasions he disappeared for about a fortnight, suddenly turning up again and resuming his habits, though more gloomy and repellent in his manner than ever. Women appeared to be objects of aversion and hatred in his eyes, and his mutterings boded no good to them. At last, he disappeared from the neighbourhood, leaving not a trace behind, and nothing was heard of him until some weeks afterwards, when he was found in a state of destitution on the outskirts of a North country town, and there died in delirium.

Meanwhile the "Jack the Ripper" scare had reached its height, and the wildest rumours were afloat. People in South Shields, however, now began to recall things connected with the young man who had led such a strange existence in their midst, and it was remembered that his periodic disappearance coincided in a remarkable manner with the date of each successive tragedy. It was known that a fast life had been his ruin, and his mutterings had led them to believe that he nursed revenge against "unfortunates." Putting various circumstances together, they came to the conclusion that he was no other than the dreaded "Jack the Ripper." And, strange as the story may appear, it is a fact that since his death no crime has been perpetrated in Whitechapel which could be without doubt ascribed to this notorious murderer. The writing that attracted so much attention has never been seen again, and nothing has been seen of the writer.

The young man in question was an outcast from his family. He had been a prodigal in every sense of the word and had even been a soldier of fortune abroad being concerned in at least one sanguinary episode. He had been well educated, he wrote in a good, bold hand, and, we believe, possessed a considerable amount of medical knowledge. His reckless career had made him callous. We do not assert that he was "Jack the Ripper," but merely state the grounds for this supposition.

Nevertheless, it is possible that his handwriting may form some clue. It will be remembered that "Jack the Ripper's" letters were reproduced in facsimile in many newspapers, and that the writing was believed to be disguised.

The Shields story as we have now stated came some months afterwards to the ears of the editor of an important journal who had accepted some articles from the individual in question. Thereupon, purely out of curiosity, he had the "copy" hunted out, and comparing it with the published facsimiles of "Jack the Ripper's" letters was struck with the singular resemblance in many of the characteristics.

Taking all the circumstances into consideration, there is some reason to suppose that the Whitechapel murderer and the destitute tramp were one and the same. The theory may be deemed far-fetched, but it has to be borne in mind that no fresh crime has been committed and nothing has actually been heard of "Jack the Ripper" since.

South Shields Gazette – 19th March 1892.

1894 – A REMARKABLE STATEMENT BY A SCOTLAND YARD OFFICER.

Two London papers, the *Morning Leader* and the *Sun* are interesting themselves just now in the whereabouts of the Whitechapel terror, known as "Jack the Ripper." Both profess to have identified and located him, and both agree that he has been incarcerated in a lunatic asylum ever since the date of the last atrocity. This is what the *Morning Leader* says:—

"I have watched the movements of this man for three years, and from the evidence in my possession I hope to bring home to him the charges of the Whitechapel atrocities." So spoke an Inspector of the Metropolitan Police to a *Morning Leader* representative yesterday afternoon. At once interesting and astonishing, the information was received with a smile of incredulity. In conversation, however, a theory was elaborated and a story so circumstantially told as to almost impel conviction. It is on the credit of a responsible officer of the Criminal Investigation Department that our representative details the following narrative. It would be impolite at this stage to disclose the name of the officer in question, but the amount of interest that he has evinced in the "Jack the Ripper" case has made him conspicuous amongst the members of the force. Briefly told, his investigations are as follows:—

"It was while I was on duty," said the Inspector, "in the vicinity of Whitechapel that I became acquainted with the outrages upon women that baffled the police and shocked the sensibility of London. I became a detective more than the ordinary sense. Dates, clues, suggestions, and theories I eagerly devoured. My pertinacity was rewarded. After a time, I secured evidence, in my judgment, ample to lay before the Scotland Yard authorities."

"What was your evidence?" inquired our representative. "Have you the knife with which he committed the deed? Have you any material evidence in support of your story?" These questions were eagerly asked and readily answered.

"I have in my possession now, and have already submitted it for inspection to the Scotland Yard authorities, the knife with which I shall endeavour to prove the Whitechapel murders were committed."

"Do the Scotland Yard authorities believe in your story?" "Well," said the Inspector, after a pause, "they believe my story to this extent, that they have allowed me a bonus for the information I have supplied. I do not, however, rest satisfied with that. If the man whom I am prepared to name is the murderer, I wish him brought to justice so that the English mind may be cleansed forever from the memory of "Jack the Ripper." "You have undertaken a large order," said our representative. "To begin with, where is the man?"

"At the present moment he is incarcerated in the Dartmoor Asylum, and has been there continuously from the date of the last Whitechapel murder," was the reply.

"Have you apprised the authorities of this?"— "Yes," said the officer.

"Have they done nothing?" There was an air of reluctance in the Inspector's manner as he answered this question. Red tape appeared to have selected him as a particular victim. "Not much," was the careless rejoinder. "In a case of that kind perhaps it would be unwise for any of the rank-and-file of the force to effect a capture."

"Ah, jealousy in the force! How then do you hope to secure his arrest and conviction?" said our representative. "Only with the aid of the Press," replied the officer, "can I hope to succeed, and you will do a public service by disclosing my story, and statements so specifically made ought easily and readily to be either confirmed or contradicted."

"Precisely. What is your evidence?" our reporter asked.

"In my possession I hold the knife, of Chinese manufacture, with which the Whitechapel crimes were perpetrated. I, at the same time, can disclose the man, whom I am prepared to name, during the intervals between the murders. I am able to trace him to the asylum after the last crime, and although he is now abandoned to insanity, he has yet remembrances of the past, and all his conversations and confessions are relating to the east End horrors."

"Surely you do not rely for a conviction upon the confessions of a man admittedly mad?" asked the Pressman. "No," was the rapid rejoiner; "I reject confessions that rely solely upon material evidence. All I wish is that the authorities may be moved to interest themselves in my investigations, so that my story may either be confirmed or refuted."

The above statement was circumstantially told to a *Morning Leader* representative by a well-placed officer in the police force, whose name can be supplied, and it seems a story that calls for investigation.

Portsmouth Evening News – 14th February 1894.

1899 – SECRET OF THE CONFESSIONAL.

To the long list of "solutions" of the great "Jack the Ripper" mystery there is now added another -possibly the final – one; possibly not.

It comes from a clergyman of the Church of England, a north country vicar, who claims to know with certainty the identity of the most terrible figure in all the blood-stained annals of crime – the perpetrator of that horrible series of East End murders which ten years ago startled the whole civilised world.

The clergyman in question declines to divulge the name of the culprit, being unable to do so without violating the secrecy of the confessional. He states, however, that he obtained his information from another clergyman to whom the murderer made a full and complete confession.

The vicar writes:- "I received information in professional confidence, with directions to publish the facts after ten years, and then with such alterations as might defeat identification.

The murderer was a man of good position and otherwise unblemished character, who suffered from epileptic mania, and is long since deceased. I must ask you not to give my name, as it might lead to identification."

The ten years were completed on November 9th last, the final murder of the "Ripper" series having taken place on November 9th, 1888, in Miller's Court.

There was a time when everybody had his pet theory as to the murders, but apart from speculation quite a number of solutions of the mystery have had a more or less substantial foundation of probability.

Major Arthur Griffiths, one of her Majesty's Commissioners of Prisons, hints, in his new book "Mysteries of Police and Crime," that the police believe the assassin to have been a doctor, bordering on insanity, whose body was found in the Thames soon after the last murder of the series. He adds, however, that this man was one of three whom the police had suspected. Then there was the madman who was traced to Broadmoor some five or six years ago, and against whom there was believed to be conclusive evidence; while Professor Bell of Edinburgh, who was a prominent figure in the investigation of the Ardlamont mystery, used to declare that he also had definitely "spotted" the culprit.

The clergyman. who now comes forward with the latest identification, declares that the assassin died shortly after the last murder of the series.

Illustrated Police News – 28th January 1899.

1901 – THE LATE HANGMAN'S THEORY.

A Bolton correspondent telegraphs:-

James Billington the hangman, whose death took place a few days ago, declared that he never hanged anybody with greater satisfaction than he did Dr. Neill Cream, whom he believed to his dying day to have been "Jack the Ripper." Dr. Cream did all could to delay the execution, and Billington becoming impatient, suddenly pulled the fatal bolt. As he did so he distinctly heard Cream say. "I am Jack__," and believed that in another second he would have confessed he was "Jack the Ripper." Certainly, as Billington put it, we never heard of the "Ripper" afterwards.

Sheffield Evening Telegraph – 18th December 1901

Printed by Printforce, United Kingdom